CINEMA AND SOCIAL CHANGE IN GERMANY AND AUSTRIA

Film and Media Studies Series

Film studies is the critical exploration of cinematic texts as art and entertainment, as well as the industries that produce them and the audiences that consume them. Although a medium barely one hundred years old, film is already transformed through the emergence of new media forms. Media studies is an interdisciplinary field that considers the nature and effects of mass media upon individuals and society and analyzes media content and representations. Despite changing modes of consumption—especially the proliferation of individuated viewing technologies—film has retained its cultural dominance into the 21st century, and it is this transformative moment that the WLU Press Film and Media Studies series addresses.

Our Film and Media Studies series includes topics such as identity, gender, sexuality, class, race, visuality, space, music, new media, aesthetics, genre, youth culture, popular culture, consumer culture, regional/national cinemas, film policy, film theory, and film history.

Wilfrid Laurier University Press invites submissions. For further information, please contact the Series editors, all of whom are in the Department of English and Film Studies at Wilfrid Laurier University:

> Dr. Philippa Gates, Email: pgates@wlu.ca
> Dr. Russell Kilbourn, Email: rkilbourn@wlu.ca
> Dr. Ute Lischke, Email: ulischke@wlu.ca
> 75 University Avenue West
> Waterloo, ON N2L 3C5
> Canada
> Phone: 519-884-0710
> Fax: 519-884-8307

CINEMA AND SOCIAL CHANGE IN GERMANY AND AUSTRIA

Gabriele Mueller and
James M. Skidmore, editors

WILFRID LAURIER UNIVERSITY PRESS

Wilfrid Laurier University Press acknowledges the support of the Canada Council for the Arts for our publishing program. We acknowledge the financial support of the Government of Canada through the Canada Book Fund for our publishing activities. Funding provided by the Government of Ontario and the Ontario Arts Council. This work was supported by the Research Support Fund.

LIBRARY AND ARCHIVES CANADA CATALOGUING IN PUBLICATION

Title: Cinema and social change in Germany and Austria / Gabriele Mueller and James M. Skidmore, editors.
Names: Mueller, Gabriele, editor | Skidmore, James Martin, 1961- editor
Series: Film + media studies.
Description: Series statement: Film and media studies | Includes bibliographical references and index.
Identifiers: Canadiana 20250287889 | ISBN 9781554585601 (softcover)
Subjects: LCSH: Motion picture industry—Germany—History—21st century. | LCSH: Motion picture industry—Austria—History—21st century. | LCSH: Motion pictures—Germany—History—21st century. | LCSH: Motion pictures—Austria—History—21st century. | LCSH: Motion pictures and globalization—Germany. | LCSH: Motion pictures and globalization—Austria. | LCSH: Social change in motion pictures.
Classification: LCC PN1993.5.G3 C553 2026 | DDC 791.430943/090511—dc23

Cover design by Blakeley Words+Pictures.
Interior design by Catharine Bonas-Taylor.
Front cover image: filmkombinat/Nadja Klier.

© 2012 Wilfrid Laurier University Press
Waterloo, Ontario, Canada
www.wlupress.wlu.ca
Paperback edition published in 2026

Every reasonable effort has been made to acquire permission for copyrighted material used in this text, and to acknowledge all such indebtedness accurately. Any errors and omissions called to the publisher's attention will be corrected in future printings.

All rights reserved. No part of this publication may be reproduced, stored in a retrieval system, or transmitted, in any form or by any means (electronic, mechanical, photocopying, recording, generative artificial intelligence [AI] training, or otherwise) without the prior written consent of the publisher or a licence from the Canadian Copyright Licensing Agency (Access Copyright).

Contents

List of Illustrations   vii

Acknowledgements   ix

1 *Gabriele Mueller & James M. Skidmore*
Cinema of Dissent? Confronting Social, Economic, and Political Change in German-Language Cinema   1

CHALLENGING VIEWING HABITS

2 *Marco Abel*
The Counter-Cinema of the Berlin School   25

3 *Sophie Boyer*
The Triumph of Hyperreality: A Baudrillardian Reading of Michael Haneke's Cinematic Oeuvre   43

4 *Morgan Koerner*
Subversions of the Medical Gaze: Disability and Media Parody in Christoph Schlingensief's *Freakstars 3000*   59

REASSESSING AND CONSUMING HISTORY

5 *Roger Cook*
Literary Discourse and Cinematic Narrative: Scripting Affect in *Das Leben der Anderen*   79

6 *Alasdair King*
Heimat 3: Edgar Reitz's Time Machine   97

7 *Joanne Leal*
   Troubled Parents, Angry Children: The Difficult Legacy of 1968 in Contemporary German-Language Film   115
8 *Mary-Elizabeth O'Brien*
   Creative Chaos as Political Strategy in Recent German-Language Cinema   133
9 *Florentine Strzelczyk*
   "Looking for an Old Man with a Black Moustache": Hitler, Humour, Fake, and Forgery in *Schtonk!*   155
10 *Peter Gölz*
   Haha Hitler! Coming to Terms with Dani Levy   173

QUESTIONING COLLECTIVE IDENTITIES

11 *Myriam Léger*
   German Fascination for Jews in Oliver Hirschbiegel's *Ein ganz gewöhnlicher Jude*   191
12 *Jakub Kazecki*
   Border, Bridge, or Barrier? Images of German–Polish Borderlands in German Cinema of the 2000s   207
13 *Michael Zimmermann*
   The Transnational Deutschkei in Yilmaz Arslan's *Brudermord*   225
14 *Alice Kuzniar*
   Diasporic Queers: Reading for the Intersections of Alterities in Recent German Cinema   245

AN INSIDER'S VIEW

15 *Barbara Pichler*
   The Construction of Reality: Aspects of Austrian Cinema between Fiction and Documentary   267

Filmography   283
Notes on Contributors   287
Index   291

List of Illustrations

Ulrich Köhler, *Bungalow*   33

Christoph Hochhäusler, *Falscher Bekenner*   37

Albrecht Dürer, *Das Traumgesicht*, 1525   44

Christoph Schlingensief, *Freakstars 3000*   68

Edgar Reitz, *Heimat 3*   108

Hans Weingartner, *Die fetten Jahre sind vorbei*   126

Marcus Mittermeier, *Muxmäuschenstill*   144

Dani Levy, *Mein Führer*   180

Dani Levy, *Mein Führer*   183

Michael Schorr, *Schröders wunderbare Welt*   212

Christoph Hochhäusler, *Milchwald*   218

Yüksel Yavuz, *Kleine Freiheit*   250

Angelina Maccarone, *Fremde Haut*   256

Ruth Mader, *Struggle*   270

Anja Salomonowitz, *Kurz davor ist es passiert*   272

Marcus J. Carney, *The End of the Neubacher Project*   277

Acknowledgements

The following agencies provided invaluable financial and logistical support for this project: the Waterloo Centre for German Studies at the University of Waterloo; the Canadian Centre for German and European Studies at York University; the Social Sciences and Humanities Research Council of Canada; the Kitchener and Waterloo Community Foundation (through its Community Fund and its Musagetes Funds); the German Academic Exchange Service; the Goethe-Institut Toronto; the Austrian Cultural Forum; the German Consulate General Toronto; Woco Foundation; the Vice-President International, the Vice-President Research, the Faculty of Arts, and the Departments of Drama, Sociology, History, and Germanic and Slavic Studies at the University of Waterloo.

The editors would like to express their sincere gratitude to all those who assisted at various stages of this project: Michael Schorr; Paul Cooke; Barbara Pichler; David G. John; Susan Ingram; Markus Reisenleitner; Janet Vaughan; John Paul Kleiner; Kyle Scholz; Leonie Schreiner; Peter Wood; Christine Wood; Betty Winge; Beverly J. Hershey; Nancy Mattes; Frank Eisenhuth; Michael Boehringer; Grit Liebscher; Barbara Schmenk; Mathias Schulze; Paul Malone; Diana Spokiene; Peter McIsaac; Mark Webber; Karin Barton; Angelica Fenner; John Davidson; Johannes von Moltke; Stefan Soldovieri; Brian Henderson and the staff at Wilfrid Laurier University Press; John Tutt and the staff at the Princess Cinema; and Myriam Léger.

1
Cinema of Dissent?
Confronting Social, Economic, and Political Change in German-Language Cinema

Gabriele Mueller and James M. Skidmore

1

In early 2009, when this volume was beginning to take shape, reports from the Berlinale, the international film festival in Berlin, attracted our attention. Already in January, the *Frankfurter Allgemeine Zeitung* was promising its readers that the event would offer a close cinematic examination of social realities "under the sign of the economic crisis"[1] ("Berlinale"). Stressing the impact of unregulated economic growth and its subsequent collapse on the thematic choices of film artists, the festival's director, Dieter Kosslick, proclaimed that "reality has really caught up with fiction this year."[2] Although he was probably referring mainly to the opening film of the Berlinale, Tom Tykwer's finance thriller *The International* (USA/Germany, 2009), many other films also focused on political, economic, and social changes and the challenges they pose both to individuals and societies in a rapidly globalizing world. Hans-Christian Schmid's *Sturm* (*Storm*, 2009), a German-Danish-Dutch co-production, for example, deals with the aftermath of the 1990s Balkan crisis and tells the story of a prosecutor at the war crimes tribunal in The Hague. Lukas Moodysson's *Mammoth* (2009), also an international production, co-financed by Sweden, Germany, and Denmark, looks at the effect globalization has on labour markets through the narrative lens of the story of a Filipino nanny who leaves her own children in order to care for those of a rich American couple.

For a number of years, the Berlinale has not only presented important cultural discourses, but it has also acted as a barometer of the state of German cinema itself, even if more innovative and thought-provoking work of German filmmakers was often found in festival sections outside the competition. In contrast to the international themes, budget, and intended audience of these co-productions, the program of the 2009 Berlinale also included a number of films with a more intimate and concentrated focus on social and political realities in Germany. But films such as the aforementioned question the usefulness of the "national" as a category for examining cinema, not only through their thematic internationalism, but also through the changing modes of film funding, production, and distribution and the increasing prevalence of transnational film practices.

Within this context it is not surprising that the German production with the programmatic title *Deutschland '09. 13 kurze Filme zur Lage der Nation (Germany '09: 13 Short Films on the State of the Nation)* prompted critics to expect the ultimate cinematic event that would help to define the nation. Indeed, even though the directors behind the project emphasized their deliberate rejection of a unified approach and favoured the production of thematically and aesthetically independent shorts, the project still seemed to be motivated by a desire, on the one hand, to sketch a profile of contemporary German society[3] and, on the other, to define their own generation's position as film artists.[4] Judging from the critics' responses to *Deutschland '09*, it seems that the film was not able to fulfill these expectations. A closer look at the project is nevertheless warranted as both the text itself and the reactions to it raise important questions that dwell at the core of any examination of contemporary German cinema.

Inspired by the simultaneous anniversaries of the founding of the Federal Republic in 1949, the student movement of 1968, and the fall of the Berlin Wall, thirteen German filmmakers joined forces and each contributed a short film to *Deutschland '09*. Dismayed by the lack of cinematic attention to the political and social consequences of these events, the directors attempted to fill that perceived gap by giving form to the state of affairs through the construction of a panorama of impressions of German society in 2009. The result of this experiment as well as the participants' ensuing assessment of the production process seem to confirm what observers of the contemporary German film scene have described as a very heterogeneous, diverse, and fragmented cinematic landscape where, in contrast to the similar project *Deutschland im Herbst (Germany in Autumn,* 1978), no single overarching theme or aesthetic approach is able to dominate.

A second argument has been made, however, that despite the impossibility of pinpointing this "single identity-shaping and definable point of friction" ("13 kurze Filme"),[5] the national is still employed as a relevant category to distinguish between the social and political realities and identities emerging at the beginning of the twenty-first century. Beyond the popular and affective cinematic reclamation of the past in the service of a "normalized" sense of national identity, cinema is still perceived as an appropriate medium for facilitating a broader critical discourse about social change in the present: "[The project] is meant as the beginning of a discussion about politics, film, and society today [...], a stimulus to start thinking about the society we live in and the society we want to live in. We have made a statement, and now we are awaiting with interest the interpretations and reactions to it"[6] ("13 kurze Filme"). This willingness, maybe even eagerness, to engage in discourses that use the national as an interpretative frame is not only reflected in critics' voices expressing disappointment at the film's inability to offer a coherent image of the nation,[7] but also in the relative ease with which the filmmakers were able early on to secure funding, in particular from the TV channel NDR. The relevance of this discourse is also demonstrated in the way most of the contributions highlight complicated interdependencies between global developments and local and/or national specificities. Even though the individual shorts display significant differences in their approach to political or thesis-driven filmmaking and in aesthetic choices, what connects the thirteen films is precisely their critical perspective of neoliberal economic structures and their exclusionary mechanisms, the consequences of globalization for the individual's aesthetic experience in urban environments, the altered perception of political activism in a society fearing terrorism, and the current relevance of utopian thinking and civil movements initiated by previous generations.

Despite (and because of) the differentiated and fragmented picture that emerges from this project, *Deutschland '09* seems to confirm a broader trend. In the early 1990s, German cinema was dominated by popular, genre-driven, and box-office-oriented films, while more innovative work, if completed, remained largely unnoticed by critics and audiences alike. This "cinema of consensus"— a term coined by Rentschler and since then frequently used as shorthand for the perceived one-dimensional film culture after unification—has given way to a more complex, formally more diverse, and thematically more critical cinematic scene. Although comedies made mainly for the domestic market (e.g., *Warum Männer nicht zuhören und Frauen schlecht einparken* [Leander Haußmann, 2007], *KeinOhrhasen* [*Rabbit without Ears*, Til Schweiger, 2007]) and "historiographically problematic and cinematically harmless" (Frey "Insecure Times") films about the Nazi past (e.g., *John Rabe* [Florian Gallenberger, 2009]) are still very profitable components of a revitalized and relatively strong film industry, the spectrum of the German-language film landscape has broadened. With more film artists re-emphasizing the value of making the social and political the narrative focus of their explorations of a changing society, some film scholars have begun identifying a new trend, the "cinema of dissent" (Hake 192). This collection of essays questions to what extent this label is justified, and, if so, whether the dissent applies to thematic or aesthetic approaches or to alternative methods of film production and distribution. Thus the authors in this collection are contributing to a growing body of academic work on contemporary German-language film that understands the current cinematic landscape as a product and agent of social, political, and technological change. Stephan Schindler and Lutz Koepnick's volume *The Cosmopolitan Screen: German Cinema and the Global Imaginary* (1–21) considers the reconceptualization of the national in post-wall cinema, while Brad Prager and Jaimey Fisher's recent book *The Collapse of the Conventional* (2010) focuses on the legacies of the New German Cinema and their impact on aesthetic approaches and political positions that are emerging in contemporary filmmaking in Germany.

Even though the films screened in 2009 could not be taken into consideration for this volume, let us return one more time to the Berlinale. When Dieter Kosslick enthusiastically praised the 2009 program claiming that "many feature films succeed in representing reality better than anything else"[8] ("Berlinale"), he emphasized the importance which a media society allocates the image as the means to understand our world, shape historical and cultural knowledge, and negotiate cultural belonging. At the same time, Kosslick's comment also problematizes the value of the image in its relationship to reality and hints at our need for narratives of unity, progress, and wholeness while simultaneously undermining our belief in the reliability and authenticity of images through its allusion to cinema's nature as constructed and better than reality. Stressing the belief in the salvation of visual narratives, it posits cinema as a means to zero in on individual, fictional stories and make sense of a reality perceived as increasingly unknowable.

II

According to social theorists, the uncertainties of this age result from fundamental social changes currently experienced by postmodern societies. If we propose to examine cinematic responses to transformations of social and political structures and processes, then what do we mean by social change? Globalization studies have attempted to unravel the factors determining the speed, dynamics, and directions of these transformations, and even though there have been contradictory interpretations from scholars, there is general agreement that these changes will question the very foundations of contemporary societies and that "we will confront profound contradictions and perplexing paradoxes; and experience hope embedded in despair" (Beck 1). Whether scholars describe a highly individualized, deregulated "risk society" (Beck 1) that places the burden of improvement and progress on the shoulders of the individual, or whether they focus on the altered political culture, on cosmopolitanism, or transnational interdependencies, they all call for a rigorous rethinking of old ideas that have now ceased to be productive as a frame of reference for societal development.

In political, economic, sociological, and cultural discourses these transformations are often reduced to one word: *globalization*. Not surprisingly, the theme of globalization has also found its way into practically all film genres of German-language cinema, from documentaries (e.g., *Unser täglich Brot* [*Our Daily Bread*, Nikolaus Geyrhalter, 2005]), to films for children (e.g., *Hände weg von Mississippi* [*Hands off Mississippi*, Detlev Buck, 2007]). Yet, the meanings of the term *globalization* and its effects on societies and individuals have been strongly contested. In his survey of scholarly literature on the phenomenon, Mauro F. Guillén identified key questions at the centre of the debate. Observers and theorists of globalization have drawn on different methodologies, empirical data, or theoretical models to interpret the transformations in radically different ways: either they see globalizing processes as producing convergences resulting in very similar economic and technological structures, or they predict growing inequalities in access to wealth. Equally controversial is the debate about the future of the nation-state. While some observers foresee the declining significance and function of the nation-state in an age of mobile global capital, others insist that the state is transformed, but not diminished, and that "globalization reinforces the importance of domestic policies, as countries engage in regionalization, sectoral protectionism, and mercantilistic competition" (Guillén 249). Often associated with neo-liberalism, the effects of globalization for the individual are also interpreted contradictorily across the ideological spectrum, either as a civilizing consumer experience of liberating prosperity or as an alienating, marginalizing, and exploitative process. Finally, a key question is whether globalization has resulted in the emergence of a global culture. Again, opinions are divided: while some theorists not only predict, but already confirm the presence of a homogenized global culture driven by mass consumerism resulting in the standardization of tastes and desires (Guillén 252), others refute this position. Though modes of cultural production may be becoming more and more similar, the outcomes, it is claimed, differ as they are shaped by regional and localized discourses and cultural traditions. In fact, as a consequence of increased migration, Elliot, Payne and Ploesch assert that "culture is progressively a marker of difference rather than of collective identity" (2).

Although Guillén finds significant disagreements in the social sciences on how to interpret globalizing processes, he stresses that most scholars agree that important changes are taking place that will fundamentally alter the way in which nation-states function and relate to each other, how knowledge within and about societies is produced and disseminated, and how individual and collective identities are constructed and negotiated within changing networks of social interaction. Yet while, according to his survey, the balance of scholarly opinion appears to suggest that none of the extreme positions can be upheld and that the complexity of global processes requires a multi-perspectival approach, popular discourses on globalization often do not offer a measured view. In contrast, they are frequently marked by fear and pessimism, by a focus on globalization's negative or unpredictable consequences, and they often express oppositional and anti-capitalist positions highly critical of unregulated transnational processes perceived as out of control and potentially irreversible.

Unpredictability, risk, and uncertainty are important factors of social change that also assume a prominent position in Zygmunt Bauman's theorization of contemporary society. Using the metaphor of "liquid modernity" to describe the fluidity of social parameters and to set the human condition within a global society apart from the traditional certainties of modernity (the age of "solid modernity"), Bauman conceptualizes the radical changes as a departure from a modernity rooted in the Enlightenment. In contrast to solid modernity with its emphasis on progress, the belief in the possibility to achieve perfection and the perception of change as a temporary state to achieve this goal, liquid society is characterized by a realization that this goal may never be achieved and, as a consequence, that change is "a permanent condition of life." In a world where work and production have been replaced by consumption and consumer culture as the central forces of the economy (Blackshaw 47), and where one dominant authority has given way to competing authorities among which individuals must choose, Bauman projects the life experience of liquid moderns as "being in an increasingly 'deregulated,' or—as the politicians' beloved cliché has it—*flexible* world: a world full of uncoordinated, often contradictory chances and voices, but devoid of clear-cut standards by which the superiority of any of them can be measured" (Blackshaw 48). Rather than being able to rely on traditions and previously acquired knowledge, individuals are required to act independently, take risks and assume responsibility for processes and outcomes beyond their control. Beck also emphasizes this connection between notions of risk and individual responsibility in the global society where "individual solutions to systemic contradictions" have to be found (Bauman 12). Yet, in the absence of a dominant political or philosophical authority, "individuals are left looking for individual recipes and models and those come mostly from the media industry" (Peterson and Monnier 14). Beck agrees with this position when he argues that the site of political discourse "is not the street but *television*," and that political participation, aided by technology, amounts mainly to the consumption of the staging of cultural symbols through the mass media (44).

Within the context of these discourses on social change, the present volume examines cinema in Germany and Austria both as a product and an agent of globalizing processes, as well as approaching it as a mediator of and an influence on notions of collective and national awareness and transnational identities. Given that, in the postmodern world, the visual image is the favoured medium for constructing identities and circumscribing cultural belonging, how do contemporary German and Austrian films contribute to or contradict the ideas and debates on social change? How does cinema represent or respond to the perceived disintegration of key concepts such as family, marriage, nation, nation-state, and community? Do filmmakers articulate social change in terms of loss, fear, and disorientation, or are they able to envision the new challenges as opportunities to creatively exercise new forms of freedom? What visions for the future development of society are projected? In their engagement with globalization discourses, do film artists lament or celebrate the effects of convergence or differentiation within the cultural sphere? How do the films comment on and contribute to the production of historical knowledge? How do changed consumer habits affect the production, distribution, reception, and marketing of the filmic product? Is film art in Germany and Austria able to develop a new cinematic language that takes into account changing modes of visualizing, seeing, and interpreting the world? What are the aesthetic strategies employed to revitalize the cinema's social function as *agent provocateur*, a purpose arguably at the heart of the *Deutschland '09* project, rather than as "consensus commodity"?

III

The impact of social transformation on contemporary cinema in Germany and Austria is evident not only in the films' themes, but also on the levels of film production, distribution, and reception. In tracing contemporary cinema's engagement with and struggle over meanings and notions of belonging in a globalizing world, most of the contributions in this volume approach questions such as those above by pursuing an analysis of cinematic representation within the context of specific cultural discourses. The authors offer close textual readings and emphasize thorough analyses of the themes, images, symbols, and narrative strategies employed to capture or challenge new formations of *Heimat*, cultural identities, and memory, and to render them visible. This does not mean, however, that the essays disregard the repercussions of these changes within the film industry itself and within production, distribution, and exhibition. On the contrary, the careful examination of the films' engagement with these discourses on the level of representation (e.g., the close attention to the recurring theme of the changing media landscape and the overt media critique present in a number of films) draws our attention to rapidly evolving economic conditions, viewing habits, market dynamics, and flows of global capital that have an impact on cinematic production. Whether addressing the correlation between public funding, box office results and aesthetics (e.g., Abel), the contentious issue of what makes a film "Austrian" (e.g., Boyer, Pichler), or the "Adolf-Bonus" (Frey "Insecure Times") and the marketability and reception abroad of films dealing with the Nazi period (e.g., Strzelczyk, Gölz, Léger), the volume's essays raise important questions about the circumstances of film production and distribution. Through their attention to the complexities of the films themselves as well as their relationship to processes of production and reception, the essays reveal the cinematic text as a product of global economies and transnational and cultural practices, and they identify crucial investigative avenues for the future study of German cinema within a global context.

A cursory glance at the cinema's more outspoken representatives and at the more glamorous events with which the film industry, particularly in Germany, celebrates itself seems to suggest that a convergence of cinematic cultures is not only occurring, but is also perceived as desirable and necessary for cinema to thrive. The producer Bernd Eichinger's remarks at the Munich film festival in June 2009 illustrate this. "The viewer must not think: OK, it is a German movie, I will have to tough it out and get through this. We want to make films where you do not see a difference with international productions"[9] ("Eichinger"). Demanding greater financial investment in the German film industry, Eichinger clearly connects homegrown cinema's perceived lack of appeal to its inability or refusal to command big production budgets. He also implies that specific national aesthetic conventions need to be overcome. Eichinger's derisory remarks notwithstanding, the German film industry appears to be booming and domestic productions in recent years have reached a respectable market share of approximately 25 percent,[10] even though this success seems to be mainly due to a relatively small number of films, among them comedies intended primarily for the domestic market, genre films, and historical films. And, although critics see the renewed strength of German-language cinema in a "new confidence" to portray "local stories and national history" (Frey "Insecure Times"), commercially successful films of recent years often display characteristics of what Randall Halle has described as a transnational aesthetic.

Paying close attention to changes in the economic mechanisms of filmmaking in a global world, Halle identifies a number of elements that result in aesthetic qualities characteristic of the "transnational artifact." One important feature is, for example, that the films target audiences beyond national boundaries: "Instead of national public spheres and ideal citizen audiences, production becomes oriented toward interest groups and subcultures that cut across national lines, marketing focus groups like 'tweens,' or social situations like the date film and summer vacation flicks. Film production attempts to pick up on trends like comedy waves or Holocaust narratives" (Halle 84). Other factors contributing to transnational cinema are the increasing importance of producers and distributors at the expense of auteurism, artistic freedom, and the influence of the director in general, as well as new modes of funding that bring together global financial flows from a variety of directions, the cinema's market orientation, and, as a consequence, the privileging of established and popular genres. These developments, however, do not render the national irrelevant as a point of reference or as an economic factor. Rather than declaring the disappearance of the national, German film scholars agree with most academics debating the general emergence of a global culture that "the reality of globalization leads to an unprecedented dynamic in which the local and the global exist in mutual interdependence" (Schindler and Koepnick 12). The way in which national tropes are modified and adapted to appeal to broader transnational audiences is particularly poignant in the historical films dealing with the Nazi period and World War II, which engage with discourses very specific to German postwar and post-wall societies. At the same time, these films also offer universalized stories of redemption, love, courage, and survival, which may appeal to broader audiences through their focus on "individualized" and "emotionalized" history and their reliance on formal elements of classic narrative cinema, e.g., verisimilitude, linear and character-driven storylines, continuity editing, and affective modes of spectator address. The often high production values and the films' marketing as "telling stories yet untold" help to find audiences abroad who are not familiar with the specificities of the discourse on the Nazi past in Germany and who approach these texts as cinematic commodities whose primary function is to entertain. *Valkyrie* (Bryan Singer, 2008), an American-German co-production with a cast of international stars, can serve as an example here: the film was advertised as a story that had never been told before, it relied heavily on the appeal of its main star, Tom Cruise, and it managed to attract almost 1.5 million viewers in Germany.

While Eichinger seems mainly concerned with audience appeal and German cinema's profitability, other observers and film scholars also see the emergence of new economic structures and dynamics that result in a transnational aesthetic as a complex set of developments enriching "the articulations of visual language" and expanding "the possibilities of cultural production" (Halle 87–88). This view is not shared by many filmmakers in Germany and Austria who, on the contrary, perceive the changing face of the film industry as restraining artistic innovation in favour of the consumability of the cinematic product. While they welcome the growing creative potential of homegrown cinema, they simultaneously bemoan the cinema's declining importance as a site of critical cultural exchange between filmmakers and audiences as a consequence of its commodification. Robert Thalheim suggests that "the cinema often has no social function, it is not perceived as a cultural site. People still go to the theatre and expect to be bored. But they do not go to the cinema"[11] (Schulz-Ojala and Tilmann). Whether this is true or not, he formulates the frustration felt by film practitioners about a pervasive attitude toward the cinema exclusively as a commodity, in contrast to the theatre which, in Thalheim's view, has retained its status as high culture and is able to pursue serious artistic ambitions.

These tensions between the fear of artistic innovation being marginalized and the attempts to ensure the economic viability and popular appeal of domestic productions permeate practically all levels of public discourse on cinema. The debates surrounding the work of the Deutsche Filmakademie (German Film Academy) illustrate these frustrations even more acutely. Even though the annual German Film Prize awards ceremony, with its glamour and self-congratulatory stance, is closely modelled on the American Academy Awards, the nomination and selection process attempts to create a public forum for critical, non-elitist dialogue and to strike a balance between recognizing innovative cinematic work and celebrating commercial success.[12] The problematic relationship many filmmakers have toward the strategies the academy uses to fulfill its mandate undermines, however, the academy's ability to hold these tensions in balance.

The academy's ability to fulfill its mandate was put to the test when Til Schweiger demonstratively resigned his membership in protest against the academy's failure to nominate his comedy *KeinOhrhasen*, despite it having sold more than three million tickets ("Schweiger verlässt Filmakademie"), or when film directors Christian Petzold and Robert Thalheim were reluctant to become members of the academy—although their films were nominated and won prizes—because they do not agree with the way in which public funds are distributed through private channels to projects not needing support (Schulz-Ojala and Tilmann). Possibly the strongest rejection of the commercial aspects associated with the Americanization of the film industry came when, two days after *Alles auf Zucker!* (*Go for Zucker!*, Dani Levy, 2004) won the Filmpreis awarded by the Deutsche Filmakademie in 2005, the first German Filmkunstpreis was awarded in Mannheim to Robert Thalheim's film *Netto*, also in 2005. This new prize was accompanied by a resolution—the *Ludwigshafener Position*—that repudiated the idea of a German-Hollywood-type film industry and insisted on defining film as art. Signed by a number of directors, producers, and actors, the resolution demanded authentic, passionate, risky, unpredictable, untamed, and artistically relevant filmmaking that should not be reined in by the fear of box office failure. It declared: "The German film will be art or it will not exist at all"[13] ("Ludwigshafener Position").

This manifesto also points to the influence of television as another element that has an impact on the visual aesthetics of contemporary cinema through the transformation of its economic foundations. When the authors of the Ludwigshafener Position declare that artists should not be afraid of low audience ratings and demand that German cinema should resist being "polished to death and strangulated by safe formulae,"[14] they are voicing the frequently heard concern that more and more often significant chunks of film budgets are made available from television companies, which then oblige filmmakers to make aesthetic compromises by conforming to the different visual requirements as well as the scheduling and exhibition policies of the small screen.[15] Critics complain that this imbues television-funded cinema with unadventurous narrative strategies aimed at a mass audience, the need for pleasurable emotion and harmony, and the reluctance toward more difficult subjects.[16] Filmmakers are also very critical about television's interference with and restriction of the range of cinematic expression. Peter Greenaway even claims that no new developments of the visual language or radical innovations in German cinema have been possible since Fassbinder, Herzog, and Straub because after 1980 "television had finally won the battle over the use of the moving image"[17] (276). Directors, although they acknowledge that television provides a much-needed platform from which they can reach wider audiences, also recognize how the cinematic landscape and working conditions for film artists have been irrevocably changed by television. Christian Petzold describes the situation as follows:

> Indeed, German cinema has become much more interesting of late. It has become really a very rich cinema—but cinema as such does not exist anymore. There are films, but there is no public for them. We have to face this without illusions; and you can't change it either. You cannot invent a film infrastructure with films, since this infrastructure is determined by television, which rules everything, certainly in Germany. The large trusts and monopolies homogenized everything; as a result, one makes films in niches. (Abel)

Television programmers and representatives, however, reject this criticism and claim, in fact, that television strengthens German-language cinema to a greater extent than does the film industry itself (Hanfeld and Seewald). Providing opportunities and funding to younger artists allows for projects to be realized which, without the support of companies such as Degeto, would never even reach the planning stage. The fact that many successful and established film directors began their careers in television is another indicator for the importance of television for German-language cinema, and, regardless of how one assesses the aesthetic and economic consequences of this dynamic interdependence, it is clear that it has been transforming modes of cinematic production and exhibition in varied and contradictory ways.

IV

If the changing economic conditions, social structures, and processes of intermedial cultural production fundamentally alter our conception of societal development and individual agency, then how has contemporary cinema responded to the challenge of rendering these transformations visible? Christian Petzold acknowledges the necessity for filmmakers to develop a new visual language that can adequately register these changes. Referring to the task of visualizing the new face of capitalism as evoked in his film *Yella* (2007), he states: "We still represent this world using old images, caricatures. We have no imagery to capture it, no story. These new images and new stories, this is what [the film] was about"[18] ("Yella"). What are the aesthetic strategies used by filmmakers to mobilize imaginaries that conjure up new narratives and construct sites of social belonging? Can artists find new ways of framing the social or do they return to, recycle or adapt older traditions of screening and seeing the world? How do film artists take into account, comment on, challenge, or play with the contemporary audience's viewing habits, attitudes, and expectations when those have been reshaped by the media, rapidly evolving technologies, and consumer society?

While all contributions to the volume address these questions, the first essays in particular focus on filmmakers in Germany and Austria who are willing to challenge conventional viewing habits. Through their films, they try to open up the image to allow for a more concentrated reflective perception of "reality" and to achieve an aesthetic experience that defies the narrowly defined role of the spectator as consumer prevalent in conventional narrative cinema. But the filmmakers discussed by Marco Abel, as well as by Barbara Pichler in the last essay of the volume, have to be seen in the context of broader developments. Both the Berlin School and Austrian documentarists can be understood as reconfiguring or responding to revitalized realist traditions and European auteurist movements that emerged over the past two decades. Cinematic narrative attention was redirected to social and political questions that had been neglected by "consensus cinema." The reputation of contemporary Austrian cinema in particular rests on its commitment to realist approaches in pursuit of the "authentic," on its willingness to seek out societal problems and to concentrate on the negative and abject as part of a tradition that John Orr has called "traductive realism" (301). Since unification, a number of German filmmakers have similarly focused on marginalized groups within a society shaken by unexpected economic and social upheaval. From the perspective of the losers of neo-liberal capitalism, the films frequently draw attention to the consequences of unemployment, social insecurity, and homelessness. Aesthetically, these socially conscious and critical texts have mainly relied on a repertoire of stylistic conventions familiar from realist cinematic traditions, e.g., documentary-style camera work or a blend of documentary and fiction elements, open-ended or episodic narrative structures, location shooting, and a reluctance to cast well-known actors or stars. Yet, in their attempts to develop a visual style that engages with contemporary social environments, the directors of the Berlin School often reject the "cinema of identification" (Abel) in favour of a specific set of formal elements. Refuting the labelling of Berlin School films as apolitical due to their formal characteristics, Abel argues that exactly because of their particular aesthetics, these films are able to shed light on social realities and mental states prevalent in contemporary Germany.

Chapters 3 and 4 also concentrate on films that address "screen realities" and comment in different ways on the emergence of a global culture. This mass culture is depicted as a visually homogenized commodity whose manipulative character prohibits the active intellectual engagement of the spectator, thereby reinforcing dominant patterns of identification and exclusion. Through provocative strategies that foreground the simulation involved in the production of the cinematic image, both Michael Haneke and Christoph Schlingensief have—throughout their careers—challenged audience understandings of the relationship between the represented and the process of representation. Sophie Boyer's essay explores ways in which Haneke's work reflects upon notions of hyperreality and subverts audience expectations by challenging the passive consumer, who is drawn to titillating and sensationalist images. Morgan Koerner examines Schlingensief's *Freakstars 3000*, a film that provokes on several levels, first as a parody and scathing critique of reality and talent shows on mainstream television, and second as an example of subversive comedy that challenges conventions of representing people with disabilities on screen in general and in sketch comedy in particular, thereby forcing the spectator into an active and (self)-reflective stance.

The next section combines essays examining shifts in the way in which contemporary cinema contributes to the discourse on German history of the twentieth century. Through their close analyses of recurring themes, motifs, and aesthetic choices, chapters 5–10 facilitate our understanding of the films' position within the complex discourses on historiography, and on the cinema's role in producing authenticity, entertainment and consumable history. Like the essays by Abel, Boyer, and Koerner, Roger Cook's contribution on *Das Leben der Anderen* (*The Lives of Others*, Florian Henckel von Donnersmarck, 2006) is similarly concerned with the hermeneutic and affective power of the cinematic image, but he discusses a different approach. Rather than attempting to open up the image and relinquish control over it as a means of engaging spectator participation in the creation of meaning, von Donnersmarck subordinates the cinematic image to literary discourse and exerts tight control over it for maximum emotional impact, thus foreclosing unexpected creative spectator responses. Maybe this strategy confirms what Greenaway calls the "tyranny of the text" (276), namely, cinema's prevailing inability to free the visual imagination from the literary text rooted in word-based knowledge production. The huge international success of this film, however, also shows that in a climate perceived as insecure and disorienting, there is still a popular desire for the comfort offered by closed narratives of redemption such as *Das Leben der Anderen*.

Assessing the international cinematic landscape in 2000, film scholar Detlef Kannapin speculated that the dearth of aesthetic creativity and the predominance of conventional filmmaking was a consequence of the loss of emancipatory ideals and utopias in a globalizing world (164). The essays in this volume demonstrate that since then the cinematic landscape has changed and that a general judgment such as this would not do justice to the diverse aesthetic approaches of the film artists discussed here. But the question remains: Is the use of unconventional or experimental aesthetics a prerequisite for the film's potential to (re)define sites of belonging and utopian spaces? Or is a conventional cinematic style equally adequate for envisioning scenarios that can, as Beck encourages, use the freedoms of uncertainties productively? Chapters 6, 7, and 8 address this question. Alasdair King examines the utopian dimension of the concept of *Heimat* in Edgar Reitz's *Heimat 3*. King reads the six episodes of *Heimat 3* as Reitz's response to the notion that *Heimat* as a spatial category has lost purchase in the age of global mobility and communication. Conceiving of *Heimat 3* as a complex visual time machine, the director reconfigures *Heimat* in temporal terms.

The attempts by filmmakers to use temporal categories to define sites of ideological belonging are also evident in the essays by Joanne Leal and Mary-Elizabeth O'Brien, which foreground questions of generational change by focusing on cinematic commentaries about the legacy of the 1968 movement. Both chapters discuss the strategies through which Hans Weingartner, Oskar Roehler, Christian Petzold, and Marcus Mittermeier articulate moral and political disorientation while at the same time contributing to and commenting on the re-evaluation of the anti-authoritarian and anti-capitalist stance of the 1968 generation. The essays also illuminate the ways in which the directors attempt to locate their own work within or outside the traditions of German-language cinema and the tensions at work in these texts between political dissent and "consensual" filmmaking.

The problematization of the generational dimension of social change equally involves the questioning of master narratives of national history and cultural memory. Given the effects of demographic and generational change on the central role of the Nazi past and the Holocaust in the fabric of memory culture and public discourse in Germany, the continued presence of these themes in German (and Austrian) cinema is not surprising, even if the younger generation of filmmakers approaches this topic differently. Since unification, the cinema's attention to matters of *Vergangenheitsbewältigung* has not only attracted significant scholarly academic scrutiny but has proved to be an important pillar of the film industry's commercial recovery.[19] Both the academic debates and the public reception of the films dealing with the Nazi period have been controversial and the discourses have often been perceived as highly problematic. Contemporary cinema's obsession with the topic has in recent years been interpreted as an expression of the process of a normalizing view of national identity, where scholars have focused on the institutionalization of Holocaust memory. It has also been read within the context of a German "victim discourse," which has emerged in Germany during the last decade. Not restricted to the cinema, German television has produced a number of high-profile dramas that emphasize the suffering of the German population during World War II.[20] Another important focus for academic enquiry has been the German version of the "heritage film" (Koepnick), which offers depoliticized and visually opulent reconstructions of the Nazi past and thus contributes to the commodification of history.

Against this background, chapters 9 and 10 trace shifts in contemporary cinematic approaches to the representation of the Nazi past. Florentine Strzelczyk takes a fresh look at Helmut Dietl's *Schtonk!* (1992) and its satirization of West Germany's fascination with fascism from a post-unification perspective. In *Schtonk!*, the film's provocative foray into the comedy genre is tempered through the visual absence of Adolf Hitler, who has otherwise become an ever-present object of fascination. By contrast, Dani Levy's *Mein Führer—Die wirklich wahrste Wahrheit über Adolf Hitler* (*Mein Führer—The Truly Truest Truth about Adolf Hitler*, 2007) breaks the taboo of representing Hitler in German comedy. Peter Gölz's analysis of the film focuses on the director's negotiation between the demands of "Holocaust etiquette" and the desire to challenge other highly emotional and overtly factual representations such as Oliver Hirschbiegel's *Der Untergang* (*Downfall*, 2004) that demand "obedience"[21] (Steinberg) of the audience through the complete suspension of disbelief.

While the ongoing cinematic preoccupation with the legacy of the past reflects changing national and even global sensibilities about the subject, discourses on national identities also find expression in films focusing on the changing social landscape of the immediate present and on the transformation of Germany into a multicultural society belonging to the European Union. Chapters 11–14 explore cinematic responses to the various forms of identity politics that have come to the fore in contemporary debates. Myriam Léger's essay on Oliver Hirschbiegel's next film *Ein ganz gewöhnlicher Jude* (*Just an Ordinary Jew*, 2006) puts into perspective the cinematic discourse on the Nazi past and its reverberations for the construction of present-day German identities. Through its analysis of the film's positioning of the spectator, the essay illuminates the debates surrounding normalization processes and the mechanisms that continue to shape German-Jewish narratives today.

Notions of European rather than national identities are increasingly invoked not only as a confirmation of the political project of European integration, but also as a means of defining a specifically European cinema as a counterweight against Hollywood and its overwhelming economic and cultural power, and as a defence against nationalist discourses within individual countries and among diasporas. A number of critically acclaimed films (e.g., *Lichter* [*Distant Lights*, Hans-Christian Schmid, 2003], *Nordrand* [*Northern Skirts*, Barbara Albert, 1999] have probed the perception of the European in German and Austrian discourses through their exploration of the cultural, social, and economic dimensions of political developments within Europe after 1989. Jakub Kazecki contributes to this debate with his essay on the representation of German–Polish relations. Concentrating on the concept of the border, he discusses films by Vanessa Joop, Christoph Hochhäusler and Michael Schorr and investigates ways in which these films comment on the sincerity and depth of the discourses on European identity.

The most visible and internationally acclaimed cinematic contributions to the discourses on transnationalism and hybridization have come with the development of a Turkish-German cinema. Emerging at the beginning of the 1990s, this "accented cinema" has shifted from a "cinema of the affected" (Burns 3), with its initial emphasis on the marginalization and victimization as dominant aspects of the immigrant experience, to a heterogeneous cinema offering much more differentiated understandings of national, ethnic, and cultural identities by exploring and celebrating more fluid, hybrid forms of identity. Against this background, Michael Zimmermann's essay examines Yilmaz Arslan's *Brudermord* (*Fratricide*, 2005). With its emphasis on the interrelations between ethnic conflict, the diaspora experience, and economic deprivation, the film attempts to reveal the grim reality of child immigrants behind the facade of official immigration policies. Alice Kuzniar's essay also explores transnational spaces constructed by recent films. Drawing on globalization studies and queer theory, she focuses on the intersections and interrelations between different forms of persecution and marginalization and offers a re-assessment of a nation-based German queer cinema.

The category of the national is also central to the analysis in the last chapter. Written by Barbara Pichler, director of the Austrian national film festival Diagonale at Graz, the essay comments on recent developments in Austrian filmmaking from a practitioner's perspective and provides insights into the mechanisms through which national interests and cultural recognition are played out in Austria's cinematic scene. Pichler's essay examines Austrian documentarists who—similar to the German filmmakers discussed by Abel and Koerner—are concerned with questions of realism. They attempt to use the cinematic medium to make visible that which in texts offered by other media remains hidden or buried under a wealth of information and which, through its sheer volume and emphasis on sensationalism, dulls the viewers' senses. Building on Austria's strong tradition in documentary filmmaking, directors such as Anja Salomonowitz and Nikolaus Geyrhalter expand the stylistic inventory of realist cinema to activate the "stories suppressed from society's quotidian consciousness" (Salomonowitz qtd. in Frey "A Cinema in-Flux") and to "provide room for thoughts and associations [...], to allow enough time for the spectator to take in sounds and images in order to facilitate the dialogue with the world"[22] (Burner). Through her exploration of recent documentaries produced by a younger generation of Austrian directors, Pichler challenges the notion of the Austrian "feel-bad cinema" and provides a more nuanced and differentiated perspective of cinema's engagement with notions of reality and realism.

The picture that emerges from the essays of this volume is one of a heterogeneous German-language cinema culture. Despite their different foci, the essays confirm a broader trend towards a more complex, critical, and formally diverse cinematic scene. Social and economic transformations pose thematic and aesthetic challenges to cinema that is itself subject to changing processes of cultural production. The analyses put forward in this volume demonstrate that the often mainly commercially oriented "cinema of consensus" of the 1990s has lost its dominance and become only one trend within a much more vibrant and multi-faceted film scene. Functioning both as product and as agent of globalizing processes, this new cinema mediates and influences important political and social debates.

The chapters illuminate these complex practices by analyzing the filmmakers' intervention in discourses on the concept of "national cinema," the effects of globalization on social mobility, and the emergence of a "global culture." At a time when cinema is primarily associated with notions of entertainment, leisure, and consumption, the essays offer insights into the strategies employed by German and Austrian filmmakers to position themselves between the commercial pressures of the film industry and the desire to mediate or even affect social change. They illustrate the variety and inventiveness of contemporary Austrian and German filmmaking and highlight the complicated interdependencies between global developments and local specificities.

Notes

1 "Mit der Kamera ganz nahe an der Realität: Die Filme der 59. Berlinale [...] zeigen, wie die Opfer und Täter von Globalisierung und Kriegen aussehen."
2 "Die Wirklichkeit hat die Fiktion in diesem Jahr wirklich eingeholt" ("Berlinale").
3 "[...] eine bestimmte Art von Quersumme der deutschen Gegenwart formulieren" ("13 kurze Filme").
4 Tykwer explained: "Diese Vorstellung hat mich nicht losgelassen: was für eine Gruppe sich in der jetzigen Generation zusammenfinden würde, um daraus eine Art von Filmkollektiv zu generieren."
5 "[...] dass es diesen einen eindeutig identitätsstiftenden und spezifizierbaren Reibungspunkt nicht mehr gibt."
6 "Es soll ja vielmehr der Anfang einer Diskussion sein, über Politik, Film und Gesellschaft heute, eine erste Sammlung. Ein Auftakt zum Nachdenken über die Gesellschaft in der wir leben, und über die, in der wir leben wollen. Wir haben hier ein Statement gemacht. Und jetzt sind wir sehr gespannt auf die Interpretationen und Reaktionen."
7 See, for example, reviews by Lueken, Worschech, and Buß.
8 "Viele Spielfilme geben die Wirklichkeit besser wieder als alles andere."
9 "Der Zuschauer soll nicht sagen: o.k.—es ist ein deutscher Film, da muss ich auf die Zähne beißen und durchhalten. Wir wollen Filme machen, bei denen man den Unterschied zu internationalen Produktionen nicht merkt."
10 See www.ffa.de for more detailed market data.
11 "Das Kino hat oft keine gesellschaftliche Funktion, gilt nicht als kultureller Ort. Man geht noch ins Theater und akzeptiert auch, dass man sich langweilt. Aber ins Kino geht man nicht."
12 For details about the mandate of the Deutsche Filmakademie and its procedures and regulations, see www.deutsche-filmakademie.de.
13 "Der deutsche Film wird Kunst sein oder er wird nicht sein."
14 "Darum darf er [der deutsche Film] nicht instrumentalisiert, zu Tode poliert und durch Sicherheitsformeln stranguliert werden."
15 For a very informative account of the relationship between television and cinema, and the impact on visual aesthetics, see Halle, in particular, chapter 6.

16 See, for example, the review of *Anonyma—Eine Frau in Berlin* (*A Woman in Berlin*, Färberböck) in which the author states: "Und doch prägt die massenkompatible Primetime-Dramaturgie mit ihren flachen Spannungskurven, ihrer Scheu vor allzu roher Emotionalität und ihren öffentlich-rechtlichen Harmoniezwängen hier eine Geschichte, die letztlich nur aus Tiefen besteht" (Kreye).
17 "Danach hat es kaum noch radikale Experimente oder Neuentwicklungen gegeben. Vielleicht war es auch gar nicht mehr möglich, denn um 1980 herum hatte das Fernsehen die Schlacht um den Umgang mit bewegten Bildern endgültig gewonnen."
18 "Aber wir stellen diese Welt noch immer dar in alten Bildern, Karikaturen. Wir haben kein Bild von ihr, keine Erzählung. Um diese neuen Bilder und neuen Erzählungen, darum ging es mir."
19 For an overview of scholarly and public debates, see, for example, Schmitz.
20 For example, *Dresden* (Richter), *Die Gustloff* (Vilsmaier), *Die Kinder der Flucht* (Blumenberg), *Die Flucht* (Wessel).
21 "Auch bei Filmen wie *Der Untergang* oder *Schindlers Liste* ist alles faktisch unterfüttert. Die Opfer und Geretteten stehen Pate, aber diese Authentizität ist auf Dauer lähmend. Ein Film, der in die Oberfläche des Dokumentarismus hineinhackt, sie aufspaltet, kann etwas zu Tage fördern. Für mich war es wichtig, etwas über die Beschaffenheit diktatorischer Autorität herauszufinden. Die Autorität des Diktators beruht auf blindem Gehorsam, und wenn Film Gehorsam einfordert, wird er gefährlich. Er setzt das Unrechtssystem mit seinen Mitteln fort."
22 "[...] genügend Raum lassen für Gedanken und Assoziationen dazu. [...] Hier soll der Blick hinter die Strukturen zugelassen werden, Zeit gegeben werden, Geräusche und Bilder wahrzunehmen und die Auseinandersetzung mit einer Welt ermöglicht werden, die unsere Nahrungsmittel herstellt und doch so verdrängt wird."

References

"13 kurze Filme. The Making of *Deutschland '09*. Ein Gespräch mit Tom Tykwer, Dirk Wilutzky und Verena Rahmig." 29 June 2009 <http://deutschland09-der-film.de/13-kurzfilme>.

Abel, Marco. "The Cinema of Identification Gets on My Nerves: An Interview with Christian Petzold." *Cineaste* 33.2 (2008), 22 June 2009 <http://www.cineaste.com/articles/an-interview-with-christian-petzold.htm>.

Bauman, Zygmunt. "Liquid Modernity." Lecture. ANSE Conference. Leiden, Netherlands. 7 May 2004. 5 March 2011 <http://www.anse.eu/html/history/2004%20Leiden/bauman%20english.pdf>.

Beck, Ulrich. *World Risk Society*. Cambridge: Polity Press, 1999.

"Berlinale im Zeichen der Wirtschaftskrise." *Frankfurter Allgemeine Zeitung* 27 Jan. 2009. 27 Jan. 2009 <http://www.faz.net>.

Blackshaw, Tony. *Zygmunt Bauman*. Ed. Peter Hamilton. New York: Routledge, 2005.

Burner, Silvia. "Der Regisseur über den Film—Ein Interview." *Presseheft zum Film* Unser täglich Brot. 1 Dec. 2006. 5 July 2009 <http://www.greenpeace.de/themen/landwirtschaft/ alternativen/artikel/geyrhalter_im_gespraech>.

Burns, Rob. "Towards a Cinema of Cultural Hybridity: Turkish-German Filmmakers and the Representation of Alterity." *Debatte: Journal of Contemporary Central and Eastern Europe* 15.1 (2007): 3–24.

Buß, Christian. "Dann Lieber Mario Barth." *Spiegel Online* 25 Mar. 2009. 30 June 2009 <www.spiegel.de>.

Deutschland '09. 13 kurze Filme zur Lage der Nation. Dir. Angela Schanelec et al. Piffl Medien, 2009.

Deutschland im Herbst (Germany in Autumn). Filmverlag der Autoren, 1978.

"Eichinger: München ist als Drehort nicht attraktiv." *Merkur Online* 29 June 2009. 5 July 2009 <http://www.merkur-online.de>.

Elliot, Emory, Jasmine Payne, and Patricia Ploesch. "Global Migration, Social Change, and Cultural Production." *Global Migration, Social Change, and Cultural Transformation.* Ed. Emory Elliot, Jasmine Payne, and Patricia Ploesch. New York: Palgrave Macmillan, 2007. 1–9.

Frey, Matthias. "A Cinema in-Flux." *Senses of Cinema* 43 (2007). 22 June 2009 <http://archive.sensesofcinema.com/contents/festivals/07/43/berlin-iff-2007.html>.

———. "Insecure Times, Confident Localities." *Senses of Cinema* 50 (2009). 25 June 2009 <http://archive.sensesofcinema.com/contents/festivals/09/50/berliniff-2009.html>.

Greenaway, Peter. "Das Kino Neu Erfinden." *Zukunft Kino. The End of the Reel World*, ed. Daniela Kloock. Marburg: Schüren, 2008. 274–86.

Guillén, Mauro F. "Is Globalization Civilizing, Destructive or Feeble? A Critique of Five Key Debates in the Social Science Literature." *Annual Review of Sociology* 27 (2001): 235–60.

Hake, Sabine. *German National Cinema.* New York: Routledge, 2008.

Halle, Randall. *German Film after Germany. Toward a Transnational Aesthetic.* Urbana: U of Illinois P, 2008.

Hände weg von Mississippi (Hands off Mississippi). Dir. Detlev Buck. Boje Buck Produktion, 2007.

Hanfeld, Michael, and Michael Seewald. "Wir müssen kein schlechtes Gewissen haben." *Frankfurter Allgemeine Zeitung* 13 Feb. 2009. 13 Feb. 2009 <http://www.faz.net>.

The International. Dir. Tom Tykwer. Columbia Pictures, 2009.

John Rabe. Dir. Florian Gallenberger. Hoffmann & Voges Filmproduktion, 2009.

Kannapin, Detlef. "Gibt es eine spezifische Defa-Ästhetik?" *Apropos: Film 2000. Das Jahrbuch der Defa-Stiftung*, ed. DEFA-Stiftung. Berlin: Das Neue Berlin, 2000. 142–64.

KeinOhrHasen (Rabbit without Ears). Dir. Til Schweiger. Barefoot Films, 2007.

Koepnick, Lutz. "Reframing the Past: Heritage Cinema and Holocaust in the 1990s." *New German Critique* 87 (2002): 47–82.

Kreye, A. "Männer—von Natur aus feige." *Süddeutsche Zeitung* 22 Oct. 2008. 5 July 2009 <http://www.sueddeutsche.de>.

"Ludwigshafener Position." *Internationales Filmfestival Mannheim-Heidelberg.* 2005. 5 July 2009 <http://www.iffmh.de/de/Festival_des_deutschen_Films/Ludwigshafener_Position/>.

Lueken, Verena. "Wo ist denn die Fraktur geblieben?" *Frankfurter Allgemeine Zeitung* 13 Feb. 2009. 30 June 2009 <http://www.faz.net>.

Mammoth. Dir. Lukas Moodysson. Memfis Film, 2009.
Mein Führer—Die wirklich wahrste Wahrheit über Adolf Hitler (*Mein Führer: The Truly Truest Truth about Adolf Hitler*). Dir. Daniel Levy. X-Filme Directors Pool, 2007.
Nordrand (*Northern Skirts*). Barbara Albert. Lotus-Film, 1999.
Orr, John. "New Directions in European Cinema." *European Cinema*, ed. Elizabeth Ezra. Oxford: Oxford UP, 2004. 299–317.
Peterson, R. Dean, and Christine A. Monnier. "Globalization as Process and Product: The Remaking of the World Witnessing 'Pregnant' Times." In *Diasporic Ruptures. Globality, Migrancy, and Expressions of Identity*, Ed. Alireza Asgharzadeh et al., Vol. 1. Rotterdam: Sense, 2007. 3–18.
Prager, Brad, and Jaimey Fisher, ed. *The Collapse of the Conventional. German Film and Its Politics at the Turn of the Twenty-First Century*. Detroit: Wayne State UP, 2010.
Rentschler, Eric. "From New German Cinema to the Post-Wall Cinema of Consensus." *Cinema and Nation*. Ed. Mette Hjort and Scott MacKenzie. New York: Routledge, 2000. 260–77.
Schindler, Stephan, and Lutz Koepnick. "Against the Wall? The Global Imaginary of German Cinema." *The Cosmopolitan Screen. German Cinema and the Global Imaginary, 1945 to the Present.* Ed. Stephan Schindler and Lutz Koepnick. Ann Arbor: U of Michigan P, 2007. 1–21.
Schmitz, Helmut. "Introduction: The Return of Wartime Suffering in Contemporary German Memory Culture, Literature and Film." *A Nation of Victims? Representations of Wartime Suffering from 1945 to the Present*. Ed. Helmut Schmitz. Amsterdam: Rodopi, 2007. 1–30.
Schulz-Ojala, Jan, and Christina Tilmann. "Willkommen in Club." *Tagesspiegel* 23 April 2008, www.tagesspiegel.de (accessed 5 July 2009).
"Schweiger verlässt Filmakademie." *Focus Online* 20 Jan. 2008. 5 July 2009 <http://www.focus.de>.
Steinberg, Stefan. "Unkenntnis der Materie ist kein guter Ausgangspunkt." *World Socialist Web Site* 30 Jan. 2007. 5 July 2009 <http://www.wsws.org/de/2007/jan2007/fueh-j30.shtml>.
Sturm (*Storm*). Dir. Hans-Christian Schmid. 23/5 Filmproduktion, 2009.
Valkyrie. Dir. Bryan Singer. United Artists International, 2008.
Warum Männer nicht zuhören und Frauen schlecht einparken (*Why Men Don't Listen and Women Can't Read Maps*). Dir. Leander Haußmann. Constantin Film Produktion, 2007.
Worschech, Rudolf. "Deutschland '09." *epd Film* Apr. 2009. 30 June 2009 <http://www.epd-film.de/33178_63133.php>.
Yella. Dir. Christian Petzold. Indigo, 2007.
"Yella. Ein Film von Christian Petzold." 5 July 2009 <www.yella-der-film.de/makingof_01.html>.

CHALLENGING VIEWING HABITS

2
The Counter-Cinema
of the Berlin School

Marco Abel

Abstract This chapter discusses the filmmaking movement known as the "Berlin School." I argue that these films constitute a counter-cinema in the sense that they manage to critically engage the neo-liberalization of contemporary Germany because of, rather than despite, their particular aesthetics. These aesthetics, which I define as "a-representational realism," allow these films both to foreground critically the issue of mobility as one of the central socio-cultural aspects affecting contemporary German political discourse and to afford their viewers a chance to become affected by a (utopian) sensation of mobility that is currently absent in their actual existing, neo-liberal social spaces.

After a quarter century of neglect, German cinema has rekindled international interest in its productions. The many awards and recognitions German films have recently garnered—I'm thinking here of films such as Caroline Link's *Nirgendwo in Afrika* (*Nowhere in Africa*, 2001), Wolfgang Becker's *Good Bye, Lenin!* (2003), Fatih Akin's *Gegen die Wand* (*Head-On*, 2004), Hans Weingartner's *Die fetten Jahre sind vorbei* (*The Edukators*, 2004), Oliver Hirschbiegel's *Der Untergang* (*Downfall*, 2004), Marc Rothemund's *Sophie Scholl—Die letzten Tage* (*Sophie Scholl—The Final Days*, 2005), and Florian Henckel von Donnersmarck's *Das Leben der Anderen* (*The Lives of Others*, 2006)—evidence this renaissance of German film culture. Only too predictably, the German press and the country's film industry representatives jumped on the opportunity to appropriate the recent success stories of German films, as if to declare that "we're somebody again." This nationalistic rhetoric eagerly espouses the belief in a German film resurgence—a convenient myth that via a synecdochical logic allowed more nationalistically minded journalists and bureaucrats to dream of the long hoped-for fulfillment of their desire to see the country itself resurge out of the long shadows cast by its totalitarian history (and post-unification economic woes) and emerge, at long last, as a "normal" country. As appealing as this view of German film history may be, it simply draws an incorrect picture, as one of Germany's leading film critics, Katja Nicodemus, asserts in response to this new-found nationalist feeling about German film productions. The mainstream press and film industry representatives, who now celebrate the success of *Der Untergang* or *Das Leben der Anderen* as ingenious entrepreneurial endeavours that almost single-handedly pulled German films into the limelight of international film culture, have always obsessively focused their attention on how well the country's film productions fare at the box office. They have rarely paid attention to developing a healthy film-cultural infrastructure capable of nurturing and sustaining a broad range of homemade productions—including artistically innovative small-scale films that usually do not rake in big returns at the box office, but that are, aesthetically, considerably more challenging than the nation's best-known productions. And yet, as Nicodemus argues, it is precisely these small films that constitute the proper "we" at the heart of German film culture, rather than the few internationally renowned mainstream successes opportunistically celebrated by the country's culture industry.

Accounting for the recent developments in German film culture, French film critics coined the phrase *nouvelle vague Allemande* (Knörer). Pleased with this positive reception across the Rhine, the German film industry un-self-critically appropriated this assessment into their own self-satisfied nationalist sentiments, all the while ignoring that for the French this term encompasses not merely films such as *Good Bye, Lenin!* but also Henner Winckler's *Klassenfahrt* (*School Trip*, 2002), Ulrich Köhler's *Bungalow* (2002), Christoph Hochhäusler's *Milchwald* (*This Very Moment*, 2003), or Angela Schanelec's *Marseille* (2004). It is films such as these—persistently ignored at home—that cumulatively demonstrate the emergence of a new film language in German cinema and constitute, according to Nicodemus, the true core of contemporary German film culture. Yet, what appeared to *Cahiers du cinéma* and *Le Monde* as a "new" wave of creatively innovative German films are, in fact, only more recent examples of a subterranean genealogy of German filmmaking that hearkens back to the first half of the 1990s. Consequently, what appears to many as a resurgence of German cinema is much better thought of as a continuation of an ongoing filmmaking process since unification—one that has predominantly taken place below the radar of the country's self-appointed cultural guardians.

This, if you will, counter-cinema, has become known in Germany as the Berlin School. The films associated with this school distinguish themselves from other post-wall German films primarily in that they constitute the first significant (collective) attempt at advancing the *aesthetics* of cinema within German narrative filmmaking since the New German Cinema of Rainer Werner Fassbinder, Werner Herzog, Wim Wenders, Alexander Kluge, Klaus Lemke, Margarethe von Trotta, Jean-Marie Straub, and Danièle Huillet, and others. So who or what is the Berlin School? The label was coined by German film critic Merthen Worthmann in a review of Schanelec's film *Mein langsames Leben* (*Passing Summer*, 2001), but was subsequently used by critics to refer to films by what is now known as the first generation of the Berlin School: Schanelec, Christian Petzold, and Thomas Arslan. All three attended and graduated in the early 1990s from the Deutsche Film und Fernsehakademie Berlin (DFFB), arguably the country's most intellectual film school, and were taught by avant-garde and documentary filmmakers Harun Farocki and Hartmut Bitomsky. As others have observed, however, the Berlin School label is somewhat misleading when its scope is widened to a second generation of filmmakers such as Köhler and Henner Winckler, graduates of the Hochschule für bildende Künste Hamburg; Hochhäusler, Benjamin Heisenberg, and Maren Ade, graduates of the Hochschule für Fernsehen und Film München; Maria Speth, who honed her skills at the HFF "Konrad Wolf" in Potsdam-Babelsberg; Valeska Grisebach, who studied film in Vienna; or Aysum Bademsoy, who studied theatre at the Freie Universität Berlin and is, like Arslan, a child of Turkish immigrants who came to Germany in the 1960s.

In short, many so-called Berlin School directors neither hail from nor learned their filmmaking skills in Berlin (even though most of them have moved there by now). Nor, I hasten to add, are many Berlin School films about, or even set in, Berlin; in fact, one of the more interesting aspects of these films is their willingness to encounter spaces outside of Germany's urban centres. Still, the label has unquestionably become part of the daily vocabulary of German film critics—so much so that discussions of the merits of individual films are often subordinated to considerations of them as examples of this school. That this de-singularization is something neither filmmakers nor more adventurous film critics are particularly fond of is understandable. Symptomatically, Olaf Möller claims in his program notes for "A German Cinema," a side series he curated for the 2007 Indie Lisboa Film Festival, that he did not include certain directors usually associated with the Berlin School at least partially, because he did not want to perpetuate already existing prejudices. He points out the danger involved in pigeonholing these directors, citing the reception of films by Arslan, Schanelec, and Petzold (*Ferien* [*Vacation*, 2007], *Nachmittag* [*Afternoon*, 2007], and *Yella* [2007], respectively), which were often discussed upon their premiere at the Berlin Film Festival (Berlinale) in 2007 only in relation to each other rather than based on their own individual merits.

Agreeing with Möller's concerns, I still think the label remains useful, because it enables the description and even advocacy of a cinema that otherwise finds itself ignored by a mainstream press more concerned with the latest box office numbers than with challenging its readers to seek out films that actively try to re-envision what German cinema could be(come). So what are these films like? Oskar Roehler, one of Germany's foremost directors of the post-wall era who decidedly does not belong to the Berlin School, characterizes these films as recalcitrant and stern. According to him, nothing much happens in films such as Arslan's *Mach die Musik leiser* (1994), Schanelec's *Plätze in den Städten* (*Places in Cities*, 1998), Petzold's *Die innere Sicherheit* (*The State I Am In*, 2000), Grisebach's *Mein Stern* (*Be My Star*, 2001), Hochhäusler's *Falscher Bekenner* (*Low Profile* a.k.a. *I'm Guilty*, 2005), or Köhler's *Montag kommen die Fenster* (*Windows on Monday*, 2006). To Roehler, these films are slow and dreary, feature hardly any dialogue, are admired by critics—and attract 5,000–10,000 viewers (Suchsland "Langsames Leben" 6). Indeed, box office receipts confirm Roehler's negative assessment. For instance, whereas films such as *Der Untergang*, Michael "Bully" Herbig's *(T)raumschiff Surprise* (2004), and Tom Tykwer's *Das Parfum—Die Geschichte eines Mörders* (*Perfume—Story of a Murderer*, 2006) attracted 4.6, 9.1, and 5.5 million theatrical viewers, respectively, Jan Krüger's *Unterwegs* (*En Route*, 2004) was seen in Germany by merely 1,200 theatrical viewers, Winckler's first feature, *Klassenfahrt* by 2,300, Schanelec's *Marseille* by 3,100, *Low Profile* by 11,600, Heisenberg's *Schläfer* (*Sleeper*, 2005) by 15,900, Grisebach's *Sehnsucht* (*Longing*, 2006) by 22,500, and Petzold's *Gespenster* (*Ghosts*, 2005) by 27,200.[1] Only Petzold's *Die innere Sicherheit*, the winner of the German film award in 2001, and, more recently, Ade's *Alle Anderen* (*Everyone Else*, 2009), winner of the Silver Bear at the 2009 Berlinale, found a considerably broader theatregoing audience, attracting a respectable 120,000 and 193,000 viewers, respectively, making them the most successful Berlin School films to date.

Yet, it would be misleading to consider this group of filmmakers merely successful with a handful of film critics in Germany and cineastes in France and England (British Film Institute's *Sight & Sound* has probably paid more attention to contemporary German cinema than any other international publication in the last five years). With a production cost that rarely exceeds 1 million euros, most of these films reach a 12–15 percent audience share during their TV screenings. Furthermore, judging by the Berlinale of the last few years, this film movement is picking up steam. For instance, among the fifty or more German films that the festival screens annually were new efforts by Arslan, Petzold, Schanelec, Grisebach, Heisenberg, Hochhäusler, Köhler, Speth, Ade, and Winckler; in fact, in 2010 the festival screened the latest efforts by Arslan, Schanelec, and Heisenberg, films that collectively were praised as being among the most interesting the festival screened that year. Even more remarkably, Grisebach's second feature-length film, *Sehnsucht*, a provocative study of longing in small-town East Germany shot with non-professional actors, was screened in the festival's main competition in 2006 rather than as part of the artistically more adventurous "Forum" or "Perspective German Cinema" series. Although Grisebach's film did not win any prizes, audiences enthusiastically applauded the film, and many critics considered it the best competition entry. Likewise, many praised Petzold's *Yella* as the best film of the 2007 competition. Yet the film's positive critical reception did not prevent it from fizzling out at the German box office at around 80,000 theatrical viewers, and as one of the few Berlin School films that received US distribution, it earned merely $30,000 since its May 2008 release in New York City. His follow-up, *Jerichow* (2009), an inspired riff on *The Postman Always Rings Twice* story, earned $60,000 on its theatrical run in the US and was seen by 100,000 viewers in Germany. Finally, Ade's widely praised *Alle Anderen* managed to cross the $100,000 mark in the United States, thus making it the biggest Berlin School hit in America to date.

To suggest that the Berlin School has become, or is at least part of, the establishment, either in Germany or elsewhere is thus clearly preposterous. Indeed, most Germans have never even heard of these directors and their films. Nor, for that matter, has this group as a whole received unanimous critical praise. In fact, their general lack of commercial success has made them vulnerable to polemical attacks from representatives of the German mainstream film industry and media. Writing for the Berlin *Tagesspiegel*, film critic Harald Martenstein, for instance, lambasted the Berlinale premiere of *Gespenster*, complaining that upon viewing the film he "felt thrown back into the hell of the German *Autorenfilm* of the 1970s, in which protagonists remain meaningfully silent and each character has to function as a metaphor for existential 'thrownness.'"[2] And Doris Dörrie, one of Germany's best-known directors ever since her breakthrough film, *Männer* (*Men*, 1985), chimed in on the ongoing backlash against the Berlin School by accusing them of hiding too much behind film theory and playing it too safe, adding, "I secretly hold against them [...] that they do not risk enough and hide behind form. I don't like this: to hide oneself behind form"[3] (Kriest 9). Even a long-time supporter such as film critic Rüdiger Suchsland eventually felt compelled to offer more critical remarks, wishing that the "Berlin

School could find the strength to destroy the impression that it is merely the cinema made by members of the well-to-do bourgeoisie in Berlin-Mitte. One wishes that the films were to clearly state what they are for rather than what they are against"[4] (Suchsland "'Gefährliches' Kino" 47).

Most notoriously, the Berlin School cinema became the implied subject of a highly visible public put-down by Günter Rohrbach, the president of the German Film Academy since its founding in 2003. Rohrbach once was an important supporter of the New German Cinema. He produced, for instance, Fassbinder's *Berlin Alexanderplatz* (1980) and also left his mark on German film culture as the producer of some of the country's commercially most successful movies, including Wolfgang Petersen's *Das Boot* (*The Boat*, 1981). In an essay originally published in Germany's leading weekly news magazine *Der Spiegel*, Rohrbach attacked German film critics as vain self-publicists for their tendency to trash commercially successful German film productions such as Tykwer's *Das Parfum* while celebrating films such as *Sehnsucht* that "wither away in the cinema."[5] Rohrbach singled out Grisebach's film because German film critics enthusiastically reviewed it and vehemently complained that this personal film, unlike Tykwer's blockbuster, received no nominations for the German Film Prize, which as of 2005 is being awarded by a body of voters resembling the Academy of Motion Picture Arts and Sciences.[6]

In addition to the charge of box office impotence, Ekkerhard Knörer reports that another common criticism of Berlin School films is that they supposedly lack interest in the political and instead present us with a "bourgeois poetics of middle-class navel-gazing."[7] According to Cristina Nord, this tendency has hypostatized in some cases into a sense of bourgeois "melancholic suffering" affecting the films' protagonists and, simultaneously, a formal mannerism affecting the films themselves. It is impossible to argue against the empirical evidence of these films' struggle at the box office; however, to charge these films with the "crime" of being apolitical strikes me as questionable. In the age of finance capitalism, the conception of the political at work in such accusations seems unproductive, not least because it nostalgically relies on a version of traditional leftist politics that may no longer have any purchase on the objects of its critique.[8] Indeed, part of the reason the Berlin School films are so compelling—and deserving of greater (inter)national recognition—is their specific cinematic nature, which renders these films political, albeit not in the traditional (content-based or agitational) sense of the term.

If one wanted a shorthand description for the films of the Berlin School, one could do worse than starting to consider how they tend to pursue an aesthetics of reduction reminiscent of the films by Robert Bresson, Michelangelo

Antonioni, Michael Haneke, the Dardenne brothers, or the second-generation directors of the French New Wave such as Maurice Pialat, Jean Eustache, and Philippe Garrel. This approach to film aesthetics is particularly striking in films such as *Milchwald*, a contemporary riff on the Brothers Grimm's fairy tale "Hansel and Gretel," set in the German–Polish border region; Winckler's *Lucy* (2005), a patiently observing study of a teenage girl's reluctance to live up to the expectations and responsibilities she suddenly faces as a new mother; Arslan's *Aus der Ferne* (*From Far Away*, 2006), his nearly voice-over-free travelogue of Turkey, his country of birth; or *Karger* (2007), a Ken Loach–like study of the fate suffered by working-class lives in the post-industrial age by Elke Hauck, another DFFB graduate. Many, though not all, Berlin School films are dominated by long takes, long shots, clinically precise framing, a certain deliberateness of pacing, sparse usage of extra-diegetic music, poetic use of diegetic sound, and, frequently, the reliance on unknown or even non-professional actors who appear to be chosen for who they *are* rather than for who they could be. In so doing, these films sharpen the viewer's attention while effortlessly creating undramatic tensions. Cumulatively, these cinematic aspects stress the characters' spatiotemporal existence—unlike the films belonging to what Eric Rentschler influentially described as the "cinema of consensus" cycle. These films unmistakably take place in a specific time and place: in the here and now of unified Germany.

Such spatiotemporal precision directs viewers' attention to the poetic texture of what could easily be mistaken for an artlessly realist *mise en scène*. These remarkably precise films solicit audience attention so that our sense perceptions are made to tune in to the extraordinary qualities of otherwise rather ordinary lives. Many of these films, that is, thematically focus on the everyday and attempt to capture normality—which is done so that in their visual intensification of normality the extraordinary at the heart of everyday-ness emerges. As Benjamin Heisenberg remarked in a conversation with me, what these films have in common is "that the camera does not allow the viewer to identify with the characters, but it is not really distancing us from them either. Instead, it creates and positions us in an in-between space that pulls us to and fro, ultimately holding us suspended in a middle space that is quite akin to the characters' own subjectivity/subject position."[9] This formal suspending that Heisenberg describes here instills a strong observational quality in his and other Berlin School films. It is as if they intentionally heeded a filmmaking adage that André Bazin once attributed to Erich von Stroheim: "Take a close look at the world and keep on doing so" ("Evolution" 27). Relentlessly focusing their camera on seemingly unremarkable events, these films exhibit a tendency to stare, thus effecting an alteration of that which they stare at from within the act of seeing (and listening) itself.

We should therefore not reduce these films to the documentary-like moniker that is so often used to describe films that call in the services of so-called realism. Certainly, as Hochhäusler says of Köhler's *Bungalow*, a distinctive feature of the Berlin School films is that they allow for an "incursion of reality into the German film" (qtd. in Rohnke). If anything, though, the Berlin School's aesthetic is more akin to what Bazin once defined as "true realism" ("Evolution" 12): these films are too obviously stylized by means of camera movement and *mise en scène* to be described as documenting reality. For instance, the sheer length of most of Schanelec's shots in *Marseille* foreground the artificial choices that give rise to the sense of reality we feel when exposed to her images: reality is not just captured, but rendered sensible through the effect her images have on the viewer. Likewise, the ambient diegetic sounds (car and street noises, the sounds of trees swaying in the wind) in Petzold's *Gespenster* or *Yella*, which often intrigue us because of their astonishing, indeed eerie, clarity, do not so much declare "that's the way reality is" as provoke in us a sense of wonder about the materiality at the heart of the everyday. These films force us to confront something that is real enough for us, but that usually remains outside of our day-to-day purview because of how our perceptive apparatus tends to block out such aspects of social reality. Rather than aiming to represent reality "as it is," these films abstract from our pre-existing clichéd perceptions of reality in order to induce a different experience of it by making reality itself appear more intensely sensible.

Along with this forgoing of any attempt at producing representational (or psychological) realism is these films' tendency to *flaner* in the Benjaminian sense with their characters, seemingly aimlessly or, perhaps better, phlegmatically, as is the case in, for example, *Lucy*, *Gespenster*, Arslan's *Der schöne Tag* (*A Fine Day*, 2001), Schanelec's *Mein langsames Leben*, or Ann-Kristen Reyels' *Jagdhunde* (*Hounds*, 2007), a film that some German film reviewers discussed in the context of the Berlin School. Köhler's *Bungalow* is in this respect one of the most quintessential of all Berlin School films. Not only is the defining feature of the film's protagonist, Paul, his utter apathy and refusal to care about the consequences of his (in)actions, but the film's *mise en scène* itself relentlessly images his refusal to engage and to live up to expectations (of the army, his brother, his friends, etc.). Consider, for instance, the film's opening sequence. For about three minutes, we witness a continuous camera movement that follows the arrival of an army truck, depicts soldiers entering and exiting a burger joint, and suddenly "refuses" to continue its movement with the soldiers, just as Paul, seemingly spontaneously, "decides" to stop his own movement and not join his troop as it leaves. Did he plan to desert? The film provides no evidence

Ulrich Köhler, *Bungalow*. © Peter Stockhaus Filmproduktion

for this. Why does Paul not rejoin his comrades? We never find out, and we do not gain the sense that Paul himself knows or cares to know. Paul's "actions" are imaged here and throughout the film not in terms of an active, conscious rejection of something in particular, but in terms of an unexplained phlegmatism (exemplified by Paul's deliberate, slow movements through the rural middle-class spaces he inhabits), his lack of emoting in his interactions with his do-gooder brother and his pretty Danish girlfriend, as well as his general indifference to how his behaviour affects his surroundings. For the viewer, the strangeness of Paul's behaviour foregrounds also the strangeness of what otherwise might simply appear as the normal, mundane environment in which many middle-class Germans dwell. In short, the Berlin School films' ethnological gaze—which they frequently direct at in-between spaces such as the border region separating Germany and Poland in *Klassenfahrt* and *Milchwald*, or the socially and emotionally transitory spaces that one frequently finds within German cities in most of Petzold's work—shows contemporary Germany as if from the perspective of a stranger.[10]

Although the Berlin School does decidedly not exhibit the traditional characteristics of avant-garde cinema,[11] these films' attitude toward reality is akin to that of an experiment whose outcome is yet to be determined. These films give the impression as if they approached the world they encounter with the assumption that they do not yet know what this object—or the other—they try to depict is. They are careful not to represent this other and thus reduce it to the pre-existing point of view of a subject that speaks from a position of superior knowledge; they instead exemplarily heed, as Theodor Adorno put it in *Aesthetic Theory*, "the primacy of the object" (145). They neither speak for this object nor make it speak; rather, in patiently engaging their objects, they create maps of the very socio-political, economic, cultural, and emotional forces that have paralyzed post-wall Germany since 1989, when the country's most recent roller-coaster ride began with the heights of the fall of the Berlin Wall and the country's subsequent unification, only to end in massive unemployment and an attending social malaise. This depression culminated around the turn of the millennium in a public debate on the Germans' unwillingness to move—to communities away from home, to different careers, to a different state of mind no longer beholden to the belief that the role of the state is supposed to be to take care of its citizens—lest the final remnants of the once well-functioning welfare state vanish, too. Indeed, it is hardly a coincidence that former German President Horst Köhler, previously head of the International Monetary Fund, felt compelled to admonish Germans in 2005 to become more mobile in a speech about which the most remarkable aspect was that it had to be delivered to begin with; after all, one of his predecessors, Roman Herzog, had already famously addressed the German nation in 1997 with the demand that Germany needed to jolt itself into action.[12] Köhler's reiteration of Herzog's original appeal simply, yet symptomatically, marked the seemingly all-pervasive paralysis that afflicted Germany once its unification party had come to an end.

The Berlin School cinematically responds to this nexus of socio-cultural paralysis. These films do so, however, neither by realistically representing such immobility nor by providing viewers with sympathetic characters who manage to escape. Their aesthetic is not emblematic of a more traditional representational realism, let alone expressive of a naïve form of political (thesis-driven) social realism. Indeed, Ulrich Köhler recently published a polemical essay in which he explains why he does not make political films. One of the surest ways to receive public funding for film productions in Germany, according to Köhler, is to make topical, message-driven films that package political enlightenment in stories. Köhler, who like many of his fellow Berlin School directors is currently struggling to find financing for his next film project, derides such *Lehrfilme* (educational films) as the embodiment of "the aesthetic program of social democratized cultural politics" (11).[13] Against this moralistic imperative to be a conscientious filmmaker who uses his art for the betterment of society, Köhler mounts a near-Adorno-esque defence of the autonomy of art in writing that "art that only wants to be art is often far more subversive" than topical art, whose popularity itself is frequently an index for its affirmation of the status quo (12).[14] Arguing against any form of liberal-bourgeois instrumentalization of filmmaking, Köhler declares, "If art is political it is political in exactly this: It refuses to be exploited by the daily round of political and social concerns. Its strength lies in its autonomy"[15] (12). Far from political acquiescence, Köhler articulates here that the job of art is not to be political (qua content) but to produce politically. In the case of cinema, producing politically today entails the (renewed) investigation of the politics of the image—not least because contemporary capitalist culture is the lightest, most image-based economic operation to which we have ever been exposed.

Rather than (moralistically) exercising the well-meaning yet ineffective operations of representational realism, the Berlin School films invent images of mobility that render visible something that is currently absent in the viewers' real social context. These films image their characters' lived refusals to either embrace the clichéd desires of individual and social security or pursue the bourgeois demand for social upward mobility—the very demand rhetorically articulated by the German presidents. Yet the experimental character of their individual encounters with reality ensures that these films ultimately differ from each other. This singularity ensues from the directors' essential attitude toward their medium—a stance perhaps best articulated by Hochhäusler when writing in the British film magazine *Vertigo* that the "goal is a cinema that makes life more intense. Every film has to let itself be measured against life. It could be said: A film is an instrument in the process of producing reality. It is therefore part of a social context. The basic question is: What is real? Each attempt at replying is a personal commitment." This strongly felt sense of personal commitment to reality results in a cinematic attitude toward reality that rejects the very clichés that have dominated German cinema, as well as its post-wall political discourse, for the last two decades.

Instead of catering toward the familiar, these films present their audiences with new, non-pre-existing images of Germany. But this imaging of novelty proceeds by intensifying its look at reality, rather than by avoiding it. These films are thus involved in inventing—or at least experimentally developing—an a-representational realism: a film style that cinematically embraces, seeks out, and non-judgmentally welcomes reality, but does so in ways that can be considered an extension of Adorno's often forgotten late-career argument about cinema in "Transparencies on Film." Putting the slightest pressure on Adorno's comments, we might say that the task the Berlin School sets itself is not to create immediacy with reality but with the (reality of the) image, so that the depicted world becomes aesthetically autonomous, abstracted from empirical reality. It is, however, just this aesthetic abstraction from empirical reality that affords viewers an intensified encounter with their own social reality, as they find themselves confronted with the necessity to rethink the very relation between what and how they see. Put differently, the (hoped-for) effect of such aesthetic intensification of the act of seeing is to bring about a momentary suspension of our habituated tendency to read images through the framework of representational realism. By affirming the image as image, the Berlin School films thus affectively transform reality, forcing viewers to engage the seemingly familiar as something unfamiliar while never alienating them from what they see. This achieved effect neither correlates to the "cinema of identification" nor embraces the imperative to create distance between image and viewer as it was advocated by what some have denounced as "grand theory."[16] While some might consider this failure to create distance between the film and our perceptive apparatus another reason for characterizing these films as, at best, apolitical, I would concur with Steven Shaviro that in a world in which the experience of life is dominated by permanent alienation, one can hardly have any faith in creating more alienation as an effective political solution to the problems caused by consumer capitalism. As Shaviro writes, "Precisely because film is already predicated on what Benjamin [...] calls the destruction of the aura, because it is already an 'alienated' art, its capacity to affect the spectator is not perturbed by any additional measure of alienation" (43). Instead of alienating us from their images in order to "get out" of them, the Berlin School films immerse us in their images (and sounds) to get us away from the clichés of reality—to affect us so that we may begin to re-see and hear again, that is, to rethink our own relation to the world that we all too often perceive in overly reductive ways.

Instead of becoming (however unintentionally) a mouthpiece for the patriarchal, neo-liberal rhetoric of Germany's past and present presidents, then, these films offer viewers sensations of what Michael Hardt and Antonio Negri, in their inspired interpretation of Herman Melville's short story "Bartleby the Scrivener," have theorized in *Empire* as "absolute refusal" of neo-liberal mobility (203–4). This sensation, articulated by Bartleby's famous "I prefer not to" reply to any request put to him, is rendered haptically through an intensive filmic actualization of mobility: it is precisely because so little movement occurs in many of the Berlin School films that the sensation of movement becomes affectively palpable at crucial moments in them. I am thinking here, for instance, of the opening and closing moments of *Bungalow*; the astonishing ending of *Marseille*, which forces us to consider the transformation the protagonist might have undergone as we look at a static, seemingly endless long shot in which she gradually disappears strolling along the Mediterranean beach; the last images of *Falscher Bekenner* in which the protagonist, who falsely claims authorship for a series of

Christoph Hochhäusler, *Falscher Bekenner*. © Heimatfilm GmbH

violent events, smiles directly into the camera as if to express that he finally managed to escape the comfortable yet boring life afforded him by his suburban, provincial upbringing; or for that matter Petzold's entire oeuvre.[17]

Although the Berlin School films tend to provide us with images that seemingly invite contemplation, their nature is not hermeneutic, since what we see is always quite lucid. The question they provoke is never, "what does this image 'mean'?"; instead, they affectively solicit our subjection to them: they provoke our fascination and expose us to their sensations. In so doing, they establish a mimetic relation in Adorno's sense between the depicted world and the reality from which the images are abstracted: instead of representing this reality and thus inevitably reducing it to the primacy of the representing subject, these films articulate an analogical similarity with this world, which becomes possible only because they heed the irreducible difference of that to which their images point. This very metonymic relation affectively expresses the cinematically fashioned provocation for us to move as well—to forge relations with our world so that the pre-existing life-world reappears as strange. This making strange of the familiar initiates in viewers material encounters with their worlds that issue forth a sense of joy and thus hope. It is as if these films were appealing to their (German) audience to start believing in their world again, rather than wallowing in nostalgia for a lost Eden—fed by memories of life in pre-unified Germany—or investing their hopes in the false utopia promised by neo-liberal demagogues.

To return to my earlier notion of the cartographic quality of the Berlin School films, the nature of the maps these films produce of contemporary Germany is untimely rather than representational. They delineate less a series of images of post-wall Germany as it is—clichéd impressions that would merely have the questionable appeal of tourist snapshots—than a network of images that, as if by accident, emerge from within the characters' subjective existence. Generative in nature, these images do not represent a pre-existing reality; they instead render visible aspects of social reality that are either inaccessible to, or simply absent in, the current "real" reality of post-wall citizens. And it is their untimeliness that finally imbues these images with a political quality: they are *of* their time only in so far as they are offered up in hopes of a better time to come. The Berlin School produces films that are politically necessary, not because these directors make political films (i.e., message-driven films such as Michael Moore's) but because they make their films politically—because their images do not so much pretend to represent some invisible knowledge of the real Germany offered up as indispensable insights as point to the future in hopes that the force of these images bears enough virtual potential for affecting yet-to-come moments with transformative energy, with the capacity to alter the very reality from within which these images initially emerged.

This aesthetic dwelling in, and intensification of, the here and now points us to one final aspect of the Berlin School. These films neither wilfully universalize their cultural-historical specificity as do, for instance, many German comedies of consensus such as Rainer Kaufmann's *Stadtgespräch* (*Talk of the Town*, 1995) nor do they sidestep the difficulties of the present by once again dutifully (re)turning to the, by now, neatly codified horrors of the past as did the recent wave of Hitler films such as *Sophie Scholl*, Dennis Gansel's *Napola* (2004), *Der Untergang*, or the made-for-TV two-part docudrama *Dresden* (Roland Suso Richter, 2006). The Berlin School instead presents us with a passionate and innovative effort to find new ways of describing and analyzing the present of a country that continues to struggle with finding its true identity six decades after the end of World War II and almost two decades after its unification. This presentism—pursued in the name of affecting the future—should not be considered a denial of history, as if this new generation of filmmakers turned its back on the horrors perpetuated by an earlier generation of Germans.[18] Rather, the films' insistence on discovering, and tapping into, the plenitude of stories available in the country's present sheds light on the very conditions of possibility in today's Germany for ethically heeding a sense of responsibility—for habituating one's capacity to become response-able before the other at the very moment when the socio-psychic environment of Germany faces great pressures from within and without in form of both the economic and psychological costs of the unification, which went anything but smoothly, and, concurrently, the brutal socio-economic effects produced by the logic of neo-liberalism, which accelerate the erosion of Germany's once celebrated social security net.

Notwithstanding their individual differences, we might view the Berlin School as undertaking the effort to create an itinerary of the present—not in order to deny history but to speculate about how a different future might be brought about. Since speculation—*specere* is Greek for "to look at"—is by definition *of* the sphere of the visual, it is only proper that these filmmakers pursue their conjecture by carefully attending to how their practices realize their medium's inherent qualities. The Berlin School films produce images that invent new lines of flight, or arrows of thought, so that viewers may pick them up in order to find solutions to their individual and collective malaise by re-seeing the problem from within their own social space. By amplifying the images' realistic concreteness to a point of abstraction, these films insist that such images are, precisely, politically necessary. It is through this process of rendering visible that the sensation of mobility or transformation emerges: at the most intensified moment of utter stasis is where things break down, where transformation, that is, the affective sensation of movement for which one then needs to forge linkages with the reality of socio-cultural space, occurs. Understood this way—as attempting to wrestle away utopian images from pre-existing social reality—the Berlin School films can be regarded as a cinema that is engaged in the difficult task to improve Germany's reality in the age of post-wall globalization by providing better images for it.

Notes

This essay is a modified version of my essay "Intensifying Life: The Cinema of the 'Berlin School,'" *Cineaste* online (Fall 2008).

1 The German box office figures are taken from http://filmportal.de and www.ffa.de. For US box office numbers cited below, I consulted http://www.boxofficemojo.com.
2 "Ich dachte in *Gespenster*, sie hätten mich wieder in die Hölle des deutschen Autorenfilms der siebziger Jahre gesperrt, wo sich die Akteure bedeutsam anschweigen und jede Figur eine Metapher fürs existentielle Geworfensein zu sein hat."
3 "Ich werfe denen insgeheim vor [...], dass sie zu wenig Risiko eingehen und sich etwas hinter der Form verstecken. Ich mag das gar nicht: sich hinter der Form verstecken."
4 "[...] die 'Berliner Schule könnte die Kraft finden und den Eindruck zerstreuen, es handle sich lediglich um das Wohlstandskino bürgerlicher Kreise aus Berlin-Mitte. Man wünscht, die Filme würden deutlich machen, wofür und nicht wogegen sie sind."
5 "[...] im Kino verkümmern."
6 For a more detailed account of this event, see Abel, "22 January 2007."

7. I should clarify this does not express Knörer's own view of the Berlin School but instead his summary of arguments made by other critics.
8. For more on this issue, see Abel, "The Cinema of Identification."
9. Personal conversation, 24 March 2007.
10. For a discussion of Petzold's oeuvre, see Abel, "Imaging Germany" and Abel, "The Cinema of Identification."
11. In the German context, I am thinking of avant-garde filmmakers such as Monika Treut, Ulrike Ottinger, or Harun Farocki, for example.
12. I am referring here to Herzog's famous "Ruck-Rede" of 26 April 1997 at the Hotel Adlon, which Köhler echoed in his speech of 15 March 2005 on the occasion of the "Arbeitgeberforum: 'Wirtschaft und Gesellschaft'" in Berlin. Both speeches are dominated by a rhetoric relying on phrases such as "Flexibilität" (flexibility) and "Mobilität" (mobility).
13. "[...] das ästhetische Programm sozialdemokratisierter Kulturpolitik."
14. "Kunst, die nur Kunst sein will, ist häufig subversiver." For Adorno's views on this matter, see his essay "Commitment."
15. "Wenn Kunst politisch ist, dann ist sie genau darin politisch: Sie wehrt sich dagegen (tages)politisch und gesellschaftlich verwertbar zu sein. Ihre Stärke liegt in ihrer Autonomie."
16. I use the term "grand theory" here merely as a shorthand for the kind of film theory emerging in the 1970s that argued for the need of films to create distance between spectator and image. For a wholesale negative assessment of "grand theory," which I do not share, see Bordwell and Carrol.
17. Using static endings is, of course, not new in the history of cinema. One of the most famous static endings is undoubtedly the zoom-in-on-freeze-frame of Antoine Doinel in François Truffaut's *400 Blows*, and fellow contemporary German filmmakers such as Fatih Akin and Andreas Dresen have also made use of this device (in *Auf der anderen Seite* [*The Edge of Heaven*, 2007] and *Willenbrock* [2005], respectively), yet the frequency with which the Berlin School films have recourse to endings of this kind strikes me as remarkable.
18. The directors of the first generation of the Berlin School were born in the early 1960s; those associated with the second generation were mostly born after 1968.

References

Abel, Marco. "The Cinema of Identification Gets on My Nerves: An Interview with Christian Petzold." *Cineaste* 33.2 (2008). 15 June 2009 <http://cineaste.com/articles/an-interview-with-christian-petzold.htm>.

———. "Imaging Germany: The (Political) Cinema of Christian Petzold." *The Collapse of the Conventional: German Films and its Politics at the Turn of the New Century*. Ed. Jaimey Fisher and Brad Prager. Detroit: Wayne State UP, 2010. 258–84.

———. "22 January 2007: The Establishment Strikes Out Against the 'Berlin School.'" *A New History of German Cinema*. Ed. Jennifer Kapczynski and Michael Richardson. Rochester: Camden House. In press.

Adorno, Theodor. Transparencies on Film." *New German Critique* 24/25 (Fall 1981/Winter 1982): 199–205.

———. "Commitment." In *Notes to Literature*. Vol. 2. New York: Columbia UP, 1992. 76–94.

———. *Aesthetic Theory*. Trans. Robert Hullot-Kentor. Minneapolis: U of Minnesota P, 1997.
Alle Anderen. Dir. Maren Ade. Euro Video, 2010.
Aus der Ferne. Dir. Thomas Arslan. Peripher, 2006.
Bazin, André. "Ontology of the Photographic Image." In *What Is Cinema?* Ed. Hugh Grey. Vol. 1. Berkeley: U of California P, 2005. 9–16.
———. "The Evolution of the Language of Cinema." In *What Is Cinema?* Ed. Hugh Grey. Vol. 1. Berkeley: U of California P, 2005. 23–40.
Bordwell, David, and Noël Carrol, ed. *Post Theory: Reconstructing Film Studies*. Madison: U of Wisconsin P, 1996.
Bungalow. Dir. Ulrich Köhler. Filmgalerie 451, 2004.
Falscher Bekenner. Dir. Christoph Hochhäusler. Indigo, 2007.
Hardt, Michael, and Antonio Negri. *Empire*. Cambridge: Harvard UP, 2000.
Heisenberg, Benjamin. Personal interview. 19 December 2005.
Hochhäusler, Christoph. "Right to Reply: A Cinema of Challenge." *Vertigo* 4.3 (2009). 15 June 2009 http://www.vertigomagazine.co.uk/showarticle.php?sel=cur&siz=1&id=773.
Jerichow. Dir. Christian Petzold. Cinema Guild, 2009.
Knörer, Ekkerhard. "Longshots: Luminous Days—Notes on the New German Cinema." *Vertigo* 4.3 (2009). 15 June 2009 <http://www.vertigomagazine.co.uk/showarticle.php?sel=cur&siz=1&id=772>.
Köhler, Ulrich. "Why I Don't Make Political Films." Trans. Bettina Steinbruegge, *Cinema Scope* 38 (spring 2009): 10–13. Originally published as "Warum ich keine 'politischen' Filme mache." *new filmkritik* 23 April 2007. 15 June 2009 <http://newfilmkritik.de>.
Kriest, Ulrich. "Die Außenseiterin—Doris Dörrie: Versuch einer Annäherung." *Film-Dienst* 5 (2008): 7–9.
Lucy. Dir. Henner Winckler. Filmgalerie 451, 2007.
Marseille. Dir. Angela Schanelec. Filmgalerie 451, 2005.
Martenstein, Harald. "Martenstein geht unter die Ausländer." *Tagesspiegel* 17 February 2005. 15 June 2009 <http://www.tagesspiegel.de>.
Milchwald. Dir. Christoph Hochhäusler. Filmgalerie 451, 2003.
Möller, Olaf. "Das Mögliche machen, so Weiteres möglich machen." *new filmkritik* 7 July 2007. 15 June 2009 <http://newfilmkritik.de>.
Nicodemus, Katja. "Grosse Figuren, grosse Gefühle." *Die Zeit* 10 Feb. 2005. 15 June 2009 <http://www.zeit.de>.
Nord, Cristina. "Notizen zur Berliner Schule." *new filmkritik* 7 July 2007 15 June 2009 <http://newfilmkritik.de>.
Rentschler, Eric. "From New German Cinema to the Post-Wall Cinema of Consensus." *Cinema and Nation*. Ed. Mette Hjort and Scott MacKenzie. New York: Routledge, 2000. 260–77.

Rohnke, Cathy. "The School That Isn't One—Reflections on the 'Berlin School'." *Goethe Institut* 2006. 15 June 2009 <http://www.goethe.de>.
Rohrbach, Günter. "Das Schmollen der Autisten." *Deutsche Filmakademie* 15 June 2009 <http://www.deutsche-filmakademie.de>.
Sehnsucht. Dir. Valeska Grisebach. Indigo, 2007.
Shaviro, Steven. *The Cinematic Body.* Minneapolis: U of Minnesota P, 1993.
Suchsland, Rüdiger. "Langsames Leben, schöne Tage: Annäherungen an die 'Berliner Schule.'" *Film-Dienst* 58.13 (2005): 6–9.
———"'Gefährliches' Kino: Spuren der 'Berliner Schule'." *Film-Dienst* 63.16 (2010): 44–47.
Worthmann, Merten. "Mit Vorsicht genießen." *Die Zeit* 27 Sept. 2001. 5 Nov. 2010 <http://www.zeit.de>.

3
The Triumph of Hyperreality:
A Baudrillardian Reading of Michael Haneke's Cinematic Oeuvre

Sophie Boyer

Abstract This chapter explores Michael Haneke's cinematic oeuvre, focusing on one of its recurring themes: postmodern society's media-manipulated reality, a theme clearly informed by French theorist Jean Baudrillard's provocative thought. My investigation starts with Haneke's application of the concepts of hyperreality and simulation; it then turns to his reflections on (and critique of) the proliferation of images and the ensuing breakdown of communication; finally, it addresses the Baudrillardian notion of fatal strategy at play in Haneke's artistic statement.

In *Le temps du loup* (*The Time of the Wolf*, 2003), Austrian film director Michael Haneke depicts the fate of a family struggling for its survival in the aftermath of an apocalyptic event left unexplained. The opening sequence confronts the viewer with the brutal killing of the family's father at the hands of strangers squatting in their country house. The mother has thus no choice but to embark on an ominous journey with her adolescent daughter, Eva, and her son, Benny; the world has now become a place ruled by terror in which everyone is held hostage. Halfway through the film, daughter Eva retreats to what seems like a former office in the abandoned train station where they have found refuge, in order to write to her deceased father: "My dear, dear Papa! It's really difficult to find words for all this, but when it's impossible to talk to anyone, it feels so stifling. [...] I guess this all must seem pretty jumbled. And it really is. In fact, that's why I'm writing. Because it's so jumbled and I hope, by writing it down, to see clearer. I want to tell you in order to try to give you an idea of life just

Albrecht Dürer, *Das Traumgesicht*, 1525. Kunsthistorisches Museum, Vienna

now."[1] While we hear Eva read the content of her letter in voice-over, the camera pauses over the remnants of a pin board: among dog-eared pictures, random invoices, and torn centerfolds hangs a reproduction of Albrecht Dürer's 1525 watercolour *Traumgesicht (Dream Vision)*. The clouds of rain threatening to flood the earth, which Dürer sketched upon waking from a nightmare some five centuries ago, unmistakably remind contemporary viewers of an atomic mushroom, an image that—regardless of the historical era—evokes catastrophe. Much like Dürer, who anticipated the end of the world in his visions, and Eva, who projects her anxieties onto the paper in a desperate attempt to bring order and structure to a dislocated world, so too is Michael Haneke pursuing a similar goal, namely, to bear witness to the malaise of postmodern reality in the face of its very disappearance, to try to give his audience an "image"[2] of life just now.

The disintegration of human relationships, the prevalence of an insidious violence in both the public and private spheres, the manipulation of reality by mass media—these are all topics that permeate Michael Haneke's work. Over the last two decades, Haneke has successfully provoked both his admirers and his detractors with nine feature films that clearly address these challenging contemporary themes. Although the majority of Haneke's films are set in his home country, Austria, the director has repeatedly cautioned against short-sighted criticism. Indeed, multi-layered alienation processes know no national boundaries and cannot be labelled as a typically Austrian phenomenon. In an interview conducted in 2005 by Serge Toubiana, director of the Cinémathèque française, Haneke explained how he always tries to be precise while avoiding being local. Concerning his first film, *Der siebent Kontinent (The Seventh Continent)* (1989), he asserted: "It's not a portrait of Austria. It's a portrait of rich countries."[3] Similarly, in a later interview conducted upon the release of *Caché* (*Hidden*, 2005), Haneke reiterated this stance when he claimed that every country had its shameful secrets (Alion 11), thereby implying that *Caché* should not strictly be interpreted as an attack upon France's colonial past, but should rather be read in a much larger context. Consistent with this universal perspective on problems that deeply affect Western society, the second half of Haneke's cinematographic productions (starting in 2000) have been made in France, while an American remake of his earlier *Funny Games* (1997)—by Haneke himself—was released in March 2008. As such, the various titles with which his films have been stamped further betray his all-encompassing way of studying the *conditio humana* in postmodern times. Indeed, while Haneke understood his first three films within the framework of a loosely conceived project bearing the ominous title of "glaciation trilogy"[4] (*Vergletscherungs-Trilogie*), film scholars have ascribed to the same cycle the equally grim title of "civil war trilogy" (*Bürgerkriegs-Trilogie*; Metelmann 142). Moreover, his fifth film, and the first one shot outside Austria, *Code inconnu: récit incomplet de divers voyages* (*Code Unknown: Incomplete Tales of Several Journeys*, 2000), introduced viewers to what he has aptly termed his cycle on world war (Gutman 5).

Haneke's films are utterly disturbing, destabilizing, irritating, and hermetic; the austere world he creates indeed often defies interpretation and certainly denies spectators the pleasure of cinematic identification and the satisfaction of clear-cut denouements. In this regard, his films can be construed as objects of pure fascination: while they echo the malaise of postmodern society, representing—and, to a certain extent, reproducing—the collapse of communication and, ultimately, of meaning within Western civilization, they simultaneously pose a challenge and call for viewers' intellectual engagement. It is precisely at such an exchange that I will aim in my chapter—an exchange that can be rendered particularly fruitful by drawing on concepts developed by French theorist Jean Baudrillard. One of the major intellectual figures of postmodern theory, Baudrillard lends himself perfectly to a dialogue with and deciphering of Haneke's work. My analysis will thus revolve around key elements at play in Haneke's cinematic oeuvre, elements that highlight dramatic societal changes and that I believe to be informed by Baudrillardian thought. While the primary focus of my attention will be placed on his concepts of hyperreality and simulation, I will also address, albeit briefly, the questions of the proliferation of images and the ensuing breakdown of communication; finally, my closing remarks will touch upon the notion of fatal strategy.

As a springboard for discussion, I have chosen to single out a four-minute sequence shot from Haneke's fifth film, *Code inconnu*, which in my view epitomizes the above-mentioned elements. Structured around fragments depicting the lives of three families of different ethnic background (French, African, and Romanian), and how they intersect with one another, *Code inconnu* features Juliette Binoche as Anne Laurent, an actress who in the following scene is auditioning for a role in a thriller.[5] Her character visits an apartment with a real estate agent, who soon reveals himself as a serial killer to whom she falls prey:

DIRECTOR: [...] We'll take it from just after he locks her in. The camera is the door. You can play it straight at us. [...] Should I read his part?
ANNE: That'd be good.
DIRECTOR: [...] You hear him lock the door. You go to make sure. The door is indeed locked. It's locked, you will never get out.
ANNE: Sorry?
DIRECTOR: You will never get out.
ANNE: What do you mean?
DIRECTOR: I mean you will die here.
ANNE: Is this a joke?
DIRECTOR: Not for me. For you neither, I'm afraid. Look at the ceiling. Do you see the light fitting? It's an inlet for gas lighting. See now why I asked if you had a lighter? You could use it to blow us both up.
ANNE: Okay, what do you want?
DIRECTOR: Nothing. I have nothing against you. Nothing at all. I like you. You just fell into my trap.
ANNE: What do you mean; I fell into your trap?
DIRECTOR: It means you're going to die. I merely want to watch you die.
ANNE: Please, stop now. You've had your fun. Now, let's forget all about it, okay? I'm expected home. I have no time for games.
DIRECTOR: Neither have I. Believe me. Can you hear a whistling noise? From the ceiling. Soon, you'll be able to smell it.
ANNE: Stop... Stop, please. Let me out! Please!
DIRECTOR: You're wasting our time.
ANNE: What do I have to do?
DIRECTOR: Show me your true face.
ANNE: What?
DIRECTOR: Your true face.
ANNE: What do you mean? What do you want?

DIRECTOR: I want to see your true face. Not your lies nor your tricks. A true expression.
ANNE: What do I have to do?
DIRECTOR: Be spontaneous. React to what's happening.
ANNE: How?[6]

Haneke's recourse here to the narrative technique of the *mise en abyme*, the film within the film, creates a cinematic metalanguage that points to the limits of the representation of reality and its eventual recession into mere simulation, a phenomenon that, according to Baudrillard, most notably characterizes postmodern society. In his essays in *Symbolic Exchange and Death* (1976) and *Simulacra and Simulation* (1994), Baudrillard distinguishes between three historically successive social orders: the first stage, that of "primitive" or pre-modern societies, is governed by the natural law of the symbolic exchange, "the uninterrupted cycle of giving and receiving" (*Mirror* 143). Modern societies make up the second stage, which is ruled by dialectical strategy and brings forth the reign of political economy and production. Finally, postmodern societies constitute the third order, in which the structuring and defining force is technology that allows for the ceaseless reproduction of reality, thus establishing the reign of simulation, and the triumph of hyperreality. Baudrillard, however, highly complicates his exploration of the representation of reality in his discussion of "The Order of Simulacra" (*Symbolic* 50–86)[7] by dividing it into—again—three historically successive stages: the counterfeit, production, and simulation. With the first order of simulacra, we are offered a copy of reality, a *counterfeit* or idealized imitation of nature. Introduced by the Renaissance artist, the counterfeit voluntarily displays its imitative nature thus subtly pointing to its distance from reality. The industrial revolution of the modern era gives way to the second order of simulacra, blurring the boundaries between reality and its representation by *producing* objects that cannot be distinguished from their real model; although the object has now become as real as the real, the existence of reality is not yet called into question. Lastly, the third order of simulacra calls for the precession of the model, the code, over reality, a phenomenon Baudrillard terms the "hyperreal": "The reality principle corresponded to a certain stage of the law of value. Today the whole system is swamped by indeterminacy, and every reality is absorbed by the hyperreality of the code and simulation. The principle of simulation governs us now, rather than the outdated reality principle" (*Symbolic* 2). While simulacrum is not only conceivable, but also present at earlier stages of historical development, it clearly takes on an all-pervasiveness in postmodern society.

With these Baudrillardian theories in mind, *Code inconnu*'s audition scene can be viewed as an illustration of these three orders of simulacra, rendered here in a simultaneous fashion: Anne Laurent, the protagonist, is asked to play a role tightly circumscribed by the requirements of the plotline. In order to obtain this role, she must to the best of her knowledge and histrionic ability counterfeit first the perplexity, then the growing anxiety and ultimately the sheer fright of the potential homebuyer turned victim. Toward the end of the audition sequence, however, the dialogue seems to momentarily shift into a disconcerting splitting of reality: to Anne's supplication to free her, her interlocutor replies: "You're wasting *our* time," thus creating confusion in the viewer who wonders whether these words are truly part of the script or rather express the director's irritation with the actress's performance, an impression further emphasized by his sudden switch from the *vous* to the familiar *tu*. This state of confusion is reinforced by Anne's lines, six consecutive questions, that point either to the character's feeling of disorientation and panic or to the actress's pleading for better defined stage direction or, perhaps, to both. The fine line dividing reality from its representation has been successfully blurred here, while we witness the conflation of both, a situation not uncommon to acting techniques such as method acting. The insistent request of the director/psychopath for truth, authenticity and spontaneity concludes the sequence, lifting it to the third order of simulacra, that of pure simulation, which operates beyond the dichotomy of the real and the false, beyond any origin anchored in reality: "The entire process is dislocated: the contradictory processes of the true and the false, the real and the imaginary are abolished in this hyperreal logic of the *montage*" (*Symbolic* 64).

The loaded message Haneke implicitly tries to flesh out in *Code inconnu*'s audition scene can thus be interpreted as twofold: on a very basic level, this scene is meant to heighten the audience's awareness of the fact that film always already represents mediated reality, its simulated version, as it were. On a more subtle level, however, this scene simultaneously reveals moviegoers' attempt to generally deny this fact: the connection with reality has not only been blurred, reality has been erased and replaced by simulation with such success that we have desperately come to believe that simulation *is* reality. The way in which the model, the code has come to precede reality has reached such a level of perfection that the origin, reality, has been lost in the process, rendering the code literally unknown, detached from its original meaning. It therefore seems logical that *Code inconnu*'s opening and closing sequences show a deaf-mute child trying in vain to convey a specific emotion via sign language to a group of children sharing the same disability. Haneke goes to great lengths to remind us that we have surreptitiously entered the third order of simulacra or hyperreality, "a society of surfaces [and] performativity" (Lane 91). The psychopath's lines ("I want to see your true face. Not your lies nor your tricks. A true expression") thus reflect first and foremost viewers' tyrannical and perverse need for authenticity and immediacy[8] in a world where, as Baudrillard points out, "the real [...] has become our true utopia" (*Simulacra* 123). In a self-referential gesture tinged with irony, Haneke holds a mirror to his viewers' self-delusion, coercing them to reflection or, as he has overtly admitted in interviews, raping them into independence. Like the victim played by Binoche, we too have just fallen into the director's trap.

In his book *The Perfect Crime*, Baudrillard further theorizes on the "murder" of reality, laying bare technological processes employed to empty the world of its meaning by saturating it with oppressive transparency and visibility. Two of the various processes he analyzes prove to be of particular importance for Haneke's artistic approach, namely, the use of real time and of high definition. While these devices both allow for what *seems* a limited manipulation of reality, complying with the viewers' perverse desire to experience the "real thing," they nevertheless remain entrenched in the realm of lies and tricks—a point Haneke himself is always intent on stressing. When challenged in an interview over the fact that the camera in *Caché* does not reveal the truth, but is rather an instrument of deception that subverts Jean-Luc Godard's famous motto that cinema is truth at twenty-four frames per second, Haneke answers point-blank: "My perspective on that, my article of faith, is that I've adapted Godard's observation to read, 'Film is a lie at twenty-four frames per second in the service of truth.' [...] Film is an artificial construct. It pretends to reconstruct reality. But it doesn't do that—it's a manipulative form. It's a lie that can reveal the truth" (Porton 51).

In his 1997 *Funny Games*, viewers are confronted with what can perhaps be argued as Haneke's best stylistic exercise in the art of the long take: in a ten-minute scene shot in "real" time, we watch the excruciating physical and moral pain inflicted upon a bourgeois couple who try to escape after having witnessed their son's death at the hands of Paul and Peter, a duo of cold-blooded killers. The feeling of authenticity viewers usually crave is delivered here, however, with such intensity that the scene becomes almost unbearable. By giving us an overdose of our own medicine, Haneke wishes, on the one hand, to foreground our collusion with the killers in our voyeuristic enjoyment of violence—an enjoyment, here, gone bad—while, on the other hand, pointing at the illusory nature of real time within the technique of the long take.[9] Indeed, such proximity of event, such extreme close-up, such entomological perspective on reality necessarily partakes of the realm of reproduction, of simulation, for as Baudrillard reminds us: "The illusion of time [...] is the objective fact that you are never entirely there at the particular moment, and that integral presence is only ever virtual. If it is true that at any point in time you are in that moment and not elsewhere, you are never at the single point where the whole event might be said to be summed up. 'Real' time does not, therefore, exist; no one exists in real time; nothing takes place in real time—and the misunderstanding is total" (*Perfect* 52). This deep conviction of the illusory nature of real time closely complies with Haneke's "article of faith" that film essentially represents a lie, a position he already exposed in an earlier interview when he states: "The media contribute to a confused consciousness through this illusion that we know all things at all times, and always with this great sense of immediacy. We live in this environment where we think we know more things faster, when in fact we know nothing at all" (Sharrett).

Another trick of contemporary cinematic trade is the use of High Definition video. While the film grain in *Code inconnu*'s audition scene informs spectators at the outset that they are about to watch a recorded version of reality, Haneke often plays at disconcerting his audience by completely erasing the image noise. Two subsequent scenes from the same film document the various stages of Binoche's character's involvement in the thriller for which she incidentally got the part: the first scene clearly establishes that we are witnessing the shooting of a film as we are allowed a peek behind the scenes, where the film crew handles clapboard, camera and microphone boom pole. The second scene, however, destabilizes, for here, the actual and the virtual's texture momentarily conflate until stylistic devices pertaining to the thriller genre (namely, sudden cuts from wide to close-up and point-of-view shots) clue us in to the *mise en abyme* situation.

An even more refined play with image texture certainly lies in Haneke's use of HD video for *Caché*, thus giving rise to repeated distancing effects. *Caché* tells the story of Georges Laurent, a Parisian literary talk-show host, and of his family, whose lives are disturbed by the anonymous delivery of threatening children's drawings and videotapes showing the Laurents' apartment filmed from outside. Georges soon comes to suspect Majid, a childhood friend, whose Algerian parents were killed in the October 1961 Parisian demonstration against the racist measures of French police. The then six-year-old Georges led his parents to believe that his friend was subject to violent outbursts. Concerned, the parents decided not to adopt the orphan, thus limiting his chances for a decent education. Despite Georges's conviction, Majid vehemently denies being the author of the videotapes. The film opens with video footage that we only understand as such five minutes later, when the image is frozen, then fast-forwarded, and Georges's and his wife Anne's comments on what they—and we—are seeing are heard in voice-over. The confusion is amplified through Haneke's use of HD for the entire film, an obviously conscious choice interpreted by one critic, Mattias Frey, as "a shift in theoretical paradigm" (Frey 31) whereby Haneke "present[s] a desubstantiated image" (Frey 33) inherent to the seamlessness of HD technology, an opinion similar to Baudrillard's when he asserts: "The highest definition of the medium corresponds to the lowest definition of the message" (*Perfect* 29). In this regard, it is interesting to note that no film by Haneke has generated as much speculation and debate as to its hidden meaning as *Caché*. Indeed, the film's open-ended conclusion leaves spectators in the dark, the author of the infamous videotapes undiscovered. Most critics have focused extensively on the question of post-colonial guilt in *Caché* (see Beugnet; Ezra and Sillars; Gilroy; Khanna; Porton; Silverman), and while I agree that the question of guilt is central to the film, I would tend to side with Georges, who claims "I have nothing to hide."[10] Indeed, tireless conjectures seem inadequate as a few perceptive critics have noted. Grossvogel, for instance, while acknowledging the undeniable political subtext, insists on drawing attention to *Caché*'s form, rather than its content (40); Ezra and Sillars share a similar view that the film's content defies interpretation. They assert, for example, that the very first exchange between Georges and Anne in the first scene (GEORGES: So? ANNE: Nothing!)[11] is symptomatic of the whole film in that it "closes off inquiry and denies the possibility of meaning" (218). In agreement with the three abovementioned critics, I contend that *Caché* represents Haneke's most subtle and refined application of a cinematic metalanguage. Indeed, *Caché* should ultimately lead viewers to reflect on the proliferation of images and their manipulative power that turn our universe into a state of surveillance in which nothing is hidden and in which humans have unlearned humanity, or as Baudrillard would put it: "This is what we do with the problem of the truth or reality of this world: we have resolved it by technical simulation, and by creating a profusion of images in which there is nothing to see" (*Perfect* 5).

The extent to which contemporary society has dramatically altered human relations is poignantly illustrated in a scene from Haneke's second film, *71 Fragmente einer Chronologie des Zufalls* (*71 Fragments of a Chronology of Chance*, 1994), in which a married man desperately attempts an intimate rapprochement with his wife:

> HANS: I love you.
> MARIA: What's the matter? Are you drunk, or what?
> HANS: Yes, why? Not very...
> MARIA: I mean, what are you getting at? You don't say "I love you" out of the blue. And certainly not you. So, what d'you want?

HANS: I thought it would be helpful.
MARIA: For what?[12]

The conversation ends when the husband gives his wife a slap to which she first reacts with surprise, but then she briefly and gently lays her hand on his forearm. What his awkward yet ingenuous declaration of love could not achieve, his recourse to violence apparently does, thus sealing in the flesh the failure of communication between humans.

Going back to Mattias Frey's argument on the "desubstantiated" image, while I concede that Haneke pushes this notion to unprecedented technical heights in *Caché*, I would argue that he has made this his specialty since the very beginning of his cinematic career. *Benny's Video* (1992), for instance, implicitly denounces contemporary youth's bulimic consumption of images to the point where the latter become randomly interchangeable, emptied of their substance. Equally impervious to the victim's fate, young Benny watches his amateur videos of a pig being slaughtered and of a girl he shot—a behaviour that reminds us of *Code inconnu*'s psychopath, who matter-of-factly admits: "I merely want to watch you die." Postmodern society's excess of visual stimuli proves inversely proportional to the lack of emotional connection to the world, a deficit Haneke hints at repeatedly.[13] In this respect, it is perhaps no coincidence that Benny's mother works at Kunstrepro, a store specializing in art reproductions, which literally plaster the family's living room wall and fill the void of an apartment otherwise emptied of familial presence. The living room thus symbolically seals the death of the family unit and must be identified "as a close correlative to Benny's techno fortress" (Grundmann 11). Among the reproductions of Warhol, Turner, and da Vinci hangs Magritte's *La reproduction interdite* (*Not to Be Reproduced*, 1937), a title that ironically reminds of and denounces Benny's criminal obsession to reproduce all aspects of reality, including death. Like the man in Magritte's painting seen from the back looking at himself in a mirror that, in its turn, reflects his back, all possibility of introspection, of facing what he did, let alone of empathy, remains foreclosed to Benny.

In the same vein, Haneke's first feature film, *Der siebente Kontinent*, stresses the emotional impairment derived from visual saturation. It portrays a family who decides to commit suicide in order to escape their collective emotional void. This void is already foreshadowed in young daughter Eva's disruptive behaviour in school: when she pretends she is going blind, her teacher rapidly unveils her scheme and informs the mother who, instead of investigating her daughter's motivations, punishes her child. Despite her work as an optician, the mother remains blind to her daughter's distress, until she finds the key to her behaviour in a newspaper article the child had hidden. Titled "Blind but

Never Again Lonely,"[14] the article recounts the story of a girl whose parents were awakened to their daughter's need for emotional support only after she lost her eyesight in an accident. Following Eva's childish but surprisingly shrewd logic, the more one sees, the lonelier one feels.

In his seminal study on violence in Haneke's oeuvre, Jörg Metelmann identifies Benny's emotional deficiency as the ontological incapacity to fathom the corporeality of pain for the human body, which does not represent in his eyes a lived reality, but rather a utopia (107).[15] The extent of Benny's emotional disability, however, seems to have been completely overlooked by film critics. Indeed, while Metelmann definitely scores a point here, I would add that Benny does not possess the psychological depth to experience in an unmediated fashion either pain or pleasure for that matter. Shortly before shooting the girl, Benny shows her his room with all its technological equipment. To the girl's inquiry about the image on the monitor, Benny first explains that his camera is filming the street below in real time, and then further impresses her by switching the camera's point of view to his bedroom. The monitor flips to a close shot of Benny's crotch revealing his nascent erection; showing a strange mixture of embarrassment and pride, the pubescent teenager then turns to the girl and smiles. Pleasure, like pain, can seemingly only be experienced through a glass pane—a phenomenon that bespeaks a radical alteration in human relations now ruled by the "cold seduction" (Baudrillard *Seduction* 162) of the digital world, yielding to "an era of fascination" (158).

Alerting viewers to the collapse of all human relations, to postmodern society's state of foreclosure, Michael Haneke champions the only counteroffensive sustainable: that of fatal strategy coined by Baudrillard. This radical position overtly aims at challenging one's adversary and, ultimately, at disrupting the system as exposed in his essay *The Spirit of Terrorism*, written in almost immediate reaction to the 9/11 terrorist attacks:[16] "Never attack the system in terms of relations of force. [...] But shift the struggle into the symbolic sphere, where the rule is that of challenge, reversion and outbidding. So that death can be met only by equal or greater death. Defy the system by a gift to which it cannot respond except by its own death and its own collapse" (17). Hyperreality's eventual reversal can thus only be hoped for by taking it to another level, redoubling it, intensifying it in an overbidding gesture. Majid's suicide in *Caché*— he slits his throat in front of Georges in one of the film's last scenes—interpreted by one very annoyed critic as "an exclusively aesthetic event, devoid of all meaning" (Gilroy 234), exemplifies perfectly what a fatal strategy entails, namely, the revenge of the foreclosed other. Despite Haneke's claim that "refusing to communicate is a terrorist act that triggers violence,"[17] Majid's highly provocative gesture of suicide-terrorism might perhaps be interpreted as a last attempt to communicate the only response possible—albeit self-destructive—to a world where nothing is at stake, where the possibility of exchange has been forever ruled out. It presents an image so radical, so catastrophic that, following the example of Baudrillard when he interprets the "pure events" of 9/11 as utterly disgusting, yet simultaneously fascinating: "We try retrospectively to impose some kind of meaning on it, to find some kind of interpretation. But there is none. And it is the radicality of the spectacle, the brutality of the spectacle, which alone is original and irreducible. The spectacle of terrorism forces the terrorism of the spectacle upon us" (*Spirit* 30).

"Defy the system by a gift to which it cannot respond except by its own death and its own collapse": Baudrillard exposes here a praxis already elaborated, word for word, twenty-five years earlier in *Symbolic Exchange and Death*.[18] With his usual ability to grasp postmodern society's most complex and most decisive issues, Baudrillard intimates the catastrophe to come when he writes in 1976 on the Twin Towers: "The fact that there are two identical towers *signifies* the end of all competition, the end of every original reference. [...] For the sign to remain pure it must become its own double: this doubling of the sign really put an end to what it designated" (*Symbolic*, 69). Haneke's highly questionable decision to replicate shot by shot his earlier *Funny Games*, to offer American audiences its simulacrum as it were, only with different actors and in English language, adheres to the Baudrillardian spirit of terrorism: to the triumph of hyperreality, Haneke responds with an even greater excess of reality to the point where all referentiality has been lost, holding the spectator hostage. Paradoxically, the ultimate success of Haneke's remake project would be achieved if viewers refused to watch it, sealing by this very fact the death of hyperreality, for as he has stated in an interview: "I've always said it's a film that you watch if you need this film. If you don't need it, you go away. If someone has stayed to the end, he needed to be tortured during that time to understand."[19] In a newspaper article published March 14, 2008, Haneke admitted taking a malicious pleasure in presenting his US remake of *Funny Games* to American audiences: "I feel like I'm inside the Trojan horse and they haven't yet figured out what's in store for them!"[20] (Lussier), thus deliberately identifying himself with the first terrorists in the history of mankind. America should consider itself warned: beware of Austrians bearing gifts.

Notes

I am grateful to the Senate Research Committee at Bishop's University for the financial support provided for this publication.

1 "Mon cher, cher Papa, c'est vraiment difficile de trouver les mots pour exprimer tout ça mais quand on n'a aucune possibilité d'en parler avec qui que ce soit on se dit qu'on va étouffer. [...] J'imagine que tout cela doit te paraître assez embrouillé. Et ça l'est vraiment. D'ailleurs, c'est la raison pour laquelle j'écris. Parce que tout est si embrouillé et que j'espère en te l'écrivant y voir un peu plus clair. Mais je vais te raconter les choses dans l'ordre et tenter de te donner une image de la vie que nous menons à présent."

2 I have deliberately chosen here to alter slightly the English translation of Eva's words to her father as they appear in the subtitles, to revert to the original text (see note 1).

3 Michael Haneke, "An Interview with Michael Haneke," *Der siebente Kontinent*, DVD, directed by Michael Haneke (New York: Kino International, 2006).

4 In view of film critics' abuse of this title, Michael Haneke has in hindsight admitted regretting ever having used it (Michael Haneke, "An Interview," *71 Fragmente einer Chronologie des Zufalls*, DVD, directed by Michael Haneke (New York: Kino International, 2006). Considering, however, that the first part of his trilogy bears the title of *Der siebente Kontinent* and that the Antarctic was the last and seventh continent to be identified as such, the term "glaciation" does seem most befitting despite Haneke's reservations.

5 The title of this thriller, *Le collectionneur* (*The Collector*), constitutes an overt reference to William Wyler's 1965 film, which also depicts a psychopath's perverse machination to hold a woman hostage. It is interesting to note that Baudrillard mentions Wyler's film in his essay *Seduction* to better explain the phenomenon of "the fetishism of the collector" (121), which he considers diametrically opposed to the game of seduction.

6 DIRECTOR: [...] Nous commencerons au moment où il vient juste de l'enfermer. La caméra, c'est la porte. Comme ça, vous pourrez jouer directement vers nous. [...] Vous voulez qu'on vous donne la réplique?
ANNE: Je veux bien, merci.
DIRECTOR: [...] Vous croyez l'avoir entendu fermer la porte et vous voulez vous en assurer. Elle est bel et bien fermée. La porte est verrouillée, vous ne sortirez plus d'ici.
ANNE: Pardon?
DIRECTOR: Vous ne sortirez plus d'ici.
ANNE: Qu'est-ce que ça veut dire?
DIRECTOR: Ça veut dire que vous allez mourir ici.
ANNE: C'est une plaisanterie?
DIRECTOR: Pas pour moi. Pour vous non plus, je le crains. Regardez au plafond. Vous voyez la fixation du lustre? Il y a une arrivée de gaz pour l'éclairage. Vous comprenez pourquoi tout à l'heure je vous demandais si vous aviez du feu? Si vous aviez du feu, vous pourriez nous faire sauter tous les deux.
ANNE: Bon, que voulez-vous?
DIRECTOR: Rien. J'ai rien contre vous, absolument rien. Vous m'êtes sympathique. Vous êtes simplement tombée dans mon piège, c'est tout.
ANNE: Bon, ça veut dire quoi ça : je suis tombée dans votre piège?
DIRECTOR: Ça veut dire que vous allez mourir. Je veux simplement vous regarder en train de mourir.
ANNE: Bon, s'il vous plaît, arrêtez. Vous vous êtes bien fait plaisir. Maintenant, vous oubliez tout ça et on arrête d'accord? On m'attend à la maison, j'ai autre chose à faire. J'ai pas l'temps d'jouer.
DIRECTOR: Moi non plus, j'ai pas l'temps d'jouer, croyez-moi. Vous entendez ce sifflement?

Ça vient du plafond. Bientôt, vous allez sentir l'odeur.
ANNE: Arrêtez... Arrêtez, je vous en prie. Laissez-moi sortir s'il vous plaît.
DIRECTOR: Vous nous faites perdre notre temps.
ANNE: Mais j'dois faire quoi?
DIRECTOR: Montrez-moi votre vrai visage.
ANNE: Quoi?
DIRECTOR: Ton vrai visage.
ANNE: Mais c'est quoi ça? Vous voulez quoi?
DIRECTOR: Je veux voir ton vrai visage. Pas tes mensonges, ni tes trucs. Une expression vraie pour une fois.
ANNE: Mais qu'est-ce que je dois faire?
DIRECTOR: Sois spontanée. Réagis à ce qui t'arrive.
ANNE: Comment?

7 Baudrillard further elaborates on the three orders of simulacra in *Simulacra and Simulation* (121–27).
8 Whether this need was first created by the film industry or, conversely, the film industry is merely feeding the public what it thirsts for is a question open for debate. I believe that, in the case of *Code inconnu*'s audition scene, Haneke wishes to stress the mirroring of the viewers' and directors' perverse desire for authenticity which, again, echoes Baudrillardian thought: "With hyperreality, [...] the active *seeing* and the passive *being seen* are one and the same position. Another way of thinking about this is in terms of the decentred structure, as it becomes impossible to locate the traditional nodes of power and subjection with the collapse of perspectival space; instead, there is a circulation of positions which, again, all appear interchangeable" (Lane 98–99).
9 In light of Haneke's own declarations on the technique of the long take, namely, that it allows for limited manipulation of the image and, therefore, of the viewer (Alion 2007, 8; Sharrett 2004), one might argue that my interpretation is skewed. To my defence, I would add that, lucid as he is, Haneke has repeatedly insisted that despite filmmakers' best intentions, the filmic medium is nonetheless condemned to remain a mediated—i.e., manipulated—rendering of the world as we know it. While Haneke is intent on having viewers reflect on the illusory nature of the filmic image by participating himself, however subtly, in the creation of illusion, he has conversely resorted to a technique of fragmentation, most notably in *71 Fragmente einer Chronologie des Zufalls* and in *Code inconnu*, explaining in an interview how he felt this technique reproduced with more intellectual honesty our necessarily fragmented understanding and perception of reality (Haneke, "An Interview," *71 Fragmente einer Chronologie des Zufalls*).
10 "J'ai rien à cacher!"
11 GEORGES: Alors?... ANNE: Rien!... Although they erroneously invert the roles, stating that Georges is the one answering Anne's query, Ezra and Sillars 2007 justly remark that the response "Nothing!" is one that recurs throughout the film. It is perhaps even more revealing, however, that the phrase "I don't know" ("Je sais pas") is uttered no less than twenty-two times, pointing less to the characters' helplessness as to an overall poorness in the dialogues that clearly mirrors the void of human relations. For a detailed script of *Caché*, see Lhuillier and Kandel.
12 HANS: Ich liebe dich.
MARIA: Was ist los? Bist du betrunken, oder was?

HANS: Ja, warum? Nicht sehr ...
MARIA: Ich mein', was bezweckst du damit? Man sagt doch nicht aus heiterem Himmel „Ich liebe dich". Überhaupt du nicht. Also, was willst du?
HANS: Ich hab' gedacht, es bringt was.
MARIA: Was?
13 In an interview, Haneke refers to studies that have proven how today's children are better at deciphering edited images than older generations. He points out, however, that these same children are considered less capable of perceiving the emotional charge behind the images, a situation he interprets as a deficit: "They can decipher [the image] ... but the depth that's behind it is lost" (Haneke, "An Interview," *Der siebente Kontinent*).
14 "Blind—aber nie mehr einsam"
15 "Er [Benny] kann mit der Körperlichkeit des Schmerzes einfach nicht umgehen, weil Körper für ihn keine gelebte Wirklichkeit, sondern im angesprochenen Sinne ebenfalls eine Utopie, ein Nicht-Ort ist."
16 Although published in book form in 2002, *The Spirit of Terrorism* first appeared as an article in the French daily newspaper *Le Monde* on 3 November 2001.
17 Michael Haneke, "An Interview with Director Michael Haneke," *Le temps du loup*, DVD, directed by Michael Haneke (New York: Palm Pictures, 2004).
18 While the English translation of this citation varies slightly from *Symbolic Exchange* (37) to *The Spirit of Terrorism* (17), probably due to the fact that they were translated by different people, the original text is identical in both essays.
19 Michael Haneke, "An Interview with Michael Haneke," *Funny Games*, DVD, directed by Michael Haneke (New York: Kino International 2006).
20 "J'ai l'impression d'être à l'intérieur du cheval de Troie et qu'ils ne savent pas encore ce qui les attend!"

References

71 Fragmente einer Chronologie des Zufalls. Dir. Michael Haneke. WEGA-Filmproduktion, 1994.
Alion, Yves. "Entretien avec Michael Haneke." *L'Avant-Scène Cinéma* 558 (2007): 7–11.
Baudrillard, Jean. *The Mirror of Production*. Trans. Mark Poster. St. Louis: Telos, 1975.
———. *The Perfect Crime*. Trans. Chris Turner. London, New York: Verso, 1996.
———. *Seduction*. Trans. Brian Singer. Montreal: New World Perspectives, 1990.
———. *Simulacra and Simulation*. Trans. Sheila Faria Glaser. Ann Arbor: U of Michigan P, 1994.
———. *The Spirit of Terrorism and Requiem for the Twin Towers*. Trans. Chris Turner. New York: Verso, 2002.
———. *Symbolic Exchange and Death*. Trans. Iain Hamilton Grant. London: Sage, 1993.
Benny's Video. Dir. Michael Haneke. WEGA-Filmproduktion, 1992.
Beugnet, Martine. "Blind spot." *Screen* 48. 2 (2007): 227–31.
Caché. Dir. Michael Haneke. Les films du Losange, 2005.
Code inconnu: récit incomplet de divers voyages. Dir. Michael Haneke. MK2 Productions, 2000.
The Collector. Dir. William Wyler. Columbia Pictures, 1965.

Dürer, Albrecht. *Traumgesicht*. Kunsthistorisches Museum Wien, Vienna.
Ezra, Elizabeth, and Jane Sillars. "*Hidden* in Plain Sight: Bringing Terror Home." *Screen* 48.2 (2007): 215–21.
———. "Introduction." *Screen* 48.2 (2007): 211–13.
Frey, Mattias. "*Benny's Video*, *Caché*, and the Desubstantiated Image." *Framework* 47.2 (2006): 30–36.
Funny Games. Dir. Michael Haneke. WEGA-Filmproduktion, 1997.
Funny Games. Dir. Michael Haneke. Celluloid Dreams, 2007.
Gilroy, Paul. "Shooting crabs in a barrel." *Screen* 48.2 (2007): 233–35.
Grossvogel, D.I. "Haneke: The Coercing of Vision." *Film Quarterly* 60.4 (2007): 36–43.
Grundmann, Roy. "Auteur de force: Michael Haneke's 'Cinema of Glaciation.'" *Cineaste* 32.2 (2007): 6–14.
Gutman, Pierre-Simon. "Michael Haneke, le provocateur idéaliste." *L'Avant-Scène Cinéma* 558 (2007): 3–6.
Khanna, Ranjana. "From Rue Morgue to Rue des Iris." *Screen* 48.2 (2007): 237–44.
Lane, Richard J. *Jean Baudrillard*. London: Routledge, 2000.
Lhuillier, Florine, and Pierre Kandel. "Découpage intégral, après montage, illustré de vidéogrammes du film *Caché*." *L'Avant-Scène Cinéma* 558 (2007): 22–67.
Lussier, Marc-André. "Funny Games, rien qu'un jeu?" *La Presse* 14 Mar. 2008. 28 Oct. 2008 <http://moncinema.cyberpresse.ca>.
Magritte, René. *La reproduction interdite*. Boijmans Van Beuningen Museum, Rotterdam.
Metelmann, Jörg. *Zur Kritik der Kino-Gewalt: Die Filme von Michael Haneke*. Munich: Wilhelm Fink, 2003.
Porton, Richard. "Collective Guilt and Individual Responsibility: An Interview with Michael Haneke." *Cineaste* 31.1 (2005): 50–51.
Sharrett, Christopher. "The World That Is Known: Michael Haneke Interviewed." *Kino-eye* 4.1 (2004). 28 October 2008 <http://www.kinoeye.org/04/01/interview01.php>.
Der siebente Kontinent. Dir. Michael Haneke. WEGA-Filmproduktion, 1989.
Silverman, Max. "The Empire Looks Back." *Screen* 48.2 (2007): 245–49.
Le temps du loup. Dir. Michael Haneke. Bavaria Film, 2003.

4
Subversions of the Medical Gaze:
Disability and Media Parody in Christoph Schlingensief's *Freakstars 3000*

Morgan Koerner

Abstract Christoph Schlingensief's 2003 film *Freakstars 3000* is explored here as an intervention in the current discourse on disability in Germany. A parody of mainstream television and the freak-show performance tradition, *Freakstars 3000* documents a casting and variety show for disabled participants. Originally shown as a series on German television and later cut into a feature film, *Freakstars 3000* critiques the exclusion of disabled actors from mainstream media. The film subverts medical definitions of disability and assumptions that preclude people with disabilities from the realm of performance, and it extends representation of them in Germany into the genre of sketch comedy.

Dear film fans!

Step right up and see cool young people who, with talent and 100 percent commitment, fulfill their dream of a big music career.

Step right up and hear German eccentrics who, while they sing, nonchalantly point to the big problem of the non-disabled.

During the shooting, actors were consistently abused and forced to portray disability. Every attack and every crackup is therefore guaranteed to be authentic and not repeatable.[1]

Christoph Schlingensief's film *Freakstars 3000* (2003) begins with the above epigraph, an ironic disclaimer that heralds both the film's aesthetic and its central theme of disability. Originally filmed as a television series in 2002 and cut into a film in 2003, *Freakstars* presents an *American Idol*-style casting show for disabled participants who are tested, evaluated, and chosen or rejected by an able-bodied jury that includes the director Schlingensief. The film's title and epigraph immediately announce two strategies at work in the film: on the one hand, *Freakstars 3000* parodies casting shows and, more generally, provides a framework in which disabled performers critique the able-bodied imperatives of mainstream television and simultaneously establish their own media presence. On the other hand, the title and epigraph also parody the freak show, a sensational form of objectification and exploitation of disabled bodies. This parodic allusion continues in the film's opening credits, which are accompanied by circus music and end with cackling laughter. The ironic references to the freak show situate the spectator in an uncomfortable position and raise ethical questions about the film. But instead of answering the question of exploitation, the film's epigraph further confuses the viewer with the claim that the performers were forced to act disabled and that their abuse makes the actions in the film more authentic. The film not only parodies mainstream media, it also raises ethical questions about disability in a highly ironic and ambiguous fashion.

The ironic and irreverent tone of Schlingensief's film is difficult to situate into recent discussions on film and disability studies. In their monograph *Cultural Locations of Disability*, Sharon L. Snyder and David T. Mitchell describe how disability and its cultural locations are viewed through the lens of science, medicine, and rehabilitation in the nineteenth and twentieth centuries (5–10). In a chapter on cinema, they add that "film spectatorship borrows from these weighty disciplinary practices in that bodies marked as anomalous are offered for consumption as objects of necessary scrutiny—even downright prurient curiosity" (157). Disability in mainstream cinema places the audience in a position similar to the medical expert who must categorize the disabled individual; depending on the film's genre, the spectator might read disability as the "body out of control" (comedy), the monstrous or avenging outsider (horror), or an object of pity and sentimentality (melodrama) (164). The cinematic emphasis on decoding individual disabled bodies, however, hides the systems of medical categorization that define disability as impairment and "discount [the disabled] from the start from being able to coexist with their non-disabled peers" (174). In other words, the spectacle of individual disabled bodies distracts audience attention from the very cultural systems that define those bodies as abnormal in the first place. Interestingly, in their brief discussion of mainstream cinematic genres, Snyder and Mitchell quickly reject comedy as a site for "freak show like titillation" and the humour of superiority (166). The implication here is that the genre of comedy cannot escape the model of corrective laughter, of humour as a means of exclusion or rehabilitation. While this generalization is perhaps understandable in the context of Hollywood cinema, it neglects comedy's ambiguous potential as a subversive force that might undermine medical taxonomies, challenge the spectator's attempts to decode disability, and open up new perspectives and possibilities for the representation of people with disabilities.

The following essay considers Christoph Schlingensief's film *Freakstars 3000* as an example of subversive comedy starring disabled actors. The film turns the tables on able-bodied mainstream media, critiques different media genres, and expands representation of disabled people into sketch comedy. At the same time, the film's parody of the freak-show format raises the question of sensationalism and the humour of superiority described by Snyder and Mitchell. While it baits the spectator to categorize the disabled performers, the film offers little information on which such a labelling might be based. In the analysis that follows, I consider the film's parody of both mainstream media and the freak-show tradition in order to articulate the film's specific intervention into the discourse on disability in Germany. Before I turn to analysis of the film, however, it will be necessary to situate Schlingensief's own work with disabled actors in the larger context of disability rights and media representation in Germany.

German Disability Rights, Media Representation, and Schlingensief's Aesthetics

Both the rights of the disabled and the discourse on disability have undergone significant changes in Germany in the past forty years. Overall, there has been a gradual shift away from the medical definition of disability and toward an understanding of disability as a social phenomenon (Heyer 725). Postwar West and East Germany treated disability largely through the lens of social welfare and medicine; the focus was on individual treatment and rehabilitation in institutions separate from the non-disabled (Heyer 726–32). As disability scholars have noted, however, the medical definition of disability as impairment and the subsequent rehabilitation approach "depoliticize disability" by sidestepping the issues of discrimination and civil rights (Snyder and Mitchell 9). The main goal of the disability rights movement in Germany was thus to change the discussion from a medical context to a social one. In the late 1960s and 1970s, the first disabled groups emerged in Germany to pursue goals such as self-determination, equal rights, integration into the community, disabled people's right to life, and the "de-medicalization of disability" (Köbsell). Today the disability rights movement can look back on several milestone victories, beginning with a 1994 amendment to Article 3 of the German constitution and culminating in 2006 in a comprehensive anti-discrimination law (the *Allgemeines Gleichbehandlungsgesetz*). As of 2006, disabled German citizens finally receive the legal protection against discrimination that other minority groups have enjoyed for years.

The shift in the legal landscape has coincided with more positive depictions in the media. Since 1983, the Munich-based Work Group for Disability and the Media (ABM: Arbeitsgemeinschaft Behinderung und Medien) has pushed for broader media representation of people with disabilities, funded television programs made for and by the disabled, and made films accessible to the public that "reveal an alternative perspective that de-emphasizes overcoming disability and validates acceptance of difference" (Poore 299). In the twenty-first century, the ABM now boasts several programs throughout the German television landscape.[2] Even mainstream German cinema has recently begun to present disability not as a metaphor for something else[3] or a tragic medical condition, but rather as a "fact of life" (Hamilton). Films such as *Jenseits der Stille* (*Beyond Silence*, Caroline Link, 1996), *Crazy* (Hans-Christian Schmid, 2000), and *Erbsen auf Halb Sechs* (*Peas at 5:30*, Lars Büchel, 2004) show disabled characters in their daily lives and, like Hollywood cinema's shift roughly a decade or so earlier, German cinema has thus begun to show disabled people whose primary concerns are issues other than disability (see Norden). Other independent films such as *Verrückt nach Paris* (*Crazy about Paris*, Pago Balke and Elke Besuden, 2003) and *Die Blindgänger* (*The Blind Flyers*, Bernd Sahling, 2004) have cast disabled actors as their protagonists and offered a unique perspective on tensions between those with disabilities and the able-bodied. These latter films signal the ongoing integration of disabled actors and the perspective of people with disabilities into German filmmaking. But, despite such positive steps toward the removal of barriers and the integration of disabled people into media representation, different disabled perspectives hardly receive extensive attention in German television and film. As Peter Radtke, head of ABM, notes, media portrayals of people with disabilities continue to focus primarily on either narratives of wonder or pity,[4] and they are rarely, if ever, interviewed on political issues other than disability.[5] While they have begun to break into the realm of media representation, they continue to remain marginalized in popular television and film.

The filmmaker, theatre director, and action artist Christoph Schlingensief has made disability a central theme in his work since the early 1990s and has integrated a number of amateur actors with varying cognitive and physical disabilities into his troupe. But, as opposed to the activist programming of the ABM and mainstream cinematic portrayals of disability, Schlingensief's approach to disability appears within a chaotic, neo-avant-garde aesthetic. Schlingensief began as a film director but gained notoriety at the theatre Volksbühne Berlin, where he staged performances that mixed media parody with avant-garde performance tactics and focused on topical themes such as unemployment, xenophobia, homelessness, and disability. But Schlingensief's performances present these issues in an anarchic format marked by comic digression and interruption, improvisation, self-reflexive subversion, and nonsense.[6] A case in point is Schlingensief's action performance/initiative/political campaign *Chance 2000*, created for the 1998 federal elections in Germany. The official goal of the project was an earnest one, namely, to call attention to people on the margins of German society including those who are unemployed, homeless, and disabled (Hegemann/Schlingensief 20). Although officially registered (and on the ballots) as a political party, *Chance 2000* inverted the strategies of political campaigns by refusing to state a clear agenda and remaining unclear about whether it was a "real" campaign or a mere performance or parody. *Chance 2000*'s nightly "election circus" at the Volksbühne's Prater stage was a mix between circus, party meeting, improvisational theatre, and avant-garde performance piece that encouraged audience participation. The performances resisted both aesthetic classification and the discourse of consensus and order in politics. The goal was not to educate the masses, state an agenda, or pursue legal changes, but rather to encourage the audience to make their voices heard by intervening in the performance. Schlingensief's performances therefore transform a democratic gesture not into a political goal or movement, but rather an integrative cacophony of voices, disruptions, and interventions that blur the boundaries between actor and audience, art and life (Hegemann 641; Fischer-Lichte 49–51). Schlingensief regularly incorporates disabled troupe members into this mix of voices and makes no attempt to contextualize their disabilities or treat them differently than his other actors. In doing so, he injects the issue of disability into his chaotic and self-subverting aesthetic and offers a further confusion for his audience, who are left in the dark about both the relationship between Schlingensief and his disabled actors and the nature of their disabilities. It is this very confusion that figures strongly in the film *Freakstars 3000*.

Parody of Able-Bodied Media Formats

Christoph Schlingensief's film is difficult to categorize. First and foremost, *Freakstars 3000* parodies mainstream television: on the one hand, it presents a casting show modelled on RTL's show *Popstars*.[7] Alongside the casting show plot, the film also features the contestants as actors in sketch-comedy style parodies of other television formats such as home-shopping presentations, a press-club discussion show, a political talk show, and advertisements for folk music. Unlike casting and sketch comedy shows, the film was not shot in a studio, but at the Tiele-Winckler-Haus in Berlin-Lichtenrade, a home for people with disabilities that emphasizes self-determined living. In a voice-over at the beginning of the film, Schlingensief immediately names the Tiele-Winckler-Haus as the site of the casting tryouts, but does not state what kind of home it is. The majority of the film's protagonists live in the home and appear as contestants on the casting show and actors in the sketches. The film also includes interviews in which the participants talk about their lives and their work, and thereby alludes to the genre of documentary cinema. Schlingensief's film blurs several genres and refuses to signal to the audience whether and when the participants are performing or not.

Freakstars 3000 parodies casting shows such as *Popstars* and Germany's version of *Pop Idol, Deutschland sucht den Superstar*. Popular in different countries around the globe, these casting shows not only dramatize the creation of pop stardom, they also involve the viewing audience in the process: after the opening elimination rounds, the audience elects the winner. *Popstars* and *Pop Idol* thus combine fantasies of stardom ("ordinary" people can become famous) with a democratic impulse (the choice comes from the people) and the authentic pretences of reality television. But, even as the audience accompanies everyday participants in their pursuit of a music career, it is made abundantly clear that opportunity is not equal for all, and we are invited to enjoy this process of inequality as it is played out as serialized spectacle. In fact, if the success myth serves to narrativize ideologies of opportunity in capitalist society, it is certainly the case that, in foregrounding the harsh nature of the audition process, it (melo)dramatizes how capitalism necessarily works for the benefit of the few at the expense of many (Holmes 158).

By staging the process of selection and elimination that precedes stardom, the *Popstars* and *Pop Idol* franchises present the importance of image and the necessity of excluding the abnormal in popular media, while they at the same time purport an "authentic" portrayal of average people's transformation into pop stars. This paradoxical mix between the ideology of success, normative exclusion, and authenticity offers a launching point for Schlingensief's exploration of the (in)visibility of disabled people in popular media. *Freakstars 3000* upends the criteria of pop casting shows. The film follows the contestants through different elimination phases and culminates in a live performance by the band of contestants at the Volksbühne Berlin. And, as is the case with *Popstars*, a voice-over (provided by Schlingensief) narrates the trials and tribulations of the contestants. But, other than the casting format and the voice-overs, *Freakstars 3000* takes a different approach than its mainstream counterparts. First of all, it is not filmed on a sound stage or studio, but rather at the Tiele-Winckler-Haus—the glamour of the *Popstars* format is missing. More importantly, the jury's criteria are completely different. At the first tryout session, the jury applauds and congratulates every song and performance without any hint of irony. Furthermore, the casting does not take place apart from the other contestants, but rather with everyone present in a communal room. Unlike mainstream casting shows, the jury focuses not on a preconceived notion of musical talent or stardom (under which most, if not all, of the contestants would fail), but rather on the uniqueness of each individual performance. While they take the form of a contest, the tryouts and subsequent phases refuse to judge the contestants according to set criteria and instead focus on the group dynamic. The tryouts take the form of a variety show that involves the encouragement and participation of the entire group. Even when contestants are "eliminated" from the competition, they continue to perform in the different sketches and appear in the film. Whereas mainstream casting shows attempt to exclude or change errors and abnormalities, *Freakstars 3000* includes atonal singing, forgotten lines, and spontaneous comments and interactions that go against the grain. Spontaneity, individuality, and personality are the primary focus. In both its open-ended format and its attention to its disabled participants, *Freakstars 3000* illuminates the forced homogeneity of mainstream television.[8]

The camera work in *Freakstars 3000* mimics and simultaneously shifts the emphasis of reality television. As is the case in many reality television shows, *Freakstars 3000* is filmed with multiple hand-held cameras, but there are two crucial differences. First of all, the camera angles repeatedly reveal the other camera operators in the room and thereby interrupt the "fly-on-the-wall documentary style" of reality TV (Holmes 161). Both in the casting tryouts and the sketches, the cameras capture the other technicians in the background as they frame the actors. They incessantly call attention to their presence in the room. The camera work thus denies a voyeuristic perspective and calls into question the "pursuit of authenticity" and the "realist codes of reality TV" (Holmes 158–59). The second main difference from reality television comes in the camera shots. On reality television, a preferred strategy for conveying authentic emotions is the close-up, which provides "a kind of super-enhanced realism offering a perspective unavailable to the naked eye" (Holmes 161). But the cameras in *Freakstars 3000* rarely zoom in on the contestants' faces. Instead, they frame the protagonists in ways that emphasize the entire group. When, for example, the contestants first perform for the jury in the community room at the Thiele-Winckler-Haus, the other contestants and residents are constantly in view behind the individual performer, who acts or sings with his or her back to the audience and the group. This strategy is repeated elsewhere in the sketches: in a parody of telethons starring Horst Gelonnek, the camera picks up other troupe members behind him even when he appears in close-up and medium close-up shots; in the talk show "Freakmann," the medium close-ups of both host and guest include audience members as well as camera operators. Instead of employing an aesthetics of individual emotion, the cameras convey a collective ludic undertaking. This technique contrasts with the emphasis on individual protagonists in casting shows, whose emotional reactions to success or failure create the show's drama. The camera work in *Freakstars 3000* refuses to isolate the protagonists from each other in a competitive spectacle and instead presents the casting show and sketches as a playful and inclusive metacomedy.

Freakstars 3000 thwarts viewers in search of narrative clarity via disruptive, non-linear editing. While the film's seventy-five minutes follow the casting-show narrative from initial tryouts to the hand-picked band's first performance, disruptive and often random interludes from interviews, sketches, graphics, and other clips constantly interrupt the main casting-show plot. The transitional graphics and disruptive editing jumps allude to the British comedy series *Monty Python's Flying Circus* and situate the film in a tradition of subversive sketch comedy. Like *Monty Python,* any given skit can be interrupted by animation and cuts to other sketches; both shows progress according to ludic, associative connections. In the DVD extras to *Freakstars 3000*, Schlingensief explains the significance of this strategy. If he were to psychologize the performers in the editing room or create a linear narrative from his own perspective, he notes, he would be forcing his viewpoint upon his performers. He continues: "As I learned in the theatre, if I have to tolerate the fact that someone is present whom I can't interrupt, whom I can't edit off the stage, then I also have to give my attention longer [to that person]. I have to accept the other in his excursiveness together with my own world and standpoint."[9] Schlingensief's experiences with live performance clearly inform his editing strategies in the film. The film's disruptive editing attempts to recreate the open-ended spontaneity of performance and allow the different voices in the film to appear in a less controlled format. The editing not only situates the disabled performers in the tradition of sketch comedy, it also attempts to provide an inclusive open-ended model for the different performers.

This open-ended model for interaction coincides with the film's mockery of political discourse on television. In a spoof of the ARD political discussion show *Presseclub*, different actors from the troupe represent different German newspapers in a discussion of "Violence in the Media" and "Love and Sex." On the one hand, the overarching tone of these sketches appears to be ridicule: the different participants in the "Violence in the Media" forum rant almost exclusively about how bad the print media are. The sketch thus offers a forum for commentary on the media by the very voices that mainstream print media tend to neglect. For example, the Tiele-Winckler-Haus resident Bernhard plays the notorious critic Franz Schirrmacher from the *Frankfurter Allgemeine Zeitung*, only to state the following about the writing in German newspapers like the *FAZ*: "When you read that stuff and so on, no, you might as well—excuse the stupid expression—go into a newspaper shop and throw a bomb!"[10] While the ridicule of the print media is clear, the model for these sketches is "anything goes" improvisational theatre. In this sense, Bernhard's suggestion to throw a bomb is not a "stupid expression" after all, but an accurate metaphor for the improvisational strategies in the sketch: each performer is given room to "explode" the constructed situation and force reactions from the others. Aside from his attempts to include all of the participants, Schlingensief does little to control the discussions. Instead, he attempts to encourage everyone to participate. As with the casting-show format, the model here appears to be an inclusive discussion format as opposed to the ordered, logical, and hence necessarily exclusive form of mainstream political discussion shows such as the ARD's *Presseclub*. Indeed, the format is so improvisational and inclusive that it, like Schlingensief's *Chance 2000*, derails into multi-vocal chaos aligned with avant-garde theatre aesthetics from the early twentieth century.

In the midst of Schlingensief's chaotic inclusivity, *Freakstars 3000* also satirizes the exclusion of disabled people from mainstream television. The film's satirical impetus is most clear in a parody of the Hessischer Rundfunk show *Friedman* entitled "Freakmann," in which the Tiele-Winckler-Haus resident Axel Silber interviews Schlingensief's troupe member Achim von Paczenski. Silber, whose musculoskeletal disability is unavoidably visible to the viewer, plays the host Freakmann and wears a suit and makeup that mimic the attire of Michel Friedman. The cognitively disabled actor von Paczenski, on the other hand, appears in the role of far right NPD representative Horst Mahler in a leather jacket and with a Hitler moustache and iconic Hitler haircut painted on his forehead. In an absurd exchange, von Paczenski/Mahler refuses to speak with the moderator Silber/Freakmann, because he is visibly disabled. When Freakmann tells him that they will take his payment away if he doesn't speak, von Paczenski storms off the stage. This scene is interesting on several levels: most obviously, it caricatures the NPD and Horst Mahler. But through the reference to Friedman—a Jewish lawyer, talk-show host, and son of a Holocaust victim—the sketch invites comparisons between Jewish and disabled identities and highlights Germany's belated *Vergangenheitsbewältigung* (coming to terms with the past) as it concerns disability. Whereas, in the wake of the Holocaust, Article 3 of the new West German constitution protected race, gender, and political and religious views against discrimination, disability was not explicitly

Christoph Schlingensief, the able-bodied director, jury member, and voice-over commentator (right), and the *Freakstars 3000* band: evocations and inversions of the "freak-show" model. Source: Copyright © Filmgalerie 451

included until a 1994 amendment. And, despite that protection, it is still difficult to imagine a physically or cognitively disabled talk-show host on mainstream television in Germany. Von Paczenski/Mahler's refusal to speak to Silber/Freakmann mirrors a broader exclusion of disabled people in the media and implicitly connects the popular media's marginalization of disabled people with fascist tendencies. But, as I will now consider, talk shows and punditry are not the only place where disabled actors are scarce in the media; at the time of Schlingensief's film, they were also invisible in the realm of irreverent and confrontational sketch comedy.

Inversions of the Freak Show and Subversions of the Medical Gaze

A constant, uncomfortable ambiguity accompanies the parodic strategies heretofore described: the consent, treatment, and status of the disabled performers in *Freakstars 3000* remain unclear throughout the film. As the title of the film as well as the sketch "Freakmann" indicates, Schlingensief constantly thematizes the objectification and commercialization of disabled performers in so-called freak shows. Despite the clear histrionics of the actors in the "Freakmann" skit, ethical questions arise about their consent and the extent of their inclusion in the creative process. While reviewers spoke positively of the film and avoided condemnation of Schlingensief's treatment of his actors,[11] public opinion was reportedly split between praise for the integration of the disabled performers and condemnation for its "degrading misuse of people with disabilities"[12] ("Wort, Bild, Ton"). Viewers on an online discussion board, for example, objected to the repetition of the freak-show model as unconscionable, claimed that the show has a derisive or degrading tone, or assumed that the actors were misused or manipulated.[13] As we shall see, Schlingensief explicitly raises these and other ethical objections in the film in order to thematize how "disability can preclude communication as its conception structures what kind of social involvement is not proper" (Kuppers 5). But the film not only highlights how the category of disability excludes people from the realm of acting and comedy, it also illuminates and subverts the source of this marginalization: the assumptions of able-bodied viewers. In its refusal to contextualize both the specific disabilities of the participants and their level of inclusion in the decision-making, the film challenges problematic assumptions about disabled people.

Schlingensief confronts audience assumptions about disabled performance by parodically invoking and inverting the freak-show model. Rosemarie Garland Thomson describes the four crucial aspects of the nineteenth-century freak show as follows:

> The four entwined narrative forms that produced freaks were, first, the oral spiel—often called the "lecture"—that was delivered by the showman or "professor" who usually managed the exhibited person; second, the often fabricated or fantastic textual accounts—both long pamphlets and broadside or newspaper advertisements—of the freak's always extraordinary life and identity; third, the staging, which included costuming, choreography, performance [...]; and fourth, drawings or photographs that disseminated an iterable, fixed, collectible visual image of staged freakishness that penetrated into the Victorian parlor and family album. (7)

Schlingensief's film mimics these strategies, albeit with a significant difference. He clearly plays the showman who gives an "oral spiel," both as the lead jury member and the voice-over commentator; he also plans and stages the different parodic performances by the disabled actors; and the film *Freakstars 3000* will certainly disseminate the images of his performers to a wider audience. Furthermore, the casting show in the film implies strategies of evaluation and categorization typical of a freak-show exhibition. But unlike the freak-show lecturer, Schlingensief refuses to contextualize or explain the disabilities of his actors. The film thereby refuses any medical or wondrous narrative of disability, yet simultaneously provokes the audience to object to its mimicry of elements from the freak-show format.

Schlingensief's *Freakstars 3000* explicitly alludes to another film with disabled performers that raised strong audience objections: Tod Browning's 1932 film *Freaks*. A groundbreaking and scandalous film for its time, Browning's *Freaks* attempted to humanize its disabled protagonists, but also sensationalized them via the horror genre (Hawkins 267–69). The special message that precedes *Freaks* betrays the film's double coding. After several paragraphs about the negative portrayal of abnormality throughout literary and cultural history, the special message concludes with the following mixed statements:

> The revulsion with which we view the abnormal, the malformed and the mutilated is the result of long conditioning by our forefathers. The majority of freaks, themselves, are endowed with normal thoughts and emotions. Their lot is truly a heartbreaking one. […] Never again will such a story be filmed, as modern science and teratology is rapidly eliminating such blunders from the world. With humility for the many injustices done to such people (they have no power to control their lot), we present the most startling horror story of THE ABNORMAL and THE UNWANTED.

Despite the assertion that most "freaks" have "normal" thoughts and feelings, the message is overwhelmingly negative. It situates the protagonists in the context of pity ("heartbreaking") and eugenics ("blunders" to be eventually solved by modern science and teratology) and closes with the insinuation that they will appear as the monsters in a "most startling horror story." Despite the film's subversive plot, which invites the audience to side with the disabled performers against able-bodied villains, it repeats the exclusionism and sensationalism of the freak-show format in its very prologue, not to mention its spectacular conclusion.

Although filmed seventy years later, Schlingensief's film *Freakstars 3000* faces a similar dilemma: how should a non-disabled director present disabled performers? As shown earlier, Schlingensief begins with a special message of his own. But, by comparison to Browning's epigraph, Schlingensief does not describe the fate of the abnormal, but rather simply announces the casting-show format. The imperative to step right up and see and hear talented singers in pursuit of a music career alludes to the call of the freak-show announcer, but otherwise the language avoids the pity and sensationalism of Browning's special message. And, when disability is first mentioned, the focus shifts to the "big problem" of the non-disabled performers. In the final line of the special message, Schlingensief then turns to the question of exploitation that Browning left unaddressed. Schlingensief states that the actors were abused and "forced" to portray disability and that "every attack and every crackup is therefore guaranteed to be authentic and not repeatable." This ironic disclaimer mocks a paradox that pervades popular cinema about disability: non-disabled method actors who train themselves to portray disability—Daniel Day Lewis in *My Left Foot*, for example—receive critical praise,[14] yet when real disabled actors appear in a film, the question of exploitation and misuse arises. Schlingensief counters such questions by categorically refusing to adopt a tone of pity or of sensationalism. The fact that a film containing cognitively disabled participants would need a disclaimer in the first place exposes lingering assumptions, above all, the notion that cognitively disabled people can neither differentiate between play and reality nor decide for themselves. Schlingensief's prologue both provokes and ridicules these assumptions.

Freakstars 3000 not only subverts assumptions about disability and performance, it also undermines the medical definition of disability and the medical gaze of able-bodied audience members. The opening credits immediately invoke the reduction of disabled people to their medical diagnoses: different animated bodies and disconnected body parts appear on the screen accompanied by circus-like music. The final images of the opening credits show an animated human head, which, in rapid succession, loses its skin and then skeleton until only a brain remains. A clamp then swings down from above like a hanging sign and fastens to the brain. Thereafter, a sign with the title of the film then replaces the brain via an animated explosion. While establishing the ludic tone of the film through the allusion to Monty Python's animated sequences, the images in this opening clip evoke a medical understanding of disability. More importantly, the final image of the clamp fastened to the brain indicates the desire to "pin down" or define disability. The "Freakstars 3000" sign in the clamp becomes the film's logo and appears as a transitional image throughout the film. At other points during the casting show, an animated brain with a number on it descends onto the screen to indicate that the next contestant will be performing—here too we have a constant reminder of the medical reduction of disabled people to their function and parts. These images, combined with the canned laughter that accompanies them, imply a tone of ridicule throughout the film that would be consistent with the freak-show model.

But within the film itself, a different picture emerges. Despite the graphics, the film focuses on the participants primarily as performers and as individuals; it presents them both in sketches, interviews, and in their own living quarters in the Tiele-Winckler-Haus, which Schlingensief mentions but never describes as a home for disabled people. The two explicit references to disability ridicule not the participants, but rather the medical gaze of the non-disabled. In the first scenario, Schlingensief and his crew are putting makeup on the actor Kerstin Grassman, when Schlingensief states: "Kerstin was schizophrenic, but you aren't anymore, right?" Kerstin replies indignantly: "No! I'm still schizophrenic." Here Schlingensief stages naïve questions that emanate from the narrative of recovery and rehabilitation. In another sequence, Schlingensief asks Achim von Paczenski what many audience members are wondering, "Achim, are you disabled? Really?" and "Where exactly are you disabled?" To the former question, Achim answers, "Yes"; to the second, he sarcastically answers, "On my ass." What sounds like a crude joke in effect refuses to give Schlingensief, who stands in for the audience here, a clear medical category. Through its treatment of the participants as individuals and refusal to pinpoint their specific disabilities, the film resists and ridicules the medical notion of disability. In this context, the clamp with the brain from the opening credits represents the audience's desire to pinpoint the nature of the disability, a desire that the film thwarts and discards. Thus understood, the canned laughter in these graphic segments is not directed at the participants, but rather at those audience members who still cling to a medical understanding of disability and use it as a means to reject or condemn the film.

Conclusion

On an aesthetic level, *Freakstars 3000* parodies different television genres and simultaneously offers an inclusive and multi-vocal alternative to mainstream television. On the level of audience reception, the film provokes a series of ethical questions. Does Schlingensief mistreat or instrumentalize the actors for his own aesthetic? To what extent are the participants active and willing actors in the performance? And to what extent do the film's title, laugh track, and graphics invite, however unwittingly, the viewer to laugh at the protagonists? By provoking such questions, the film sets a trap for able-bodied spectators: as I have argued, the objections to the film expose problematic assumptions about disabled people that continue to pervade German and, for that matter, North American culture. Objections to the treatment of protagonists imply that they, as an entire undifferentiated group, cannot speak for themselves, that they, as a group, cannot differentiate between play and reality, and that they should not be treated the same as able-bodied actors. By exposing these assumptions and simultaneously subverting the medical model of disability, the film critiques still-prevalent beliefs that preclude full inclusion of disabled people into the realm of visual representation.

Finally, it is important to note yet another possible objection to the film, namely, that it deals with the topic of disability in a too ludic, ironic, irreverent, and chaotic fashion. This point of contention brings us back to the issue of the graphics, music and voice-overs, which evoke both the freak-show format and the sketch comedy show *Monty Python's Flying Circus*. The objection implies that disabled people should not participate in such a show, because it runs the danger of repeating the freak-show tradition and evoking the laughter of superiority that Snyder and Mitchell see in Hollywood cinema. But this is a danger that comedy and parody always run when they cite and repeat different taboos in an irreverent manner. In closing, I would like to argue that another service of *Freakstars 3000* has been to expand media representation of disabled performers into the terrain of sketch comedy. Proof that this strategy has already born fruit can be found in the television show *Para-Comedy*, launched in 2006 on Comedy Central Germany. A candid-camera-style show in which actors with different disabilities play pranks on able-bodied passersby, *Para-Comedy* exposes and contradicts the assumptions of non-disabled Germans in a highly irreverent and amusing manner. *Freakstars 3000*, it seems, has ousted the taboo against comedy and disabled performance in mainstream German television and film.

Notes

1 "Liebe Filmfreunde! Sehen Sie coole junge Menschen, die mit Talent und hundertprozentiger Hingabe ihren Traum von der großen Musikkarriere wahr machen. Hören Sie deutsche Originale, die so ganz im Vorbeisingen auf das große Problem der Nicht-Behinderten hinweisen. Während der Dreharbeiten wurden Akteure konsequent mißhandelt und zur Darstellung von Behinderung gezwungen. Jeder Anfall und jeder Zusammenbruch ist deshalb garantiert authentisch und nicht wiederholbar."
2 The *ABM* currently supports six different television programs that focus on disability issues and the lives of people with disabilities. See http://www.abm-medien.de for more information.
3 See David T. Mitchell's essay on "Narrative Prosthesis."
4 "Batman oder Bettler—zwischen diesen beiden Polen scheint es nichts zu geben, was es wert wäre, vermittelt zu werden. Beide Tendenzen sind gleich weit vom Ziel einer zusammengehörenden Gesellschaft entfernt, indem sie den Betroffenen entweder auf ein Podest stellen oder umgekehrt außerhalb jeglicher sozialen Verpflichtung als ausschließlich Nehmenden" (Radtke 9).
5 "Ich habe noch keine einzige Fernseh-Straßenumfrage erlebt, in der ein behinderter Passant über Alltagsprobleme zu Wort gekommen wäre, wie die Öffnung der Ladenzeiten oder die gegenwärtige politische Situation. Dem Wortgeklingel von Integration—die Problematik des Begriffes wurde bereits angesprochen—steht die Wirklichkeit der gedanklichen Aussonderung und Beschränkung auf die Behinderung entgegen" (Radtke 10).
6 For a summary of Schlingensief's oeuvre and analyses of specific films and performances, see Tara Forrest and Anna Teresa's Scheer's edited volume *Christoph Schlingensief: Art Without Borders*.
7 In *Popstars*, which began in New Zealand and Australia, and was then localized in countries around the globe, a jury and the viewing audience hand-pick a new pop group over an extensive period of tryouts and eliminations. Its spinoff, *Pop Idol*, has become a sensation in the United States under the title *American Idol* and in Germany as *DSDS (Deutschland sucht den Superstar)* (Holmes 149).

8   In "Productive Discord" 2010, Tara Forrest uses Adorno's writings on atonality to explain the film's open-ended format and parodic displacements of televisual homogeneity. Forrest describes the film as an "atonal re-enactment" that questions the exclusion of people with disabilities from mainstream television.
9   "Wenn ich aber—was ich durchs Theater gelernt habe—aushalten muss, dass da einer ist, den ich nicht unterbrechen kann—den kann ich ja nicht wegschneiden auf der Bühne oder so—dann muss ich auch länger hingucken [...] das muss ich akzeptieren in seiner Sprunghaftigkeit zusammen mit meiner Welt, aus der ich komme."
10 "Ja wenn man det so liest und so weiter, ne, da kann man gleich—entschuldige, blöden Ausdruck—in einen Zeitungsladen gehen und 'ne Bombe werfen!"
11 See the reviews by Harald Fricke, Florian Malzacher, and Johanna Straub. Even Christiane Müller-Lobeck's more skeptical review avoids objecting to Schlingensief's use of cognitively disabled protagonists.
12 "Die Meinungen, ob das Integration oder ein entwürdigender Missbrauch der behinderten Menschen ist, gehen weit auseinander" ("Wort, Bild, Ton").
13 The following postings offer a sampling of typical objections: "Ich denke schon allein der Titel *Freakstars* ist Aussage genug um die Sendung als verachtend gegenüber Behinderten zu klassifizieren." DerBlob. "Re: Freakstars 3000." Online posting. 1 July 2002. 20 Jan. 2009 <http://www.xpbulletin.de/t1383-0.html>; "Ein solches Projekt untergräbt ganz klar die Würde dieser Menschen. Das dürfte eigentlich sogar ein Fall für die Staatsanwaltschaft sein." Phoinix. "Re: Freakstars 3000." Online posting. 29 June 2002. 20 Jan. 2009 <http://www.xpbulletin.de/t1383-0.html>; "Wenn Leute, die das offensichtlich nicht selbst einschätzen können, dazu gebracht werden und vor der 'Nation' bloßgestellt werden, dann ist das schon ziemlich pervers und kann auch nicht mehr mit dem Kunstcharakter gerechtfertigt werden." SnooP. "Re: Freakstars 3000." Online posting. 30 June 2002. 20 Jan. 2009 <http://www.xpbulletin.de/t1383-0.html>.
14 "Similar to black-face actors, non-disabled people can prove the 'mastery' of their craft by 'acting disabled,' whereas disabled actors are often denied work opportunities" (Kuppers 54).

References

Fischer-Lichte, Erika. "*Quo Vadis?* Theater Studies at the Crossroads." *Modern Drama. Defining the Field.* Ed. Ric Knowles et al., 48–66. Toronto: U of Toronto P, 2003.

Forrest, Tara. "Productive Discord: Schlingensief, Adorno, and *Freakstars 3000.*" *Christoph Schlingensief. Art Without Borders.* Ed. Tara Forrest and Anna Teresa Scheer. Bristol: intellect, 2010. 123–35

Forrest, Tara, and Anna Teresa Scheer, ed. *Christoph Schlingensief. Art Without Borders.* Bristol: intellect, 2010.

Freaks. Dir. Tod Browning. Metro-Goldwyn-Mayer, 1932.

Freakstars 3000. Dir. Christoph Schlingensief. volksbühne films, 2003.

Fricke, Harald. "Die hohe Kunst der Vermischung." *Tageszeitung* 20 Nov. 2003. 20 Jan. 2009 <http://www.taz.de>.

Hamilton, Elizabeth C. "No Longer Unreasonable: Disability in German Cinema." *Disability Studies Quarterly* 24.3 (2004): n. pag.

Hawkins, Joan. "One of Us: Tod Browning's *Freaks*." *Freakery. Cultural Spectacles of the Extraordinary Body*. Ed. Rosemarie Garland Thomson. New York: New York UP, 1996. 265–76.

Hegemann, Carl. "Das Theater retten, indem man es abschafft? Oder: Die Signifikanz des Theaters." *Maschinen, Medien, Performances. Theater an der Schnittstelle zu digitalen Welten*. Ed. Martina Leeker. Berlin: Alexander, 2001. 638–49.

Hegemann, Carl, and Christoph Schlingensief. *Chance 2000. Wähle dich selbst*. Cologne: Kiepenheuer & Witsch: 1998.

Heyer, Katharina C. "The ADA on the Road: Disability Rights in Germany." *Law & Social Inquiry* 27.4 (2002): 723–62.

Holmes, Su. "'Reality Goes Pop!': Reality TV, Popular Music, and Narratives of Stardom in Pop Idol." *Television New Media* 5.2 (2004): 147–72.

Köbsell, Swantje. "Towards Self-Determination and Equalization: A Short History of the German Disability Rights Movement." *Disability Studies Quarterly* 26.2 (2006). 16 June 2006 <http://www.dsq-sds.org>.

Kuppers, Petra. *Disability and Contemporary Performance: Bodies on Edge*. New York: Routledge, 2003.

Malzacher, Florian. "Dramaturgie des Leerlaufs; 'Freakstars 3000' nun als Film." *Frankfurter Rundschau* 18 Nov. 2003. 20 Jan. 2009 <http://www.451video.de/451/d_set_frameload.htm?content/prod/freakstars_texte.html~content>.

Mitchell, David T. "Narrative Prosthesis and the Materiality of Metaphor." *Disability Studies. Enabling the Humanities*. Ed. Sharon Snyder et al. New York: MLA, 2002. 15–30.

Müller-Lobeck, Christiane. "Die Nichtbehinderten sind das Problem: Schlingensiefs *Freakstars 3000* im Lichtmeß." *Tageszeitung* 14 Oct. 2004. 20 Jan. 2009 <http://www.taz.de>.

Norden, Martin F. "The Hollywood Discourse on Disability: Some Personal Reflections." *Screening Disability: Essays on Cinema and Disability*. Ed. Christopher R. Smit and Anthony Enns. Lanham: UP America, 2001. 19–31.

Poore, Carol. *Disability in Twentieth-Century German Culture*. Ann Arbor: U of Michigan P, 2007.

Radtke, Peter. "Zum Bild behinderter Menschen in den Medien." *Bundeszentrale für politische Bildung*. 2003. 3 Feb. 2009 <http://www.bpb.de>.

Snyder, Sharon L., and David T. Mitchell. *Cultural Locations of Disability*. Chicago: U of Chicago P, 2006.

Straub, Johanna. "Schlingensiefs 'Freakstars 3000.' Wir sind alle krank." *Spiegel Online* 19 Nov. 2003. 20 Jan. 2009 <http://www.spiegel.de>.

Thomson, Rosemarie Garland. "Introduction: From Wonder to Error—A Genealogy of Freak Discourse in Modernity." In *Freakery: Cultural Spectacles of the Extraordinary Body*. Ed. Rosemarie Garland Thomson. New York: New York UP, 1996. 1–19.

"Wort, Bild, Ton—auch für Menschen mit geistiger Behinderung?" *Lebenshilfe Berlin*. 2002. 20 Jan. 2009 <http://home.snafu.de/m.franke/referenzen/lebenhilfe-text.pdf>.

REASSESSING AND CONSUMING HISTORY

5
Literary Discourse and Cinematic Narrative:
Scripting Affect in *Das Leben der Anderen*

Roger Cook

Abstract This chapter examines how *Das Leben der Anderen* juxtaposes the state-propagated literature in the East to the free literary production of the West. I argue that in keeping with its bias in favour of a *Bildungsliteratur* cut from a Western mould, von Donnersmarck's film subordinates cinema as a visual medium imbued with presence to the textual semiotic of literary narrative. I then analyze how this embrace of literary discourse situates the filmic text with respect to the circulation and modulation of affect in the free-market "society of control" in contemporary Germany.

Meticulously composed and constructed by the first-time director/screenwriter Florian Henckel von Donnersmarck, *Das Leben der Anderen* (*The Lives of Others*, 2006) has won uniform praise and the 2007 Oscar for best foreign language film. Most critics have focused on what A.O. Scott called in his *New York Times* review, "Mr. von Donnersmarck's brilliant exposition of the Orwellian logic of East German Communism." The film achieves this in part with a storyline that recalls Bertolt Brecht's classic play *Der gute Mensch von Sezuan* (*The Good Woman of Setzuan*, 1943). Von Donnersmarck turns the tables on Brecht's critique of capitalism, focusing the attention on a "good person" who is caught in the bind of trying to advance the worthy goals of socialism within a corrupt communist system. His protagonist is a Stasi agent devoted to the cause of rooting out the enemies of socialism. As he begins to question his commitment to the German Democratic Republic (GDR), the film poses a question similar to that at the heart of Brecht's play: How can a good person negotiate a social order that makes it impossible to consistently do the right thing? The film makes this connection to Brecht and his play explicit in several ways. Not only do the theatre and its role in the cultural politics of the GDR play prominently in the story, but also the film's other protagonist is a famous playwright who, like Brecht, supports the GDR despite an underlying ambivalence.[1] And the key musical piece and literary work in the film have a title, *Die Sonate vom guten Menschen* (*Sonata for a Good Man*), that alludes unmistakably to Brecht's play.

Das Leben der Anderen not only reverses the thrust of Brecht's play, it also eliminates almost all ambiguity in its black-and-white depiction of the moral juxtaposition between East and West. While its portrayal of the totalitarian machinations of the East German state is indeed precise and powerful, I want to examine the film with another question in mind. What does it say about the forms of social control that exert pressures on the individual in the free-market democracies of the West? Keeping the film's direct allusions to Brecht in mind, my analysis focuses first on the stark distinction it makes between the state-propagated literature in the East and the free literary production of the West. Then I look at the use of voice-over to give filmic presence to these two opposing approaches to literary practice. Turning to the question of the film's place in the cultural landscape of the Federal Republic, I examine how *Das Leben der Anderen* subordinates cinema as a visual medium imbued with presence to the textual semiotic of literary narrative. And finally, I ask how this embrace of literary discourse situates the filmic text as a cultural agent in the circulation and modulation of affect in the free-market "society of control" in contemporary Germany.

Love, Literature, and Coming to Terms with the Present

Das Leben der Anderen tells the story of the Stasi officer Gerd Wiesler, who has been assigned the task of spying on the successful playwright Georg Dreyman. The latter has always been loyal to the communist cause, but begins to question his stance after learning that his lover and the lead actress in his new play, Christa-Maria Sieland, has been coerced into having an affair with a member of the Communist Central Committee, Bruno Hempf. This, together with the suicide of his friend Albert Jerska, who had been banned from working as a theatre director for ten years, drives Dreyman to anonymously author a magazine article critical of the GDR. Wiesler, while monitoring Dreyman and his circle of friends, begins to gain new perspectives from the lives of others, and he begins to have moral reservations about his career as a Stasi agent. The plot summary on the website *movie.de* gives this short list of the positive influences he encounters while spying on Dreyman: "The immersion into *Das Leben der Anderen—*

into love, literature, free thinking and free speech—makes Wiesler aware of his own meagre existence and opens up to him a whole new world that draws him ever more into its sphere"[2] ("Das Leben"). Of the four aspects mentioned here the film's treatment of literature is the most intricate and most significant for the contrast drawn between East and West. Although the film portrays in depth the extensive measures the GDR took to control the expression of ideas, the practice of free speech seems to have relatively little effect on the changes in Wiesler. The events of the film story lead us to question the idea that free speech is essential to the overthrow of an oppressive regime. The film implies that the freedom enjoyed in the democratic West is necessary for the individual to find the right course. Conversely, Wiesler's ability to free himself from the ideological hold of the socialist state displays a moral agency of the individual that is at least to some extent possible regardless of the social or national context. Although the love between Dreyman and Sieland leads to the tragic event at the heart of the film story, it is the pointed juxtaposition of life in the East versus the West that brings this point home. Wiesler's almost grotesquely portrayed session with a state-sanctioned prostitute sets his dismal love life off against the intimacy experienced by Dreyman and Sieland, which he then sees destroyed by the jealous Hempf's corrupt use of government authority.

The film's complex treatment of literature situates it as the pivotal cultural instrument in the East–West divide. It is apparently literature in conjunction with the other arts that provided Dreyman and his group of cultured friends the ability to develop their own private realm of free thinking. Literary works appear prominently throughout the film. For the most part, they are books from the West, mainly contraband that the Stasi agents find in Dreyman's apartment, but consider inconsequential. And, of course, there is the one important new book that appears at the end of the film, also a product of the West. As far as the East goes, there are key references to the state-propagated literature of the GDR and to the relationship between the writer and the state. But with one key exception, a volume of Brecht's poetry, it is the absence of East German books that is more telling. Yet, without a final push from this literary giant, it is unclear whether Wiesler would have made the step from an indoctrinated agent of the state to liberated, autonomous individual.

The GDR's narrow prescription for the role the writer and literature should play in a socialist state provides the backdrop for the film's engagement of Brecht and for its own vision of literature. In his speech at the celebration of the premiere of a Dreyman play, the party boss Hempf proclaims: "The writer is the engineer of the soul. Georg Dreyman is one of our most important engineers."[3] When Dreyman defends his friend Jerska and suggests that the authorities should lift the *Berufsverbot* (ban against him directing plays) that has been placed on him, Hempf criticizes the sentimental optimism of his writing: "But that is what we all love about your plays, your love for mankind and your belief that people change. Dreyman, no matter how often you say it in your plays, people do not change."[4] The film story sets out to demonstrate not only that he is wrong about this, but also that literature is an effective means of shaping and moulding the individual into a different, and indeed a better person. It, however, rejects the idea that a programmatic form of literary production, whether one proscribed by the cultural arm of an autocratic government or not, can fulfill this higher purpose. The film includes an instance where literature delivers on the promise of aesthetic education. Shortly after the failed meeting with the prostitute, Wiesler enters Dreyman's apartment and explores it slowly with a personal interest that not only goes beyond the interests of the state, but even betrays them. In the following scene, we see him reclining on a sofa reading Brecht's poem from a book he took with him from Dreyman's apartment. Its place in the sequence of scenes leading up to Wiesler's decision to protect Dreyman clearly indicates that this poem was an important element in his conversion.

While Brecht's poetry plays a key role in Wiesler's transformation, the film also carries an implied critique of Brecht's turn to literary writing for the socialist cause. Von Donnersmarck has Wiesler read from the work of the most prominent literary figure to choose the GDR over the West. He has him read, however, not from his writings that promoted the goals of the communist movement, but rather from an early love poem, "Die Erinnerung an Marie A." (The Memory of Marie A.). After the *Wende,* Dreyman stops writing for the theatre, turning his back on the genre that Brecht had made the literary vehicle par excellence for the support of socialism. The scene at the premiere of Dreyman's play highlights von Donnersmarck's reservations about drama. As a literary genre designed for public performance in a stratified cultural environment, drama can be easily co-opted by and for social or political groups or causes. Hempf's speech at the party following the premiere puts this on display. When we see Dreyman at the theatre again after the *Wende,* he runs into Hempf. The presence of this corrupt leader from the fallen regime, now obviously "reformed" and moving in the circles of respectable society, calls to mind the deception that informs theatrical performance. The character flaw that drives Sieland to betray Dreyman is also linked to her career as actress. When Wiesler approaches her in the bar, he praises her as a beloved actress: "Many people love you because you are who you are." Her response, "Actors are never 'who they are,'"[5] offers a partial explanation of her moral weakness and her ability to deceive Dreyman despite their intimacy. Sieland's life in the theatre is implicated in her downfall, and we are left to assume that this was one reason why Dreyman decided to give up drama after he learned of her betrayal.

Rather than taking up poetry, Dreyman turns to a German literary form with a long established history, the *Bildungsroman*. The title of his novel, *Die Sonate vom guten Menschen*, alludes to one of Brecht's best-known plays, *Der gute Mensch von Sezuan*. It does so not in homage, but rather to challenge the play's message. The film suggests that Brecht got it wrong, that the individual can find and follow the right path even within a corrupt social order. It shows that, contrary to the central lesson of Brecht's play, fundamental changes in the socio-economic foundations are not a prerequisite for the viable existence of the good person. A logical literary corollary of the film's thesis supports Dreyman's rejection of the theatre in favour of the novel. If literature, or film, can promote such moral edification, then it will occur as *innere Bildung*, a change spurred best by individual reception and reflection rather than as part of a public discourse featuring competing ideas. Moreover, it suggests that literature in the GDR was part of a social and cultural experiment that went wrong, a detour away from a rich literary tradition that can still be invoked to shape and guide the "good German."

The film not only advocates in favour of the literary tradition of aesthetic education, it also sacrifices its medium specificity to produce a fictional world that could be created almost identically in a novel. *Das Leben der Anderen* is, one could say, the perfect film adaptation of a novel that does not exist. Or, more precisely, it is the film adaptation of *Die Sonate vom guten Menschen*, Dreyman's fictional *Bildungsroman*. His novel, like the film itself, functions as an act of redemption that tells the story of the good person trapped in a malignant social order. As we can deduce from the fictional context of the film, Dreyman's novel tells the story of Wiesler's heroic sacrifice of his career to protect Dreyman and Sieland from the tyrannical oppression of the East German state. Von Donnersmarck's film tells not only this story, but also the story of Dreyman's novel and the set of circumstances that produced it. Like the fictional novel, the film too is a *Bildungswerk* directed primarily at the former citizens of the GDR, who must make sense of their past complicity in the evils of the state in order to come to terms with their new lives in the Federal Republic. The message in each case is that the blame lies not with the individual, at least those who were simple *Mitläufer* (followers), but rather with the failed system. Dreyman's turn back to a classical tradition of German literature after the fall of the Wall recalls a similar reaction in the Federal Republic in the years following the collapse of the Third Reich. As a work of aesthetic and moral *Bildung*, the film attempts to overcome a crisis of the present, one that inhibits the integration of eastern Germans into the social order of the West. In this case, the message is more of an implied connotation as opposed to the carefully constructed message about the failings of the GDR. It goes something like this: the difficulty you are experiencing in becoming fully enfranchised citizens of the Federal Republic is not your individual fault, nor is it the fault of the new social order. It is a lingering effect of your lives in the GDR; and the cathartic effect of this film is to exorcise this past and enable full integration.

Voice-/Sound-Over and Social Control

There are four key instances of voice-over readings from written texts in *Das Leben der Anderen*. Two of these lend support to the film's characterization of the despotic state control by the communist party in the GDR. The other two show the power of free literary expression or journalistic writing to effectively counter this form of control. To analyze their purpose and effect I want to turn to Michel Chion's well-known discussion of the off-screen voice. He coined the term *acousmêtre* for the voice of an unseen character that is always on the verge of making its appearance and its power manifest in the film. None of the four voice-overs in *Das Leben der Anderen* fits Chion's definition exactly, and yet each exhibits the powers he ascribes to the disembodied voice that is not connected to either a visible character or a known off-screen body: "First, the *acousmêtre* has the power of *seeing all*; second the power of *omniscience*; and third, the *omnipotence* to act on the situation" (129–30). In each case of acousmatic voice-over in *Das Leben der Anderen,* the voice reading the written text is that of one of the characters who is already well known to the viewer. All four texts are also diegetic and play an integral role in the plot. Still, von Donnersmarck uses the voice-over readings to establish an invisible source of power much like that described by Chion.

The two opposing pairs of voice-over readings play off each other to underscore the power of free literary expression as a form of opposition to totalitarian control. The first is a voice-over recitation of the love poem by Brecht that Wiesler is reading alone in his apartment. The second is the voice-over of Wiesler reading his colleague's report of Sieland's return to the apartment after her conversation with him in the corner bar. As we hear Wiesler's voice reading the report, the typewritten text is transposed over slightly veiled footage of her and Dreyman making love. Not only does the terse, objective style of the report fail to capture the intensity of the scene that unfolds behind it, but the report also misses the subversive content of their pillow talk following sex. Wiesler's colleague misinterprets Dreyman's repeated avowal that he will now have the strength to do something as referring to his stalled progress on a play to commemorate the fortieth anniversary of the GDR. The subsequent scene shows him acting on this resolve, while a voice-over situates the writing as an act of moral indignation at the destruction of lives in the GDR. It is a voice-over in Dreyman's voice of the article he writes about the high suicide rates in the GDR. It begins at the funeral scene as the camera is fixed on his face during the ceremony and forms a sound bridge across a sequence of shots that lead into an image of him at the typewriter actually composing the text. The voice-over leads us—as readers of the film—to assume that he had begun to formulate it in his head as he mourned the loss of his friend Jerska. His decision to smuggle this text over to the Federal Republic for publication in *Der Spiegel* leads to the pivotal event in the story, Wiesler's decision to conceal his identity as its author.

The final voice-over comes late in the movie, after the fall of the Wall, and serves both to reveal the full scope of the spying and to dispel its power, which had been on display throughout the movie. When Dreyman goes to the Stasi archives to read his files, we see him sitting at a table stacked high with the extensive reports, and we hear voice-over readings of excerpts from the files, always in the voice of the person who entered the account (Wiesler, his boss Grubitz, Sieland). With respect to the film story, this episode enables Dreyman to learn how Wiesler had protected him from being revealed as the author of the *Spiegel* article criticizing the high suicide rate in the GDR. It also lets the viewer see the cryptic smudge of red ink that Wiesler had left as a signal for Dreyman, suggesting that he had the prescient hunch that one day the Stasi files would be open to their victim—which in turn implies that he had gained a certain faith in the work of those in the circle of intellectuals and literati he had been monitoring. The spying had already been clearly established in the course of the film, but this scene serves to demonstrate just how thorough and extensive it had been. Also, even though the voice belongs to characters known to the viewer, the acousmatic voice-over points to the site of central power in the GDR that exerted its control everywhere while remaining invisible. The reading of Sieland's signed statement about her lover in her own voice dramatizes the ability of the state power to infiltrate into the most private realms, even wedging itself between intimate lovers. This final voice-over also functions to defuse the ominous authority of the GDR state, much in the way the appearance of a figure onscreen diminishes the aura evoked by an earlier *acousmêtre*. As Chion wrote: "An inherent quality of the *acousmêtre* is that it can be instantaneously dispossessed of its mysterious powers [...] when it is *de-acousmatized*, when the film reveals the face that is the source of the voice" (130).

These acousmatic voice-overs of written texts in *Das Leben der Anderen* establish a dual structure to the powers they represent. The two pairs are set off against each other in a way that produces a static juxtaposition of opposing forces and over-determines the role of human agency in the control exerted by a society. To illustrate this last point, I want to contrast these instances with another prominent example of *acousmêtre* in German film. In one of the best-known scenes of New German Cinema, a radio voice-over plays for the last eleven minutes, including the rolling of the credits, of *Die Ehe der Maria Braun* (*The Marriage of Maria Braun*, Fassbinder, 1979). This voice-over is the actual radio broadcast of the frenetic final minutes of the 1954 soccer World Cup final in Berne between Germany and Hungary. As Germany scores the winning goal against their favoured opponents and then hangs on to win the title, the voice of the announcer becomes increasingly frenzied. His almost crazed anticipation of the final whistle reflects a state of affect shared by the entire nation after nine years of working through a traumatic relationship with the recent past and now standing on the threshold of a new legitimacy. Unlike the voice-overs of written texts in *Das Leben der Anderen*, this radio *acousmêtre* does not reference the efforts of either an individual or group vying for control or influence over the German people. It represents diverse forces that are transmitted circuitously through various channels and unintentional agents. The final radio voice-over is but the last in a constant cacophony of disruptive sound-overs throughout *Die Ehe der Maria Braun*—radio broadcasts, the loud clacking of typewriter keys, jackhammers involved in the frenetic reconstruction of Germany, among others. As physical effects of the rapid economic transformation occurring in the Federal Republic, they are eruptions of systemic capitalist forces that produce virulent new affective flows and volatile, uncontrollable forms of subjectivity.

This contrast produced by these different forms of acousmatic voice- and sound-overs is only to be expected in that von Donnersmarck's film is depicting the control exerted by the centralized authority of a totalitarian regime in the GDR. Each style seems appropriate for the respective social order that the film reproduces. *Das Leben der Anderen* captures the totalitarian form that the modern, bureaucratically regulated "disciplinary society" took in an East German state under communist control. In *Maria Braun* we see a free-market "control society" (Deleuze *Postscript* 3–7) take shape out of the chaos and destruction in postwar Germany. On the level of representation, acousmatic voice and sound is used effectively in both films to depict social and political forces that shape affective flows and produce subjectivities at a juncture in recent Germany history. But how does each film function as a cultural mediation of affective flows in its own social context? How does the textual fabric of the film structure, inhibit, convey, or unleash intensities of affect? And how do these constructs relate to the way such affects are modulated and controlled in the society that produced the films? To answer these questions, I turn now to the tight narrative structure of *Das Leben der Anderen* and the control it exerts over the image. I examine in particular the priority von Donnersmarck gives to literary traditions over the iconic film image and the effect this has on the film's mode of visuality.

Narrative, Image, and Affect

Von Donnersmarck approaches filmmaking with a bias toward language and literature. He follows in the tradition of those who "think" of cinema as a visual medium whose texts merely translate the meaning of linguistic, and particularly written, discourse into an image stream enhanced by synchronized sound. Because of the influence of this paradigm, mainstream narrative film conforms largely to aesthetic principles derived from nineteenth-century literary prose. Consequently, we tend to "read a film text" much as we would literary narrative, piecing together its signs according to a set of differences that correspond to written texts. My discussion of *Das Leben der Anderen* offers such a reading, interpreting it as a highly discursive text that presents complexly structured arguments about life and culture, and particularly literary culture, in the two Germanys.[6]

What enables the film to function discursively much like a literary text is the predominant role played by narrative. As Keith Cohen wrote, "Narrativity is the most solid median link between novel and cinema, the most pervasive tendency of both verbal and visual languages. In both novel and cinema, groups of signs, be they literary or visual signs, are apprehended consecutively through time; and this consecutiveness gives rise to an unfolding structure, the diegetic whole that is never fully *present* in any one group yet always *implied* in each such group" (4). Cohen's account is convincing, but it is based on a central presupposition. It assumes that the filmmaker works with film images as signs in a semiotic system designed to produce narratives. Even if film viewing necessarily includes a stream of consecutive images, "the unfolding structure, the diegetic whole" that Cohen references presupposes a semiotic construction aimed at a coherent, unified narrative. As opposed to literary discourse, or writing per se, film has the potential to show a "posited world" without the kind of interrelation of the images as signs described by Cohen. While in practice cinema is almost always narrative, and usually conforms to a set of classical principles that demand coherence, continuity, and closure, there is always the potential that it includes autonomous images that do not fit into the narrative structure of the whole. In *Das Leben der Anderen,* von Donnersmarck takes great pains to fold any such potentially autonomous images back into its highly structured complex of textual signs. Not only each event, but also every image in the film, is a visual sign integrated into the unfolding of a narrative film world consecutively through time.[7]

To illustrate this I want to look at two scenes. Each includes an audio text that threatens the hegemony of narrative, but in both scenes the subordination of the visual image to the film story leaves the dominance of the latter intact. The first shows Wiesler reading the book of Brecht's poetry, while his voice-over is heard reading from "Die Erinnerung an Marie A." As this scene plays itself out, the actual verses of the poem are less important than the role Brecht's poetry plays in influencing Wiesler to protect Dreyman. The poem, written by Brecht at the age of twenty-two, describes how the memory of first love fades in comparison to the beauty of the experience. One could argue that the sentiment expressed in the poem fed into Brecht's decision to take up the communist cause. That is, if nothing in human experience has a higher or lasting value, not even the ecstasy of first love, then life in a meaningless present could be sacrificed for the hope of a better future. But, apparently Wiesler, like von Donnersmarck, reads the poem against the grain of this disillusionment, moved rather by the description of the ecstatic moment of the original love experience. The voice-over includes only the first of the poem's three stanzas, which recounts a romantic moment when the poet was together with his lover and caught sight of a passing cloud. It is not until the second stanza shifts the time frame to the present that the poet admits that he can no longer recall his lover's face and does not remember what happened to their love. In the context of the film, the lyrical force of the voice-over yields to the poem's place as a narrative signifier. During the reading the viewer's attention is trained on Wiesler's face and what it reveals about the poem's effect on him. The stanza is recited in an emotionally charged tone that reveals how he has been moved by his encounter with Brecht's poetry. The viewer is left to conclude that the love poem has given Wiesler a new appreciation of the love relationship between Dreyman and Sieland and clinches his decision to protect Dreyman. The single word *Brecht* visible on the cover also situates the scene as part of the film's discursive engagement of GDR literary culture. The juxtaposition with the previous scene, Wiesler's grotesquely portrayed encounter with the prostitute, provides the viewer a detached perspective from which to compare the two societies. This context, along with the clear signs pointing to the effect of the poem on Wiesler, inhibits the potential for the words of Brecht's poem to open up a free play of imagery in the mind of the spectator.

The lyrical power of music suffers a similar fate. Although Dreyman expressly claims that it has an exceptional power to induce moral behaviour, the film does not actually allow the music to work its influence. After hearing the news of his friend's suicide, Dreyman plays the sonata that Jerska had composed for him as a birthday gift. The context in which the sonata is played, however, renders the musical event secondary to its function in the narrative. Following shortly after the voice-over reading of Brecht's poem, the playing of the sonata serves as a narrative event that reinforces the point about the power of lyrical poetry. Cut in between the shots of Dreyman playing the piano is an extended shot of Wiesler in the attic listening to it. His motionless face expresses a deep sadness, with tears visible on one cheek. When Dreyman is finished, he first tells Sieland that he is reminded of Lenin's statement that he could not listen to Beethoven's piano sonata "Appassionata," because if he did he would not be able to complete the revolution. He then comments: "Whoever listened to this music, I mean really listened to it, could not be a bad person."[8] The two statements firmly fix the significance of the music for the story. Having just seen Wiesler listening intently to the music and being moved by it, the viewer is led to conclude that Jerska's sonata has helped transform him. In the larger context of the history of communist rule in Russia and its satellite state in East Germany, we are also to conclude from Dreyman's first comment that it would have been better had Lenin listened to Beethoven rather than carried through with the revolution. And by inference, this idea supports the previous scene's point that Brecht's poetry, rather than his theatre works that promote the communist movement, have the power to produce genuine good. But again the delimiting narrative context forecloses on any free affective flows that may have been set in motion by the music. We see the sonata have this effect on Wiesler, but the act of reading its significance interferes with the music actually having the same effect on the viewer.

In both these instances, von Donnersmarck rejects the potential of film as a medium in favour of a more literary aesthetic. Despite the difference in media, cinema can move away from the immanently visual and toward narrative representation that is commensurate with literary texts. Dudley Andrew provides a good description of how the two converge: "Generally film is found to work from perception toward signification, […] from the givenness of a world to the meaning of a story cut out of that world. Literary fiction works oppositely. It begins with signs (graphemes and words), building to propositions that attempt to develop perception" (100). In the two examples just discussed, the vivid aural perception of first a poem and then a piano sonata is compromised in the rush to fix their meaning in the film story. The associative power of the poetic imagery or of the musical passages could have been enhanced by autonomous images that are de-associated from the narrative context.

As a cultural medium, cinema is well suited for the evocation of free-floating affect-images. Stirring a sense of presence, of being in the (virtual) reality presented by the moving image, film produces perception-images in the viewer that initiate a motor response and calls forth a rich array of corresponding memory-images and affective states. In the usual situation of conscious life, this complex network of multiple and overlapping impulses undergoes a process of elimination designed to produce an action-image that can best guide our bodily responses.[9] In the case of film reception, the viewer does not respond to the virtual action-images, but rather remains silent and still in the darkened theatre. In this passive condition that has often been compared to a state of waking fantasy, affect gains a greater degree of autonomy. There is also the call to another kind of action, however, that intervenes in this fantasy-effect—that is the cognitive act of making sense of the film text. In *Das Leben der Anderen*, the strong pull toward hermeneutic intervention demands intense attentive recognition and cuts off the free play of affect, memory, and virtual sensations that could lead to new ways of seeing. Wiesler reads Brecht's poem in a voice that connotes his own affective state rather than allowing the poem to evoke autonomous word-image affects in the viewer. Similarly, the scene where the "Die Sonate vom guten Menschen" is played foregrounds the piece's significance for the meaning of the story rather than allowing the music to combine with autonomous film images and produce new constellations of affect and memory.

The narrative in *Das Leben der Anderen* enfolds the image so completely that one shot alone stands out as unattached to the story and the actions of its characters. It is a moving vertical camera shot looking up through the tops of trees, shot presumably from a car as it passes along a tree-lined boulevard. It begins when the camera cuts away from Dreyman holding Sieland's lifeless body in the street in front of his apartment and ends with a cut to a shot of Wiesler pulling up to a stop in his car to drop off Grubitz. The subsequent scene marks it as a transition shot taken from Wiesler's car as he drove away from the site of Sieland's death. While it has no apparent narrative significance, it is also not designed to enhance the power of the image to convey affective intensities directly to the viewer in a way that multiplies and prolongs the embodied play of autonomic responses. Coming immediately after the emotionally charged sequence of events that include the search of Dreyman's apartment by Grubitz, Sieland's death, and Dreyman and Wiesler's presence together at the scene of the accident, this shot offers a momentary respite before the narrative picks up again. And the narrative resumes immediately when Grubitz tells Wiesler that his career is finished, and that he will spend the next twenty years steam-opening letters.

But even this image is worked back into the narrative system of the film. After the *Wende*, Dreyman follows Wiesler along his delivery route in a taxi, stopping and getting out at one point apparently with the intention of speaking to him. He then changes his mind, gets back into the taxi and instructs the driver to take him back to his apartment. As the taxi drives slowly down the boulevard, we see Dreyman's face inside the closed back window, shot from a camera attached to the outside of the taxi. In addition to Dreyman, leaning his face toward the window with a thoughtful expression, the shot catches the moving reflection in the car window of the treetops and buildings along the boulevard. The shot begins before the taxi stops and resumes after Dreyman gets back in and heads home. Not only does this image recall the earlier moving shot of the treetops, but it also works that image into a new shot with complexly structured meaning for the film story. Although we are not given direct access to Dreyman's thoughts, it is clear that he is pensive about meeting Wiesler, with the reflections in the car window mirroring his own mental reflections. When he stops and then gets back in the taxi, it is also clear that he has changed his mind. Again we are not privy to his thoughts as the taxi heads toward his apartment, at least, not until the following and final scene of the movie. A transposed title tells us that it is two years later as we see Wiesler on the same job delivering magazines and advertising supplements. When Wiesler sees the advertisement for Dreyman's book on the shop window of the Karl Marx Bookstore, he goes in to see it and discovers the dedication to his Stasi cryptonym, HGW XX/7. At this point we realize that behind the reflections on the taxi window, Dreyman was hatching his plan that is at the heart of the film story, the plan to write a novel about Wiesler. This visual technique to represent the origins of the novel in Dreyman's thoughts corresponds to the earlier voice-over of the *Spiegel* text that indicate he decided to write the piece while at Jerska's funeral.

The tight control over affect extends to the unconscious effect exerted by less determined aspects of the image. In his historical research for the film, von Donnersmarck read that the GDR eliminated pigments of brighter colours such as red and blue from many of their manufacturing processes. It did so to disassociate itself from the capitalist production and marketing processes in the West, which favour these colours, because they tend to generate stronger intensities of affect and increase sales. Von Donnersmarck then tried to reproduce the look and feel of the GDR by using predominantly yellow, brown, and green hues in his set design and shot selections. And this was apparently successful. Many former East Germans have commented that the film captures the "feeling" of life in the GDR in an almost eerie manner, and von Donnersmarck attributes this success in large part to the colour schemes.[10] In evoking this feeling, the film short-circuits certain affective capacities of the image. They become linked with certain complexes of memory before their immediate sensory reactions can circulate autonomously in the spectator. Rather than providing "space" for the intensities of colours (what Gilles Deleuze called "colour-force" [*Francis*

Bacon 94–97]) to evoke and combine more freely with memory-images, von Donnersmarck associates them with an already formed "feeling" that defines past experience. Where capitalist production favours colours that register high intensity levels and can stir the desire for new consumer products, von Donnersmarck eliminated them in order to evoke latent memories tinged with nostalgia. This actually constitutes a two-level remove from affect as pure intensity. The former resident of the GDR first recognizes the emotion as a familiar feeling, thus rendering it an act of re-cognition that eclipses the free play of affect. The feeling is then also associated with a particular historical and social context—a style of life that once existed in the GDR. Rather than images, the film produces imagery that functions much like description in literary prose. It serves the purpose of describing the cultural environment in the GDR in a way that supports the film's thesis about state control over the lives of its citizens. In this case it does so pictorially via the *mise en scène* without interrupting or delaying the forward movement of the narrative.

Conclusion

In the end, Dreyman's *Bildungsroman* puts the final touches on the film's construction of the East–West divide. It stands in contrast to the state-dictated literary production of the GDR. Until the final scenes that take place after the *Wende,* the freedom of the West is for the most part only implied. But once Dreyman has been emancipated from the stifling oppression of the socialist state, he discovers the full authorial power of the creative writer (*Dichter*). His conversation with Hempf in the lobby of the same theatre where his play had premiered early in the film frames this difference and sets the stage for his decision to write his *Bildungsroman*. Noting his surprise that Dreyman had stopped writing, Hempf continues: "And that after we invested so much in you. But I understand you in a way. What is one supposed to write in this Federal Republic? There is nothing to believe in, nothing to rebel against. It was nice in our little republic. Many realize that now."[11] Dripping with an irony that reveals the corruption of the GDR leadership to be even more outrageous than we had seen throughout the film, Hempf's statement tries to twist the disappointment in the West felt by many former East Germans into support of the GDR leadership's most cynical policies. Dreyman expresses his disgust in a parting remark: "To think that people like you once ruled a country."[12] But he finds the most appropriate and effective response when he takes up writing again. Born of the literary freedom in the West, the novel he writes serves to redeem the "good man" who had been a victim/perpetrator of GDR oppression. As the reformed former agent buys *Die Sonate vom guten Menschen* at the Karl Marx bookstore, the sales clerk asks if he wants it gift-wrapped. His response, "No, it's for me,"[13] accompanied by the film's final shot of Wiesler's face expressing a deep satisfaction at the book's private praise of his noble deed, puts the final touch on the film's affirmation of the German literary tradition of aesthetic education over and against literature in the service of political ideology. It also asserts the power of Dreyman's *Bildungsroman* to atone for the life lost in service to the GDR.

Like other recent German films—*Sonnenallee* (*Sun Alley*, Leander Haußmann, 1999), *Good Bye, Lenin!* (Wolfgang Becker, 2003)—*Das Leben der Anderen* depicts life in the GDR in an attempt to bridge the divide between eastern and western Germans in the unified Federal Republic. It is in this regard that the fictional novel stands in for the film itself. More crucially, however, Dreyman's *Bildungsroman* also serves to redeem the disenfranchised subject of Western capitalism, the new Wiesler, the door-to-door distributor of commercial printed matter. The film in turn acts to sanction the status of former GDR citizens who have yet to gain a full share in the affluence and benefits of the German free-market society. As Wiesler walks along the boulevard outside the Karl Marx Bookstore, we hear a jackhammer on the sound track. While perhaps an allusion to similar sound-overs in *Die Ehe der Maria Braun*, the sound here is not nearly as loud or as obtrusive as in Fassbinder's film. It has rather more the opposite effect. Instead of questioning the role of a fragile national psyche in the frenetic pace of reconstruction, it suggests a steady, robust rebuilding of eastern Germany in the image of the West. Rather than agitate and unsettle the affective intensities of the eastern German viewer, it promotes assimilation to the free-market dynamism of the West through the physical regulation of affect.

In contrast to the oppressive power of the GDR state that it exposes so well, *Das Leben der Anderen* exerts its own bio-political form of control on the level of affect. Like the lyrical text of Brecht's poem, Gabriel Jared's musical theme for Jerska's piano sonata, and the *mise en scène* construction of the GDR past, the final sound-over of the jackhammer does not stir the free play of affect. The tight control of narrative reduces the film experience to what is already known and can be recaptured semiotically. Rather than disrupt the pervasive control of a market-driven production and regulation of affect, the film leaves them intact underneath a veneer of representation that yields re-cognition. Fassbinder, on the other hand, subjected them to change, in terms of both narrative control and embodied response. The explosion that sends Maria Braun's house, marriage, and her entire cumulative existence up in smoke and flames also dissolves everything that had accumulated with the progress of the film's linear narrative. The viewer's investment in the fate/marriage of Maria Braun, not only emotionally, but also on the level of pre-emotion bodily affect, is unleashed.

The suddenly free-floating affective capacities acquire the potential to produce as yet unknown virtual images and unexpected calls to action. As I watch Wiesler distributing the products of the Western media, I feel nostalgia for the radio *acousmêtre* of Fassbinder's *Die Ehe der Maria Braun*. I long for chaotic soundovers that express with full affective force our subjection to the dissonant forces of global capitalism. Instead, the film offers restrained energies and a carefully articulated picture of harmony.

Notes

1 For a discussion of this ambivalence, see Davies and Parker, 181–95.
2 "Das Eintauchen in *Das Leben der Anderen*—in Liebe, Literatur, freies Denken und Reden—macht Wiesler die Armseligkeit seines eigenen Daseins bewusst und eröffnet ihm eine nie gekannte Welt, der er sich immer weniger entziehen kann." http://www.movie.de. See also Horn, 143.
3 "Der Dichter ist der Ingenieur der Seele, und Georg Dreyman ist einer der bedeutendsten Ingenieure unseres Landes." Hempf is quoting Stalin, who declared the writer to be the "engineer of the soul." For an account of how the leaders of the GDR applied this phrase to their own cultural and political context, see Schichtel, 30.
4 "Aber das lieben wir auch alle an Ihren Stücken. Die Liebe zu Menschen, die guten Menschen. Sie glauben, dass man sich verändern kann. Dreyman, ganz gleich wie oft Sie das in Ihren Stücken schreiben, Menschen verändern sich nicht."
5 "Viele Menschen lieben Sie, weil Sie sind, wie Sie sind." "Ein Schauspieler ist nie so, wie er ist."
6 For an excellent discussion of how we read films according to the hermeneutic practices established by literary texts, see Nayar, 140–55.
7 In countering the possible objection that the "narrative is rather too neat and closed," Cheryl Dueck argues that a simple, closed narrative can work therapeutically to help mitigate "the trauma inflicted by the Stasi." Setting aside the question whether the therapy of narrating trauma would work on a collective trauma that derives from life in the GDR, I see another problem with this argument. It affirms a West German narrative that places the entire responsibility for the trauma and the entire need for therapeutic treatment in the lap of former East Germans. This implies, wrongly I would claim, that former West Germans are not implicated in this trauma in any way and are well situated to write a "healing" narrative for their Eastern counterparts (607). Mary Beth Stein also misses the issue of a West German narrative about the East, when she claims that the film "attributes to art and literature the power of *self-healing* [emphasis added] and the possibility for political reconciliation" (577).
8 "Kann jemand, der diese Musik gehört hat, ich meine, wirklich gehört hat, ein schlechter Mensch sein?"
9 For an account of how the interplay of perception-images, sensorimotor-responses, memory-images, and action-images determines our bodily perception of and response to the external environment, see Bergson, 77–90 and 127–31.
10 Recounted by von Donnersmarck in a National Public Radio interview on *Fresh Air*, broadcast 7 February 2007 on WHYY, Philadelphia.

11 "All, das unser Land in Sie investiert hat. Man könnte Sie verstehen, Dreyman. Was soll man noch schreiben in dieser BRD. Nichts mehr, woran man glauben kann, nichts mehr, worüber man rebellieren kann. Es war schön in unserer kleinen Republik. Das verstehen viele erst jetzt."
12 "Dass Leute wie Sie wirklich ein Land geführt haben!"
13 "Nein. Es ist für mich."

References

Andrew, Dudley. *Concepts in Film Theory.* Oxford: Oxford UP, 1984.

Bergson, Henri. *Matter and Memory.* Trans. Nancy Margaret Paul and W. Scott Palmer. New York: Zone Books, 1991.

Chion, Michel. *Audio-Vision: Sound on Screen.* Trans. Claudia Gorbman. New York: Columbia UP, 1994.

Cohen, Keith. *Film and Literature: The Dynamics of Exchange.* New Haven: Yale UP, 1979.

Das Leben der Anderen (The Lives of Others). Dir. Florian Henckel von Donnersmarck. Arte et al., 2006.

"*Das Leben der Anderen*: Kurzinhalt." *Movie.de.* 28 November 2008 <http://www.movie.de>.

Davies, Peter, and Stephen Parker. "Brecht, SED Cultural Policy and the Issue of Authority in the Arts: The Struggle for Control of the German Academy of the Arts." *Bertolt Brecht: Centenary Essays.* Ed. Steve Giles and Rodney Livingstone. Amsterdam: Rodopi, 1998. 181–95.

Deleuze, Gilles. *Francis Bacon: logique de la sensation.* Paris: Éditions de la différence, 1981.

———. "Postscript on the Societies of Control." *October* 59 (1992): 3–7.

Dueck, Cheryl. "The Humanization of the *Stasi* in *Das Leben der Anderen.*" *German Studies Review* 31.3 (2008): 599–609.

Die Ehe der Maria Braun (The Marriage of Maria Braun). Dir. Rainer Werner Fassbinder. Film Verlag der Autoren et al., 1979.

Good Bye, Lenin! Dir. Wolfgang Becker. X-Filme Creative Pool et al., 2003.

Horn, Eva. "Media Conspiracy: Love and Surveillance in Fritz Lang and Florian Henckel von Donnersmarck." *New German Critique* 35.1 (2008): 127–44.

Nayar, Sheila J. "*Écriture* Aesthetics: Mapping the Literate Episteme of Visual Narrative." *PMLA* 123.1 (2008): 140–55.

Fresh Air. NPR. Washington, DC, 7 February 2007.

Schichtel, Alexandra. *Zwischen Zwang und Freiwilligkeit: Das Phänomen Anpassung in der Prosaliteratur der DDR.* Opladen, FRG: Westdeutscher Verlag, 1998.

Scott, A.O. "A Fugue for Good German Men." *New York Times* 9 February 2007: E1.

Sonnenallee (Sun Alley). Dir. Leander Haußmann. Boje Buck Produktion, 1999.

Stein, Mary Beth. "*Stasi* with a Human Face? Ambiguity in *Das Leben der Anderen.*" *German Studies Review* 31.3 (2008): 567–79.

6
Heimat 3:
Edgar Reitz's Time Machine

Alasdair King

Abstract According to filmmaker Edgar Reitz, we are experiencing the end of the provincial in spatial terms and must instead reconfigure Heimat as a temporal category. *Heimat 3* works as a complex filmic "time machine," recording the changing nature of everyday life after the fall of the Wall, chronicling the social impact of historical change in Germany, and registering the being-in-time of its key characters. The third part of his trilogy is an attempt by Reitz to use cinema to construct a "safe home" in time, a Heimat composed of time-images—everyday, historical, durational.

Introduction

Edgar Reitz's *Heimat 3: Chronik einer Zeitenwende* (*Heimat 3: A Chronicle of Endings and Beginnings*, 2004) was first shown at the Venice Film Festival in September 2004. It completed Reitz's monumental trilogy of films on the changing nature of provincial life in the twentieth century that was initiated with the release of the much-discussed *Heimat* in 1984, an exploration of modernization within the particular spaces of the Hunsrück region in western Germany where Reitz originated. In his second film cycle, *Die zweite Heimat: Chronik einer Jugend in 13 Filmen* (*Heimat 2: Chronicle of a Generation*, 1992), Reitz moved away from these village landscapes in order to explore the urban environment of Munich in the 1960s, particularly the utopian potential of the student avant-garde there. With the six episodes of *Heimat 3* (which constituted a running time of almost twelve hours),[1] Reitz returned to the Hunsrück to address the changing German landscape over the decade between the fall of the Wall and the millennium celebrations.

This chapter seeks to explore Reitz's assertion that in our contemporary epoch of increased transit and instant communication, we are experiencing the end of the provincial in spatial terms. In this current period of globalization, according to Reitz, a sense of belonging is possible only if we reach a new understanding, not of the spatial ties that defined community in the first *Heimat*, nor of the artistic experiments of the avant-garde that were mooted as an alternative in *Die zweite Heimat*, but of a shared sense of *time* as Heimat, as the structuring principle of community. Reitz claims in this context that *Heimat 3* explores the notion of a "Zeit-Heimat" and acts as a filmic time machine that registers the substantial social changes in both eastern and western Germany in the decade after unification. *Heimat 3* concerns an exploration of the role of cinema in constructing a Heimat built on local time-images as a counterpoint to the placelessness of the globalized world.

Questions of Space and Time

With this assertion of the significance of time in thinking about the contemporary location of Heimat, Reitz seems initially to be moving against a tide in the arts and social sciences, which has attempted to answer some of the political challenges of late modernity by arguing for the prioritizing of space over time as a fundamental building block in conceptualizing contemporary society. This trend—the so-called "spatial turn"[2]—has given impetus to productive research in film analysis, which considers not only the representation of Germany's troubled history on film, but also the significance of the symbolic and real landscapes within which events take place, and which have always featured so prominently in German cinema. It is of particular use in considering both the Heimatfilm itself as a genre with its emphasis on the construction of territories, borders, inclusions and exclusions at specific historical moments,[3] and also Reitz's response to these central generic concerns in his own *Heimat* film cycle. The earliest waves of scholarly reception after the first *Heimat* in 1984 centred, often negatively, given the sensitivity toward such issues in the years of the *Historikerstreit* in West Germany, almost exclusively on the relationship of Reitz's filmmaking to questions of historiography and of the politics of memory. Until recently, little attention was given to Reitz's spatial constructions, despite the foregrounding of territorial questions in the very title of the trilogy. Matters of geography remained largely unexplored until Johannes von Moltke's "spatial reading" of the first *Heimat*, published in 2005, in which he attempts to shift the focus on Reitz's work to a discussion of what he termed the director's "spatialization of history."[4] As the cultural geographer Mike Crang has recently argued, however, the rush to embrace newly fashionable spatial paradigms among researchers in the last decade should be welcomed, but not if it implies the renunciation of attention to temporal aspects altogether. Crang's point, which, to paraphrase Edward W. Soja's formulation, amounts to a reassertion of the temporal in spatial theory, is that "rather than a disciplinary celebration that social theory seems to have noticed geography, we need to unpack how space and time interact" (202).[5] Indeed, fellow geographer Doreen Massey's recent work *For Space* makes a strong case for thinking space and time as mutually implicated, with space defined as "a simultaneity of stories-so-far" (9), always under construction and within time. For Massey, places do not just exist as points or areas on maps, but "as integrations of space and time; as spatiotemporal events" (130).[6] For those of us working with film, this implies not a return to prioritizing the representation of historical events over the landscapes in which they occur, but of looking instead at how time and space are utilized within and across moving images. To look at how film registers time and space in images and sequences also raises ontological,[7] as much as directly sociological, questions about the nature of cinema at this juncture in its evolution, questions that Reitz seems inclined to explore.

The "New Placelessness" and the Time-Heimat

Reitz's attempt to foreground the temporal rather than the spatial dimensions of belonging to a particular Heimat in *Heimat 3* are significant in the context of other forms of cultural expression emerging in Germany at this time. The attention paid by the director to the temporal dimension of experiencing key events initially suggests parallels with the increasing focus on generational models used by many contemporary writers in works exploring German identity in the decade or more after unification. Reitz's focus on the joint or common experience of time and of specific key historical moments as constitutive of shared identity, as well as his long-standing commitment in the *Heimat* trilogy overall to a form of "history from below" by means of a family narrative, finds an echo in literary and critical discourses prominent in the "Berlin Republic," where the differences in outlook between generations are used as a way to register and make meaningful distinctive formative experiences. These include, for instance, how the new Berlin's emerging topographies are experienced differently across generations, according to the age of the central protagonists (particularly concerning whether or not they have any direct experience of the National Socialist era or of the political turbulence of 1968 and after) and according to any wider prior experience of a socialist (East German) or consumer-capitalist (West German) or even migrant childhood and upbringing before living in the newly unified city.[8] These generational differences are, of course, part of a recent burgeoning culture of "memory contests," which have registered deeply in debates about the search for identity in German culture after 1990. The idea of generation as a hugely decisive category in these debates has been discussed at considerable length by literary and cultural critics exploring the threads that constitute Germany's increasingly pluralistic memory culture.[9] The concept of the determining generation has been explored in detail recently with the upsurge of family narratives that chart changing responses to the National Socialist era on the part of several generations and that give rise to new understandings of the implications of the politics of memory.[10] Indeed, Reitz's post-unification exploration of Heimat in *Heimat 3* is concerned to register significant variations in how unification and the increasingly globalized environment, which feeds into the provincial locale at the heart of the film, are experienced across several generations.

In his initial notes from May and June 1998, Reitz recorded how the idea of a *Generationsvertrag* (contract between generations) (*Drehort* 208) might form a central theme of his new project, within which he could explore notions of inheritance and of the legacies passed on to the younger protagonists. Significantly, Reitz wanted not just to consider generational differences, but also how the relationship between differing generations might change with time. For Reitz, the decade after unification seemed to be a time in which the whole idea of setting up large-scale projects that might take several generations to complete, and that therefore relied on some kind of contractual obligation between generations, had ceased to resonate, with the consequence that younger generations claimed the right to refuse to complete the work of their elders. Reitz argues that historical events of the twentieth century—two world wars, the collapse of ideologies and religious affiliations—have changed the nature of our relationship to projects that exist in a time-span exceeding that of a single generation. These early ideas are picked up in *Heimat 3*, in the refusal of Hartmut to fall into line with his father's wishes concerning the management of the Simon-Optik factory, and, alternatively, in Lulu's drive to establish a physical site to house her uncle Ernst's art collection. Ernst's relationship with the young Matko Misic also hangs on his desire to find a son or, at least, an heir.

Thus, Reitz's third installment of his trilogy is marked by a concern for the differing expectations and actions of several generations, and so can be viewed in part in the context of a wider exploration of generational issues in post-unification culture. However, his work explores not just the more familiar tropes of the unfolding of history and the dynamics of memory, which feature so prominently in the memory contests mentioned above, but also by an ontological earnestness regarding both the experience and the aesthetic reconstruction of time itself—which seems to mark it out from many of its literary counterparts. Because of this, it is useful to consider Reitz's cinema as part of a longer aesthetic undertaking in cinema to register time and duration in the visual image and not to elide it too readily within wider and more sociologically oriented considerations of generational perspectives on German identity.

This can be seen in Reitz's interest in the idea of a "Zeit-Heimat." In his early sketches for *Heimat 3*, he was adamant that although Hermann had returned to Schabbach, ostensibly making it once again the centre of the world that it had been through most of the first *Heimat* series, the defining sense of place, of a spatial repository of shared experiences that Schabbach had offered to its inhabitants previously, could no longer be assumed in the late twentieth century. The reasons for this could be found less in any great changes internal to the provincial village (which is represented across the trilogy not as an untouched and timeless rural idyll, but explicitly, and increasingly in *Heimat 3*, as a meeting point of various economic, technological, migratory flows), but more in the expanded dimensions of everyday life experienced by the main protagonists. Hermann and Clarissa, principally, but also many other key characters, are seen as typically in transit in a space that now assumes continental and even global physical (as well as virtual) dimensions. Reitz argues that Schabbach has become a "symbolic place for the new placelessness" (209). As a consequence, Heimat for characters like Hermann is no longer a spatial category, but must instead be sought in a relationship to time (210).

Reitz's notes echo many of the central ideas concerning the replacement of spatial bonds with temporal ones aired by the sociologist Bernd Guggenberger, whose articles on the new placelessness were appearing regularly in *Die Zeit* and the *Frankfurter Allgemeine Zeitung*, and who had published his pessimistic book *Das digitale Nirwana* in the same year (1997). For Guggenberger, it did not matter where one lived: territorial borders no longer marked out distinct and shared identities as people meeting up online from far-flung places had, potentially, far more connecting them in terms of a shared experience of recent history than the nearest of (geographical) neighbours. What mattered far more was when one was born, went to school, enjoyed formative experiences, encountered and used new technologies, and so on. Guggenberger's categorization of this new placelessness resonates in Reitz's thinking. Whereas Schabbach had been the main *Schauplatz* (setting) of the first *Heimat* series, Reitz indicates that in *Heimat 3*, rather than a location, the setting is intended to be more a period of time. In his notes, he initially specifies the period as from 23 September 1999 leading up to 1 January 2000, and that these one hundred days would form the central narrative space for his new cycle. He, however, specifically changes the usual German orthography of *Zeitraum* to the hyphenated and capitalized term, *Zeit-Raum* or time-space, and utilizes the phrase *Zeit-Heimat* to describe the context in which his characters will be functioning (209). Consciously reworking Ernst Bloch's celebrated statement in *Das Prinzip Hoffnung* (The Principle of Hope), that Heimat is something "which shines into the childhood of all and in which no-one has yet been" (1,376), Reitz commented that the third part of his *Heimat* trilogy would take place "in this new space, a sense of time [...] in which no-one has yet been" (209). Reitz reported how greatly conceptions of Heimat had changed in the years since the fall of the Berlin Wall:

> Barely ten years ago, it meant, at least as I remember it, a specific place. Now, on the eve of the millennium, our yearning desire has changed into wanting to remain "children of this time," not to be driven out of it, when the world no longer has any borders and places have become arbitrary. We no longer look for Heimat in landscape or village, but in time, which we want to belong to even more intensively than previously. The wonderful feeling of belonging to a time, which most of us only know from our youth, has become the new world-wide sense of Heimat. Heimat is no longer a spatial category, it has become a temporal category, and thereby fully a theme for films.[11] (220)

Although Reitz's sense of how to categorize Heimat in his third film series is markedly different from his previous two constructions, what is notable is how again Heimat is configured in elegiac terms in *Heimat 3*, associated with a sense of loss for the disappearance of what has been taken for granted formerly. In the first *Heimat*, this was clearly constructed around the secure space of the rural village, and, in the second, linked to a belief in the utopian potential of aesthetic creation.[12] In the third series, what comes to constitute the contemporary Heimat, and what then is under threat and will disintegrate as the series progresses, is a shared sense of being-in-time, which, for Reitz, the film camera is uniquely placed to register (220).

"The Camera Is Not a Clock": Reitz on Film and Time

In an essay written in 1979, before filming the first *Heimat* series, Reitz had argued that time should not be thought of as the regular, linear, unfolding of a unidirectional chronology, a second passing, then a minute, then an hour, all in regular transitional beats that once sounded are lost forever. Time is complex, more varied and more personal, effectively the subjective experience of moments encountered:

> I think it's a lie to say that time is a smoothly flowing stream in which all of us and all things move at the same speed. Time as we measure it with clocks, as we register it with calendars, or as we define it in metres of film, does not exist. Every living

thing and every object lives in its own time and this personal time does not flow continuously, but rather stands still at times, proceeds only haltingly, sometimes with incredible velocity, that is to say, it is irregular. What is past is not past, the future does not lie before us, but just as much behind us. The present is not the time in which we live. Anyone working with the medium film has to deal with the problem of time. ("Camera" 140–41)

Although, as Reitz argues forcefully, the "film camera is not a clock" (140), it does act as a kind of time machine, as the medium is able to make sense of this complex qualitative being-in-time as a whole, registering and reawakening these moments experienced and holding them together in their richness, so that moments experienced are not simply consigned to some lost past, but become fully part of an experienced present duration. This redemptive power of film, and the echoes of Kracauer's *Theory of Film* are here notable, is down to the camera's ability to record onto celluloid events in the world as they occur and extend in duration, "to salvage them from the march of time" (137). Moreover, Reitz makes a significant point about the "always pastness" of the work of the camera. The moment of making an image already contains the awareness that the moment of screening that image will occur at a different temporal moment, that what is present in the image is also in part already its future pastness. This is also the case with the events of *Heimat 3*, told from the perspective of the new century.[13] For Reitz, film acts in parallel with the human capacity to recollect experience, registering and constructing a web of moments from differing time periods and allowing them to play out together on a public and externally accessible screen, interacting with present experiences (137).

The idea of the cinema as "the first really functioning time machine" (Reitz "Film und Zeit" 3) recurs at several important points around the making of *Heimat 3*. Reitz notes how this third *Heimat* cycle will register substantial changes in everyday life over a short period of time. In the globalized and increasingly homogenized spatial environment, Reitz sees little difference between previously distinct places, but the film camera is able to follow the changes that occur now more markedly in time rather than in space in terms of the changing appearance and texture of everyday life—cars, clothes, architecture, technologies, and so on (*Drehort* 218). This concern with film and time was aired again after the making of *Heimat 3*, on the occasion of the award to Reitz of an honorary doctorate at the University of Perugia in 2006. He devoted his acceptance speech to this theme and acknowledged that time was at the heart of his filmmaking career. Growing up as the son of the village clockmaker, the family house was filled with clocks in every room, to the extent that the hundreds of clocks at home all ticked loudly, measuring the passage of the minutes and hours ("Film und Zeit" 2). Reitz explained that the aesthetic specificity of film's relationship with time owes much to the ability of the camera to register one-off gestures and utterances occurring at a singular moment and to provide a transportable duplicate of these events-in-time, which can be accessed and re-presented at subsequent moments (2). Moreover, film is able to register duration as experienced by objects as well as people in a way that the photograph, which can only capture the singular moment, cannot. Film can therefore conserve and replay time, and register the temporal reality of an object even if there is no visible movement or other event in the filmed images. Film's distinct aesthetics also entail the capacity to reconfigure the fleeting fragments of our everyday experience of the world into a coherent and meaningful whole. Reitz argues that we cannot make sense of the fleeting perceptions of the world we encounter as our perspective is always already clouded by our preconceived opinions, and here Reitz again echoes Kracauer's *Theory of Film* (3). In its ability to narrate these "real time fragments,"[14] (4) the film camera acts as a machinic intermediary in the flow of time. The more imperceptible and transient a captured filmic moment, the more the camera has, in a sense, become itself as an aesthetic technology (4). For Reitz, again echoing Kracauer's redemptive film aesthetics, the camera allows the viewer for the first time to fully experience life in time, to perceive how valuable every second in our everyday experience of the world around us can be, to accelerate and slow down, or reverse, the passage of time and even, with montage, to cut into little pieces the time continuum. The filmmaker, in this way, becomes a researcher and explorer, the "discoverer of countless secrets which elude the consensus of the everyday" (4). Crucially, Reitz suggests that the camera is able to bring us closer to an understanding of the full power and dimensions of time. Moving toward a philosophical position that hints at a kinship with Bergson and with Deleuze's discussion of the various time-images constructed in cinema, Reitz grants an important status to the aesthetics brought into being by the film camera:

> The camera can free itself from the limits of human perceptions of time and puts us in the position of making research trips into the heart of time. Time reveals itself to be more than causality [...]. Many of its properties indicate that it possesses its own form and that the "Space-Time" talked about by physicists is curved in on itself as an indivisible continuous shape.[15] (5)

Despite not fully drawing out the implications of this proposition, he does insist that time is more complex than simply the passing of events in a causal relationship: linear chronology is an invention that enables filmmakers to explain how one event follows another, meaning that chronology is dependent on causality, not time itself. Film, Reitz suggests, can reveal the true nature of the richness of time, and, like Kracauer again, he maintains that the time-images made accessible by the film camera are necessary to live life fully as each film produces its own time-images, can set its own temporal rules, and can combine time fragments freely in aesthetic combinations. Reitz suggests that filmmakers can use time fragments with the freedom of composers, and that film can work in a similar fashion to the conventions established in music for notes and phrasing (6).

Reitz's Heimat of the Time-Image

Reitz's rather Deleuzian understanding of his own filmmaking as the setting in circulation of time-images connected as narratives loops back in interesting ways to Deleuze's taxonomy of modern European cinema. It has rarely been noted that Deleuze's account of the emergence of the cinema of the direct time-image from that of the dominant movement-image returns repeatedly to German spaces, histories, and films. Deleuze's account in *Cinema 2* draws in part on his viewing of the prehistory of the New German Cinema, on Lang, Murnau, and Riefenstahl in particular (131–32). The historical setting necessary (but not in itself determinant) for the emergence of a new cinema of the time-image, which, for Deleuze explicitly includes the New German Cinema of Wenders, Herzog, Syberberg and Straub, is that of the desolate landscapes of Germany in the aftermath of National Socialism, the haunted nihilistic destruction within the perimeters of the concentration camps, the bombed-out cities, and deracinated public spaces (131–32). These German city-deserts, as Reitz's early critics repeatedly objected, never appeared fully despite the obsessive attention to historical detail in the first *Heimat*. Deleuze does not mention Reitz's films, writing his *Cinema 2* before the first *Heimat* series was screened on French television,[16] but he takes care to praise the time-images in the work of the *Autor*-driven Young German Cinema of the 1960s and 1970s out of which Reitz emerged, particularly Herzog's "crystal images" and Straub's archaeological layering of time in his "stratigraphic landscapes" (72, 234).

Arguably Reitz's task as a filmmaker would be to chronicle the major historical events of the decade following the fall of the Wall, while simultaneously indicating that our experience of time is not reducible to the chronological ordering of history, given his long-standing suspicions of the narratives produced in the name of history ("Camera" 137–38). Is it possible, then, that with *Heimat 3*, Reitz has attempted to use the camera as a filmic time machine in a complex way, not necessarily to represent history, but rather to record the changing texture of everyday life, to register the impact of major public events, and to express our lived understanding of time at a moment when its movement becomes so noticeable? Did he try ultimately to show how our shared lived experience of time is our chance of Heimat, a Heimat of the time-image? There are several points in *Heimat 3* that point toward just such a complex treatment of time and duration. There is the well-known switching from black and white to colour stock to indicate public history as opposed to private experience of lived time, the use of which Reitz explains as relating to a division between personal stories and the more general unfolding of shared historical events (*Drehort* 292). Most Deleuzian perhaps are Reitz's idiosyncratic *mise en scène* constructions, which often rely on dividing the spaces of the frame with glass screens or mirrors, with which he produces an image of a tectonic layering of time experienced by key characters.

Three Images of Time

If time is the structuring principle of community in *Heimat 3*, then the unexpected breach in the flow of history, which sees the dramatic opening of the Berlin Wall, is the catalytic event-in-time that throws the key characters together. The new Heimat community will comprise Hermann and Clarissa, reunited from *Die zweite Heimat* together with the East German craftsmen, Gunnar, Udo, Tillmann, and Tobi, who are able to take up the couple's offer to come and work in the Hunsrück on the Günderrode house. Their stories-so-far join up with the wider dynastic saga of the extended Simon family gathered again around the aging patriarch, Anton, who still is in conflict with his brother Ernst. Also drawn into the network of stories unfolding in this time fragment are characters such as Lulu, Hermann's daughter; Matko, a young refugee from Bosnia; and Galina, married to a Russo-German and newly immigrated. If the fall of the Wall marks the opening of the new Zeit-Heimat for this particular community, it closes with them reuniting after a decade to celebrate the new millennium at the restored Günderrode house.

Heimat 3 begins with the credits set out on a black screen, while the sound of distant cries and cheering and then voices precedes our reintroduction to Hermann. In a typical Reitz image construction, Hermann is surrounded by panes of glass, here the glass doors and long window of the Berlin Philharmonic concert hall through which we see him in conversation just after he has finished conducting. Hermann in voice-over articulates that he registers the significance of this moment in time through his nervous system; his body senses that the moment is one of epochal change for Germany, experienced as "a strange vibration"[17] in the night air. He is embraced by an East Berliner in the street near Savigny Platz, but at this moment Hermann can only imagine that the man's motive might be to steal his wallet. Not until Hermann gets back to his hotel is he able to comprehend more fully what is going on. Standing in the lobby of the Hotel Kempinski, and surrounded by, but not in direct communication with, a number of other hotel guests and visitors, he sees history unfolding again against panes and glass screens. A Trabant drives slowly amid a crowd of celebrants up the street outside, which Hermann views through the extensive glass frontage of the hotel, while on the television screen in the lobby an announcer comments on the evening's events and on the decision to relax the travel restrictions on East Germans who wish to leave the GDR. As the camera pulls back its close-up on the television screen to take up a position just behind Hermann and pans slowly to the right, we become aware at the same time as Hermann that he has found himself standing next to Clarissa, thus reuniting, after a gap of seventeen years since their last meeting, the central couple of *Die zweite Heimat*.

This is a highly melodramatic scene, overly romanticized in its intertwining of public and private histories. Indeed, Heinz-Peter Preusser argues that Reitz's central concern in *Heimat 3* is to construct a foundational myth for the newly unified Germany, which draws on both the couple's freshly reawakened romance for its narrative frame, and on Germany's Romantic traditions in literature, art, and music at key points. There are certainly parallels between Hermann and Clarissa's reunion and the unification of the two German states, but Reitz also seems to be at least allowing a reading of this chance meeting, where viewers are offered reasons from the beginning of *Heimat 3* to question this over-romanticized perspective on German history and also the naïvety of Hermann and Clarissa with regard to their investment in reconstructing their lives so exclusively and suddenly around each other.[18] Crucially, they are reunited against the backdrop of immense historical events, yet are hardly part of the forces and currents that surround them because of the way that Reitz chooses to seal them off throughout this sequence through his use of glass panes. This could be read as Reitz's first key time-image, which holds together an experience of present time opening out for them into a reawakened past but simultaneously separating them from the public flow of historical events. They belong to a different order of unfolding time, part of their private experiences and recollections rather than fully in the stream of history. They inhabit a strange hermetic space, spinning each other around the floor of the hotel lobby in a passionate embrace, so different from Hermann's cold reaction to the East German's hug moments before. It is, of course, fully a part of their lifestyle as sought-after professional musicians that this nomadic and deracinated couple should meet up at a hotel, one of a number of key spaces that they occupy that belong to what Marc Augé has termed the "non-places of supermodernity," the sites in the contemporary globalized world of transit, travel, and economic transactions. Other key spaces

Edgar Reitz, *Heimat 3*. © Edgar Reitz Filmproduktion GmbH

for Hermann and Clarissa in this film include the airport lounge, the expensive car, the train or taxi, the concert hall, the recording studio, and the post-concert reception, all of which parallel Augé's topographies of supermodernity.[19]

The glass screens that contain Hermann and Clarissa separate their own experience of time from that of the greater population beyond these spaces, not least the images playing out uninterrupted on the television screen. The director consistently places them at a remove from the crowds using glass screens: their bodies are reflected in the television screen, where the celebrating masses are pictured climbing the Wall. Similarly, Hermann and Clarissa choose to stay in their hotel room, whose glass windows and doors seal them off in their own world and keep them apart from the people below. This shared solipsism is maintained for Hermann's claim that "this is all just for us," as the camera refocuses narrowly in close-up on the faces of Hermann and Clarissa to the exclusion of the world outside. Reitz's camera work here distances viewers from identifying too readily with Hermann's assertion, and suggests that the director is allowing an ambiguity, at least, in the idea that Hermann and Clarissa's highly emotional reunion should be viewed too sentimentally, even if it is constructed as a symbolic parallel to the political events of German unification. Reitz's camera work allows viewers the possibility of reading this moment as ironized, as already flawed in its blind optimism. As Peter Blickle has pointed out more generally, the mode of irony, if that is what is present here in part, is one that is not typically part of the Heimat tradition, which seeks instead to overcome distance and alienation in modernity (28). The culmination of their encounter is an erotic consummation in the hotel bedroom, wrapped up in sheets and gazing from each other to the events playing out on the television screen and, from time to time, outside their hotel window. Reitz captures Hermann's face reflected back from the television screen, layered over the faces of the celebrating masses climbing the Berlin Wall. Reitz's purpose, from this opening sequence, is to accompany Herman and Clarissa in their quest to move from the atomized space of the non-place, the hotel lobby, and to attempt to construct a new (or regained) Heimat constituted by shared time as much as space.

A second key image of different sheets of time coalescing around a particular space occurs with the reconstruction of the Günderrode house on the banks of the Rhine and its claim to anchor itself in a mythic version of German history. The Günderrode project, a meeting of west German investment, risk, and drive, and east German craftsmanship, hard work, and attention to detail, clearly symbolizes in part the project of German unification.[20] It is also connected, however, with how time is understood and experienced by Hermann and Clarissa. After visiting the house for the first time as a couple, they spend the night in a local hotel room, and, in a scene that reworks the Berlin hotel room conversation, find themselves in a space that is surrounded and fragmented by mirrors. The linear unrolling of time is interrupted, as the voice-over of Clarissa draws attention to the way that suddenly the passage of history has reached a unique singularity, when time has opened up a whole new range of possibilities and potential paths. Clarissa's attempt to step outside the temporal boundaries of late globalized modernity are clearly romanticized, with her commitment to the Günderrode myth and delight in the gaze that the house offers over the Rhine and toward the famed Lorelei rock. Although Preusser maintains that the romantic relationship of Hermann and Clarissa at the beginning of *Heimat 3* is part of a wider indebtedness in the series to German Romanticism, the euphoric romanticization presented here by Reitz is debunked very swiftly. He allows the owner of the ruined house to scotch any rumours circulating (and picked up so eagerly by Clarissa) that the ruin, known locally as the Günderrode house, actually did belong at one time to the Romantic poet Karoline von Günderrode with his statement: "All of Romanticism is a misunderstanding."[21] He relates the difficulties he had with various local authorities in getting planning permission and in having reconstruction work costed up. He also notes that there are rumours about the house being haunted.

Hermann's step out of contemporaneity is—albeit unconsciously—back toward the security and familiarity of his childhood environment. This he realizes on the first morning as the couple walk out from the ruined house that he is suddenly, almost magically (note the mysterious rider on the white horse coming out of the early mists) on the threshold of his childhood Heimat, Schabbach. Hermann has not been placed directly back in his childhood home, but slightly at a distance from it, and, in terms of the exact site of the house, with his back to it. The liminal position of the house, directly on the border where the Hunsrück region meets the Rhineland, allows Hermann initially to believe that he has not in fact returned to the landscape of his childhood, that he still belongs to a wider, less parochial world. But, as time passes, and particularly evidenced in his conversations with Ernst and Matzko, it becomes clearer that Hermann has gradually returned to his Hunsrück roots (*Drehort* 252).

Far from being the house-as-Heimat that Clarissa has romanticized, *Heimat 3* ultimately narrates how the house becomes *unheimlich*, and how the Zeit-Heimat community that coalesces around its construction gradually falls apart in the ensuing decade. Despite the craftsmanship involved in the reconstruction of the house, and the beauty of the finished house, the idyllic nature of its setting is often punctuated by unexplained occurrences and unwelcome interventions from the outside world, a mood underscored by the frequent use of eerie and discordant music to accompany images of the house. It comes to represent containment and confinement to Clarissa, who begins an affair with a fellow performer on tour. Hermann is only able to become fully creative again in the house after his temporary estrangement from Clarissa. She is able to return to the house, but subsequently is diagnosed with cancer and spends a long period at a clinic in Mainz. Anton and Ernst die prematurely, Ernst's line-of-flight from the constraints of Heimat take him into a fatal air crash into the Lorelei rock, also the setting of Matko's suicidal leap. Lulu's boyfriend Lutz is killed in a road accident, and the Simon-Optik factory falls prey to venture capitalists. In the final episode, "Abschied von Schabbach," the survivors meet up at the Günderrode house to celebrate the millennium, with Clarissa performing a scene-stealing version of the song "Maybe This Time" from *Cabaret*, with its acknowledgement of the repetitious nature of the passing of time and hope for future good fortune. As much of *Heimat 3* concerns the varying legacies of the older Simon brothers and the inability or unwillingness of the younger Simon clan to take up the responsibilities of their inheritance (208), the cycle closes fittingly with a focus on Lulu, participant in the disastrous attempt to construct an underground museum to house Ernst's plundered art treasures. She is shown walking through the early morning grey mists by the river Main in Frankfurt with her dying friend, Roland, who makes a series of predictions about the coming century, which includes the abandonment of all clocks. Lulu returns to her son in the Günderrode house, whom she discovers playing Hermann's piano, with the party guests mostly still asleep. Reitz closes his trilogy with a time-image constructed in medium shot moving to extreme close-up on Lulu's face, gazing through another pane of glass out past the camera, a framing held for some seventy seconds that registers the past she carries with her, her inability to identify with the Zeit-Heimat created by her father, and, even in this present, her anticipation of a bleak future time.

In conclusion, *Heimat 3* claims to be a complex kind of filmic time machine, recording the new patterns of everyday life in the decade after the fall of the Wall, chronicling the impact of historical change in Germany, and also registering the being-in-time of its key characters. *Heimat 3* captures the changing nature of German society in the decade following unification in terms of surface phenomena such as the altered visual nature of Germany's cities and villages, new consumer goods and technologies, changing architecture, yet also in terms of significant structural changes brought about by this larger Germany's place within a more globalized economy, with the emergence of venture capitalists and new waves of migration from countries situated to Germany's east. The third part of Reitz's trilogy, perhaps in this way the filmic correlative of the Günderrode house, is also an attempt by the director to construct a safe home in time, a stable location or Heimat composed of time-images—everyday, historical, durational—which, like the house, is a project that tries to transcend the flux of time passing. As the nature of image-making changes with the increasing replacement of analogue cinematic processes with digital, Reitz's stubborn commitment to analogue filmmaking in *Heimat 3* and his attention to time and duration mark the final part of his trilogy as a significant exploration, not only of what Germany has been in this past decade, but also of the likely passing of a distinct kind of cinema. Reitz argues that digital images are free from the natural laws that govern film's relationship to time. Everything about a digitally constructed representation is easily manipulated, particularly how "the unity of space and time is revoked" (*Film und Zeit* 7), so digital images no longer carry the ontological status of being documents of a specific event in space and time.[22] As David Rodowick has argued recently, as digital fantasy and inventiveness come to replace analogue filmmaking's ability to focus on everyday objects and people in their duration, "What we have valued in film are our confrontations with time and time's passing" (*Virtual Life* 73). For Reitz, as analogue filmmaking evolves into a digital future, the final word: "The search for lost time, in the way that Proust began it at the time of the invention of cinematography, has come to an end. [...] I see in the cinema a time machine with which we can travel after our memories, to gather them up and to take firm possession of them" ("Film und Zeit" 7).[23]

Notes

1. The DVD release in the UK claims to run to 761 minutes; Reitz complained that the TV release in Germany was cut to six ninety-minute episodes.
2. The "spatial turn" is often associated with the groundbreaking volume on *Postmodern Geographies* published by Edward W. Soja in 1989, coincidentally the temporal starting point of *Heimat 3*. Soja's subtitle *The Reassertion of Space in Critical Social Theory* could stand as a programmatic statement for something of a paradigm shift that has been felt far beyond its original field of cultural geography and across into a number of other disciplines.
3. See King, and on the history and key generic concerns of the *Heimatfilm*, see von Moltke, *No Place Like Home*, particularly 1–18 and 21–35.
4. See von Moltke, 203–26.
5. Crang's examples include Barbara Adam's work on the temporal landscape or "timescape" as a way of understanding the complexity of how events occur in a variety of temporal dimensions (213).
6. For a stimulating application of some of Massey's arguments to contemporary German cinema, see Koepnick.
7. For a detailed discussion of the ontological questions raised by film's relationship to time passing, see Harbord or Rodowick, particularly Chapter 12: "An Ethics of Time," 73–87.
8. See Broadbent.
9. See Fuchs and Cosgrove, *The Quest for Identity in Literature, Film and Discourse since 1990*, 1–21. See also Fuchs and Cosgrove, *German Life and Letters*.
10. See here particularly Fuchs, *Phantoms of War in Contemporary German Literature, Films and Discourse: The Politics of Memory*. Fuchs's wide-ranging and stimulating study includes a chapter that links these generational debates to issues of Heimat, but there is no mention in the book at all of Edgar Reitz or his *Heimat* trilogy, which arguably prefigures much contemporary discussion. On the post-wall *Generationsroman*, see Ganeva.
11. "Noch vor zehn Jahren war damit, zumindest in der Erinnerung, ein fester Ort gemeint. Nun, an der Schwelle zur Zeitenwende, richtet sich unser sehnsüchtiges Verlangen danach, Kinder der Zeit zu bleiben, nicht aus ihr vertrieben zu werden, wenn die Welt grenzenlos und die Orte beliebig werden. Heimat suchen wir nicht mehr in Landschaft und Dorf, sondern in der Zeit, der wir noch intensiver als früher angehören möchten. Das wunderbare Gefühl, dazuzugehören, das die meisten von uns aus der Jugend kennen, ist das neue, weltweite Heimatgefühl geworden. Heimat ist kein Ortsbegriff mehr, sondern ein Zeitbegriff und damit ein ganz und gar filmisches Thema."
12. On Reitz's elegiac tendencies in *Heimat*, see Santner, 97–99. On the sense of loss captured in aesthetic performance in *Die Zweite Heimat*, see von Moltke, 124.
13. See also Reitz, 210.
14. "realen Zeitfragmenten"
15. "Die Kamera kann sich von den Begrenzungen der menschlichen Zeitwahrnehmung befreien und setzt uns in die Lage, Forschungsreisen ins Innere der Zeit zu unternehmen. Zeit erweist sich als etwas, das mehr ist, als nur Kausalität [...]. Manche ihrer Eigenschaften deuten darauf hin, dass sie eine eigene Form besitzt, und dass die Raumzeit, von der die Physiker sprechen, als untrennbares, zusammenhängendes Gebilde in sich gekrümmt ist."
16. Wikipedia France suggests that it was first screened in its entirety in eleven episodes on TF1 starting on 9 January 1987. It may have been screened in 1986 in four parts in French cinemas.
17. "eine eigenartige Vibration."

18 See Preusser, 240–43, and Schmitz, 99.
19 See Augé, particularly 75–115.
20 See also Preusser, 240–43.
21 "Die ganze Romantik ist ein Missverständnis."
22 Reitz's post-*Heimat* filmmaking has been dedicated to a number of digital projects with his son Christian.
23 "Die Suche nach der verlorenen Zeit, wie sie Proust zur Zeit der Erfindung des Cinematographen begonnen hat, ist zu Ende gegangen. [...] Ich sehe im Kino eine Zeitmaschine, mit der wir unseren Erinnerungen hinterher reisen können, um sie einzusammeln und zu einem festen Besitz zu machen."

References

Augé, Marc. Non-places: *Introduction to an Anthropology of Supermodernity*. Trans. John Howe. London: Verso, 1995.

Blickle, Peter. Heimat: *A Critical Theory of the German Idea of Homeland*. Woodbridge, Suffolk: Camden House, 2002.

Bloch, Ernst. *The Principle of Hope*. Vol. 3. Cambridge, Mass.: MIT Press, 1986.

Broadbent, Philip. "Generational Shifts: Representing Post-*Wende* Berlin." *New German Critique* 35.2 (2008): 139–69.

Crang, Mike. "Time: Space." *Spaces of Geographical Thought: Deconstructing Human Geography's Binaries*. Ed. Paul Cloke and Ron Johnston. London: Sage, 2005. 199–220.

Deleuze, Gilles. *Cinema 2: The Time-Image*. Trans. Hugh Tomlinson and Robert Galeta. London: Continuum, 2005.

Fuchs, Anne, and Mary Cosgrove, ed. *German Memory Contests*. Spec. issue of *German Life and Letters* 59.2 (2006): 163–322.

Fuchs, Anne, Mary Cosgrove, and Georg Grote, ed. *German Memory Contests: The Quest for Identity in Literature, Film and Discourse since 1990*. Rochester: Camden House, 2006.

Fuchs, Anne. *Phantoms of War in Contemporary German Literature, Films and Discourse: The Politics of Memory*. Basingstoke: Palgrave Macmillan, 2008.

Ganeva, Mila. "From West-German *Väterliteratur* to Post-Wall *Enkelliteratur*: The End of the Generation Conflict in Marcel Beyer's *Spione* and Tanja Dückers's *Himmelskörper*." *Seminar* 43.2 (2007): 149–62.

Guggenheimer, Bernd. *Das digitale Nirwana*. Hamburg: Rotbuch, 1997.

Harbord, Janet. *The Evolution of Film: Rethinking Film Studies*. Cambridge: Polity Press, 2007.

Heimat. Eine Chronik in elf Teilen. Dir. Edgar Reitz. Edgar Reitz Film Productions, 1984.

Heimat 3. Chronik einer Zeitenwende. Dir. Edgar Reitz. Edgar Reitz Film Productions, 2004.

King, Alasdair. "Placing *Green Is the Heath* (1951): Spatial Politics and Emergent West German Identity." *Light Motives: German Popular Film in Perspective*. Ed. Randall Halle and Margaret McCarthy. Detroit: Wayne State UP, 2003. 130–47.

Koepnick, Lutz. "Free Fallin': Tom Tykwer and the Aesthetics of Deceleration and Dislocation." *Germanic Review* 82.1 (2007): 7–30.
Kracauer, Siegfried. *The Mass Ornament: Weimar Essays*. Trans. and ed. Thomas Y. Levin. Cambridge: Harvard UP, 1995.
———. *Das Ornament der Masse. Essays*. Frankfurt am Main: Suhrkamp, 1963.
———. *Theory of Film: The Redemption of Physical Reality*. Princeton: Princeton UP, 1997.
Massey, Doreen. *For Space*. London: Sage, 2005.
Moltke, Johannes von. "Home Again: Revisiting the New German Cinema in Edgar Reitz's *Die zweite Heimat* (1993)." *Cinema Journal* 42.3 (2003): 114–43.
———. *No Place Like Home: Locations of Heimat in German Cinema*. Berkeley: U of California P, 2005.
Preusser, Heinz-Peter. "Eine romantische Synthese und ihr notwendiges Scheitern. Edgar Reitz' filmische Chronik *Heimat 1–3*." *Seminar* 43.2 (2007): 234–50.
Reeh, Henrik. *Ornaments of the Metropolis: Siegfried Kracauer and Modern Urban Culture*. Trans. John Irons. Cambridge: MIT, 2006.
Reitz, Edgar. "The Camera Is Not a Clock (Regarding My Experiences Telling Stories from German History)." *West German Filmmakers on Film: Visions and Voices*. Ed. Eric Rentschler. New York: Holmes and Meier, 1988. 137–41.
———. *Drehort Heimat. Arbeitsnotizen und Zukunftsentwürfe*. Ed. Michael Töteberg, Ingo Fliess, und Daniel Bickermann. Frankfurt am Main: Verlag der Autoren, 2004.
———. "Film und Zeit." Doctoral speech. University of Perugia, Perugia, Italy. 6 Dec. 2006. 14 Feb. 2008 <http://www.edgarreitz.de/cms/index.php?option=com_content&task=view&id=190&Itemid+97>.
Relph, Edward. *Place and Placelessness*. London: Pion, 1976.
Rodowick, D.N. *Gilles Deleuze's Time Machine*. Durham: Duke UP, 1997.
———. *The Virtual Life of Film*. Cambridge: Harvard UP, 2007.
Santner, Eric. *Stranded Objects: Mourning, Memory, and Film in Postwar Germany*. Ithaca: Cornell UP, 1989.
Schmitz, Helmut. "Introduction." *Seminar* 43.2 (2007): 95–99.
Soja, Edward W. *Postmodern Geographies: The Reassertion of Space in Critical Social Theory*. London: Verso, 1989.
Vidler, Anthony. *The Architectural Uncanny: Essays in the Modern Unhomely*. Cambridge: MIT, 1992.
———. *Warped Space: Art, Architecture and Anxiety in Modern Culture*, Cambridge: MIT, 2001.
Die zweite Heimat. Chronik einer Jugend in 13 Filmen. Dir. Edgar Reitz. Edgar Reitz Film Productions, 1992.

7
Troubled Parents, Angry Children:
The Difficult Legacy of 1968 in Contemporary German-Language Film

Joanne Leal

Abstract This chapter investigates ambivalent responses to 1968 and its aftermath in three recent German-language films that are—to differing extents—also critical of social and political developments in post-unification Germany. Specifically, it demonstrates how Oskar Roehler's *Die Unberührbare*, Christian Petzold's *Die innere Sicherheit*, and Hans Weingartner's *Die fetten Jahre sind vorbei*, even while they disparage the role played by the 1968 generation at different moments in the development of the Berlin Republic, evaluate more positively the ideological legacy of the student movement, offering a critique of contemporary Germany from a perspective not dissimilar to the 1968 generation's own anti-authoritarian, anti-capitalist, and anti-imperialist stance.

In a recent exploration of the representation of the West German student movement in contemporary fiction, Ingo Cornils argued for the continued significance of this phenomenon, at least as it manifests itself discursively in contemporary Germany, claiming that "one of the constituent debates of the post-unification period has centred on the impact of the generation of '68 [...] on the culture, politics and society of both the "old" West Germany and the "new," post-1990 Federal Republic" (91). Reflecting on the nature of this debate, in which competing claims have been put forward, on the one hand, for the continued resonance of the transformatory cultural politics of 1968 in today's Germany and, on the other, for the student movement's absolute irrelevance in a contemporary context, Cornils concludes that current assessments tend in general to favour the latter view. "By the late 1990s, some thirty years after the events of '68, a process of historicization had begun which, for the most part, appeared to undermine the political agenda and self-image of the former student radicals" (91).

Since the beginning of the new millennium, German cinema can be said to have contributed substantially to such critical reassessments of the student movement and its legacy. A number of films have appeared that can be understood both as interventions in debates about the impact of the 1968 generation on the development of post-unification Germany and as contributions to a process whereby its aims, ideals, and actions are exposed to critical reassessment. Oskar Roehler's *Die Unberührbare* (*No Place to Go*, 2000), Christian Petzold's *Die innere Sicherheit* (*The State I Am In*, 2000), and Hans Weingartner's *Die fetten Jahre sind vorbei* (*The Edukators*, 2004) are three such films that I will examine in detail here. Others include *Die Stille nach dem Schuss* (*The Legends of Rita*, Volker Schlöndorff, 2000), *Black Box BRD* (*Black Box FRG*, Andres Veiel, 2000), *Baader* (Christoph Roth, 2002), *Was tun, wenn's brennt?* (*What to Do in Case of Fire*, Gregor Schnitzler, 2001), *Elementarteilchen* (*Atomized*, Oskar Roehler, 2006), and *Der Baader Meinhof Komplex* (*The Baader Meinhof Complex*, Uli Edel, 2008). The majority of these focus on the violent legacy of 1968 in the form of Red Army Faction (RAF) terrorism, and as such they follow thematically in the footsteps of those films of the New German Cinema that tried to understand the terrorist phenomenon in its immediate aftermath. In her analysis of four such recent films, Rachel Palfreyman has noted that they are particularly concerned, like those that I will examine here, with "the question of how the legacy of the Bonn Republic can be understood in the political climate of the Berlin Republic" (15).

My aim here is to demonstrate that, in line with the contemporary historiographical tendency identified by Cornils to re-evaluate negatively the legacy of the student movement, each of the three films with which I am concerned passes decidedly critical judgment on the actions of 68ers, both as individuals and as a group. As I shall show, however, they also open up alternative perspectives on that debate. Their overall response to 1968 as an ideological whole is in fact marked by a deep-seated ambivalence. All three films are—albeit to differing extents—distinctly critical of social and political developments in post-unification Germany and, even while they disparage the role played by (elements of) the 1968 generation at different moments in the development of the Berlin Republic, they nevertheless evaluate in positive terms the student movement's broader ideological legacy. What is more, each can be seen to offer a critique of contemporary Germany from a perspective that shares marked similarities with the 1968 generation's own anti-authoritarian, anti-capitalist and anti-imperialist stance.

This is perhaps surprising in view of the fact that each of these films is the work of a filmmaker too young to have adult experience of the political upheavals of the late 1960s or their radical aftermath in the form of Baader-Meinhof terrorism: Oskar Roehler was born in 1959, Christian Petzold in 1960, and Hans Weingartner in 1970. Each film thus represents, more or less explicitly, an engagement with the legacy of an older, (quasi-)parental generation. In this respect too, they can be seen to follow broader trends in the discussion about the significance of 1968, described by Monika Shafi as an "emotionally charged, even explosive" debate in which "different generations vie for the task of delivering the interpretive framework that will shape cultural memory" (204). Each of the films is in fact constructed around a confrontation between parents and children, allowing them to explore the legacy of 1968 on an (inter)personal as well as a political level. In this respect, the films demonstrate that the contemporary re-evaluation of the student movement is marked by a generational conflict that bears some similarities at least to that which characterized the 68ers response to their parents, not least in respect to a critique of suspect ideological allegiances.[1] I intend here to read each film in detail with a view to determining the nature of the intergenerational clash represented, to identifying the varying significance each film attaches to patterns of (generational) conflict and violence for an understanding of German history, and to determining how each assesses the relevance of these patterns to processes of social change within contemporary Germany.

Anti-Capitalist Critique in *Die Unberührbare*

Hanna Flanders, the central figure of *Die Unberührbare*, is based on the filmmaker's mother, the left-wing novelist Gisela Elsner, who published her debut novel, *Die Riesenzwerge* (*The Giant Dwarfs*), to critical acclaim in 1964. Elsner found herself firmly in step with the countercultural developments of the 1960s, a period with which she continued to associate herself both ideologically and emotionally until her suicide in 1992, despite—or perhaps because of—the fact that her left-leaning novels of the 1970s and 1980s failed to find a readership in the West and were eventually published only in the GDR. In what can be assumed to be self-ironizing fashion, Roehler stages a fictionalized encounter between himself and his mother in the film, one which makes clear the dysfunctional nature of their relationship as well as their very different responses to developments in contemporary Germany: while the son is thrilled by the fall of the Berlin Wall—the moment at which the film's narrative begins—his mother is only depressed. It is precisely this response to contemporary events that indicates the representative status that attaches to the Elsner/Flanders figure, as Julia Hell and Johannes von Moltke have argued:

> For all of the film's autobiographical overtones, Hanna Flanders functions as an allegory [...]. With the figure of his mother, Roehler brings to the screen an admittedly

idiosyncratic representative of the West German Left to remind us that many of its members experienced unification not as a cause for celebration but as a traumatic event that shattered long-held imaginary projections. (84)

Through this character the film attempts to understand those members of the 1968 generation who continued, throughout the life of the Federal Republic, to criticize the state from a left-wing perspective and to view socialism as a viable alternative to capitalism, and it explores the response of such unreconstructed members of the old Left to the end of the communist experiment in East Germany.

During the film's credit sequence we hear the sound of emotional voices and honking Trabis associated with the television coverage of the fall of the Wall. The first visual sequence shows Hanna on the telephone, clutching a bottle of arsenic and two lit cigarettes, stating her intention to kill herself. These images are intercut with television pictures, implying a connection between Hanna's obvious distress and the euphoria of the rest of the population. Why she should take the fall of the Wall so badly emerges in an interview with a young reporter, who has come to record her views on these historic events. She experiences them as the triumph of capitalism and therefore as the betrayal of truth:

> It makes me sick to see these clones all over the place. It nauseates me how they rummage through the underwear, grabbing at things. Now, suddenly, I have realized the depressing truth that they're fighting for Mon Cheri chocolates, and so that they can stuff Western tampons, bananas and Coca Cola bottles into their cunts. They are not fighting ... in Lenin's sense ... for the truth.[2] (Roehler, 42)

In the course of the film, Hanna's perspective is exposed as hypocritical, anachronistic, and ultimately self-destructive. The product of an upper-middle-class family, she lives in relative luxury in Munich and is happy to indulge in the kind of consumerism she criticizes so forcefully here as a way of protecting herself against loneliness and the recognition of her failures, both artistic and personal. Her relationship with her son is only one of many that she is unable to sustain, not least because she seems incapable of responding to him as someone who changes over time. Similarly, her relationship to political and ideological realities remains in limbo. She is unable to adjust her understanding of the GDR as "the better Germany," even after an encounter with an East German family whose members respond enthusiastically to the fall of the Wall, an event that for them represents a first taste of freedom.

This critical portrayal of an old 68er out of step with contemporary reality is doubled when Hanna encounters her former husband, Bruno. Both embrace this chance meeting as an opportunity to hide from an unsatisfactory present by recreating the past, a realm he seems largely to inhabit. He too couches his disillusionment with contemporary reality in political terms, invoking the names of female terrorists to give expression to his frustration that the present has no place for the political radicalism of his youth. As Hell and von Moltke note: "The failed reunion of an emblematic couple from the New Left of the 1960s and the invocation of the RAF's female icons once again presents the Left's paralysis in the wake of unification as a critical subtext of Roehler's film" (85). As with Hanna, Bruno's trauma manifests itself above all as a sense of self-alienation, existential loneliness, and personal failure. The film presents the inability of both characters to adapt either ideologically or emotionally to contemporary reality as self-destructive and, in Hanna's case, as ultimately fatal: in the film's final sequence, she falls to her death from a hospital window.

Significantly, while *Die Unberührbare* certainly passes scathing judgment on Hanna's failings, both personal and political, it also provides scope for her to be viewed as a victim of West German capitalism and the isolation, hypocrisy, and exploitation it demonstrably promotes. Because she has a product unwanted in the German market place, Hanna suffers economically under capitalism and is shown struggling to finance her existence. She also suffers emotionally as a member of a consumer society that is shown to exploit the desire it helps to promote for youth and beauty. It presents anything as possible if enough money is available, but human relationships are shown to have atrophied. The film highlights lack of compassion as a central characteristic of Western society by contrasting the scene in which Hanna, in the process of buying a Dior coat, is fawned over by sycophantic shop assistants anxious for a sale with the one in which her attempt to return the coat is met with icy disdain despite her obvious financial and emotional distress. Conversely, there is an apparently anticapitalist glorification of what is presented as a specifically East German sense of honesty, warmth, and community. The film might reject Hanna's understanding of the East as the (politically) better Germany, but it seems at the very least to want to suggest that ordinary Easterners are the (morally) better Germans. Counterparts to the mostly men who make Hanna's life difficult in the West are the women who are prepared to help her in the East: like the young mother who rescues her when she is traumatized by a sleepless night, greeting her with the words: "You look terrible. But that doesn't matter"[3] (Roehler 93). This statement suggests that, as an East German, the young woman adheres to a value scheme in which surface appearance is less important than the evidence of human need. The warmth of the welcome Hanna is offered by this family would seem to provide further evidence of a supportive social environment that has flourished, at least at a local level, under socialism. Their unadulteratedly enthusiastic response to the fall of the Wall means, however, that they can only provide Hanna with a temporary refuge from the evils of capitalism.

Given that the film's portrayal of a capitalist reality is essentially negative and given that it was made a decade after the *Wende* for an audience well aware that Easterners' initial enthusiasm for the promises of the West had waned, it is hard not to read the euphoria of the East German family as deeply naïve. One might want to argue that their ideological naïveté is merely the counterpart of Hanna's—and that of other 68ers like her—who were also prepared to embrace a political system of which they had no concrete experience. This would support a reading of the film as essentially critical of the ideological obsessions of its central figure and the generation to which she belongs. Given that in its critique of capitalism, however, the film presents the values of its East Germans as superior to those of its West Germans, one could argue that it opens up the possibility that Hanna's ideological allegiances—if not the way she practises them—can be read more positively.[4]

Die innere Sicherheit and Countercultural Discourses

While *Die Unberührbare* allows for at least a degree of uncertainty as to how 68er ideology should be judged in contemporary Germany, Petzold's *Die innere Sicherheit* appears to insist not just on the anachronism, but also on the moral bankruptcy of those who cling to outdated political views. Clara and Hans, a couple who have engaged in unspecified terrorist activities presumably in the late 1970s, and who have subsequently lived abroad in hiding with their now fifteen-year-old daughter, Jeanne, belong to that small group of former student activists who took their allegiance to the ideology of 1968 to violent extremes.

A robbery at their apartment in Portugal forces the couple to return to Germany at the beginning of the new millennium, where they are brought face to face with their own irrelevance. Their ideological convictions—and those of the generation to which they belong—seem to have left no discernible trace on the Germany they encounter, a country whose political and economic agendas have changed substantially. Thus, when the police raid a motorway service station at which the family have stopped, they are there to catch not former terrorists but illegal migrants; and when Hans digs up the cash box containing the proceeds of earlier illegal activities, it is full of outdated D-Mark (a new series of banknotes replaced the 1960s series in 1990), good only—like the ideology that has inspired the terrorists—for "history lessons," as Hans says.

Hans's and Clara's choices are measured against those of two other old 68ers and former terrorist sympathizers to whom they turn for help. Klaus is potentially willing, although his continued support for the couple is apparently based on his lasting affection for Clara, rather than his continued faith in their cause. But as an alcoholic, who has failed to capitalize on the Federal Republic's prosperity, he can offer little—the pressures of capitalist competition mean that he has been forced to sell the publishing company that should have made him rich to a larger organization. The other former colleague they encounter wants nothing to do with them. Having traded his ideological views for financial success and social integration, he is presented as a hypocrite and attacked first verbally by Clara and then physically by Hans.

Set against—and largely at odds with—this morally disoriented older generation are a younger generation, represented primarily by Jeanne, who is clearly marked in the film as the victim of her parents' convictions. Wanting to escape the twilight world, to which their allegiance to an anachronistic ideology condemns her, and desperate to experience instead the banality of teenage normality in the here and now, she eventually betrays them, confessing their underground existence to Heinrich, her first love. At the end of the film, the white car in which the family is fleeing is surrounded and forced from the road by three black cars, causing an accident in which Hans and Clara can be assumed to perish. Petzold has described this sequence as one in which healthy antibodies destroy a foreign body: "A body fights the viruses that have attacked it. My idea was: they travel in a white car on the motorways and roads like a virus that has penetrated a body and the black cars that gather around them are the antibodies that eliminate the virus"[5] (qtd. in Homewood 132). This would seem to imply that the film argues for the eradication of 1968 ideology—or at least its more extreme versions—as vital to the health of contemporary Germany in general and to the future of its youngest generation in particular. This view is reinforced by the film's final sequence—one which Petzold has described as "like a birth"—in which a bloodied and battered Jeanne, who has been thrown clear of the car, stands up to face the future bathed for almost the first time in the film in bright sunlight.[6] Rachel Palfreyman has described this as a "symbolic ending, where the guilty parental generation is literally exploded" (18).

Die innere Sicherheit—while it refrains from any kind of direct moralizing and while it provides a not unsympathetic portrayal of its terrorists as "the living dead" (Petzold)[7]—would thus seem unequivocal in its conclusion, offering a wholesale condemnation of the left-wing extremism of the previous generation and a plea for the liberation of the younger generation from the political demands of their parents in order to enable them to embrace life in a normalized Berlin Republic. Like *Die Unberührbare*, however, the film opens up at least a degree of ambiguity in its relationship to the ideology of 1968. The overriding characteristic of the new Germany, as it manifests itself in *Die innere Sicherheit*, is its materialism and Jeanne's longing to be part of mainstream society is represented as a desire to possess the consumerist trappings that mark various kinds of identity within a capitalist society. Thus, many of the arguments with her parents crystallize around the question of what she should wear, and she steals CDs and clothes to emulate Pauline, daughter of Hans and Clara's financially successful former colleague. While one might simply want to read this as normal teenage behaviour, the film does signal the exclusionary, and thus potentially socially divisive, ways in which consumerism determines choices and identities in contemporary Germany, drawing attention to the inequalities on which capitalist societies thrive. Not only do we see the illegal migrants bundled into the back of a police van, presumably destined to be denied access to Western prosperity, the film also reveals the very different opportunities available to German children by contrasting the comfort of Pauline's bourgeois home with the rather less luxurious existence of the orphaned Heinrich, whose sense of social inadequacy leads him to invent a life in an opulent villa to impress Jeanne. In this sense, the film "remains implacably critical of the unified Germany as a divisive consumer society" (Palfreyman 21). The materialism of the new Germany can be taken, on the one hand, to provide evidence of the lack of impact the ideology of 1968 has had on the construction of the country post-unification; on the other, however, the emphasis the film places on rampant consumerism could also imply the need for the kind of alternative to it that the aims and ideals of the protest generation once offered.

A similar degree of ambiguity also attaches to the film's depiction of contemporary responses to the Nazi past. Craving contact with young people her own age, Jeanne follows a student with whom she has fallen into conversation into her history class, where she sits through a screening of Alain Resnais's *Nuit et brouillard* (*Night and Fog*, 1955) before becoming a target for the teacher's ire, because she is unable to answer a question on what she has just seen. The teacher then berates Jeanne and the class for their apparent unwillingness to take German history seriously and, as a consequence, she flees the classroom. Several commentators have noted that this sequence references a parallel one in Margarethe von Trotta's *Die bleierne Zeit* (*Marianne and Juliane*, 1981) in which the film's two sisters, characters based loosely on real-life siblings Christiane and Gudrun Ensslin, are left distressed and nauseous by the same film. In reality it did in fact contribute substantially to the politicization of the 1968 generation and their sense of conflict with their parents.[8] Petzold has suggested that Jeanne is unfairly treated by the teacher, because she "is made responsible for something about which she knows a lot. Basically she's punished for something that's in her very bones."[9] Just at the moment she attempts to escape her parents' influence, she is confronted with precisely the punishing attitude to the German past she has experienced at home: "She always had to suffer from this politicization,"[10] as Petzold notes. While we might possibly sympathize with Jeanne here, neither her flight, nor the slightly bemused silence of the other students, nor the disillusioned teacher's diatribe, in which he refers to *Nuit et brouillard* as a *Filmchen* ("a little film"), seem appropriate. This could imply that, for all their efforts, the 68ers—including the teacher here whom Petzold describes as a "disappointed left winger"[11]—have failed to keep alive a meaningful discourse on the crimes of the immediate past, the remembrance of which has deteriorated into a kind of self-flagellating and ultimately meaningless ritual. But, if that is the case, then it also implies the need for new kinds of counterhegemonic discourses in the new Federal Republic to fill the gap left by the failures of the student movement generation.

That the film, for all its thoroughgoing critique of anachronistic political extremism, nevertheless aligns itself, at least in part, with more moderate countercultural discourses, is signalled precisely by its referencing of *Die bleierne Zeit*. In fact, both *Die innere Sicherheit* and *Die Unberührbare* locate themselves in relation to the cinematic traditions of the New German Cinema, itself partially a product of the ideological concerns of the student movement. Roehler's film references Rainer Werner Fassbinder's cinema both thematically and aesthetically. As Paul Cooke has identified, with "its use of high-contrast black and white and symbolically-laden camera angles" (37), it is reminiscent of *Die Sehnsucht der Veronika Voss* (*Veronika Voss*, 1982), but it also cites *In einem Jahr mit dreizehn Monden* (*In a Year of Thirteen Moons*, 1978), the film the director himself claims as one of *Die Unberührbare*'s antecedents. Roehler's film follows a pattern common to both in its representation of the life of an isolated and unloved protagonist as symptomatic of a widely spread social malaise in the Federal Republic.[12]

In his much cited and highly critical review of developments in German cinema in the ten years preceding the release of *Die Unberührbare* and *Die innere Sicherheit*, Eric Rentschler identifies, as characteristic of the decade, cinema "as mass diversion" rather than as "a moral institution or a political forum," dubbing its filmic output "the post-Wall cinema of consensus" (264). Significantly, Rentschler characterizes the protagonists of this cinema—in explicit contradistinction to the troubled heroes of the New German Cinema—as oriented exclusively on a present and a future that are endlessly open to new definition, not least because they are no longer experienced as uniquely defined by German history in the same disquieting sense in which they were for their New German Cinema predecessors: "Repeatedly the Cinema of Consensus presents characters whose primary sense of person and place is rarely an overt function of their national identity or directly impacted by Germany's difficult past" (272). Clearly, Hanna's inability in *Die Unberührbare* to untie her sense of self from the existence of a divided Germany, as well as Hans's and Clara's morbid relationship in *Die innere Sicherheit* to an anachronistic ideology, aligns each of these figures more closely with the protagonists of the New German Cinema than with those associated with Rentschler's conception of contemporary film. Equally, other aspects of each film locate them both aesthetically and thematically within the territory of the political filmmaking of the 1970s: *Die Unberührbare*'s carefully constructed black-and-white images and its interest in the psychological consequences of social and political change; and *Die innere Sicherheit*'s reconstruction of the muted colours and sombre mood of *Die bleierne Zeit*, as well as its critical engagement with the themes of terrorism, consumerism, and memory. What the engagement of these films with an earlier tradition of politicized filmmaking implies is that cinema can still provide a much needed space for the probing of the kind of counter-hegemonic discourses—including those associated with the 1968 generation—that otherwise seem largely to have disappeared from contemporary reality as the films themselves portray it.

1968 Revisited: *Die fetten Jahre sind vorbei*

Made four years after *Die Unberührbare* and *Die innere Sicherheit*, *Die fetten Jahre sind vorbei* is the product of a changed political environment, both nationally and globally. It came after then Foreign Minister Joschka Fischer was outed as a former left-wing radical in early 2001, reopening debates about the legitimacy of political violence, and it also came after the massively more significant events of 9/11. This changed context might explain the fact that while *Die Unberührbare* and *Die innere Sicherheit* are content to probe the possibility of countering consumerism with alternative cultural discourses within the cinematic realm, the main concern of *Die fetten Jahre sind vorbei* is to explore whether interventionist political action on the 1968 model can change a world shown to be drastically in need of correction. It might also account for the fact that while it explores generational conflict in Germany, nowhere is this linked to the Nazi past, perhaps because this film—unlike its two predecessors—is interested in social injustice and political action on more than just a national scale. Possibly also as a consequence, it eschews a serious tone and sober aesthetics, opting instead for a mixed genre form that incorporates elements of the thriller and the romantic comedy to construct a kind of political cinema quite different to that associated with the 1970s, one which has been celebrated as "in keeping with the times"[13] (Borcholte). As Weingartner himself said: "The main reason why I wanted this film to have an optimistic tone and to reproduce the comedy of life was that I didn't want to make a classic political film. I wanted to break with that tradition a little bit"[14] (qtd. in Dzugan and Jaeger). One could argue therefore that, in contrast to *Die Unberührbare* and *Die innere Sicherheit*, *Die fetten Jahre sind vorbei*, in its desire for a broad popular appeal, works more conventionally within the framework of the kind of aesthetics of mainstream cinema criticized by Rentschler. While this would seem confirmed, on the one hand, by the film's lush colours and relatively conventional editing, it is also deliberately and explicitly counteracted by the fact that it is shot with a hand camera, allowing for a great deal of fluidity and mobility, which gives the finished product a spontaneous, often intimate, and sometimes unconventional feel. This allows the film to combine popular appeal with an aesthetic that can run counter to the Hollywood norm, and therefore to bring its visual effects in line with its critical perspective on the spread of global capitalism, something to which, of course, mainstream cinema makes a significant ideological contribution.

Die fetten Jahre sind vorbei confronts radical youth—in the form of three young people angry at social inequalities as they exist both within Germany and in the broader global environment—with the middle-aged conformity of an ex-member of the old Left in a post-unification Germany, which has embraced whole-heartedly global capitalism. While Jule distributes leaflets protesting the exploitation of the cheap labour that fuels Western economies, Peter, Jule's boyfriend, and his friend, Jan, draw attention to social injustices in a more subversive fashion: they break into the villas of the wealthy, rearrange their belongings in ways that unsettle and disorient the returning homeowners, and leave behind a message—either "Your days of plenty are numbered" or the even more direct "You've got too much money," signing themselves "the Edukators." All three, however, and particularly the group's intellectual, Jan, are disillusioned by the lack of resonance their protest actions find—in part the result of consumer society's ability to co-opt and commodify the revolutionary ideas and actions of previous generations. As Jan puts it: "Rebellion is more difficult now. Before all it took was dope and long hair and the establishment was automatically against you. What was considered subversive then, you can buy in the shops today—Che Guevara T-shirts or anarchy stickers."[15]

While discussing the effectiveness of earlier attempts at youth revolt, Jan makes a direct connection between personal and political transformations: "Even if some didn't work, the most important thing is that the best ideas survive. The same goes for personal revolts. What turns out good, what survives in you, that makes you stronger."[16] Nevertheless, problems arise precisely at the moment when the two fields collide: while Peter is away, Jan and Jule, whom the film presents as a victim of the same kind of social inequalities against which

Hans Weingartner, *Die fetten Jahre sind vorbei*. © Celluloid Dreams

she protests, undertake a revenge attack on the home of wealthy businessman Hardenberg, to whom Jule owes 100,000 euros, having written off his Mercedes in an uninsured car. In the process, Jule and Jan fall in love. When Hardenberg returns and recognizes Jule, she and Jan call Peter for help, and the three take off, with Hardenberg gagged and tied, to Jule's uncle's hut in the mountains.

Thus the stage is set for an encounter between young would-be revolutionaries and an apologist for capitalism-at-its-most-ruthless, one who in fact turns out to have an ultra-left past as a leading member of the Socialist German Student Union (Sozialistischer Deutscher Studentenbund). While the kidnapping of Hardenberg is an act born of desperation, it potentially propels the three friends along a path toward violent political extremism already pursued by the Red Army Faction before them. The leap they have taken from violence against property to violence against people is highlighted in a plan that contains more than a hint of the RAF's dehumanization of its victims:

> What about a 1970s-style political kidnapping? We'll put a sign around his neck—prisoner of the Edukators—make a film of it and send it to the television stations. That way we can finally test our methods on a living example, can't we?[17]

While the group rejects this extreme course of action almost immediately, they are, at least initially, unable to identify an alternative to it. Temporarily paralyzed, they engage instead in a series of confrontational debates with Hardenberg. These increasingly come to represent an encounter with a symbolic father, despised for his current position as part of the capitalist elite and yet a figure of respect in view of his radical past, and for this reason gradually able to turn the debates to his own advantage. This development highlights precisely the dilemma of the younger generation: they want to rebel against parents who repel any attack by invoking their status as the ultimate rebels. Moreover, they have no language in which to couch their rebellion other than that of their fathers. As Katja Nicodemus has put it: "Vital to the film is the contradiction inherent in the desire to overcome the difficulties of the world here and now with the mouldy vocabulary of yesterday."[18] Nevertheless, via the kidnap and the political debates it provokes, in which the arguments of the protest generation are appropriated by the young radicals and reworked for contemporary purposes, the film would seem to imply that both the bloody legacy of the RAF and the sell-out of the 68ers must be confronted and overcome if the younger generation are to find their way toward an effective political future in which the ideals that inspired the previous generation can be productively reactivated and reconceived in the fight against global capitalism.

Their interactions with Hardenberg and each other in the course of the kidnap enable the three to go some way toward achieving this, as they develop both morally and politically as a result of their experiences, to the point where they can recognize that the kidnapping represents not a legitimate political action, but a personal one—born initially of Jule's desire for revenge. They must return Hardenberg unharmed, if they are to stand any chance of fighting the kind of social injustices for which they hold him responsible. Once the kidnapping is resolved, Jule reiterates Jan's claim that "the best ideas survive." The question remains, however, whether for the younger generation to achieve their aims, those ideas must be totally liberated from their originators and potential betrayers: the 1968 generation themselves.

The answer will vary depending on which version of the film one takes, as Weingartner significantly altered the original conclusion for the film's international release. In its final version, Hardenberg, as the representative of the 1968er generation in the film, proves himself, in contrast to his three antagonists, incapable of further development, having lost the capacity to relate to the ideals of his youth in any way other than nostalgically. He might enjoy smoking a bit of dope with his captors, talk about abandoning his well-heeled existence to become a teacher, and even agree to write off Jule's debt, but in the final instance he reverts to authoritarian type and betrays the three to the police. He sits in a waiting car—wearing a suit once more—when special forces, acting on his tipoff, raid Peter's and Jan's flat. There they find pinned to the wall a note with the message "Some people never change." While, on the one hand, this can refer to the young protagonists' recognition that Hardenberg is far too integrated and implicated in capitalist structures to side with them, it also signals their own determination to do a better job of staying true to their political ideals than the previous generation had done. Hope—but only of the most speculative sort—that this might indeed be possible is offered by the film's admittedly somewhat fairy-tale-like conclusion.

In the final sequence, the three—miraculously transported to Spain—are shown sleeping peacefully in a wide, white bed as the police batter down the door of the Berlin apartment. Their escape from the clutches of the law provides compelling testimony to the potentially utopian power of their friendship, which has survived the shift of Jule's affections from one man to the other, and which might provide an alternative, non-materialistic vantage point from which to oppose contemporary capitalism. In this respect, one could argue they are indeed living out the ideal represented by the "1968 catchwords such as authenticity, desire, dream, freedom and their counter-values of alienation, repression, everyday bourgeois existence" (Shafi 204). In a final twist, however, an image of satellite dishes emerges slowly behind the credits in a reference to Jan's long-term plan to disrupt Europe's entire television network. The image might imply the continuation of the group's fight against injustice on a global scale, but it might equally point to its inevitable failure given that it demonstrates the omniscience and potential omnipotence of the forces they oppose.[19]

The film's other ending is substantially more utopian, both in relation to the possible success of the group's revolutionary activities and potentially also to the political integrity of the 1968 generation. In the final sequence, Jan, Jule, and Peter are shown studying plans of the European satellite station they intend to destroy before boarding the luxury yacht that will transport them to it. That the boat belongs to Hardenberg is confirmed by a close-up shot of his identity documents on board. Whether he is a willing participant in the group's revolutionary plans is ultimately less clear. The fact that he might just be opens up a new possibility: the statement "some people never change" might actually refer to the fact that at least some of the 68ers are capable of finding a way back to the political ideals of their youth. The subsequent change of ending can perhaps be accounted for by the fact that this more positive, and less likely, conclusion was received unenthusiastically by critics. It was described typically by one, for example, as "a tacked-on piece of chic posturing, which fails to do justice to the wonderfully delicately narrated drama which precedes it and which it in fact undermines"[20] (Koll).

Conclusion

What my analysis of *Die Unberührbare, Die innere Sicherheit,* and *Die fetten Jahre sind vorbei* has demonstrated is that all three films are similarly critical of the materialist nature of contemporary German society. They also have in common the fact that they link this development to the failure of the 68er generation (although in the case of *Die fetten Jahre sind vorbei,* this critique is far more explicit in its later version). Within the framework of familial conflict—autobiographical in *Die Unberührbare,* symbolic in *Die fetten Jahre sind vorbei*—members of the older generation are judged, and found wanting, in relation to their own ideological aims, exposed as failures or hypocrites, or both. Hanna pays only lip service to ideals she is effectively unable to live out. In taking their ideals to an unacceptable extreme, Clara and Hans deny themselves and potentially the next generation any kind of political effectiveness; and in *Die fetten Jahre sind vorbei,* the 68er sell out and consumerist appropriation of revolutionary practices threaten to paralyze a generation potentially willing to protest. As heirs to the ideological legacy of 1968, the younger generation are seen struggling to find ways to confront the repressive authoritarianism, the aggressive capitalism, and even the (culturally) imperialist ambitions of the contemporary Germany their parents have helped to create. All three films imply the necessity of resistance on the part of the younger generation to this development, but only one, *Die fetten Jahre sind vorbei,* suggests that resistance might be possible in the real world rather than only within the framework of the kind of countercultural discourses cinema can construct. Where all three films come together is in their insistence that if any of the hope once associated with utopian politics is still alive, then it no longer resides with the 68er generation.

Notes

1. Hans-Joachim Hahn has noted a similar tendency to structure representations of the student movement in literature around family conflicts, both in the immediate aftermath of 1968 and more recently (Hahn 135).
2. "Mich macht es krank zu sehen, wie diese Einheitsmenschen sich hier breitmachen, es ekelt mich an, wie die in den Unterhosen wühlen, wie die raffen. Mir ist jetzt erst schlagartig die deprimierende Wahrheit bewußt geworden, daß die für 'Mon Cherie'-Pralinen kämpfen und damit sie sich Westtampons, Bananen und Colaflaschen in ihre Fotze stopfen können. Die kämpfen noch nicht ... im Sinne von Lenin ... für die Wahrheit."
3. "Sie sehen schrecklich aus. Aber das macht nichts."
4. For an extended version of this argument, see Leal.
5. "Ein Körper bekämpft die Viren, die ihn befallen haben. Meine Vorstellung war: In einem weißen Auto fahren die als eingedrungener Virus über die Autobahnen und Straßen, und die schwarzen Autos, die sich um sie herum gruppieren, sind die Antikörper, die den Virus eliminieren."

6 Petzold's comment, "wie eine Geburt," is taken from Petzold, Christian. "Commentary." *Die innere Sicherheit*, DVD. Directed by Christian Petzold. MC-One, 2001.
7 See Homewood for a discussion of Petzold's use of vampire imagery.
8 On the relationship between Petzold's and von Trotta's films, see Homewood.
9 Jeanne "wird [...] für etwas verantwortlich gemacht, wovon sie unheimlich viele Ahnung hat. Sie wird im Grunde genommen für etwas bestraft, was sie im ganzen Körper drin hat." From Petzold, Christian. "Commentary." *Die innere Sicherheit*, DVD. Directed by Christian Petzold. MC-One, 2001.
10 "Unter dieser Politisierung hat sie immer leiden müssen." Petzold in *Der Tagesspiegel*.
11 Petzold's comment, "entäuschter Linke" is taken from Petzold, Christian. "Commentary." *Die innere Sicherheit*, DVD. Directed by Christian Petzold. MC-One, 2001.
12 Palfreyman has argued that a thematic concern with terrorism is one factor that creates a direct link between the contemporary films she examines and the New German Cinema: "In exploring contemporary German identity via the West German past, the new films allude to the cinematic tradition of the New German Cinema both by taking up the genre of terrorism film and by consciously alluding to the aesthetics and politics of the earlier generation of films" (12).
13 "Zeitgemäß."
14 "Der Hauptgrund, warum ich wollte, dass der Film eine optimistische Grundstimmung hat und auch die Komik des Lebens widerspiegelt, war, dass ich keinen klassischen politischen Film machen wollte. Ich wollte ein bisschen aus der Tradition ausbrechen."
15 "Das Rebellieren ist halt schwieriger geworden. Früher brauchtest du nur zu kiffen und lange Haare zu haben und das Establishment war automatisch gegen dich. Was früher subversiv war, kannst du heute im Laden kaufen—Che Guevara T-Shirts und Anarcho-Sticker."
16 "Klar, im einzelnen hat es vielleicht nicht funktioniert. Aber das Wichtigste ist doch, dass die besten Ideen überlebt haben. Genau so ist es bei den privaten Revolten auch. Das, was davon gut ist, und das, was davon in dir überlebt, das macht dich stärker."
17 "Wir wär's dann mit einer politischen Entführung in 70er Style. Wir hängen ihm ein Schild um den Hals 'Gefangener der Erziehungsberechtigten', filmen das ab und schicken es ans Fernsehen. Das ist doch jetzt die Gelegenheit, mensch. Endlich können wir unsere Methoden an einem lebenden Exemplar testen, oder?"
18 "Der Film lebt nun mal vom Widerspruch, der Welt von hier und jetzt und heute mit dem angeschimmelten Vokabular von gestern beizukommen."
19 Weingartner expands his critique of the media—specifically in this case German television—in his next film, *Free Rainer—Dein Fernseher lügt* (*Free Rainer*, 2007), where he also continues the exploration begun in *Die fetten Jahre sind vorbei* of the potential for success of the revolutionary action of a few against an all-powerful establishment.
20 "So bleibt die Schlusspointe des Films lediglich eine schicke aufgesetzte Pose, die dem zuvor so wundersam leicht erzählten Drama nicht gerecht wird und es eher konterkariert."

References

Die bleierne Zeit (*Marianne and Juliane*). Dir. Margarethe von Trotta. Bioskop Film, 1981.
Borcholte, Andreas. "Anarchie und Alltag." *Spiegel Online* 24 Nov. 2004. 1 Dec. 2008 <http://www.spiegel.de>.

Cooke, Paul. "Whatever Happened to Veronica Voss? Rehabilitating the '68ers' and the Problem of *Westalgie* in Oskar Roehler's *Die Unberührbare* (2000)." *German Studies Review* 27 (2004): 33–44.
Cornils, Ingo. "Literary Reflections on '68.'" *Contemporary German Fiction Writing in the Berlin Republic*. Ed. Stuart Taberner. Cambridge: Cambridge UP, 2007. 91–107.
Die fetten Jahre sind vorbei (*The Edukators*). Dir. Hans Weingartner. Y3 Film, 2004.
Free Rainer—Dein Fernseher lügt (*Free Rainer*). Dir. Hans Weingartner. Coop 99, 2007.
Hahn, Hans-Joachim. "Die Studentenbewegung und die RAF als deutscher Familienroman. Jüngste litererarische Erkundungen einer jüngeren Vergangenheit." *Seminar* 43 (2007): 134–48.
Hell, Julia and Johannes von Moltke. "Unification Effects: Imaginary Landscapes of the Berlin Republic." *Germanic Review* 80 (2005): 74–95.
Homewood, Chris. "Von Trotta's *The German Sisters* and Petzold's *The State I Am In*: Discursive Boundaries in the Films of the New German Cinema to the Present Day." *Studies in European Cinema* 2 (2005): 93–102.
———. "The Return of 'Undead' History: The West German Terrorist as Vampire and the Problem of 'Normalizing' the Past in Margarethe von Trotta's *Die bleierne Zeit* (1981) and Christian Petzold's *Die innere Sicherheit* (2001)." *German Culture, Politics and Literature into the Twenty-First Century. Beyond Normalization*. Ed. Stuart Taberner and Paul Cooke. Rochester: Camden House, 2006. 121–35.
In einem Jahr mit 13 Monden (*In a Year of 13 Moons*). Dir. Rainer Werner Fassbinder. Film Verlag der Atuoren, 1978.
Die innere Sicherheit (*The State I Am In*). Dir. Christian Petzold. Schramm Film, 2000.
Leal, Joanne. "Time, Transformation and Tradition in Oskar Roehler's *Die Unberührbare*." *German as a Foreign Language* 1 (2006): 76–89 <www.gfl-journal.de>.
Koll, Hans Peter. "*Die fetten Jahre sind vorbei.*" *Film-Dienst* 25 Nov. 2004. 1 Mar. 2009 <http://www.filmportal.de>.
Nicodemus, Katja. "Denn sie wissen, was sie tun. Hans Weingartners Film *Die fetten Jahre sind vorbei* sucht mit seinen Helden nach der Revolution von morgen." *Zeit* 25 Nov. 2004. 1 Dec. 2008 <http://www.zeit.de>.
Nuit et brouillard (*Night and Fog*). Dir. Alain Resnais. Argos Films, 1955.
Palfreyman, Rachel. "The Fourth Generation: Legacies of Violence as Quest for Identity in Post-Unification Terrorism Films." *Cinema since Unification*. Ed. David Clarke. London: Continuum, 2006. 11–42.
Petzold, Christian. "*Die innere Sicherheit*: Nach dem Schiffbruch—Christian Petzold im Gespräch." *Tagesspiegel* 24 Jan. 2001. 1 Dec. 2008 <http://www.tagesspiegel.de>.
Rentschler, Eric. "From New German Cinema to the Post-Wall Cinema of Consensus." *Cinema and Nation*. Ed. Mette Hjort and Scott Mackenzie. London: Routledge, 2000. 260–77.
Roehler, Oskar. *Die Unberührbare. Das Orignal-Drehbuch*. Cologne: Kiepenheuer & Witsch, 2000.

Die Sehnsucht der Veronika Voss (*Veronika Voss*). Dir. Rainer Werner Fassbinder. Laura-Film, 1982.

Shafi, Monika. "Talkin' 'bout My Generation: Memories of 1968 in Recent German Novels." *German Life and Letters* 59 (2006): 201–16.

Die Unberührbare (*No Place to Go*). Dir. Oskar Roehler. Distant Dreams Film Produktion, 2000.

Weingartner, Hans. "Kein Zeichen von Dekadenz." [Interview with Roberto Dzugan and Frédéric Jaeger]. *critic.de*. 24 Nov. 2004. 1 Dec. 2008 <http://www.critic.de>.

8
Creative Chaos as Political Strategy
in Recent German-Language Cinema

Mary-Elizabeth O'Brien

Abstract Against the two-sided coin of political idealism with its call for a perfect society and its use of force to obtain such lofty goals, this chapter examines two films that present "creative chaos" as a strategy to protest against the loss of utopian dreams. Hans Weingartner's *Die fetten Jahre sind vorbei* and Marcus Mittermeier's *Muxmäuschenstill* are black comedies about young people who want to teach ordinary citizens about equality, civility, and responsibility in a world beset with injustice. These films reflect a growing discomfort with the lack of political and moral high ground, and they seek creative means to redefine German national identity in a globally responsible framework.

The fall of the Berlin Wall and the demise of communism in Europe have contributed to a growing sense that currently there is no politically viable alternative to capitalism. Living in a world in which the clear lines between bipolar superpowers have been erased and nearly every imaginable youth rebellion has failed to overthrow the system, what is left for a young generation to do to eradicate social injustice? A look at recent German-language films shows that many of the ideals embodied in the 1968 student revolts remain a powerful undercurrent in the Berlin Republic. One of the most enduring notions is that capitalism is inherently unjust and that the establishment uses consumerism as a strategy to distract citizens with self-indulgence, thereby averting their attention from serious social problems. In post-millennial Germany, counterculture movements share with 68ers the conviction that mass media form a cog in the wheel of global capitalism. Demonization of the media, especially television, as the system's tool to pacify the masses and dull their senses has become an increasingly popular theme in motion pictures, as the following examples demonstrate.

A scathing critique of mass media can be found in the omnibus film *GG 19: 19 gute Gründe für die Demokratie* (*GG 19: Nineteen Good Reasons for Democracy*, 2007), made by Harald Siebler and eighteen other directors. Siebler called on scriptwriters to propose six-minute stories about the fundamental civil rights embodied in the first nineteen articles of the constitution. In response 482 scripts were submitted to a jury for consideration, and over 1,500 individuals participated in making the 19 episodes that make up the 149-minute film. In the segment "Adrenalin Flash" (Johannes von Gwinner), which is devoted to Article 1 guaranteeing the inalienable right to human dignity, a man is attacked in his home, tied up, and forced to watch on a monitor as his wife and children are tortured, only to learn that he is an unwitting contestant on a bizarre reality television show. In *Egoshooter* (Christian Becker and Oliver Schwabe, 2004), the main character, Jakob, is obsessed with creating a video diary and uses his camera like a vital appendage of his body and mind, as if his thoughts and actions make sense only through the camera lens. Jacob and his friend believe that in a world saturated with images, the media manipulate the youth and prevent them from organizing and working for social change. Finally, Hans Weingartner's *Free Rainer: Dein Fernseher lügt* (*Free Rainer: Your Television Is Lying*, 2007) is a satirical critique of the television industry, in which a ruthless trash-television producer recognizes that his shows contribute to the dumbing down of the masses and begins a clandestine campaign to change viewers' habits and the industry's offerings.

Within this context, this essay examines Hans Weingartner's *Die fetten Jahre sind vorbei* (*The Edukators*, 2004) and Marcus Mittermeier's *Muxmäuschenstill* (*Quiet as a Mouse*, 2004). Both films also seem to display a growing dissatisfaction with political and cultural processes in contemporary society. Against the two-sided coin of political idealism with its call for a perfect society and its use of force to obtain such lofty goals, both films present "creative chaos" as a strategy to protest against the loss of utopian dreams. Creative chaos can be understood as a form of political engagement, whereby established patterns of behaviour are disrupted through playful or innovative acts in the hope of generating widespread cognition of society's failures and the need for a new social order.

Die fetten Jahre sind vorbei and *Muxmäuschenstill* were both low(er)-budget productions that quickly became box-office hits. From its cinematic release on November 25, 2004, until the end of 2005, *Die fetten Jahre sind vorbei* sold 873,935 tickets in German theatres, ranking it slightly behind the critically acclaimed *Sophie Scholl: Die letzten Tage* (*Sophie Scholl: The Final Days*, Marc

Rothemund, 2005) with 1,096,026 tickets sold and *Alles auf Zucker* (*Go for Zucker*, Dani Levy, 2005) with 1,038,631. Released in German cinemas on July 8, 2004, *Muxmäuschenstill* garnered 90,000 viewers in its first ten days. By the end of 2005, it had sold 306,820 tickets, thus achieving an excellent audience share, considerably stronger than the average German production, but not comparable to the blockbusters of that year like *(T)raumschiff Surprise – Periode 1* (*Dreamship Surprise: Period 1*, Michael Herbig, 2004) with an attendance of 9,137,506; *7 Zwerge: Männer allein im Wald* (*7 Dwarfs*, Sven Unterwaldt, 2004) with 6,486,540 and *Der Untergang* (*Downfall*, Oliver Hirschbiegel, 2004) with 4,521,903.[1]

Both films are black comedies about young people who want to teach ordinary citizens about equality and civility at home and about their global responsibility in a world beset with injustice. Weingartner's film features rebellious "educators" (*Erziehungsberechtigte*), who break into villas, not to steal anything but to rearrange the furnishings and jolt the residents out of their comfort zone. While their imaginative acts are intended to teach the rich that possessions cannot guarantee security, their tactics begin to resemble those used by the Red Army Faction (RAF). In a postmodern society where traditions are recycled and socialism has been discredited, the educators must come to grips with the history of 1968 and determine which ideas are worth saving. *Muxmäuschenstill* likewise deals with a vigilante, Mux, who seeks out wrongdoers and dispenses justice at will. Mux oversees a network of informants, monitors suspicious individuals, films his "pedagogical measures," and archives them with a zeal rivalling the Stasi. Inspired by the German enlightenment and classicism, Mux is nonetheless a psychopath obsessed with modern media and the adrenaline rush of control. These films reflect discomfort with the lack of political and moral high ground in the present and look to the past for guidance. Finding paradigms in different historical periods, 1968 and the late eighteenth century, respectively, they introduce creative means to redefine German national identity in a globally responsible framework. The question that arises is whether these characters achieve an original form of social engagement that can be viewed as "poetic resistance" or whether they succumb to the ancient pitfall of violence routinely associated with forcing others to do the right thing.

Hans Weingartner's *Die fetten Jahre sind vorbei* shares with many recent films an interest in young people who are searching for meaning in an alienating environment.[2] While contemporary films tend to depict the everyday lives of adolescents in a gendered pattern with boys more cognizant of and eager for social or political group membership and girls more focused on fitting into secure familial and sexual relationships, the teenagers have many common existential problems. Along with the typical lack of control particular to their age group as minors, these young people suffer from absent and ineffectual parents, unstable living conditions often bordering on homelessness, the lack of education and job training, which leads to little interest in or prospects for the future, and a general lethargy that can only fleetingly be overcome through shopping, drugs, sex, or violence. Without guidance and a sense of purpose, they go through life as phantoms, never knowing in which direction they should head, but acutely aware that they want out of this state of limbo.

Weingartner taps into this prevailing sense of existing in a world without orientation, but what separates his film from others is that it proposes underground activism as a possible solution to the youthful malaise. *Die fetten Jahre sind vorbei* encourages nonconformity to the wisdom of mainstream society and offers pedagogical lessons on how to change societal thinking. In contrast to a "cinema of consensus" (Rentschler 264) that avoids difficult issues and seeks common ground, Weingartner wants his work to contribute to a cinema of consciousness that challenges the status quo and is unabashedly educational.[3] He sees himself as a diagnostician of an unhealthy culture: "My task as a filmmaker is to look at where it hurts"[4] (qtd. in Aust). Touching the open wounds of German society, he prescribes a simple remedy: dissatisfied individuals must band together to demand change.

Die fetten Jahre sind vorbei identifies global capitalism as the disease and the educators as the cure. Jan and Peter are masked crusaders who resemble the character Neo in the blockbuster film *The Matrix* (Andy and Larry Wachowski, 1999). Like Neo, the educators are morally righteous, perceptive individuals who can see the structure of oppression and are intent upon fighting injustice. Jan recognizes in Peter's girlfriend Jule the same superpower: she can see the façade, while others believe in a web of illusions. Whereas in the Wachowski brothers' cult classic, the unsuspecting masses are content to live in a make-believe world, because it shelters them from the bitter reality that they serve as human batteries for alien machinery, in Weingartner's film Jan acts like the computer hacker Neo to break society's codes, alerting the public to the numbing effect of endless consumption, which keeps people trapped in a mere simulacrum of reality and prevents them from living authentic lives. Jan explains: "That is the matrix. You see it and can't live in it. Me neither."[5] Jan and Peter's nightly break-ins are based on *The Matrix* principle that the enlightened must awaken the cataleptic masses. The public does not question the morality of capitalism, because the system is so entrenched it seems natural, and therefore it is the educators' duty to alert others to the true nature of this phenomenon. By turning expensive furniture into unexpected arrangements, they hope to shatter the protective bubble of privilege surrounding the power elites and force them to recognize the injustice of their status. The educators' playful performance art has a serious purpose: they want to strike fear in the hearts of the rich. The staging of break-ins as spontaneous happenings and enjoyable, if mischievous, symbolic exhibitions rather than acts of violence leaves little doubt with whom the audience should identify and sympathize. The contrast between an empty palatial residence devoid of human warmth and the likeable educators, who have transformed everyday objects into artistic installations, makes it eminently easier to accept the film team's characterization of the break-ins as a symbolic action contributing to "poetic resistance." Hans Weingartner claims that the educators are not criminals but rather creative individuals who use subtle forms of humour: "At first glance they create chaos, but there is meaning in the chaos. Just like in many poems. Therefore, one could call what they are doing 'poetic resistance'"[6] (Weingartner). Consciousness-raising is ultimately dependent upon accepting the notion that property is theft.

The educators adhere to a set of ideas associated with groups like ATTAC (Association for the Taxation of Financial Transactions for the Aid of Citizens). ATTAC was founded in France in 1998 to advocate for the worldwide institution of the Tobin tax on currency speculation, in order to create a development fund. Currently, ATTAC has an estimated 90,000 members in over fifty countries and under its motto, "The world is not for sale," their activities have expanded to include monitoring the World Trade Organization, the International Monetary Fund, and the Organization for Economic Development and Cooperation, demonstrating at G8 meetings, and championing a wide variety of projects relating to sustainable development, Third World debt relief, environmental concerns, and social justice.[7]

Even though the educators do not belong to any such organized political group, their ideological positions seem similar. For example, when Jule explains that she has destroyed a Mercedes belonging to the multi-millionaire Hardenberg, and argues that it is her moral responsibility to pay 100,000 euros in restitution, Jan counters that this kind of bourgeois morality is a weapon the establishment uses to maintain its power. Jan claims that a poor waitress driving without insurance cannot be considered a transgression, because the real crime is conspicuous over-consumption. After Jan and Jule are caught in the act of creating chaos in Hardenberg's home, and they kidnap him, Jan confronts the millionaire directly: "We're living in a dictatorship of capital. Everything you own you've stolen."[8]

The educators recognize that the protest movements of the 1960s and 1970s already attempted revolutionary action with little change in the socio-economic order. In the post-cold-war, postmodern condition, they wonder how their generation can be original, let alone successful. If one looks closely at what these young people know about recent history, it becomes clear that they have a selective memory about the 68er student movement and the Red Army Faction. Although they are prolific with slogans, they reject the type of public demonstrations popularized by 68ers as ineffective, and refuse to work within the political system or create an alternative forum like the Außerparlamentarische Opposition (extra-parliamentary opposition). While never referring specifically to the *Kommune 1, Spaßguerrilla,* or the Situationists International, the educators embrace the basic strategies of these historical groups.[9] Staging imaginative pranks and utilizing the establishment's power against itself to derail it (e.g., arranging things in new configurations to illustrate the absurdity of property) positions them as heirs to figures like Dieter Kunzelmann, Rainer Langhans, Fritz Teufel, and Guy Debord.

Invoking the vocabulary of the RAF kidnapping of Hanns-Martin Schleyer, Jan asks Hardenberg how he likes it in the *Volksgefängnis* (people's prison). Only half jokingly, Peter suggests that they take a lesson from the RAF, hang a sign around Hardenberg's neck reading "prisoner of the educators," film it all, and send it to a television station. They quickly reject the idea of ransoming or killing their captive as the RAF did in the past. More importantly, they refuse to see any similarity between their own development and the gradual formation of the Baader Meinhof gang from activists staging a T-shirt demonstration to firebombers protesting consumerism to terrorists using kidnapping and murder to force change. When Hardenberg reminds them that they are using the same methods as the RAF to frighten their enemies, the educators dismiss the comparison and offer the seemingly empty platitude that they are unassuming and original. Originality and creativity are, however, vital elements in their self-definition, because these qualities ensure that the young generation is unique and can counteract postmodern cynicism. Since the educators refuse to ransom or kill Hardenberg, admit that kidnapping him was an act of self-preservation devoid of political intent, and set him free, their crime is sublimated from an actual offence to a mental miscalculation. Intention rather than deed becomes the standard for evaluating whether something is a crime, and since they admit their mistake, it somehow disappears, and they absolve themselves of any wrongdoing.

Hardenberg functions to a great extent as a witness to history, explaining his trajectory from a student revolutionary to a multi-millionaire manager. Smoking a joint with his captors, he reminisces about his youth in the student movement and about being a leader in the SDS (Socialist German Student Union). He recalls how he knew Rudi Dutschke personally, lived in a commune, and experimented with free sex. But then he followed the path of many, got married, had children, found a good job, bought a house, and slowly his determination to change the world eroded and his energy was funnelled into maintaining his wealth and the status quo. Surprised by his own development and the conservative transformation of the 68er generation, he admits that conformity sneaks up on you, "and suddenly you catch yourself in the voting booth making a cross for the Christian Democratic Union."[10] Being kidnapped by the educators is depicted as a positive thing for Hardenberg. Transported from the hectic pace of Berlin to the peaceful surroundings in the Tyrolean Mountains, he is given the chance to reflect upon his life. He has the opportunity to stop working and reminisce about a time when he still believed in changing the world and was able to have fun. Indeed, he begins to see his normal life as a prison, and wonders if he should drop out, become a teacher in an isolated village, and live a simple but authentic life. The sincerity of Hardenberg's transformation, however, is put into question by his subtle gestures and intense gaze that the young people fail to notice. Although Hardenberg seems to flourish in this space beyond his normal reality, he remains a gifted observer and strategist, ready to assume command.

Apart from looking to the past for lessons on what type of activism works, it is the intellectual legacy of 1968 that makes the greatest impression on these young people. Although they do not cite specific historical references, they are deeply indebted to Theodor W. Adorno and Max Horkheimer's critique of the culture industry and Guy Debord's *Society as Spectacle*. It is interesting to note that many critics (e.g., Dietrich Kuhlbrodt) commended the educators for not belonging to a group, because it implies that they are spontaneous and authentic. Tobias Kniebe also thinks that the educators' individual acts of rebellion demonstrate that they will not be caught up in a political movement that could lead to the type of dictatorship that plagued twentieth-century Germany ("Generation Nix"). In a somewhat similar vein, Matthias C. Müller argues that the educators lack a believable political language and are charming exactly because they are so hapless, naïve, and speechless. Katja Nicodemus likewise notes that Jan represents a generation that seeks change, but that refuses to rely on old ideologies, and thus rages against the system in a soulful, if inarticulate, manner. Yet, at the same time, the educators' statements and actions also demonstrate an acute awareness of arguments put forth by Naomi Klein in *No Logo* and Kalle Lasn in *Culture Jam*. Jan's tirade against Hardenberg, for example, almost sounds like a synopsis of Lasn's book, in which the author offers the following prediction:

> We will strike by smashing the postmodern hall of mirrors and redefining what it means to be alive. We will reframe the battle in the grandest terms. The old political battles that have consumed humankind during most of the twentieth century—

black versus white, Left versus Right, male versus female—will fade into the background. The only battle still worth fighting and winning, the only one that can set us free, is The People versus The Corporate Cool Machine. (xvi)

Echoing Lasn, Jan claims that children all around the world who live in slums and watch American action films will one day rise up and rage against the machine, and he warns: "At some point you can't keep sedating them with game shows and shopping."[11]

The question of whether the educators' actions should be considered violence or poetic resistance is addressed at numerous points in the film, and, in their responses to the film, it divided the critics who either saw the educators as non-violent resisters (e.g., Tobias Kniebe, Thomas Klingenmaier, Dominik Kamalzadeh) or who considered them to be terrorists, dangerous criminals, or misguided and ineffectual activists (e.g., Ulrike Frick, Michael Kohler, Ekkehart Krippendorff, Juli Zeh). Jan provides the group's definitive answer to this question when he tells Hardenberg: "Our meagre break-ins are completely ridiculous compared to the violence people like you commit."[12] Defining capitalism as a state-sanctioned form of collective violence, they justify their behaviour by redefining it in euphemisms. Breaking into people's homes, kidnapping Hardenberg, threatening him with a weapon (albeit a fake one), stealing his yacht, and sabotaging television satellites are all acts of violence. If these acts are not committed by likeable characters, it seems unlikely that the audience and critics would accept these acts as "ceremonial destruction."

The final scene in the original film, however, features the educators as innocent angels, draped in white, peacefully sleeping in their cloudlike communal bed, as a modern-day version of Leonard Cohen's song "Hallelujah" plays over the scene. Most reviewers applauded the educators for using creativity instead of violence, and Michael Althen's remarks were typical: "Smart idea, sexy actors, great music ... what more do you want from German film?"[13] The film's second ending, a puzzling and incongruent coda rewritten after the premiere at Cannes, includes a finale that is stylistically inconsistent and jarring in its pace and glamour. In a scene rivalling a Hollywood adventure blockbuster, the trio of attractive, well-dressed heroes wearing sunglasses board Hardenberg's luxury yacht to the upbeat rhythms of pulsating music. The young rebels have become the epitome of radical chic and speed off into the horizon to intensify their struggle against the establishment. As the credits roll over a silhouette of satellites followed by the familiar image of television static and the lingering afterglow of being unplugged, it becomes clear that the educators have succeeded in halting television transmission throughout Europe. As Althen's remarks suggest and the film's conclusion illustrates, Weingartner straddles the fine line between, on the one hand, popular media styles that appeal to mass audiences exactly because they deliver tried and true patterns and, on the other, a message of resistance to established behavioural norms, economic systems, and political structures that demand new ways of thinking.

Based on a script by Jan Henrik Stahlberg, who also starred in the title role, *Muxmäuschenstill*, Marcus Mittermeier's debut film, was a surprise hit. The film's black humour, politically incorrect protagonist, largely amateur cast, and pseudo-documentary camera work lent it an underground quality, and its unusual production history contributed further to its subversive status. Mittermeier and Stahlberg, two actors with no previous experience in directing and screenwriting, applied to subsidy boards and television stations, but were refused funding. They eventually made the film for 40,000 euros, using digital cameras, hundreds of untrained performers, and often shooting without the required permits, leading film critic Hanns-Georg Rodek to call it a "perfect example of the new digital guerrilla filmmaking"[14] ("Ich muxe").

In an attempt to generate a pre-premiere buzz along the lines of the *Blair Witch Project* (Daniel Myrick and Eduardo Sánchez, 1999), Mittermeier and Stahlberg created a website at www.denunziant.de to recruit a network of informants like Mux does in their film. Presenting themselves as a group of young Berliners fed up with people constantly breaking the rules, they admonished their fellow citizens to accept responsibility for shaping society.[15] In the first three days online, twenty people filled out application forms, agreeing to spy on others and denounce wrongdoers. Although the website was quickly exposed as a publicity stunt, even after the film appeared in cinemas, some viewers thought that *Muxmäuschenstill* was a documentary about a real organization and inquired about becoming members of the fictional *Gesellschaft für Gemeinschaftsinn* (Society for Public Spirit). Mittermeier saw these reactions as evidence "that denunciation falls on fertile ground," and Stahlberg added: "What we saw is that our film is much closer to reality than we thought"[16] (Lehnartz). Mux's politically incorrect idea that Germany needs a domestic spy network to police ordinary citizens was intended as a satire, but it resonated with at least some members of the audience as a reasonable remedy for social ills. Despite the all too familiar historical precedent of a public willing to inform on others to the Gestapo and the Stasi, the notion of moral surveillance as a practical means to maintain social order continues to have its supporters. This concern seemed to be confirmed when, in February 2008, Christel Wegner, a parliamentarian representing the Left Party in the state of Lower Saxony, made a statement on national television justifying the Berlin Wall and arguing that Germany once again needed an official agency like the Stasi to keep tabs on the population. Wegner reasoned: "I think that ... if one is to establish another social form, then one needs once again an agency, because one has to protect against other forces, reactionary forces, that will use the opportunity and weaken the state from within"[17] (qtd. in Hengst and Wittrock). The Left Party removed Wegner from her seat in the state parliament, but the question of whether her remarks reflect a broader public sentiment is open to debate.

Mux, the former philosophy student turned vigilante, scours the streets of Berlin looking to catch individuals who transgress against the norms of good behaviour. Inspired by Kant, Goethe, and Kleist, this modern moralist is a psychopath intent on forcing others to follow his own rigid notion of decency. Equipped with a digital camera, a pistol, and an unwavering moral certitude, Mux becomes a self-appointed sheriff, judge, and avenger. No one is safe from his watchful eye; he catches people who ride the subway without a ticket, shoplifters, pet owners who fail to pick up after their dogs, exhibitionists, rapists, and murderers with equal zeal. Accompanied by his videographer Gerd, Mux punishes offenders in increasingly humiliating ways in order to teach them manners and obedience. *Muxmäuschenstill* thus works on much the same principle as *Die fetten Jahre sind vorbei*, introducing a self-appointed do-gooder to shake up society and educate the masses in unexpected, creative ways.

Mux has two pedagogical goals, to punish violators so that they will learn that crime does not pay and to present the larger community with a terrifying example as a preventative measure. Beyond this common didactic mission, Mux and the educators part ways. Whereas Weingartner's characters remain generally sympathetic, Mittermeier's protagonist begins as an admirable if odd character who turns out to be a megalomaniac and murderer. At first this straightlaced avenger carries out the kind of street justice that viewers may secretly imagine doing. Stopping speeders and taking away their steering wheel may be a wickedly enjoyable if socially unacceptable form of wish-fulfillment. At some point, however, Mux's pedagogical measures become sadistic and deadly. He shackles a wheelchair-bound man to a signpost for crossing the street on a red light, and spray-paints a graffiti artist in the face, which results in the blinded teenager being run over by a train. Mux bases his crusade on a misguided reading of Kant's categorical imperative. What in theory is the foundation of individual responsibility and moral behaviour becomes in practice the exact opposite of what he set out to achieve. In his zeal to right all wrongs, Mux becomes a demagogue who disregards the rights of others. The filmmakers wanted to illustrate that this aberration originates from a distinctly German intellectual heritage. Mux's ideas are rooted in the German philosophical traditions of the Enlightenment as much as in National Socialism's preoccupation with order, obedience, and duty. The filmmakers readily admit that Mux has fascist aspects, but they contend: "He is not a child of the brown soup, he is a child of classicism, of unhinged romanticism, of German persnicketiness"[18] (Körner).

Mux's understanding of the classics is partial at best, and he turns to literature for more than spiritual edification. He patterns his own life on famed literary figures as if these steadfast fictions could provide him with a set of ideals and a genuine personality. He venerates the Enlightenment as demonstrated by the Kant breviary on his bedside table, but he is also fascinated with romantic notions of suffering and the special lonely nature of the artist. A self-described loner who is alienated from conventional society and seeks respite in nature, Mux resembles Werther, and shares with Goethe's sentimental figure unrequited love and a fascination with the folk. Just as Werther admired the peasants' simple and genuine lifestyle, Mux frequents traditional pubs and socializes with those he perceives as the lower class in his quest for authenticity. Mux's sentimental nature is revealed as utter kitsch in a scene where he bids a final farewell to his neighbour Trude. The old woman lies dying in her bed, while a group of friends keeps vigil. A grief-stricken Mux weeps as a sombre requiem plays, but when the music suddenly stops, he calmly reaches for the tape recorder at her bedside and turns the cassette over. Staging emotion with the accoutrements of a sappy melodrama, Mux ensures that reality conforms to his romantic world outlook. It is easy to imagine that a man who wants nothing more than justice and champions unconditional obedience to a higher order has read Heinrich von Kleist's *Michael Kohlhaas* and *The Prince of Homburg* as a venerable catechism on integrity and duty. Like Kohlhaas, the relentless man obsessed with righting a wrong, or Prince von Homburg, the dreamer consumed with notions of duty and just punishment, Mux cannot live in a world where other people break the rules. Kleist's description of Kohlhaas as "one of the most upright and atrocious men of his time"[19] is an equally fitting characterization of Mux (9). In the end, like the tragic figure Kohlhaas, Mux's preoccupation with justice will cost him his life.

With his noble ideas and zeal bordering on insanity, Mux also resembles Don Quixote. Like Cervantes's legendary figure, Mux imagines himself to be a knight errant fighting for justice, and he is accompanied by his faithful servant, Gerd, who has the rotund look and dim-witted nature of Sancho Panzo. Mux stylizes his girlfriend, Kira, as his Dulcinea, a pure and innocent young girl who needs to be protected. Mux's romanticized view of the perfect woman is an unobtainable fiction he has learned from reading the German classics. His first words to Kira are, "Do you know *Faust*?" and this ominous question foreshadows her tragic fate. Like Gretchen, Kira will lose her life because she had the misfortune to become involved with a man who literally believes that the eternal

Marcus Mittermeier, *Muxmäuschenstill*. © Schiwago Film

feminine will lead him to paradise. Mux imagines Kira as an angel, and she is often lit from above creating a halo effect and dressed in white clothes that give her a virtuous appearance. Mux's vision is predicated on Kira remaining silent and compliant, in essence adopting the role of Mux's quiet little mouse as indicated in the film's title. When Mux goes to sleep at night surrounded by his books and accompanied by the reoccurring melody of "Tomorrow Belongs to Me" from *Cabaret* (Bob Fosse, 1972), Kira appears in his dream as a beatific figure. Bathed in sunlight and radiating youth, she is shown in slow motion as if existing in a vacuum. Kira's function is to be Mux's muse, and when she fails to meet his expectations, he eliminates her from the picture. Mux kills Kira but does not have the courage to commit suicide. Instead, he calls on his faithful servant, Gerd, to bury the body, allowing his crime to go unpunished.

From the film's opening scene, the act of creating images and documenting reality is problematized as a highly suspect endeavour. Before the credits roll by, Mux is seen filming a video diary, rehearsing his lines before he is satisfied with his performance. After several takes, he speaks directly into the camera as if he were spontaneously explaining his mission: "I am part of a society in which we have lost our ideals, in which there is no longer a utopia of a more just society. And therefore I am here: to help with the first step, so that people regain the power to accept responsibility for their behaviour."[20] The wobbly hand-held camera promises immediacy and authenticity, but in Mux's hands it turns out to be a carefully staged element to simulate spontaneity. With the aid of his apprentice, Mux captures people in the act of committing crimes and administers punishment, carefully filming his actions as evidence. The violator's name, the date, category of crime, and index number are imprinted on the videos, which are carefully archived to document misconduct. This fanatic attention to detail, categorizing people, and keeping meticulous records is an integral part of Mux's fascistic personality, but equally important is his obsessive need for images of domination and control.

At first Mux polices mostly traffic violations and inconsiderate behaviour, but after he falls in love with Kira, he directs his attention to sexual crimes with ever greater frequency. Shifting the focus from identification of lawbreakers to voyeuristic pleasure, Mux is seized by a compulsive need to watch sexual violence. Mux catches a shoplifter and insists the woman take off the bra she has stolen in front of him. Naked and vulnerable, her shame is intensified by the staging of her punishment. In a prism of looks, Gerd watches and films Mux watching a woman forced to undress, and he multiplies the degrading image by having both the victim and her punisher reflected in the dressing-room mirror. Afterward Mux admits that the scene was erotically stimulating, because he had humiliated the woman, and there was nothing she could do but submit to his authority. Equating voyeurism with psychopathy, *Muxmäuschenstill* thus implicates both the media that deliver a steady stream of visual input and the viewers who are never satiated and demand ever more bizarre and stimulating imagery. As the film progresses, the editing style changes from a relatively moderate pace, giving adequate time to the identification of crimes, to a point of acceleration where each incident becomes a blur in a rapid succession of violent and largely sexual images. With its shifting focus, the film replicates channel switching at hyper speed.

This type of montage also characterizes Mux's diatribe against society's insatiable desire for media images at the cost of living authentic lives. In a sequence introduced by a TV reporter stating that the station is going live to the Gendarmenmarkt in downtown Berlin, where Mux is being interviewed by the press, the truth value of the news is brought into question, since Mux is seated at the back of the room while his entire office watches him appearing "live" on television. The "live" press conference shown on the office television segues into the Gendarmenmarkt scene itself and then into a rapid montage of clips from news commentaries, talk shows, reality TV, superstar contests, game shows, and pornography that illustrate television's mindless fare. In this minute-long sequence consisting of nearly thirty television clips, images of Arnold Schwarzenegger giving a speech next to his beaming wife, Maria Shriver; a man dressed in a bodysuit made of meat cutlets being eaten by a pack of German shepherds; Dieter Bohlen gleefully humiliating a contestant on *Deutschland sucht den Superstar*; and a group of naked middle-aged party-goers drinking champagne in a communal hot tub underscore Mux's notion of corruption and his disgust over the relentless barrage of titillating images demanded by an insatiable public. Strongly associated with Mux's point of view via the framing devices and voice-over, the sequence ironically employs the very qualities of trash-TV programming that Mux criticizes as debased—the stringing along of shocking, mindless, or droning surface images without depth, insight, or artistry. He sees his own filmmaking as an educational mission and rejects the content of trash-TV, but not the medium of film or even television. In his last will and testament, Mux reserves his final criticism for populist political figures and pop-culture icons: "Enough with this public idiocy. If I am right, then all the Roland Kochs, Dieter Bohlens, and Stefan Raabs, all the obsolete models of this republic, had better prepare themselves for a rough ride."[21]

As Mux expands his operations, opening up new branches of the Society for Public Spirit and hiring an army of reformed delinquents to inform on others, he turns to the Internet to advertise with unexpected results—a sequence that provides a biting satire. His employee Bjorn proudly presents an Internet trailer for the proposed website that looks like a slick TV commercial for a new cop show. The black-and-white, fast-paced sequence features Mux running along the Oberbaum Bridge as if he were the lead in Tom Tykwer's cult classic *Lola rennt* (*Run Lola Run*, 1998). Dressed in a trench coat, he is shown in slow motion drawing his pistol in a rage, and calmly firing his gun directly at the audience. The ticking of a clock segues into a pulsating musical score and a commentary spoken in the deep voice and steady cadence of a typical television announcer: "Inside you it is ticking. You are alone. You are afraid—but you have eyes. You have ears. And offenders will lose their hearing and sight. Because you find offenders simply awful."[22] The trailer ends with a spectacular car crash and bright red explosion as the background for the title words: "www.denunziant.com" and the directive: "Denounce your neighbour!" Mux reacts with anger and dismay that Bjorn has mistakenly substituted "denouncer" for "informant," because as he has to explain to the clueless Bjorn, the term "'denouncer' leaves a bad aftertaste in Germany."[23]

The Internet trailer and Mux's entire operation play on the prevailing fear for one's safety, which is a double-edged sword: the public fears for its security due to (at least the perception of) rampant crime and terrorism and looks to the government for protection, but the authorities, both domestic and international, threaten to institute a system of obsessive surveillance and curtail civil rights to solve the problem. The security dilemma in Germany carries the historical weight of the Gestapo and Stasi legacies, but in a post-9/11 world, the implications are global, and the collective solution may well be worse than the original problem. Mux taps into this fear of surveillance by offering ordinary people the opportunity to turn the tables. Rather than tolerating the government's clandestine oversight of its citizens, he suggests that they can be empowered to scrutinize the lives of others and transfer the state's monopoly on the use of violence to a morally upright individual. Mux argues that his plan is even good for the economy, because he transforms perpetrators into informants and actually creates jobs. Wedding his critique of the "New Economy," where everyone greedily speculates, to his self-help employment package that will solve the security dilemma, Mux seems to offer the public exactly what it wants, because he is heralded in the press as an innovative thinker and morally upright leader. Pointing to Gerd, "the epitome of a person who has accomplished nothing in his life,"[24] as an example of how he can transform even the most pathetic loser into a productive member of society, Mux purports to have a concrete method to remedy the country's pressing social and economic problems. He recognizes that Germany desperately needs a modern-day hero but laments: "I am not a hero, because every country has the heroes it deserves. Michael Schumacher is a hero because he can drive around curves quickly and he doesn't pay taxes. Poor country."[25]

Without heroes in the present, Mux tries to bring to life the noble ideas of the past, so that Germans can see themselves as a nation of upstanding citizens who inspire others. But, as is generally the case, reanimating utopian visions from the past can lead to disastrous results. Mux is the archetypal fool who voices common-sense wisdom, a psychopath who prescribes a cure for the world's insanity. In this satirical look at contemporary society through the eyes of a lunatic, the rational need for moral responsibility taken to its logical extreme provides hilarious moments, but it also reveals a lingering sense that a system of shared values and governance has somehow gone astray.

Hans Weingartner and Marcus Mittermeier see their films as documents of the time, which reflect a general malaise and discomfort with the lack of political and moral high ground. Weingartner laments: "I think that my generation is the generation of helplessness and reorientation. Nowadays, there is a new generation, in the framework of the anti-globalism movement—with which I strongly sympathize—and which is developing new strategies"[26] (qtd. in Arnold). Mittermeier confers: "*Muxmäuschenstill* is a reflection of the new spirit of the times, the general crisis atmosphere. For a long time now Germany has found itself in a state of social upheaval. However, only when the majority is doing poorly, do people begin to ask questions. We are still a 'fat' country, but the economic euphoria of the 1990s is long over. What remains is the moral hangover after the soaring flight. We are reacting to this with our film"[27] (qtd. in Wach 9). Screenwriter Jan Henrik Stahlberg echoes these sentiments: "Since the fall of the Wall there no longer exists an alternative to this form of society we are living in now. Even the idealist Mux has no alternative to offer. He is writing a manifesto and is stuck in the first chapter. He becomes violent and a psychopath because the ventilating mechanism of a utopia is missing"[28] (Schwichert).

Both directors criticize turbo-capitalism and the mass media, and they present vigilantes who adopt creative chaos as a strategy to change the way people think. Weingartner and Mittermeier develop a similar visual aesthetic by means of hand-held digital cameras, little or no constructed sets, and no artificial lighting, which lend their films a documentary-like air of authenticity. They both worked under similar production conditions, employing a small crew on a modest budget and relying on improvisation or amateur actors. These artistic choices, primarily the result of limited financial resources, give their films the look of an indie production and contributed largely to their reception as anti-mainstream cinema. Yet, although they both use comedy, they embrace different comedic genres and have very different intentions for their films. Mittermeier uses satire and acknowledges that his character is a violent criminal despite his good intentions. Far from promoting a model for the audience to emulate, he wants viewers to leave the cinema and contemplate the complexities of social change. Confronted with a sociopath who identifies a pervasive lack of respect for the law, but offers up a remedy that results in tyranny, audiences are not given an easy answer to society's problems. Conflicts are left unresolved and open to discussion. Whereas *Muxmäuschenstill* is a cautionary tale that warns against moral vigilantism as a looming threat to civil liberties, *Die fetten Jahre sind vorbei* is a plea for change and concludes with a clear-cut answer to social problems: collective grassroots activism. Weingartner plays down the potential threat of violence inherent in the educators' playful anti-establishment happenings, and emphasizes that these disturbances are a necessary means to raise awareness and change the world. He presents a humorous look at social injustice through highly sympathetic characters and argues that moviegoers should pattern themselves after these rebels. His film combines aspects of independent and mainstream filmmaking, with its jerky mobile camera and grainy image quality juxtaposed to identification, emotional engagement, and conflict resolution—this mixture complicates the notion of a stark contrast between a "cinema of consensus" and a "cinema of consciousness." Weingartner tries to bridge the gap, openly embracing the more attractive aspects of popular filmmaking to demonstrate that political activism can be fun. He wants viewers to imitate the educators and believes that motion pictures can create a revolutionary mindset that leads to political change. His film has already inspired imitators in real life: in Hamburg people wearing *Edukator* T-shirts went into expensive restaurants and stole food off the tables. He maintains:

> This is something I'm really quite happy about, something I dreamt about. So I'm very proud that *The Edukators* is not just abstract art, but has jumped down from the screen and become real. Just imagine if those forty people become thousands, then you have a real revolution like in East Germany, which started out with only twenty-five demonstrators. After two years, there were millions. The regime ordered soldiers to shoot at them, but they didn't because how can you shoot at two million people? The next day the Wall came down." (qtd. in Rowland)

While the details of Weingartner's history lesson are less than exacting, he ironically uses the historical uprising against Marxism to justify further Marxist-inspired activism and aligns fictional acts of resistance with real ones, suggesting that imagined stories can spark an uprising of the same magnitude as the 1989 revolution. If the 68er rally cry "All power to the imagination!" holds even a grain of truth, then a closer look at the political ideology behind the educators' "poetic resistance" is warranted.

Both *Die fetten Jahre sind vorbei* and *Muxmäuschenstill* conspicuously end outside of Germany with the educators and Mux travelling to other countries where people are equally in need of enlightenment. Whether sailing the Mediterranean Sea intent on destroying European television satellites or campaigning against speeders on Italian country roads, these characters venture beyond their own borders, implying that national concerns over inequality, consumption, media manipulation, surveillance, and the security dilemma have broader implications in an increasingly globalized, interconnected world. Underlying these films is a lament over the current state of affairs in which modern society, despite its laudable achievements and profound historical consciousness over past failed political regimes, still cannot guarantee safety, security, prosperity, and justice for all.

Taken together, these films reflect a fundamental dilemma that has captured the popular imagination in unified Germany and has played out in various modes ranging from the media campaign commemorating the fortieth anniversary of 1968 to the cinema's ongoing fascination with the GDR and the RAF. Mediated engagements with the immediate past make clear that the general public has lost faith in the type of political utopia that engendered twentieth-century dictatorships and terrorism, but doggedly continues to long for a collective solution to society's imperfections. Confronted with a national history of two dictatorships fuelled by grandiose plans for social engineering, this longing for utopia often wavers between cynicism and naïve faith, creating a nearly schizophrenic mindset. This tension is evident in contemporary German cinema with *Muxmäuschenstill* and *Die fetten Jahre sind vorbei* representing different approaches to the same dilemma. Stuck between disappointment with failed utopian experiments and a relentless desire to strive for the perfect society, the public is confronted with films that examine the positive and negative consequences of creative chaos as a possible way out of the quandary.

Notes

1. For statistics on audience shares, see the Filmförderungsanstalt [German Federal Film Board] http://www.ffa.de.
2. See, for example, Sylke Enders's *Kroko* (*Crocodile* 2003), Christian Becker and Oliver Schwabe's *Egoshooter* (2004), Christian Petzold's *Gespenster* (*Ghosts*, 2005), Mirko Borscht's *Kombat 16* (2005), Henner Winckler's *Lucy* (2006), Bettina Blümner's *Prinzessinnenbad* (*Pool of Princesses*, 2007), and the omnibus film *Berlin 1. Mai* (*1st of May: All Belongs to You*, 2008) by Sven Taddicken, Jakob Ziemnicki, Carsten Ludwig, and Jan-Christoph Glaser.
3. Eric Rentschler argues that mainstream filmmaking in unified Germany strives for common ground and consensus building over uncomfortable and provocative challenges to the status quo. Rentschler applauds New German Cinema directors because "they interrogated images of the past in the hope of refining memories and catalysing changes" (263–64). By contrast, the majority of contemporary German directors "want cinema to be a site of mass diversion, not a moral institution or a political forum" leading to a "cinema of consensus" (264).
4. "Meine Aufgabe als Filmemacher ist es, da hinzugucken, wo es wehtut" (Aust).
5. "Das ist die Matrix. Du siehst sie und kannst in ihr nicht leben. Ich auch nicht." Hans Weingartner has acknowledged the centrality of this pop-culture reference and considers himself a central player: "I see myself as a submarine in the matrix." ("Ich sehe mich als U-Boot in der Matrix." [Stolz]). For further references to the matrix, see Borcholte, and Gansera and Göttler.
6. "Auf den ersten Blick erzeugen sie Chaos, aber in dem Chaos liegt eine Bedeutung. So wie bei vielen Gedichten. Deshalb könnte man das, was sie tun 'poetischen Widerstand' nennen." See also Kammerer.
7. For an excellent study of how mass-media reporting on ATTAC protests at the 2001 European Summit in Gothenburg and the 2001 G8 Summit in Genoa helped to bolster the group's reputation and increase its membership in Germany, see Kolb.
8. "Wir leben in einer Diktatur des Kapitals. Alles, was du besitzt, hast du gestohlen."
9. Founded in France in 1957 the Situationist International (SI) was a Western avant-garde, Marxist movement that sought to overcome the traditional boundaries between art, politics, and daily existence. The SI decried modern society as a monolithic spectacle and advocated creating situations that drew attention to the constructed nature of everyday life in order to bring about social change. Guy Debord, one of the Situationist's most renowned theorists, argued: "The whole life of those societies in which modern conditions of production prevail presents itself as an immense accumulation of spectacles. All that once was directly lived has become mere representation" (12). The Munich-based group SPUR was part of the SI, and SPUR member Dieter Kunzelmann was instrumental in developing the Kommune 1 in Berlin. Together with Fritz Teufel, who coined the term *Spassguerrilla* referring to playful happenings meant to expose entrenched rituals and encourage the public to reflect upon and change unjust social structures, Kunzelmann and other Kommune 1 members planned

the so-called pudding assassination attempt on US Vice-President Hubert Humphrey. The group planned to attack Humphrey with a variety of non-lethal projectiles including smoke bombs, paint, flour, and the vice-president's favourite dessert, pudding. Ironically, the attack never took place, but it produced so much publicity that it turned into a virtual event that defined the Kommune I. For an overview of this international movement, see Wollen 1989. Simon Teune presents an informative analysis of the Kommune I's use of humour as a political strategy. A useful resource is the anthology by Dreßen, Kunzelmann, and Siepmann.

10 "Und plötzlich ertappst du dich in der Wahlkabine, wie du das Kreuzchen bei der CDU machst."

11 "Die könnt ihr irgendwann nicht mehr mit Gameshows und Shopping betäuben." Compare further with Kalle Lasn's prognosis: "America is no longer a country. It's a multi-trillion-dollar brand. America TM is essentially no different from McDonald's, Marlboro or General Motors. It's an image sold not only to citizens of the USA, but to consumers worldwide" (xii). Finally, Lasn argues that one must adopt the tactics of the Situationists and their strategy of "*détournement*—a perspective-jarring turnabout in your daily life," akin to the creative chaos practised by the educators (xvii).

12 "Das bißchen Einbrechen von uns, das ist komplett lächerlich gegen die Gewalt, die Leute wie du ausüben."

13 "Smarte Idee, sexy Schauspieler, super Musik ... Was will man mehr vom deutschen Film?"

14 "Paradebeispiel des neuen, digitalen Guerilla-Filmemachens."

15 For details on the Internet presence, see Lehnartz.

16 "daß Denunziantentum immer noch Nährboden hat" and "Was wir gesehen haben, ist, daß unser Film viel näher an der Realität ist, als wir dachten."

17 "Ich denke, ... wenn man eine andere Gesellschaftsform errichtet, dass man da so ein Organ wieder braucht, weil man sich auch davor schützen muss, dass andere Kräfte, reaktionäre Kräfte, die Gelegenheit nutzen und so einen Staat von innen aufweichen."

18 "Er ist kein Kind der braunen Suppe, er ist ein Kind der Klassik, der verstörten Romantik, der deutschen Pingeligkeit." See also Rodek, "Man muss Stellung beziehen."

19 "einer der rechtschaffensten zugleich und entsetzlichsten Menschen seiner Zeit."

20 "Ich bin Teil der Gesellschaft, in der wir unsere Ideale verloren haben, in der es keine Utopie mehr gibt von einer gerechteren Gesellschaft. Und dafür bin ich da: beim ersten Schritt zu helfen, daß die Menschen die Kraft wiederfinden, für ihr Verhalten Verantwortung zu übernehmen."

21 "Es reicht mit dem öffentlichen Schwachsinn. Wenn ich Recht habe, können sich all die Roland Kochs, Dieter Bohlens und Stefan Raabs, all die Auslaufmodelle dieser Republik, warm anziehen."

22 "In dir tickt es. Du bist allein. Du hast Angst, aber du hast Augen. Du hast Ohren und Straftätern wird Hören und Sehen vergehen. Denn Straftäter findest du einfach nur noch ätzend. [...] Denunziere deinen Nächsten!"

23 "'Denunziant' hat in Deutschland einen fahlen Beigeschmack."

24 "der Inbegriff eines Menschen, der es in seinem Leben zu nichts gebracht hat."

25 "Ich bin kein Held, denn jedes Land hat die Helden, die es verdient. Michael Schumacher ist ein Held, weil er schnell um die Kurven fahren kann und keine Steuer zahlt. Armes Land."

26 "Ich glaube, meine Generation ist die Generation der Ratlosigkeit und der Umorientierung. Da kommt jetzt eine neue Generation, im Zuge der Anti-Globalisierungsbewegung—mit der ich stark sympathisiere—die neue Strategien entwickelt."

27 "*Muxmäuschenstill* ist eine Reflexion des neuen Zeitgeistes, der allgegenwärtigen Krisenstimmung. Deutschland befindet sich schon länger im gesellschaftlichen Umbruch. Doch erst, wenn es den meisten schlechter geht, fangen sie an, Fragen zu stellen. Wir sind zwar noch immer ein 'fettes' Land, aber die wirtschaftliche Euphorie der 1990er-Jahre ist längst vorbei. Geblieben ist jedoch ein moralischer Kater nach dem Höhenflug. Darauf reagieren wir mit unserem Film."

28 "Aber seit dem Fall der Mauer existiert keine Alternative mehr zu dem Gesellschaftsbild, in dem wir jetzt leben. Auch der Idealist Mux hat keine Alternativen zu bieten. Er schreibt ein Manifest und bleibt im ersten Kapitel stecken. Er wird gewalttätig und zum Psychopathen, weil ihm das Ventil der Utopie fehlt."

References

Althen, Michael. "Wildes, freies Leben: *Die fetten Jahre sind vorbei.*" *Frankfurter Allgemeine Zeitung* 24 Nov. 2004. 6 Nov. 2009 <http://www.faz.net>.

Aust, Bettina. "'Fernsehen ist Lebensersatz:' Medienkritiker Hans Weingartner." *Spiegel Online* 16 Nov. 2007 <http://www.spiegel.de>.

Borcholte, Andreas. "Anarchie und Alltag: *Die fetten Jahre sind vorbei.*" *Spiegel Online* 25 Nov. 2004. 6 Nov. 2009 <http://www.spiegel.de>.

Debord, Guy. *The Society of Spectacle*. Trans. Donald Nicholson-Smith. New York: Zone Books, 1994.

Dreßen, Wolfgang, Dieter Kunzelmann, and Eckhard Siepmann. *Das Nilpferd des höllischen Urwalds. Situationisten–Gruppe Spur–Kommune I*. Gießen: Anabas, 1991.

Egoshooter. Dir. Christian Becker and Oliver Schwabe. Reverse Angle Factory, 2004.

Die fetten Jahre sind vorbei (*The Edukators*). Dir. Hans Weingartner. Universum Film, 2004.

Filmförderungsanstalt (German Federal Film Board) <http://www.ffa.de>.

Free Rainer. Dein Fernseher lügt (*Free Rainer: Reclaim Your Brain*). Dir. Hans Weingartner. Coop99 Filmproduktion, 2007.

Frick, Ulrike. "Parolen von damals: Hans Weingartners kleiner Schlaumeier-Film." *Münchner Merkur* 24 Nov. 2004. 6 Nov. 2009 <http://www.merkur-online.de>.

Gansera, Rainer, and Fritz Göttler. "Jede Aktion ist eine positive Aktion: Hans Weingartner über Trauma und Utopie und die Prüfungen der Freundschaft in seinem neuen Film *Die fetten Jahre sind vorbei.*" *Süddeutsche Zeitung* 23 Nov. 2004. 6 Nov. 2009 <http://www.sueddeutsche.de>.

Hengst, Björn, and Philipp Wittrock. "Eklat in Niedersachsen: Linken-Abgeordnete hat Sehnsucht nach der Stasi." *Spiegel Online* 14 Feb. 2008. 6 Nov. 2009 <http://www.spiegel.de>.

Kamalzadeh, Dominik. "Revolution auf der Almhütte: Hans Weingartners *Die fetten Jahre sind vorbei* fragt nach den politischen Möglichkeiten der jüngsten Generation." *Standard* 25 Nov. 2004. 6 Nov. 2009 <http://derstandard.at>.

Kammerer, Dietmar. "'Die private Revolte ist nie privat:' Der Regisseur Hans Weingartner hofft auf eine junge Generation, die wieder Lust hat zu kämpfen. Mit seinem neuen Film *Die fetten Jahre sind vorbei* will er selbst einen Anfang machen. Ein Gespräch

über das Gefühl von Wut, poetischen Widerstand und einen vereinnahmenden Kapitalismus." *Tageszeitung* 25 Nov. 2004. 6 Nov. 2009 <http://www.taz.de>.
Klein, Naomi. *No Logo: Taking Aim at the Brand Bullies*. Toronto: Knopf Canada, 2000.
Kleist, Heinrich von. *Sämtliche Werke und Briefe*. Ed. Helmut Sembdner. Vol. 2. Munich: Hanser, 1984.
Klingenmaier, Thomas. "*Die fetten Jahre sind vorbei*: Revolte gegen den Wohlstand." *Stuttgarter Zeitung* 25 Nov. 2004. 6 Nov. 2009 <http://www.stuttgarter-zeitung.de>.
Kniebe, Tobias. "Generation Nix: Hans Weingartner ergründet die Jugend in seinem Film *Die fetten Jahre sind vorbei*." *Süddeutsche Zeitung* 24 Nov. 2004. 6 Nov. 2009 <http://www.sueddeutsche.de>.
———. "Mit Hans Weingartner in Cannes: Der Welt wird nichts erspart." *Süddeutsche Zeitung* 21 May 2004. 6 Nov. 2009 <http://www.sueddeutsche.de>.
Kohler, Michael. "Vorrecht der Jugend: Geschichte und Klassenkampf wiederholen sich als Burleske: Hans Weingartners *Die fetten Jahre sind vorbei*." *Frankfurter Rundschau* 25 Nov. 2004. 5 Nov. 2008 <http://fr-online.de>.
Kolb, Felix. "The Impact of Transnational Protest on Social Movement Organizations: Mass Media and the Making of ATTAC Germany." *Transnational Protest and Global Activism*. Ed. Donnatella della Porta and Sidney Tarrow. Lanham: Rowman and Littlefield, 2005. 95–120.
Körner, Andreas. "Provokation ist hohl: Kino-Gesprächsstoff: Marcus Mittermeier und Jan Hendrik Stahlberg zu *Muxmäuschenstill*." *Sächsische Zeitung Online* 8 July 2004. 6 Nov. 2009 <http://www.sz-online.de>.
Krippendorff, Ekkehart. "Wohlstandsgefängnis: *Die fetten Jahre sind vorbei*: Die Alt-68er, die erwachsen werden mussten in dieser Gesellschaft." *Freitag: Die Ost-West-wochenzeitung* 26 Nov. 2004. 6 Nov. 2009 <http://www.freitag.de>.
Kuhlbrodt, Dietrich. "Für alle Fälle Magerquark: Die 3 von der Wohngemeinschaft und der böse Mercedesfahrer: Hans Weingartners globalisierungskritische Digitalvideofabel *Die fetten Jahre sind vorbei* probt den poetischen Widerstand—in Berliner Villen genauso wie auf der österreichischen Alm." *Tageszeitung* 25 Nov. 2004. 6 Nov. 2009 <http://www.taz.de>.
Lasn, Kalle. *Culture Jam: How to Reverse America's Suicidal Consumer Binge—And Why We Must*. New York: HarperCollins, 2000.
Lehnartz, Sascha. "Vendetta gegen Schwimmbad-Pinkler: Um für ihren Film *Muxmäuschenstill* zu werben, haben dessen Macher im Internet zum Denunziatenum aufgerufen – mit erstaunlichem Erfolg." *Frankfurter Allgemeine Zeitung* 8 Feb. 2004. 6 Nov. 2009 <http://www.faz.net>.
Lola rennt (*Run, Lola, Run*). Dir. Tom Tykwer. X Filme Creative Pool, 1998.
The Matrix. Dirs. Andy and Larry Wachowski. Groucho II Film Partnership, 1999.
Müller, Matthias C. "*Die fetten Jahre sind vorbei*: Die Sprachnot charmanter Weltverbesserer." *Stuttgarter Nachrichten* 25 Nov. 2004. 6 Nov. 2009 <http://www.stuttgarter-nachrichten.de>.
Muxmäuschenstill (*Quiet as a Mouse*). Dir. Marcus Mittermeier. Warner Home Video, 2004.

Nicodemus, Katja. "Denn sie wissen, was sie tun: Hans Weingartners Film *Die fetten Jahre sind vorbei* sucht mit seinen Helden nach der Revolution von morgen." *Die Zeit* 25 Nov. 2004. 6 Nov. 2009 <http://www.zeit.de>.

Rentschler, Eric. "From New German Cinema to the Post-Wall Cinema of Consensus." *Cinema and Nation*. Ed. Mette Hjort and Scott Mackenzie. London: Routledge, 2000. 260–77.

Rodek, Hanns-Georg. "Ich muxe, du/er/sie muxt, wir muxen." *Die Welt* 5 July 2004. 6 Nov. 2009 <http://www.welt.de>.

———. "Man muss Stellung beziehen: Marcus Mittermeier und Jan Henrik Stahlberg über ihre Groteske *Muxmäuschenstill*." *Die Welt* 8 July 2004. 6 Nov. 2009 <http://www.welt.de>.

Rowland, Sarah. "Revolutionary Remodelling: *The Edukators* Director Hans Weingartner and Actor Daniel Brühl Explain Why Rearranging Furniture Is a Great Way to Protest." *Montreal Mirror* 28 July–3 August 2005. 6 Nov. 2009 <http://www.montrealmirror.com>.

Schwickert, Martin. "Nicht wackeln! Marcus Mittermeier und Jan Henryk Stahlberg über ihr Regie-Debut." *Ultimo auf draht* (no date). 6 Nov. 2009 <http://www.ultimo-bielefeld.de/homepage.htm>.

Stolz, Matthias. "Sind Sie in Cannes auf dem Teppich geblieben?" *Die Zeit* 30 Dec. 2004. 6 Nov. 2009 <http://www.zeit.de>.

Teune, Simon. "Humour as a Guerrilla Tactic: The West German Student Movement's Mockery of the Establishment." *International Review of Social History* 52 (2007): 115–32.

Wach, Alexandra. "Schiefe Welt, schräger Gang: Gespräch mit Marcus Mittermeier über *Muxmäuschenstill*." *Film-Dienst* 8 July 2004: 9–10.

Weingartner, Hans. *Die fetten Jahre sind vorbei. Offizielles Program im Wettbewerb Cannes 2004*. Press booklet.

———. "'Ich suche die Herausforderung:' Gespräch mit Hans Weingartner über Politik, Liebe und seinen neuen Film." Interview with Frank Arnold. *epd Film* 11 (2004): 24–25.

Wollen, Peter. "The Situationist International." *New Left Review* 174 (1989): 67–93.

Zeh, Juli. "Sixties würzig, Sixties light: *Die fetten Jahre sind vorbei*: Die Cabinet-Generation wird politisch, aber deshalb noch lange nicht erwachsen." *Freitag: Die Ost-Westwochenzeitung* 26 Nov. 2004. 6 Nov. 2009 <http://www.freitag.de>.

9
"Looking for an Old Man with a Black Moustache"
Hitler, Humour, Fake, and Forgery in *Schtonk!*

Florentine Strzelczyk

Abstract Helmut Dietl's 1992 comedy *Schtonk!* evokes Hitler's incessant presence in postwar Germany of the early 1980s and exposes the German fascination with fascism by fictionalizing the 1983 scandal around the Hitler diaries. Hitler and the Third Reich as the main objects of desire in the film remain absent, yet are also ever-present through the fetishes that the characters of the film are invested in. *Schtonk!* plays with notions of original and forged Nazi relics to point satirically to Germany's contemporary fetishization, simulation, and commodification of Third Reich history.

Hitler, Humour, Memory

From Chaplin's rendition of Hitler in *The Great Dictator* (Chaplin, 1940) to Donald Duck's in *Der Fuehrer's Face* (Kinney, 1942), laughing at Hitler has been a way to deflect and at least morally to minimize the threat that Nazism posed to the world. Yet comic relief resulting from poking fun at Nazi Germany can, depending on the political-historical circumstance, be perceived as either acceptable, or frivolous and shameful. Humour, in other words, is not a timeless concept, but closely bound to the circumstances in which it occurs. A case in point is the diametrically opposed reception accorded to the two most well-known Hollywood anti-Nazi satires, Charlie Chaplin's *The Great Dictator* and Ernst Lubitsch's *To Be or Not to Be* (1942). Both took a pre-war approach, mocking the pompous visual appearance of Third Reich officials and pageantry while at the same time claiming seriousness. Yet these works were received in diametrically opposite ways because of timing (Doherty 126). When *The Great Dictator* was released in mid-October of 1940, its humour could be received and welcomed in the United States with the uninvolved stance of a neutral bystander. *To Be or Not to Be*, on the other hand, released in March of 1942, had to face a number of historical political events such as the invasion of Russia and American retreats in the Pacific, against which the film's approach seemed outmoded and ill-suited. Widely thought of today as the more sophisticated film of the two, its wit, irony, and black humour were rejected as untimely and dangerous naïveté (Doherty 126–27). Humour, then, is produced by and limited to a certain Zeitgeist; under certain circumstances, works intended as entertainment can be received as tasteless annoyance.

For the longest time, renditions treating Hitler, the Third Reich, or the Holocaust as comedy have belonged most often to other national cinemas (*La vita è bella [Life Is Beautiful]*, Roberto Benigni, 1997; *Train de vie [Train of Life]*, Radu Mihaileanu, 1998). Making Hitler and the Nazis laughable under the dominant German discourse of *Vergangenheitsbewältigung*, the introspection into the nation's guilt and responsibility for the atrocities of the Third Reich, equalled an unspoken taboo that extends to representing Hitler on film altogether. During the postwar era, play-acting Hitler on film, comedy notwithstanding, seemed to a nation of perpetrators morally questionable, if not psychologically alarming. In fact, few German feature films between 1945 and 1990 have had leading Nazi figures in the narrative centre. Humanizing Hitler and his henchmen was considered as explaining away guilt and responsibility; explaining them "as people" facilitates explaining "away the ultimate evil inherent in their ideology and actions" (Haase 191). Another representational conundrum, identified in the 1970s and 1980s by critics such as Susan Sontag, Saul Friedländer, and Alvin Rosenfeld, lies in the reproduction and perpetuation of the seductive glamour of National Socialism's visual self-representation on film. Before 1990 there is only one feature film focusing on Hitler, G.W. Pabst's *Der letzte Akt* (*The Last Act*, 1955), and two much debated documentary-style films: Hans Jürgen Syberberg's seven-hour epic, *Hitler—ein Film aus Deutschland* (*Hitler: A Film from Germany*, 1977), and Christoph Schlingensief's *100 Jahre Adolf Hitler—die letzte Stunde im Führerbunker* (*100 Years of Adolf Hitler*, 1989), a film that is more a mockumentary in that it avoids lecturing and focuses on the absurd and surreal. The oeuvre of the recently deceased Schlingensief will certainly be re-evaluated in the next few years beyond his own description of his aesthetic program as "total irritation" (Grimes B12). To be sure, *100 Jahre Adolf Hitler*, shot in 1989 in one day, features Hitler, Braun, Göring, Goebbels, and others playing "Death in the Führer's Bunker" and celebrating Christmas. Sex and violence mingle with pettiness and juvenile games: the person who catches Hitler's moustache will be chancellor. During the premiere of the film, fights broke out in the audience; the reception of the film has been highly controversial with some critics accusing it of being an adolescent rebellious prank without depth, while others credit it with an uncanny ability to represent the banality of evil beyond the initially superficial humour that the film seems at first to encourage (Roth 29). The reception of Schlingensief's film clearly highlights the ethical and aesthetic issues at stake, both with mocking Hitler on film and presenting the German dictator on film at all (Vander Lugt).

Helmut Dietl's film comedy *Schtonk!* (*Stench*, 1992) is, in many ways, more a product of the immediate unification period than the above-mentioned production by Christoph Schlingensief. It received numerous state film prizes and was nominated for Golden Globe and American Academy Awards for best foreign film of 1992. The film was shot in 1991, and although it refers to a West German incident, the Hitler diaries, it was praised as a successful East–West collaboration. *Schtonk!* was the most elaborate German production since Wolfgang Petersen's *Das Boot* (*The Boat*, 1981), with a star cast that included Götz George, Uwe Ochsenknecht, Harald Juhnke, Veronica Ferres, and Christiane Hörbiger, but also featuring many prominent East German actors such as Ulrich Mühe, Rolf Hoppe, and Dagmar Manzel. The topic, the confrontation with the German past, i.e., the Third Reich, had little if any humorous dimension in either East or in West Germany during the postwar decades leading up to 1989. Both states attempted in very different ways to address guilt and responsibility resulting from the Third Reich, yet both considered the discourse of *Vergangenheitsbewältigung* as central to their national identity (Niven 1–9). That *Schtonk!* focuses its satirical humour less on the Nazi past itself and more on the way of approaching it, marks the film as sensitive to post-unification sensibilities: it leaves importance of the Third Reich to both countries' pasts intact and attests to the crucial role that the legacy of the Third Reich played during the first years of unified Germany. The immediate post-unification period was marked not only by increased neo-Nazi activities, but also by historic events such as the regaining of Germany's pre-war sovereignty in the "Two Plus Four Treaty" in 1990. This treaty ended all German claims on formerly German and now Polish territory, and included the decision to relocate Germany's capital back to Berlin, and recognized the successful compensation claims of Jewish victims of Nazism. The topic of *Schtonk!*—the approach to the Nazi past—was central to the forging of an all-German identity after 1990, and the fact that the film applies humour to attitudes toward the past rather than the past itself speaks to the opportunities and limits of humour in connection with the Third Reich during the immediate post-unification period.

The Film about the Book by the Führer

The comedy *Schtonk!* reveals humour about Hitler as part of a parodic-ironic play with and about German history: its facts and fictions, its originals and fakes, its presence and absence in postwar Germany of the early 1980s. *Schtonk!* restages the 1983 press scandal in which the German magazine *Stern* spent millions of dollars to acquire and then publish the infamous *Hitler Diaries*. They were shortly thereafter revealed to be a forgery. The scandal took on international dimensions as it involved *Newsweek* magazine and the *Washington Post* newspaper; both publications exploited the marketing opportunity extensively, establishing a climate of monumental expectation while they were already suspecting a sensational fraud (Haywood 45). The word *Schtonk* is an homage to Charlie Chaplin's famous comedy *The Great Dictator*, in which the dictator utters the nonsensical word several times; the film's title thus gives the first indication of the kind of humour regarding National Socialism in which the film situates itself. The word also sounds like a Southern German dialect version of *Gestank* (stench). The full title of the film, *Der Film zum Buch vom Führer: Schtonk! (The Film about the Book by the Führer: Schtonk!)*, assigns *Schtonk* the function of a commentary regarding the forged diaries. The film's ironic title teases collective German memory about the not-so-distant and embarrassing incident surrounding Hitler's assumed "book" that from the beginning reeked of forgery.

Schtonk! begins with Hitler's death. In the last days of the Third Reich, a few faithful dart around Hitler's bunker in a Berlin under siege to burn the bodies of the Führer and Eva Braun. After showing a few unsuccessful attempts to do away with the Third Reich's most prominent icon, the film switches to the immediate postwar era where self-appointed Prof. Dr. Knobel, whose voice-over commentary characterizes the first part of the film, begins his artistic career as a young boy selling the Führer's "Sonntagsmütze," complete with certificate of authenticity to numerous eager members of the American forces. Knobel then upgrades from selling to fabricating Nazi relics to feed an ever-growing appetite for things Hitler in the Federal Republic of Germany. That is when his chosen career path crosses with the one of *Stern* reporter Hermann Willié. The sleazy reporter, known both for his talent of fabricating journalistic blockbusters and for his unsavoury investigative approaches, is also an admirer of Hitler and a collector of Hitler memorabilia and paraphernalia. So when Knobel sets out to write several volumes of Hitler diaries, Willié sells them to HHpress, using his healthy profit as middleman to restore Hermann Göring's former yacht. *Schtonk!*

follows Willié and Knobel to the heights of success until the discovery of the forgeries, when Knobel flees to Switzerland, and Willié extends his pursuit of Nazi remnants to the international scene. The film's director, Helmut Dietl, tells the story of the diaries by conjuring up the context of the so-called *Hitlerwelle* of the 1970s and 1980s that resulted in a new obsession with Third Reich paraphernalia and profanities (Dönhoff 1). Tired of confronting the burdensome analysis of guilt and responsibility, the West German public turned to Hitlerabilia and spin-off products and events. *Schtonk!* successfully evokes Hitler's incessant presence in postwar Germany of the early 1980s by paradoxically playing up an absence compensated for by fetishes, forgeries, and fakes.

Despite the evidence that humour unfolds in distinct cultural contexts and environments, major theories of humour largely disregard historical specifics that influence when, how, and under which circumstances we do or do not find things funny. The superiority theory of humour can be traced back to Aristotle, whose thoughts on the nature of comedy revolve around the malicious pleasure of sorts that occurs when observing the misfortune and ignorance of others. Relief theories go back to Freud and describe humour as part of a tension-release model and focus on the psychological processes. Incongruity theories base humour on the perception of an incongruity, with Henri Bergson's essay on laughter as the most influential formulation of this theory; and play theorists consider humour a form of play, often tracing the development of humour back through evolution. While all these major theories on humour could be applied productively to a film such as *Schtonk!*, they do not advance an understanding of humour as a product of a specific cultural-political-historical situation—in the case of *Schtonk!*, the Hitler wave of the 1970s and 1980s perceived through the lens of the post-unification 1990s. The humour in *Schtonk!* is a by-product or effect of the film's mocking, mimicking, and parodying a major event in German cultural history of that era—the discovery of the Hitler diaries—as forgeries in order to reveal and critique a twofold problem: the unwieldy fascination with National Socialism despite and underneath an officially normative memory culture, and the inherent fake in all postwar representations of the Third Reich, be they documentary or feature film, as a means to get closer to the "reality" of the Third Reich.

In discussing Helmut Dietl's *Schtonk!*, rather than attempting to define humour along the lines of the established humour theories, I will examine the parodic structures and the ironic dimensions of the film's narrative. According to Linda Hutcheon, parody refers to "another work of art or form of coded discourse" as its primary aim, while satire has "the moral and social in its focus" (16). Parody mocks texts and satire critiques the social order. Parody, according to

Hutcheon, speaks doubly, first its message and second, the form it mimics (16). Postmodern parody can be considered an ironic satirical quotation and appropriation of historical contexts; it both "is and represents" the historical. By ironically quoting the historical context of the 1983 scandal around the Hitler diaries, *Schtonk!* mimics and appropriates the events to expose the extent to which the German Nazi past has become commoditized in German society of the 1980s. *Schtonk!* self-consciously plays with Hitler as a marketable fake. The film both is and represents *Vergangenheitsbewältigung* and critiques its ideological implications. *Schtonk!* quotes, affirms, re-appropriates, and unsettles the absence and presence of Hitler in postwar Germany, the original and fake historical artifacts, the love object Hitler and its substitutes, and the reality and fiction of the Third Reich, all in a parodic-satirical manner. The film offers a "contesting revision or rereading of the past that both confirms and subverts the power of the representation of history" (Hutcheon 95).

Fake & Forgery

Schtonk! begins with a flashback of Berlin during the last days of World War II. The credits roll in front of a greyish grainy screen accompanied by a radio news report, announcements, Nazi leader speeches, and the sounds of marching boots. Then Zarah Leander's popular song, "Davon geht die Welt nicht unter" ("It Isn't the End of the World"), from the 1942 feature *Die grosse Liebe* (*Great Love*, Hansen), can be heard while documentary footage from the war flashes by, depicting the German defences and the retreats from burning buildings. The upbeat, enthusiastic manner of Leander's song insisting that none of this can cause the world to end clashes with the images, which testify that it did. As Eric Rentschler highlights in his discussion of the film, there is a smooth and seamless cut from these documentary segments to feature film fiction (204). The transition is almost invisible as fiction produced in a 1990s studio mimics the documentary in style, editing, *mise en scène*, and set. In the twilight, we see uniformed figures rushing back and forth, and, as the camera draws closer, the bodies of Eva Braun and Hitler being placed into a pit to be burned. As the camera leaps to a close-up of Hitler's face, we are shown a dummy awkwardly lit to expose its artificiality and dressed to look like Chaplin's great dictator. When one of the officers carefully combs Hitler's hair and fondly removes flakes from his infamous moustache, there is no longer any doubt that we have been duped and lured to leap from fact to fiction and from past to pop (or prop). "This film about an act of forgery thus begins with its own act of forgery in which National Socialism is extended and prosthetically enhanced," argues Rentschler aptly (204). When one of the many historical newsreel sound bites announces seconds earlier that "Hitler is once again in our midst," the performance of the Hitler-dummy points ironically to the dilemma inevitably inherent in all visual re-enactments of the Third Reich: although still at the centre of German memory politics and identity, one can never see or experience the Third Reich for what it was; we will always encounter Hitler as a prop of history, a representation, a copy, or a fake. *Schtonk!*'s extraordinary leap from documentary footage to postwar studio mimicry of the Third Reich self-consciously and self-critically draws attention to both its subject—Hitler and the Hitler wave—and its own cinematic status as a doubtful and problematic representation of history and not history itself.

Eric Rentschler's argument can be taken one step further. *Schtonk!*'s play with forgery and fake at the beginning of the film invites a reading of the film as both a fake documentary and a feature film. Fake documentary, in Hutcheon's terms, "both is and represents" documentary and, according to Jesse Lerner and Alexandra Juhasz, like satire, it "both is and feigns documentary's referent, the social, political," or, as in this case, the historical. Fake documentaries "do and undo" the documentary form, the film's subject, and the moral and social orders (2). Fake documentaries reveal the documentary genre's certainties about reality and history to be formative and visible lies in that they mirror, mimic, and thereby critique the hidden fabrications and constructions of documentaries (2). *Schtonk!* targets Hitler and the way his persona has unfolded mainly in and through mediatized forms of representations (Rentschler 206). Beginning with Riefenstahl's films that pose as documentaries (while they are thoroughly mediated and stylized) to the Führer's postwar life and posthumous fame onscreen and in TV documentaries (Chow), Hitler has not just been a brand name for a product but also an industry.

Schtonk!'s posing as a fake documentary acknowledges that Hitler, to a certain extent, has always existed as a "function of media, a mediatized performance and a special effect" (Rentschler 206). The Third Reich cannot be understood by searching for "history as it had really been," as Leopold von Ranke so famously postulated for the historicism of the nineteenth century (45). *Schtonk's* documentary beginning points to the impossibility of visual media, including the documentary genre, to ever capture and reveal the reality of the Third Reich "the way it had really been." Such an endeavour is doubly fraught at the outset: film, as Saul Friedländer, Thomas Elsaesser, and others have pointed out, with its filmic conventions and effects and its libidinal investments in sex and power, is a medium susceptible to the lure of National Socialist images. Secondly, National Socialism not only transformed "the technological means by which the state reproduces its own legitimacy before individuals" (Kaplan 34), but, according to Rey Chow, it could be considered as a "form of technology" (25). Hitler, then, can be considered a cultural phenomenon, whose power and success can only unfold within technology, especially the medium of film. *Schtonk!*'s self-conscious parodic-satirical self-introduction as fake documentary draws attention to its noticeably flawed parodic-satirical performance and points to the failure of film per se to represent and explain adequately National Socialism as history, memory, or truth. *Schtonk!* parodies the thoroughly mediatized persona of Hitler to mock reality and the postwar era's Hitler wave that indulges in and fetishizes excesses and relics of National Socialism underneath the patina of *Vergangenheitsbewältigung*. In its ironic-satirical mode, the film cleverly points to the difficulties of producing knowledge about history on film, particularly about an era that has been so thoroughly mediatized, commodified, and imbued with suppressed desires and longings as the Third Reich has been.

In *Schtonk!* a crucial scene takes place just before the diaries are revealed to be forgeries. HHpress, just as the publishers group Gruner + Jahr did in 1983, holds an international press conference with fifteen camera teams and journalists from eighty-four countries. While the sequence initially replicates closely the available documentary footage of the 1983 press conference, it rapidly dereels into parody and satire: Willié holds up one volume of the diary and the crowd whistles and cheers—Hitler's presumed bequest to posterity elicits audience reactions reserved for celebrities and stars only. The absent Hitler thus radiates into the present. Willié then climbs on the desk, attempting to master the exhilarated masses as Hitler once did from above his podium; the camera circles Willie's desk in Riefenstahlian fashion. As executor of Hitler's will, Willié waves the diary in one hand, makes the sign of V for victory with the other, and bathes in the borrowed power and the media limelight of his role model, Hitler. In the course of the surreal scene captured in slow motion sequence, Willié's gestures mutate more and more into a Hitler greeting. By appropriating the Riefenstahlian manner of capturing Hitler from below, admired by the masses, *Schtonk!* grafts the fascinating performance that has become Hitler's signature image onto the representation of the 1983 press scandal around the diaries. *Schtonk!* successfully highlights that documentary is less to be understood as an expression of a pre-existing genre and more as a set of performative actions or movements that produce the genre of documentary as an effect (Lerner and Juhasz 7). *Schtonk!* then apes the iconic conventions of this other textual system while simultaneously marking it with doubleness (9).

The most poignant marker of this doubleness is the play with the presence and absence of Hitler in the postwar societal setting of the film. Except for the beginning of the film that dupes the audience's expectation to see a realistic representation of Hitler on film "as he had really been" or might have been, Hitler is absent. Throughout the film, however, the absent Hitler is ubiquitously present in a number of parodic mutations, similarities, and identifications that push and play with the notion of fake, copy, imitation, caricature, and counterfeit. Willié sports a moustache and Hitler's hairdo; Knobel, in the course of forging the diaries, turns more and more into Hitler, adopting Hitler's speaking style, while complaining that he does not know anymore who he is. He starts wearing an old army coat, and with a Hitler moustache made with smeared ink on his upper lip, he repeats phrases from the diaries he forged, admitting that he now masters Hitler's handwriting better than his own. *Schtonk!*'s initial posing as a documentary not only undoes the documentary as a cinematic form by questioning the genre's ability to deliver historical truth; the film also critiques the genre known as period piece or history film. According to Lerner and Juhasz, any fake documentary is "at least in part" also a "fiction film" (8). In fact, it is received as "more than a fiction film plus a documentary" with the "two systems referring to and altering the other's reception" (9). While *Schtonk!* starts out as a documentary it falls, as the film progresses, more and more into fiction film mode with less references to the actual events of 1983 and with more techniques to suture the audience into the fictional universe of HHpress and the emotional hyperbolic world of the forger Knobel and the yellow press reporter Willié.

Schtonk!'s play with and circulation of "Hitlerabilia" reads like a film scripted by Jacques Derrida and produced by Jean Baudrillard. If parody refers to "another work of art or form of coded discourse" as its primary target (Hutcheon 16), *Schtonk!* derives its irony and parody not just from staging the presence and absence of Hitler in postwar Germany, but also from the playful unsettling of our normative expectations about original and copy. Jacques Derrida spent a significant part of his life thinking about the undoing of dominant oppositions in Western thought: speech/writing, inside/outside, and original/copy, to name a few. The interplay and contradictions between original and copy are particularly intriguing in *Schtonk!* Derrida asserts that a truly perfect imitation can only be an original, hence "a perfect imitation is never an imitation" for imitation "affirms and sharpens its essence in effacing itself" (*Dissemination* 139). Much like a signature, an original is supposed to be unique, yet, much like a signature, it gains validity foremost through the act of repeating it. The signature is a prime example of the reproducibility of a singular "pure" event (Derrida *Margins* 328–29). Copies, if deconstructed, are not inferior to the original; they could be considered as central in giving meaning to originals. To copy cell for cell or word by word, then, could be considered an act of creation (Groom 22). Walter Benjamin in his 1936 essay, "The Work of Art in the Age of Its Technological Reproducibility," and Judith Butler in her influential 1990 *Gender Trouble*, among others, have sought to rethink the relationship between copy and original: the parodic repetition of an "original reveals the original to be nothing other than the parody of the idea of the original" (Butler 22). What fuels *Schtonk!*'s parodic irony is not so much the scandal about forged artifacts that are being sold as originals, but the fact that their value for a market hungry for Hitler memorabilia lies precisely in what Derrida called the "accurate repetition" of the copy (*Dissemination* 139). The forgeries that the film shows as circulating en masse in German society are imitations of originals that only exist as ideas or conceptions about what the public perceives the Third Reich to have been about; they gain their validity or "market value" through their reproducibility as proof for historical events. Once Knobel realizes that his first volumes of Hitler diaries are in fact validated by market demand, he does not just repeat the act and produce sixty-two volumes, but he also forges other historical artifacts and memorabilia. Rentschler thinks of Knobel as "the embodiment of the free market economy that satisfies the consumer appetite for Führer-related artifacts" (205), but he can also be thought of as the master of simulacra, the resourceful creator of copies that do not have originals, but only imitate, mimic, and counterfeit the idea of an original. The parody lies in the audience witnessing the clumsy process of forging and faking, whereas the clients of Knobel do not want to read the textual signs of forgery, or they buy into it because of expected profit. *Schtonk!* thus initiates a chain of meanings that defer the meaning of original (or an original Hitler) to copy, plagiarism, imitation, counterfeit, mimesis, and forgery. From today's perspective *Schtonk!* seems to foreshadow, albeit anachronistically, the current debate about Germany's status as a nation of victims or perpetrators which, in their extreme forms, point to the constructedness of these positions that seem to prevent rather than facilitate access to and understanding of the "real/original" German past.

As his first major act of forgery, Knobel delivers a portrait of a naked Eva Braun in front of a pastoral mountain idyll to a collector of Nazi memorabilia. Previously we had witnessed Knobel's desperate search for a muse that would supply the naked body for Eva Braun's face on the canvas. Knobel's bricolage, from historical photos of Eva Braun and the handmaid Martha's body, parodies and questions the creative process that results in originals. The finished portrait is an imaginary original in the double sense that we know that it is patchwork, but also in the more fundamental sense that painting as an art form is always already a representation or imitation of nature (Derrida *Dissemination* 138). Yet Knobel's bricolage of Eva Braun is recognized by a known art expert, Strasser, as "absolutely most authentic Hitler." Strasser insists that he himself was an eyewitness to the creation of the painting and indicates precise date and time. Strasser invents a romantic setting: "I was a summer guest at the Berghof. It was a beautiful summer day, the 7th of July, 1939, in the afternoon, it must have been around five. I was walking through the vast meadow, through the cornflowers behind the Berghof and suddenly there he stood and painted her—as God created her." Strasser's fictional endorsement is excessive; he claims to have not just witnessed Hitler painting Eva, but also gazed at Eva's nude body as she was being painted. Strasser's narrative functions as a copy of Knobel's copy that both imitates and entices the fantasies of the collectors of Hitlerabilia. Strasser's authentication gives Knobel not only the idea to create more Hitlerabilia, but also highlights the possibility of circulating expert advice the way that the forgeries circulate in the marketplace, with one endorsing the other. When Knobel's diaries finally have to undergo authentication themselves, his copies are compared to other copies by his hand. One copy confirms the other; they have become copies without originals—simulacra, in other words.

Here Jean Baudrillard's thinking proves productive for the discussion of the film. Baudrillard argues that the obsessive re-creation of Nazism marks a simulation of history that is more and more characterized by the decline of referentiality. History is transformed into what Baudrillard calls the hyperreal, where history is merely simulated, fetishized and re-enacted onscreen within new and traditional media. With our Western societies' move into the simulated worlds of the hyperreal, history has become our lost referential, the last great myth that particularly the cinema pursues with a vengeance (*Simulacra and Simulations* 43). In "perfect remakes" and "extraordinary montages," contemporary film simulates history (44–45). In *Schtonk!* the fetishization of history, i.e., the desire for Hitler memorabilia, culminates in a hyperreality in which copies or forgeries without originals simulate history during the Nazi era "as it had really been" without getting any closer to this most enigmatic of historical eras. In this context, Nazism can be understood as a simulacrum of its own kind. Baudrillard defines a simulacrum as a system of signs that no longer bears any relation to reality; it is an image that has become its own world of self-referential signs (*Selected Writings* 170). In the case of the Third Reich, the real and its representation form a curious relationship in which the Third Reich as real history is vanishing continuously, while its images refer less and less to history and more to a history of images. In fact, they have initiated a fantastic tradition in their own right as *Schtonk!*'s quotations of and allusions to Third Reich newsreels, Riefenstahl's signature shots, and Hitler's iconic looks illustrate.

Fetish and Fake

In *Schtonk!*, Nazi simulacra create desire and take on fetish functions for the different characters of the film. According to Freud, fetishism is a category ascribed to those (men) who develop erotic attachments to objects rather than to people, and who seek sexual gratification with and through that object. The act involves not only finding a substitute object, but also a subsequent act of forgetting the act of substitution. Alexander and Margarete Mitscherlich, in their 1967 *Die Unfähigkeit zu trauern* (The Inability to Mourn), argued that under National Socialism, Hitler became a projection of an individual's ideal-ego that turned Hitler into a narcissistic love object. The loss of this ideal-ego, they argue, caused postwar Germany's suffering—attempting to avoid the pain of melancholia stemming from the Hitler's death and the collapse of National Socialism had negative psychological effects. They observed how Germany changed into a nation that was apolitical and conservative, in which "the restoration of the economy has been the average German's pet concern" (9). *Schtonk!* presents Germany of the 1980s as a space in which the former love for Hitler has been displaced onto fetish objects that are not only equally gratifying for the characters in the film, but that also allow for a highly lucrative alliance between fetish and economic gain that fuels Hitler's commodification into marketable desire. The Führer's hat, his painting of naked Eva Braun, his diary entries about flatulence and bad breath, Göring's bathrobe and his sunken and then restored yacht, silver spoons embossed with Third Reich insignia, even Hitler's niece, Freya von Hepp, everything and everyone who has been touched by the Führer and is connected to his era has the power to arouse sexually, provoke love and allegiance, give the illusion of authority, raise social status or, most profanely, make money.

Having succumbed to one of the many conspiracy theories about Hitler still being alive, Willié, in the final sequences of the film, steers Göring's now restored yacht, *Carin II*, out of Hamburg harbour, consulting a dictionary of European languages as he prepares for his search abroad. Practising first his Spanish, then his English, he stutters, "Hello, my name is Willié, I am looking for a man with a brown moustache," thereby perpetuating and accentuating the film's play with Hitler's omnipresence through fetish objects, the fetishization of the history of the Third Reich, and the indeterminacy of the real Hitler and his simulations in postwar restaging and re-enactments. Just as the beginning of the film parodies the way postwar Germans stage the fantasy of the Third Reich, the ending of the film in its original movie version has reality and film fiction interfere with each other. On the altered TV/DVD version, the film ends as the harbour police accompany the *Carin II* out of Hamburg harbour. The original movie version has an officer of the harbour police board Willié's yacht. The officer was played by Gert Heidemann, the *Stern* reporter who had discovered and acquired the Hitler diaries for *Stern* magazine, and on whom the character of Willié was modelled in the film. The authentic/real Heidemann puts an end to the filmic farce by ironically impersonating law and order and stopping the fictitious Heidemann alias Willié in his criminal tracks. While the blatant and rather unsophisticated conflation of reality and film fiction might have accounted for the decision to alter the ending for the TV version, the original version perpetuates the interrogation of the nexus between history and its representation and between the authentic and fake.

Conclusion

From its post-unification vantage point, *Schtonk!* takes leave of postwar attempts to define, understand, and preserve the Third Reich "as it had really been." *Schtonk!*'s parody of imagined originals, of the 1983 scandal surrounding the Hitler diaries, is an ironic and humorous departure not only from World War II as the last grand narrative of our time, but also from the grand narrative of German responsibility for the memory of the Third Reich. Not by accident does the ending of the film point to the continuous circulation of Hitlerabilia in other places: North America, South America, Europe. *Schtonk!* situates itself comfortably within postmodern and post-histoire discourses concerning the loss of grand narratives, the indeterminacy of history and its increasing commodification. This discourse has certainly become more intense over the decade and a half that lies between 1992 and the present day.

Contemporary Germany has been characterized by the emergence of a number of new competing narratives and discourses about the past. These are played out in the public sphere, on the Internet, but also in literature and cinema. They are related to a sharply perceived shift in the way memory, specifically the memory of and the attitude toward the National Socialist past, is debated in post-unification culture, and the way this shift has had an impact on theoretical discussions and concepts of memory. When addressing the German discourse of memory, Anne Fuchs, for example, highlights that memory debates since 1968 into the late 1980s were marked by what she calls the fetishization of trauma. Fuchs argues that this both public and academic focus on trauma and repression of guilt (most famously expressed in Alexander and Margarete Mitscherlich's *Die Unfähigkeit zu trauern* [1967] and applied to films from the 1980s in Eric Santner's *Stranded Objects* [1990]) should also be looked at from a generational perspective. According to Aleida Assmann, the current trend in German culture to revisit German suffering during and after World War II can be explained as a form of "memory contests," which offers a complex understanding of the structure of memory involving different classes and generations. Assmann asserts that this new social frame regarding memory allows room for "new conflicts about symbols, concepts, representations, and the normative value of memories" (199). These new and recent memory contests negotiate, as

Assmann stresses, new spaces for social memory and help shape national memory in more complex ways. These larger trends and debates regarding the reconstruction of the National Socialist past also account for the changing representation of National Socialism's central figure, Hitler, and the modes in which these representations take shape.

While some recent German films (such as Oliver Hirschbiegel's much debated feature *Der Untergang [Downfall]*, 2004) have broken not only the unspoken taboo against representing Hitler and focused more on Germans as victims, others have also explored the connection between Hitler and humour, and should be considered a function of the current re-mapping of the parameters of social change in the discourse of German memory as discussed above. Films other than *Schtonk!* such as *Goebbels und Geduldig* (Kai Wessel, 2001), *Speer und er* (*Speer and Hitler: The Devil's Architect*, Heinrich Breloer, 2005) or *Mein Führer—Die wirklich wahrste Wahrheit über Adolf Hitler* (*Mein Führer: The Truly Truest Truth about Adolf Hitler*, Dani Levy, 2007) also show Hitler, his henchmen, or the Third Reich as laughable, shrinking their towering dimensions down to human proportions. While the small number of such films, compared to the majority of dramatic representations of the National Socialist past in feature film period pieces, does not entirely warrant discussing them as part of an emerging trend in the comedic genre, the issues concerning the presentation of Hitler on film and the connection between humour and the Third Reich in general, have found other alternate outlets that are, by many, still considered irreverent.

Most notable are comics, cabaret, and Internet environments in which the humorous engagement with visual representations of the Third Reich takes place. Walter Moers, a bestselling German comic-book author, published a two-part comic, *Adolf*, in 1998 and 1999 respectively, in which Moers infamously does away with Hitler's and, by extension, German guilt. "Dann verjährt endlich seine Schuld...," the first panel announces laconically. Moers, unperturbed by the etiquette of the politically correct, shows Adolf pondering which strategy might have secured him military victory. Equally infamous and irreverent toward the discourse of *Vergangenheitsbewältigung* is Moers's animation short, *Der Bonker (The Bunker)*, which accompanied the 2005 cartoon publication of the same name in which Adolf can be seen in the bathtub with Blondie lamenting his situation. *Der Bonker* achieved cult status on YouTube, presently the Internet's most popular site for sharing video clips. On YouTube, humour about Hitler and the Third Reich is a common feature, in such videos as "Heil Hitler, das Schwein ist tot" ("Heil Hitler, the pig is dead"), a well-known satirical narrative that also exists in different versions targeting other political leaders such as G.W. Bush. The Moers video was also screened on the ZDF (one of Germany's two state-sponsored TV stations) cultural magazine *Aspekte* in July 2006, reaching around 800,000 viewers ("Netz schlägt TV" 95), yet its Internet presence in popular German and international video portals can be estimated to be around five to six million. In Germany, readings by Serdar Somuncu, a German of Turkish origin, have become popular. Since 1996 Somuncu has toured Europe reading excerpts from Hitler's *Mein Kampf* that turn into spectacular performances unmasking racial hatred and hollow propaganda.

The heated discussion about Moers's music video, *Der Bonker* (Melzer 37) and other alternative forms of humour is not always a laughing matter. Perceiving Moers's Adolf as hilarious depends on generation, ethnic origin, education, political leaning, and cultural/national background, and on a preferred medium, which is perceived as best for receiving humour. While humour about Hitler takes place mainly in a visual domain, feature films only present a small part of a much larger production that unfolds mainly in live performances and video concoctions in alternative media. What these different forms, including film, have in common, however, is that they forge new spaces and generational outlets for alternative ways of addressing the German past beyond the stifling discourses of either guilt or victimhood.

References

100 Jahre Adolf Hitler—die letzte Stunde im Führerbunker. Dir. Christoph Schlingensief. DEM, 1989.
Assmann, Aleida. "On the (In)Compatibility of Guilt and Suffering in German Memory." *German Life and Letters* 59.2 (2006): 187–200.
Baudrillard, Jean. *Selected Writings*. Ed. Mark Poster. Stanford: Stanford UP, 1988.
———. *Simulacra and Simulations*. Trans. Sheila Faria Glaser. Ann Arbour: U of Michigan P, 1994.
Benjamin, Walter. *The Work of Art in the Age of Its Technological Reproducibility, and Other Writings on Media*. Cambridge: Belknap Press of Harvard UP, 2008.
Butler, Judith. *Gender Trouble*. New York: Routledge, 1990.
Chow, Rey. "The Fascist Longings in Our Midst." *Ariel* 26.1 (1995): 23–50.
Derrida, Jacques. *Dissemination*. Trans. Barbara Johnson. Chicago: U of Chicago P, 1981.
———. *Margins of Philosophy*. Trans. Alan Bass. Chicago: U of Chicago P, 1982.
Doherty, Thomas. *Projections of War: Hollywood, American Culture, and World War II*. New York: Columbia UP, 1993.
Dönhoff, Marion Gräfin. "Was bedeutet die Hitlerwelle?" *Die Zeit* 2 September 1977: 1.
Elsaesser, Thomas. "Subject Positions, Speaking Positions: From *Holocaust, Our Hitler*, and *Heimat* to *Shoah* and *Schindler's List*." *The Persistence of History: Cinema, Television and the Modern Event*. Ed. Vivian Sobchack. New York: Routledge, 1996. 145–83.

Freud, Sigmund. *Three Essays on the Theory of Sexuality*. 4th ed. Trans. James Strachey. New York: Basic Books, 1975.
Friedländer, Saul. *Reflections of Nazism. An Essay on Kitsch and Death*. 1982. Trans. Thomas Weyr. Bloomington: Indiana UP, 1993.
Fuchs, Anne. "From 'Vergangenheitsbewältigung' to Generational Memory Contests in Günter Grass, Monika Maron and Uwe Timm." *German Life and Letters* 59.2 (2006): 169–86.
Der Fuehrer's Face. Dir. Jack Kinney. RKO Radio Pictures, 1942.
Goebbels und Geduldig. Dir. Kai Wessel. SWR, 2001.
The Great Dictator. Dir. Charles Chaplin. United Artists, 1940.
Grimes, William. "Christoph Schlingensief, Artistic Provocateur, Dies at 49." *New York Times*, 26 August 2010: B12.
Die Grosse Liebe. Dir. Rolf Hansen. Black Hill Pictures, 1942.
Groom, Nick. *The Forger's Shadow: How Forgery Changed the Course of Literature*. London: Picador, 2002.
Haase, Christine. "Ready for Close-up? Representing Hitler in *Der Untergang* (Downfall, 2004)." *Studies in European Cinema* 3.3 (2006): 189–99.
Haywood, Ian. *Faking It: Art and the Politics of Forgery*. New York: St. Martin's, 1987.
Hitler—ein Film aus Deutschland. Dir. Hans Jürgen Syberberg. Omni Zoetrope, 1977.
Hitler, Adolf. *Mein Kampf*. Trans. Ralph Manheim. London: Hutchinson, 1974.
Hutcheon, Linda. *A Theory of Parody*. London: Methuen, 1985.
Kaplan, Alice Yaeger. *Reproduction of Banality: Fascism, Literature and French Intellectual Life*. Minneapolis: U of Minnesota P, 1986.
Lerner, Jesse, and Alexandra Juhasz. "Introduction: Phony Definitions and Troubling Taxonomies of the Fake Documentary." *F Is for Phony: Fake Documentary and Truth's Undoing*. Minneapolis: U of Minnesota P, 2006.
Der letzte Akt. Dir. G.W. Pabst. Columbia Film, 1955.
Mein Führer—Die wirklich wahrste Wahrheit über Adolf Hitler. Dir. Daniel Levy. X-Filme Creative Pool, 2007.
Melzer, Chris. "Walter Moers: Hitler-Satire sorgt für Wirbel." *Stern* 18 September 2006: 37.
Moers, Walter. *Adolf: Äch bin wieder da!!* Frankfurt am Main: Eichborn, 1998.
———. *Adolf 2: Äch bin schon wieder da!* Frankfurt am Main: Eichborn, 1999.
———. *Adolf: Der Bonker*. München: Piper, 2005.
Mitscherlich, Alexander and Margarete. *Die Unfähigkeit zu trauern. Grundlagen kollektiven Verhaltens*. Munich: Piper, 1967.
"Netz schlägt TV." *Spiegel* 2 October 2006: 95.
Niven, Bill. *Facing the Nazi Past: United Germany and the Legacy of the Third Reich*. London: Routledge, 2002.
Ranke, Leopold von. *Geschichte der romanischen und germanischen Völker von 1494 bis 1514*. Vol. 1. Leipzig: Georg Reimer, 1824.

Rentschler, Eric. "The Fascination of a Fake—The Hitler Diaries." *Cultures of Forgery: Making Nations, Making Selves*. New York: Routledge, 2003. 199–212.
Rosenfeld, Alvin H. *Imagining Hitler*. Bloomington: Indiana UP, 1985.
Roth, Wilhelm. "100 Jahre Adolf Hitler—Die letzte Stunde im Führerbunker." *epd Film* (August 1989): 29–44.
Santner, Eric L. *Stranded Object: Mourning, Memory and Film in Post-war Germany*. Ithaca: Cornell UP, 1990.
Schtonk! Dir. Helmut Dietl. Constantin Film, 1992.
Sontag, Susan. *Under the Sign of Saturn*. New York: Farrar, Straus and Giroux, 2002.
Speer und er. Dir. Heinrich Breloer. WDR, 2005.
To Be or Not to Be. Dir. Ernst Lubitsch. United Artists, 1942.
Train de vie. Dir. Radu Mihaileanu. AB International Distribution, 1998.
Der Untergang. Dir. Oliver Hirschbiegel. Constantin Film, 2004.
Vander Lugt, Kristin T. "An Obscene Reckoning: History and Memory in Schlingensief's *Deutschlandtrilogie*." *Christoph Schlingensief: Art Without Borders*. Ed. Tara Forrest and Anna Teresa Scheer. Chicago: U of Chicago P, 2010. 39–56.
La vita è bella. Dir. Roberto Benigni. Ascot Elite Entertainment, 1997.

10
Haha Hitler!
Coming to Terms with Dani Levy

Peter Gölz

Abstract While Dani Levy's *Mein Führer—Die wirklich wahrste Wahrheit über Adolf Hitler (Mein Führer—The Truly Truest Truth about Adolf Hitler*, 2007) continues the tradition of Hitler comedies such as *The Great Dictator*, it is the first feature comedy made in Germany that pokes fun at the Nazi dictator. The degree to which the film either succeeds or fails as a comedy will be discussed in this chapter. While representations of Hitler humour in other media remain acceptable to the broader audience, this feature film challenges the notions of what constitutes "acceptable" *Vergangenheitsbewältigung* in Germany.

At the beginning of the twenty-first century, the previous century's most notorious dictator has become a Web phenomenon and laughing stock. The *Deutsche Welle* reports: "Move over Paris Hilton—Hitler is the hottest thing on Web 2.0" (Chase). *Maclean's* magazine tells us that "Hitler comedy is in" and declares: "If Hitler comedy is starting to become popular in Germany, it's absolutely thriving in other parts of the world" (Weinman 51). The author describes its various guises, from the musical and movies *The Producers*, also known by the title *Springtime for Hitler*, to Hitler-themed episodes of *The Simpsons* and *Family Guy*,[1] from innumerable YouTube postings to the self-explanatory website catsthatlooklikehitler.com.

While comedic treatments of Hitler and his surroundings are becoming more acceptable outside Germany, *Vergangenheitsbewältigung* made in Germany still evokes strong reactions. The production of Dani Levy's *Mein Führer—Die wirklich wahrste Wahrheit über Adolf Hitler* had barely begun when heated discussions about its appropriateness flared up, and they have not stopped since. While German cinema has a long and internationally respected tradition of *Vergangenheitsbewältigung*, coming to terms, coping, or dealing with its Nazi past, no major German filmmaker had yet approached the topic as a comedy. Many questioned its suitability, others welcomed the fact that laughing about Hitler might actually dethrone him and "rob him of the metaphysical, demonic capabilities that the postwar apologists attributed to him" (Herzog qtd. in Weinman 51). Dani Levy defended his project by stressing that a fresh look at the past, not endless repetition of what we know, was needed ("Director's Point" 209). Helge Schneider, the famous German comedian who plays Adolf Hitler, stressed that as a genre, comedy was more subversive than tragedy (Schneider).

To understand the debate surrounding *Mein Führer*, however, it will be necessary to place this film within the historical context of presenting Hitler as a comedic figure. The term "Hitler humour" will thus be applied to humorous depictions of Adolf Hitler as a person, his politics, and his immediate surroundings. The musical and films *The Producers*, for example, would not fall in this category because, although they include a ridiculed Hitler character, the overall focus is not on ridiculing the Nazis and their ideology but on skewering Broadway, and, by implication, Hollywood commercialism.

Making fun of Adolf Hitler is, of course, not a recent invention. Rudolph Herzog showed in his documentary *Heil Hitler, das Schwein ist tot!* (*Heil Hitler, The Pig Is Dead!*, 2006), released first as a monograph in 2006 and followed by a TV documentary, how widespread Hitler jokes already were in the dictator's lifetime. Of the many reported cases from the 1940s, one of the most famous was that of Marianne Elise K., who was reported to the authorities and sentenced to death in 1943 for telling the following joke: "Hitler and Goering stand atop the Berlin radio tower. Hitler says he would love to please the people of the city. What to do? To which Goering replies: 'Go ahead, jump!'" (Herzog 186).

But while telling *Flüsterwitze* (whispered jokes) about Hitler in Nazi Germany was punishable by imprisonment in a concentration camp or death, to laugh or not to laugh about Hitler was never a question in Hollywood. A milestone in film history and the first feature-length Hitler comedy, Charlie Chaplin's 1940 *The Great Dictator* presents a crazy Adenoid Hynkel ballet dancing with a globe. This film, Chaplin's first talkie and his biggest commercial success, appeared in the same year as the Three Stooges' slapstick short *You Natzy Spy*. Two years later, the exiled Ernst Lubitsch released *To Be or Not to Be*, and Walt Disney followed with the Donald Duck cartoon *Der Fuehrer's Face*. American audiences enjoyed these films, Lubitsch explained, not "because they underestimate [the Nazis'] menace, but because they are happy to see this new order and its ideology ridiculed" (Paul 243).

Making fun of Hitler and the Nazis in America in the 1940s was, of course, untainted by subsequent historical developments. As Sander Gilman explains, these comedies were popular exactly because they "historically pre-figure[d] the Shoah" (287). When Chaplin was asked about his portrayal of Hynkel twenty years later, he said that "had I known of the actual horrors of the German concentration camps, I could not have made *The Great Dictator*; I could not have made fun of the homicidal insanity of the Nazis" (qtd. in Gilman 287).

It is interesting to note that Chaplin does not distinguish between his Hynkel/Hitler character, Nazi atrocities, and the Holocaust. The conflation of all three paved the way for the serious treatment of the so-called Third Reich in postwar film productions. The marginalization of the comedy genre led to widely accepted and internalized codes, which deemed any other depictions inappropriate. This "Holocaust-Veritas" school (Laster and Steinert 193), with its "Holocaust etiquette" (Des Pres 218), was based on the following assumptions and regulations:

1. The Holocaust shall be represented, in its totality, as a unique event, as a special case and kingdom of its own, above or below or apart from history.
2. Representations of the Holocaust shall be as accurate and faithful as possible to the facts and conditions of the event, without change or manipulation for any reason—artistic reasons included.
3. The Holocaust shall be approached as a solemn or even a sacred event, with a seriousness admitting no response that might obscure its enormity or dishonour its dead. (Des Pres 217)

Such a fact-driven, mimetic, and solemn approach, however, only allowed for an oscillation of cinematic representations situated somewhere between Claude Lanzmann's *Shoah* and Steven Spielberg's *Schindler's List*. This began to change with the international success of Art Spiegelman's graphic novels *Maus I* and *Maus II* for which the author received the Pulitzer Prize Special Award in 1992. Roberto Benigni's *Life Is Beautiful* presented a similar challenge to "Holocaust etiquette," when it was released in 1997. The film also won numerous awards, among them the Cannes Grand Jury Prize, the Jerusalem Film Festival Award, and, in 1999, three Academy Awards. This trend continued with the release of other films, for example, *Train de vie* (*Train of Life*, 1998) by director Radu Mihaileanu and the new version of *Jakob the Liar* (1999), directed by Peter Kassovitz.[2]

In *Laughing about Hitler*, Kathy Laster and Heinz Steinert added two conditions to Des Pres's list to explain the intense reactions to Benigni's film, which are central for the present discussions surrounding *Mein Führer*. They concluded that to be widely accepted and to be taken seriously, representations of Hitler and the Holocaust had to be part of what was perceived as high culture. "Popular cultural products are automatically suspect and considered less important. Comedies mostly appeal to audiences that are not necessarily highly educated, and, therefore, they are less likely to be considered 'high culture'"[3] (Laster and Steinert 186). And, if artists were involved in such art forms, they had to show at least "an appropriate motivation and attitude: altruism, best intentions, the right moral and educational goals. Even if the product belongs to the comedic genre, the artist should demonstrate appropriate levels of seriousness"[4] (190).

The fundamental binary oppositions of high and low culture, tragedy and comedy, seriousness and fun, factual mimetic representations and artistic play explain the limits of Holocaust etiquette and decorum. In light of the growing impact of postmodernism in the final decades of the last century, however, it comes as no surprise that such censoring dichotomies were bound to be questioned sooner rather than later. With the ubiquitous proliferation of information access, new media, and popular culture studies, internalized self-censoring did not remain unchallenged. The German film *Schtonk!* (1992), for example, managed to popularize the discussion and to allow a non-serious treatment of *Vergangenheitsbewältigung* by separating Hitler and the Holocaust, and more so, by focusing on the media mania surrounding the supposed discovery of Hitler's diaries and the ensuing commercial frenzy around the Hitler persona and its ridiculed followers.[5]

Challenging not only how the past is presented but also how present audiences interact with the post-memory (Hirsch) of perceived correct or appropriate depictions, all representations are thus based on a "transfixed 'code'" (Lentin 1), which is always fictitious. As such, all "staged reality,"[6] a term repeatedly used by Goebbels in *Mein Führer*, points to (cinematic) historic representations as mediations of questionable and ultimately unattainable aspirations. Levy clearly questions and distances himself from cinematic attempts to achieve historic authenticity: "*Mein Führer* is not about historical facts, but about staged reality"[7] (qtd. in Westphal). A true mimesis can never be presented and is at best a common agreement on pre-established values and codes. The title of Levy's film, *Mein Führer: The Truly Truest Truth about Adolf Hitler*, exemplifies and ridicules this Veritas aspect and also points to the popular and populist Hitler humour that has attracted broad audiences throughout Germany in recent years.

Walter Moers, for example, published the comic book *Adolf, Äch bin wieder da!!*, based on the character first introduced in his comic *Adolf, die Nazisau* (Adolf, the Nazi Pig), which sold 170,000 copies in Germany (Herzog 251) in the late 1990s. The 2005 follow-up, *Der Bonker*, was not only another success as a comic but also resulted in the cult video *Adolf, You Nazi Pig—I Cower in My Bunker*.[8] Many German top comedians have performed Hitler jokes; for example, "Little Hitler" showed up in the German comedy sketch show *Bullyparade*, the comedy series *Zack* had numerous Hitler skits, and the ever-popular Harald Schmidt presented a *Downfall* spoof. The Norddeutscher Rundfunk broadcasts the *Neueste Nationale Nachrichten* as part of *Extra3*, in which an angry Hitler screams at members of the Nationaldemokratische Partei Deutschlands members and makes fun of them.[9] This shrinking-down-to-size (*"Schrumpfkur"*), as Brauer called it in *Der Spiegel*, was supposed not only to ridicule and shrink Hitler and his past followers down to size, but even more so the present neo-Nazis.

While these are all examples from German television, Hitler humour on the Web is even wider spread. The search term "Adolf Hitler" on YouTube lists 106,000 hits (of which many are pro-Hitler), while the term "Hitler" results in 290,000 (most of which are spoofs).[10] The most popular of these parodies are famous scenes with new subtitles, such as the many clips from Hirschbiegel's *Der Untergang*, now called "Hitler reacts to Canucks missing playoffs," "Somebody stole Hitler's car," "Hitler: Vista Problems," "Linux vs Windows," etc. There are also many Hitler clips with new sound tracks, from Village People's "YMCA" to the Black Eyed Peas.

The most famous YouTube clip, however, is by the German film student Florian Wittmann, who took a scene from *Triumph of the Will* and added a routine by Bavarian comedian Gerhard Polt, in which he bitterly complains about the leasing contract with his car dealer. Harald Martenstein reports Henryk M. Broder's claim that a short video like this one about the leasing contract might actually tell us more about Hitler than some anti-fascist features. The *Deutsche Welle* even advised its readers to "forget the new film *Mein Führer*. The most successful Hitler parody on film is a short in which Adolf moans about a dishonest car salesman. It has attracted more than half a million hits on YouTube" (Chase).[11] Actually, while there are various postings of this clip, one posting by ddrdieter alone has attracted millions of views and thousands of comments.[12]

Preceding the present wave of Hitler humour on the Web, Serdar Somuncu has been touring the German Republic since the mid-1990s with highly provocative cabaret and stand-up performances. His readings from and comments on *Mein Kampf* have been very successful. At the beginning of the program, he asks the audience if one should laugh about Hitler. "No!" is his answer, "but," he adds, "one just can't help it." And then he shows the power of humour dethroning if not deconstructing Hitler the seducer [*Ver-führer*]. But neither

Somuncu's tours nor the YouTube postings have caused an international debate like the release of Dani Levy's *Mein Führer*. The intense reactions to Levy's film can be explained in terms of the continuing high–low dichotomy of cultural production—cartoons, YouTube videos, or TV sketches do not cause the same stir as a feature film.

Dani Levy gave many interviews before and after *Mein Führer*'s release. He places himself within the Hitler humour tradition by thanking Roberto Benigni in the credits, and by stating that he would like to continue where Chaplin and Lubitsch had left off: "I am happy to continue their tradition. It is no coincidence that I consider Charlie Chaplin and Ernst Lubitsch as my intellectual fathers"[13] ("Brief" 177). The real impetus, however, to make *Mein Führer* did not come from any classic comedies. Rather, an intense reaction to Oliver Hirschbiegel's *Der Untergang* (*Downfall*, 2004), the first German film that humanized the monster motivated Levy to make his film. Hirschbiegel's Oscar-nominated feature conservatively and traditionally followed the Holocaust-Veritas etiquette by emphasizing historical verisimilitude, but at the same time challenged it by presenting Hitler the private person rather than the public persona. While this fuelled many national and international discussions, for Dani Levy it was the film's "forced seriousness"[14] and its attempt to be merely authentic that provoked and inspired him to counter with something "small, quick, rude, and politically incorrect."[15]

Der Untergang was such an important influence on *Mein Führer* that one critic claimed Helge Schneider's Hitler was really a response to the earlier film. "Levy does not satirize the Holocaust, but its reduction in media representations. It is no coincidence that this was only possible after someone else had broken this taboo—through the humanizing portrayal of Hitler in *Der Untergang*. Eichinger's production is the target of Levy's attack. Helge Schneider does not parody Hitler, but Bruno Ganz playing Hitler"[16] (Kothenschulte). The other main inspiration Levy mentions is the Swiss psychoanalyst Alice Miller's *Am Anfang war Erziehung* (*For Your Own Good*) in which she describes Hitler's childhood abuse by his father as the explanation for his later behaviour. These two main intertexts are complemented by the story of Paul Devrient, Hitler's acting and speech coach who travelled with him in 1932 and who inspired Bertolt Brecht's *Arturo Ui* (Zander), and the comedian Fritz Grünbaum, who lost his life in Dachau and was known for his *Doppelconférence* act, playing around with the dialectics of master and servant (Rotthaler).

While *Flüsterwitze* had secretly ridiculed Hitler's authority, *Mein Führer* was going to challenge the authority of the cinematic Hitler-Holocaust-etiquette and representations of history in general. Laughter was going to be employed to "mock *what is* [and to] deflate or even cancel the authority of its object" (Des Pres 220). Freud had described the purpose of hostile jokes in the same way: "By making our enemy small, inferior, despicable or comic, we achieve in a roundabout way the enjoyment of overcoming him" (103) or, in Jean-Paul Sartre's words: "Freedom produces jokes and jokes produce freedom" (qtd. in Freud 11).

While laughing about Hitler will not necessarily cost one one's life these days, it certainly might kill one's career. A Forsa survey undertaken a week before the film opened asked Germans whether they thought a German Hitler comedy was a good idea. The result was quite overwhelming: only 38 percent of the participants from West Germany and a mere 22 percent of East Germans said yes. Once the film was released, the media reaction was largely negative, with few exceptions. The responses most often quoted were by Rolf Hochhuth, who talked about the "transfiguration" [*Verklärung*] of Hitler ("Kritik an Hitler-Satire") and by Stephan Kramer, the General Secretary of the Central Council of Jews in Germany, who called the film "superficial, superfluous and even dangerous" (8). Kramer also stressed that in his opinion this was "the wrong time for this kind of attempt to deal with the past in a country which invented and carried out the Holocaust."[17] The historian Hans-Ulrich Wehler said that he preferred serious films like *Schindler's List* and that if Hitler had to be ridiculed, one film had already accomplished that—*The Great Dictator*—and that that was quite enough ("Historiker wünscht"). Others, such as Christina Nord in *Die Tageszeitung*, criticized the film for not going far enough or not being funny enough: "It almost seems as if he lost courage halfway through the film. Therefore, *Mein Führer* is a timid film. Despite its fictitious elements, it still tries to cling to some safety net."[18] This echoes Broder's comments on Levy's previous film *Alles auf Zucker* (*Go for Zucker*, 2004). In contrast to *Mein Führer*, here the critic felt that *Alles auf Zucker* had been successful and "effective as a comedy because Levy didn't have the handbrake on, even if he ran the risk of being misunderstood" (Broder).

The critics who talked positively about the film stressed the relevance of the film for today's audiences due to the liberating smile it caused and through the film's exposure of the commodification of history in the media (Kothenschulte). Rabbi Walter Rothschild, one of the few commentators paying attention to the film's cinematic qualities, mentioned the "healing humour" of the film and proposed that maybe German audiences should look at Hitler the seducer rather than Hitler the leader (*Verführer* instead of *Führer*).

Yet, while Levy had the admirable aim of presenting a fresh perspective, he also adhered to the Holocaust etiquette by continually stating his good intentions in making this film. In various interviews and in the companion volume, which was released one week before the film opened, he repeatedly explained his motivations. He even posted a statement on the film's official website to counter the overwhelmingly negative response (Landler), even by people who had not actually seen the film (Brumlik). But perhaps good intentions do not produce good art, and laughter is a dangerous weapon that can also backfire. None of Levy's statements could prevent naysayers from fundamentally opposing a humorous depiction of the unfathomable. Comedy lives and feeds on incongruity, bringing together what does not conventionally belong together, but, in this case, that kind of suspension of disbelief proved to be too much for too many.

What is it about Levy's film that robs the comedy of its humour? *Mein Führer* is set in the final days of 1944, just before Hitler is supposed to deliver a New Year's speech in Berlin. Goebbels decides, in a last-ditch attempt to re-establish faith in the Nazis and in Hitler in particular, to lift Hitler's spirits and to prepare him for the speech by getting help from acting coach Prof. Adolf Israel Grünbaum, presently interned in the concentration camp Sachsenhausen. Comedic moments arise naturally when Hitler is reduced to an acting student wearing a jogging suit, or down on all fours and barking like a dog, or when he plays out

Dani Levy, *Mein Führer*. © X Verleih

the Alice Miller–inspired suffering child who never managed to cope with his authoritarian father. The comedic potential, however, is never allowed free play, because the audience knows that, on the other side of the one-way mirror in the Führer's office, lurk the real power players who are quite literally behind it all. Grünbaum's therapeutic sessions with the ailing Hitler are never allowed to become the sole focus and to let the audience enjoy pure comic relief. Rather, the tragic elements surrounding Goebbels's control on the other side of the mirror and the immediate or implied presence of Grünbaum's family are constant reminders that, while we might watch comedic interactions, a tragic seriousness is always present. Even the confusion of the two Adolfs, Grünbaum and Hitler, is not played out to a degree that would allow a shift in focus. When Grünbaum's wife shouts out her husband's first name and the masses awaiting the Führer mistake her call for an imminent appearance of Adolf Hitler, the comedic potential is restricted and never allowed to transcend the basic premise, a tragic situation that is sprinkled with comedic elements.

Throughout the film, Grünbaum literally plays with Hitler, testing the limits of showing a diminished, humanized, suffering, and ultimately quite ridiculous persona. The tragic elements always overpower what could be, but never is, comic relief. When Grünbaum toys with the shrunken and seemingly powerless Hitler, he entertains the idea of killing him with a knife or a gold bullion. In either case, though, the potentially powerful comedic elements give way to a tragic pity he feels for the person at his feet. This is particularly pronounced when Hitler crawls into bed with Grünbaum and his wife, and she attempts to smother Hitler with a pillow. Grünbaum stops her by arguing that killing Hitler would not put an end to the Nazi regime and that, after all, he is just another abused child.

The film opens with images of a Nazi parade, where Hitler is greeted by cheering crowds. The black-and-white documentary footage is accompanied by Adolf Grünbaum's voice-over narration which, through its irony and incongruity, tries to set the tone of the satire and establish the Jewish character as the main focus of the narrative: "No doubt about it, the Führer has seduced the German nation.... But I don't really want to talk about Herr Hitler, I want to tell you *my* story."[19] As a result of the voice-over narration, the spectators align themselves with Grünbaum's perspective while watching the story unfold. This alignment is strengthened further when a close-up shot of Grünbaum's smiling face, peeking through a curtain and whispering directly to the spectators, is inserted into the documentary footage. This black-and-white image of Grünbaum then gradually turns to colour, while blood begins to run down his face.

Established and ultimately reinforced by this frame, his sad and tragic story is a reminder that Grünbaum is only staging a comedic potential, watched by the power players who are always ready to put an end to the farce. In much the same way the Hitler comedy is not allowed to transcend Holocaust etiquette. The real tragedy of Grünbaum's character is his hope of making a difference while at the same time everybody around him, especially his wife and his eldest son, as well as the film's audience, see through the game that is played with him, while he continues to believe in a power he never has. The idea that Adolf Grünbaum is in charge of his story and his voice-over frame is thus an illusion. While he thinks that he can manipulate Hitler, he is the one who is constantly manipulated. The space he occupies with his acting student Hitler only serves the purpose of a defeated regime: Grünbaum is a pawn in the regime's game, and tragedy triumphs over comedy. Similarly, the ridiculed Nazis with their unfailing Hitler salutes and confusion about the exact ranks of their fellow officers are stuck on a superficial level. They will never gain the awareness needed to question the basic assumptions and dichotomies of the situation portrayed in this film.

In the end, when Grünbaum delivers Hitler's speech for the ailing and literally speechless Führer, he presents Hitler as the helpless and hopeless person he has encountered during their acting lessons. But his dying words to the one million spectators—"Heal Yourself!"—fall on deaf ears. Grünbaum's hopes, and the hopes of the spectators of the Hitler comedy, are shattered by the shots of Hitler's supporters. Grünbaum never really had a chance of making a difference.

Grünbaum's story, then, is an expression of a potential comedy that does not come to fruition. The violent death of a mistaken humanist with high hopes of making a difference clearly situates the film within a Holocaust and Hitler etiquette that, at least for now, does not allow for a radical new perspective. Grünbaum's story is ultimately tragic and sad, and the comedic elements only add to its tragic aspects rather than transcend them. At the moment of his greatest power, being allowed to put words into the Führer's mouth, Grünbaum is silenced forever, and his story is presented as an illusion that cannot break rigid internalized borders. As such, while it attempts to break new ground, *Mein Führer* does not allow the audience to break free of a pre-established etiquette and to present a ridiculed, satirized, and parodied Hitler. Grünbaum's story, while trying to take a humoristic view of Hitler, does exactly the opposite by showing the impossibility of breaking away from pre-established notions of what can and cannot be shown in German theatres. Grünbaum made fun of Hitler, literally on his knees, but his story is ultimately tragic, and his death spells the end of an arguably well-intended attempt at a Hitler comedy made in Germany.

While the Grünbaum frame ultimately restricts and limits the film's potential, *Mein Führer*'s initial cut presented quite a different perspective. The first director's cut failed miserably. This version, framed and narrated by a 117-year-old Adolf

Hitler living in a Wellness Hotel in Berchtesgarden, was shown to an audience of 400, who thought the film privileged Hitler's voice ("Schneider distanziert"). Instead of what might have been a funny introduction presenting a ridiculous character still rambling on about the old days and commenting on the present political system in Germany, the Hitler frame did not go over well, to say the least, and Dani Levy was forced to reconsider the basic premise of the film. On the DVD, he comments on the deleted frame (and on the deleted plot line of Eva Braun as Goebbels's mistress), and explains the decision by pointing out the cynicism that would have been created had he kept the Hitler frame. Instead, he opted for what he terms "a simpler story and a more honest film" (Levy, DVD commentary).[20] In an interview, the director explained that initial responses to the original cut had convinced him that shifting the focus to the Jewish character and his fate would make it easier for the spectators to watch the film with a clear conscience ("Dani Levy").[21]

The new Grünbaum frame, however, turns the potential comedy into an odd tragi-comedy that does not succeed in either genre. Instead of having the ridiculed Hitler have the final say, the film now ends, somewhat like *Schindler's List*, with various people making statements about Hitler—from small children to people who lived during the Third Reich. Their answers cover the broad spectrum from "I don't know who Hitler was" to "I'd rather not talk about it."

Dani Levy, *Mein Führer*. © X Verleih

Most comments show either a lack of information or a refusal to share the information. But even then, Levy wants to ensure that the original Hitler frame is erased and replaced by the other Adolf. In a second round of interviews, he asks the interviewees what they know about Adolf Grünbaum. Yet, as the answers to the Grünbaum question mirror the first round of responses in their ignorance, it is doubtful whether Levy achieved this effect. While this epilogue does draw attention to the precariousness of "appropriate" collective memory, it could also be read as an implication of similarities between the two Adolfs that go beyond their names, a suggestion that irritated reviewers of the film.

The uneven relationship between comedy and tragedy—just like the uneven Hitler–Grünbaum narrative—is a safety net that does not allow a new and radical perspective. "There are two parts to Dani Levy's comedy about Hitler," Henryk Broder wrote, "one absurd and the other moral. Unfortunately the rest is a balancing act not even the Führer himself can pull off" (Broder). In the end, *Mein Führer* does not accomplish what it sets out to do. While it challenges our perceptions of representations of the Third Reich and Adolf Hitler in particular, it attempts to provoke but does not want to offend. The film's final cut and its reception illustrate the still widespread Holocaust Veritas wall-in-the-head, and how hard it is to break out of it, both for German filmmakers and audiences. Laughing about Hitler, it seems, is still only possible (and acceptable) on the small screens, the television and the personal computer. *Mein Führer* aims high and hits the ceiling of *Vergangenheitsbewältigung*. It attempts to go where no German feature film had gone before, but in the end it does not go far enough. At the same time, it makes a significant contribution to the ongoing attempts of coming to terms with the past. As Adolf Grünbaum says in his dying words, "We want to understand what we will never understand."

Notes

1 For a comprehensive list of film and TV references, see <http://en.wikipedia.org/wiki/Adolf_Hitler_in_popular_culture.>
2 For a detailed analysis of these films, see Loshitzky. A detailed filmography of comedies and satires of Holocaust representations can be found in Loewy.
3 "Darstellungen des Holocaust sollen im Bereich der "Hochkultur" stattfinden. Populäre Produkte sind automatisch verdächtig und jedenfalls weniger bedeutend. Komödien sprechen meist ein Publikum an, das nicht zwangsläufig hoch gebildet ist, und haben es daher schwerer, zur Hochkultur gerechnet zu werden."
4 "Der Künstler soll die richtige Haltung und die richtige Motivation haben: Altruismus, beste Absichtern, die richtigen moralischen und didaktischen Ziele. Selbst wenn das Produkt komisch ist, soll der Künstler angemessene Ernsthaftigkeit zeigen."
5 See Florentine Strzelczyk's essay in this volume.
6 "inszenierte Realität."

7 "Es geht in *Mein Führer* ja nicht um historische Fakten, sondern um inszenierte Realität."
8 "Adolf die Nazisau: Ich hock in meinem Bonker" (2006) was written by Walter Moers and Thomas Pigor and performed by Pigor. See <http://de.youtube.com/watch?v=17Jg1 Jjzwoo> (accessed 22 April 2008).
9 I'd like to thank Miriam Winkels, FU Berlin, for her help tracking down these references.
10 These numbers are from 23 April 2008.
11 "But not everyone's a fan. Polt's publisher sued Wittmann for breach of copyright, which ended up costing him 2,000 euros ($2,586) in legal fees" (Chase).
12 <http://youtube.com/watch?v=q-7QoiOH9r0> (accessed 2 March 2008).
13 "Ich knüpfe gern an diese Tradition an. Nicht umsonst sind Charlie Chaplin und Ernst Lubitsch meine geistigen Väter" (Levy, "Brief," 177).
14 "Der Film ist handwerklich und künstlerisch wirklich gut gemacht. Aber diese angestrengte Ernsthaftigkeit, bloß authentisch sein zu wollen, das hat mich provoziert" (Adorján).
15 "... dem etwas Kleines, Schnelles, Freches, politisch Inkorrektes entgegenzusetzen" (Adorján).
16 "Levy persifliert nicht den Holocaust, sondern seine mediale Verkürzung. Dass dies erst nach einem Tabubruch Anderer möglich wurde—der menschelnden Darstellung Hitlers in DER UNTERGANG—ist kein Zufall. Die Eichingerproduktion ist Levys Angriffsfläche. Helge Schneider parodiert nicht Hitler, sondern Bruno Ganz als Hitler."
17 "Dies ist nicht die Zeit für eine solche Form der Auseinandersetzung mit der Vergangenheit in dem Land, in dem der Holocaust erfunden und exekutiert wurde."
18 "Ganz so, als habe ihn auf halbem Weg der Mut verlassen. *Mein Führer* ist deshalb ein schüchterner Film. Noch in der Fantasie knüpft er sich ein Sicherheitsnetz."
19 "Kein Zweifel, der Führer hat das deutsche Volk verführt ... Aber eigentlich will ich Ihnen nicht die Geschichte des Herrn Hitler erzählen, sondern meine."
20 "Und einen zynischen Film wollte ich auch gar keinen Fall machen. Und deswegen ist ein neuer Rahmen enstanden. [...] Das hat den Film vereinfacht und gleichzeitig ehrlicher gemacht" (from Levy, Dani. "Commentary." *Mein Führer—Die wirklich wahrste Wahrheit über Adolf Hitler*, DVD. Directed by Dani Levy. Berlin: X Filme, 2007).
21 "Levy verzichtete nach ersten Probevorführungen auf diese Rahmen-Perspektive, da die nun vorliegende Kinofassung mit der Fokusverschiebung auf das jüdische Schicksal besser geeignet sei, den Zuschauern 'Gewissenssicherheit zu geben,' wie er in einem Gespräch am 8. Januar 2007 auf 3sat erklärte" ("Dani Levy").

References

"Adolf Hitler in Popular Culture." Wikipedia. 2008. 23 Apr. 2008 <http://en.wikipedia.org>.

Adorján, Johanna. "Dürfen wir über Hitler lachen? Interview mit Dani Levy." *Frankfurter Allgemeine Sonntagszeitung* 17 Dec. 2006: 25. 24 Apr. 2008 <http://www.faz.net/>.

Alles auf Zucker! (*Go for Zucker!*). Dir. Dani Levy. X-Filme, 2004.

Brauer, Wiebke. "Schrumpfkur für Hitler." *Spiegel Online* 4 July 2006. 23 Apr. 2008 <http://www.spiegel.de>.

Brecht, Bertolt. *Der unaufhaltsame Aufstieg des Arturo Ui*. 1941. Frankfurt am Main: Suhrkamp, 2004.

Broder, Henryk M. "Dani Levy's Failed Hitler Comedy." Trans. Christopher Sultan. *Spiegel Online International* 9 Jan. 2007. 8 Feb. 2008 <http://www.spiegel.de/international/>.

Brumlik, Micha. "Im Bett mit Adolf. Zu Levis Film *Mein Führer*." *Frankfurter Rundschau* 17 Jan. 2007: 17.

Chase, Jefferson. "Hitler's Rant about a Leasing Contract a Hit on YouTube." *Deutsche Welle Online*. 23 Apr. 2008 <http://www.dw-world.de>.

Conrad, Vera, ed. *Mein Führer: Materialien für den Unterricht*. 23 Apr. 2008 <http://www.meinfuehrer-derfilm.de/downloads/MEINFUEHRER_Schulheft.pdf>.

"Dani Levy." *Wikipedia*. 2008. 24 Apr. 2008 <de.wikipedia.org>.

Des Pres, Terence. "*Holocaust Laughter?*" *Writing the Holocaust*. Ed. Berel Lang. New York: Holmes and Meier, 1988. 216–33.

Freud, Sigmund. *Jokes and Their Relation to the Unconscious*. Ed. and trans. James Strachey. New York: Norton, 1963.

Der Fuehrer's Face. Dir. Jack Kinney. Walt Disney Studios, 1942.

"The Germans." *Fawlty Towers*. Dir. John Howard Davies. BBC, 1975.

Gilman, Sander L. "Is Life Beautiful? Can the Shoah Be Funny? Some Thoughts on Recent and Older Films." *Critical Inquiry* 26.2 (2000): 279–308.

The Great Dictator. Dir. Charlie Chaplin. Charles Chaplin Productions, 1940.

Herr Meets Hare. Dir. Friz Freleng. Warner Brothers, 1945.

Herzog, Rudolph. *Heil Hitler, das Schwein ist tot! Lachen unter Hitler—Komik und Humor im Dritten Reich*. Berlin: Eichborn, 2006.

Heil Hitler, das Schwein ist tot! Dir. Rudolph Herzog. Ilona Grundmann Filmproduction, 2006.

Hirsch, Marianne. *Family Frames. Photography Narrative and Postmemory*. Cambridge: Harvard UP, 1997.

Hochhuth, Rolf. "Kritik an Hitler-Satire. Der komische Führer." *Süddeutsche Zeitung* 9 Jan. 2007. 24 Apr. 2008 <http://www.sueddeutsche.de>.

Jacob the Liar. Dir. Peter Kassowitz. Tri Star Pictures, 1999.

Kramer, Stephan J. "Mein Führer"—oberflächlich, überflüssig, gefährlich. Warum ich über die Hitler-Satire von Levy nicht lachen kann." *Tagesspiegel* 11 Jan. 2007: 8.

Kothenschulte, Daniel. "Heil mich selbst: Lachen über Hitler—die Filmkomik stieß bei diesem Thema an Grenzen / Dani Levys aktueller Film bezieht den heutigen Umgang der Medien mit dem NS-Regime ein." *Frankfurter Rundschau* 8 Jan. 2007. 24 Apr. 2008 <http://www.fr-online.de>.

Landler, Mark. "In Germany, a Hitler Comedy Goes Over with a Thud." *New York Times* 11 Jan. 2007. 24 Apr. 2008 <http://www.nytimes.com>.

Laster, Kathy, and Heinz Steinert. "Eine neue Moral in der Darstellung der Shoah? Zur Rezeption von *La Vita e Bella*." *Lachen über Hitler—Auschwitz-Gelächter? Filmkomödie, Satire und Holocaust*. Ed. Margrit Frölich, Hanno Loewy, and Heinz Steinert. Frankfurt am Main: edition text + kritik, 2003. 181–98.

Lentin, Ronit. "Postmemory, Received History and the Return of the Auschwitz Code." *Eurozine*. 6 Feb. 2008 <http://www.eurozine.com>.

Levy, Dani. "Ein Brief an die Filmförderung." *Mein Führer—Die wirklich wahrste Wahrheit über Adolf Hitler.* Ed. Michael Töteberg. Hamburg: Rowohlt, 2007. 175–78.

Levy, Dani. "Director's Point. Dani Levy im Gespräch." *Mein Führer—Die wirklich wahrste Wahrheit über Adolf Hitler.* Ed. Michael Töteberg. Hamburg: Rowohlt, 2007. 209–14.

Levy, Dani. *Mein Führer—Die wirklich wahrste Wahrheit über Adolf Hitler.* DVD Commentary. X-Filme, 2007.

Life Is Beautiful. Dir. Roberto Benigni. Cecchi Gori Group Tiger Cinematografica, 1997.

"Little Hitler." *Bullyparade.* 21 Apr. 2008 <http://www.leechvideo.com>.

Loewy, Hanno (with Margrit Frölich and Heinz Steinert). "Komödie und Satire in der filmischen Repräsentation des Holocaust: Eine Filmografie." *Lachen über Hitler—Auschwitz-Gelächter? Filmkomödie, Satire und Holocaust.* Ed. Margrit Frölich, Hanno Loewy, and Heinz Steinert. Frankfurt am Main: edition text + kritik, 2003. 335–82.

Loshitzky, Yosefa. "Verbotenes Lachen: Politik und Ethik der Holocaust-Filmkomödie." *Lachen über Hitler—Auschwitz-Gelächter? Filmkomödie, Satire und Holocaust.* Trans. Margrit Frölich. Ed. Margrit Frölich, Hanno Loewy, and Heinz Steinert. Frankfurt am Main: edition text + kritik, 2003. 21–36.

Martenstein, Harald. "Adolf auf der Couch." *Zeit* 4 Jan. 2007. 23 Apr. 2008 <http://www.zeit.de>.

Mein Führer—Die wirklich wahrste Wahrheit über Adolf Hitler (*Mein Führer: The Truly Truest Truth about Adolf Hitler*). Dir. Daniel Levy. X-Filme Creative Pool, 2007.

Miller, Alice. *Am Anfang war Erziehung.* Frankfurt am Main: Suhrkamp, 1980.

Moers, Walter. *Adolf. Äch bin wieder da!!* Frankfurt: Eichborn, 1998.

Moers, Walter. *Adolf. Der Bonker.* Munich: Piper, 2006.

Moers, Walter. "Adolf die Nazisau: Ich hock in meinem Bonker." 22 Apr. 2008 <http://de.youtube.com>.

Nord, Christina. "Ein schüchterner Film." *Tageszeitung* 10 Jan. 2007: 15. 24 Apr. 2008 <http://www.taz.de>.

Paul, William. *Ernst Lubitsch's American Comedy.* New York: Columbia UP, 1983.

The Producers. Dir. Mel Brooks. Crossbow Productions, 1968.

The Producers. Dir. Susan Stroman. Universal Pictures, 2005.

Rothschild, Walter. "Ich spüre Sie nicht, mein Führer. Vielleicht kein feiner Humor, aber ein heilsamer: Der Berliner Rabbiner Walter Rothschild über Dani Levys Hitler-Film, der nächste Woche startet." *Tageszeitung* 6 Jan. 2007. 24 Apr. 2008 <http://www.taz.de>.

Rotthaler, Viktor. "Frühling für Hitler. Dani Levys historische Vorbilder." *Frankfurter Rundschau* 13 Jan. 2007: 15.

Schindler's List. Dir. Steven Spielberg. Universal, 1993.

"Schneider distanziert sich von Hitler-Film." *Spiegel Online* 4 Jan. 2007. 24 Apr. 2008 <http://www.spiegel.de>.

Schneider, Helge. "Komödie ist das einzige Ausdrucksmittel, mit dem man so eine Geschichte vorführen kann." *Mein Führer—Materialien für den Unterricht.* 19–20. 20 Apr. 2008 <http://www.meinfuehrer-derfilm.de/downloads/MEINFUEHRER_Schulheft.pdf>.

Schrecklichkeit, Dr. *Struwwelhitler—A Nazi Story Book.* 1941. Autorenhaus, 2005.

Shoah. Dir. Claude Lanzmann. Historia, 1985.

Somuncu, Serdar. *Aus dem Tagebuch eines Massenmörders: Mein Kampf.* Random House Audio, 2006.

Spiegelman, Art. *Maus I: A Survivor's Tale: My Father Bleeds History.* Pantheon: 1986.

———. *Maus II: A Survivor's Tale: And Here My Troubles Began.* Pantheon: 1992.

To Be or Not to Be. Dir. Ernst Lubitsch. Romaine Film Corporation, 1942.

To Be or Not to Be. Dir. Alan Johnson. Brooksfilms, 1983.

Töteberg, Michael, ed. *Dani Levy. Mein Führer—Die wirklich wahrste Wahrheit über Adolf Hitler.* Hamburg: Rowohlt, 2007.

Train de vie (*Train of Life*). Dir. Radu Mihaileanu. Belfilms, 1998.

Triumph des Willens (*Triumph of the Will*). Dir. Leni Riefenstahl. Leni Riefenstahl Produktion, 1935.

Der Untergang (*Downfall*). Dir. Oliver Hirschbiegel. Bavaria, 2004.

"Der Untergang." *Harald Schmidt Show.* 22 Apr. 2008 <http://de.youtube.com/watch?v=yCLralhpcdI>.

Wehler, Hans-Ulrich. "Historiker wünscht dem *Führer* eine Nullquote." *Frankfurter Neue Presse* 11 Jan. 2007. 21 Apr. 2008 <www.zeitgeschichte-online.de/portals/_rainbow/documents/pdf/presse_levy.pdf>.

Weinman, Jaime J. "Hitler is Hilarious." *Maclean's* 26 Feb. 2007: 51–52.

Westphal, Anke. "Jedes Volk sucht sich seinen Diktator." *Berliner Zeitung* 6 Jan. 2007. 23 April 2008 <http://www.berlinonline.de>.

You Natzy Spy. Dir. Jules White. Columbia Pictures, 1940.

Zander, Peter. "So ist Dani Levys *Mein Führer.*" *Welt* 5 Jan. 2007. 24 Apr. 2008 <http://www.welt.de>.

QUESTIONING COLLECTIVE IDENTITIES

11
German Fascination for Jews
in Oliver Hirschbiegel's *Ein ganz gewöhnlicher Jude*

Myriam Léger

Abstract This chapter discusses Oliver Hirschbiegel's film as the site both of an imagined contemporary struggle for German-Jewish identity and the construction of the spectator's problematic involvement in it. As the Jewish protagonist unravels the powerful discourse of postwar German–Jewish relations in which he feels trapped, the chamber-drama style of the film as well as its cinematography mark the spectator as a fascinated and implicitly German observer, who gazes at the protagonist's intimate engagement with his troubled self-image. This film comments on the existing cultural alienation between Germans and Jews that continues to shape this discourse, and perpetuates a German fascination for "things Jewish."

Shortly after Oliver Hirschbiegel attracted international attention with his 2004 box-office success *Der Untergang* (*Downfall*), he directed the chamber-drama-style film *Ein ganz gewöhnlicher Jude* (*Just an Ordinary Jew*) with Ben Becker, which was released in 2006. While *Der Untergang* attempts to depict Hitler's last days in the bunker from a historical and, according to film producer Bernd Eichinger, authentic viewpoint, *Ein ganz gewöhnlicher Jude* redirects the discussion to a contemporary setting, where the effects of this period have created a discourse of German–Jewish relations based on political correctness and cultural difference. It is striking that Hirschbiegel chose to direct a film about the difficulties of Jewish life in postwar Germany only two years after directing *Der Untergang*, a film that had repeatedly been accused of depicting the character of Adolf Hitler in an inappropriately human light, evoking pity and compassion. Before considering the possibility that Hirschbiegel took on

Ein ganz gewöhnlicher Jude in order to counter such criticism, it is important to note that, as Hirschbiegel pointed out in an interview in 2006 with Hanns-Georg Rodek, it was rather due to the elaborate preparations for *Der Untergang* that the production as well as release of *Ein ganz gewöhnlicher Jude* were delayed considerably. In the same interview, Hirschbiegel was asked whether he followed a particular strategy when choosing his films, whereupon he explained that "[I] like jumping between themes and genres. I do not follow money but subject-matter."[1] Although other reviewers, such as Peter Zander, have noted that the film "almost seems to be an afterthought because he was criticized for having deliberately avoided any reference to the Holocaust in his bunker drama,"[2] it seems evident that any relationship between these two films, similar to other films about Germany's postwar legacy, can only be established in terms of their criticism of contemporary German discourses about guilt, victimhood, and contrition.

From the outset of *Ein ganz gewöhnlicher Jude*, the rather uncommon genre of the chamber drama turns the spectator into an intimate witness of the protagonist's furious speech about German–Jewish relations, made while he is alone in his Hamburg apartment. As the son of Holocaust survivors who has lived all his life in Germany, Emanuel Goldfarb demands for himself an ordinary life that allows him to avoid any participation in the German–Jewish dialogue. An invitation from the high-school teacher Emanuel Gebhardt to speak about his life as a "Jewish fellow citizen" (*jüdischer Mitbürger*), however, deprives him of his ordinariness and marks him as standing outside of the ordinary. Furious about this request, Goldfarb begins dictating a letter addressed to Gebhardt to refuse the invitation. The ensuing dialogue with the imaginary interlocutor dominates the film as he comes to terms with his troubled self-image as a Jew in Germany, who feels trapped in the powerful discourse of postwar German–Jewish relations. As will be shown, the film's rather simple storyline constitutes an interesting counterpoint to the film's cinematography. As Goldfarb speaks about his albeit problematic wish to be just an ordinary Jew, the camera constructs the spectator as curious observer who, implicitly identified as German, is fascinated by Goldfarb's exotic appearance. The spectator's fascination is created through the identification of the camera's gaze at Goldfarb with the spectator's gaze at the images captured by the camera. This cinematographic construction of the spectator-protagonist relationship crafts the spectator's fascination as an intense but questionably reserved interest in Goldfarb and his Jewishness. Underlying both Goldfarb's identity struggle and the problematic relationship between him and the spectator is a tension grounded in the cultural space shared by Jews and non-Jewish Germans in Germany. In order to further explore the workings of this cultural space, I will draw on theoretical concepts introduced by Michel Foucault, Stuart Hall, and Homi Bhabha, who examine the cultural dimensions and dynamics of ideology, communication, and identity.

For the cinematic adaptation of his screenplay,[3] Charles Lewinsky was hoping to win Ben Becker for the role of Emanuel Goldfarb. The reason for his preference, stated in a TV interview in 2008, speaks to the problematic issue of representing Jewishness within the given context: "And exactly because he [Ben Becker] does not conform to the cliché of a Jew, he reveals that the cliché lies with the others. That it does not even benefit him to look like a blond SA officer. Once the cliché comes into existence, he is seen only as the typical Jew even though he is not"[4] ("Autor Charles Lewinski"). Lewinsky intended to confront the audience with their own racial stereotypes about Jews by presenting a Jewish character who shares more physical features with a stereotypical Nazi official than with a stereotypical Jew. The identification of Emanuel Goldfarb as a Jew is thus not based on racial stereotypes reflected in his appearance. Although the actor playing Emanuel Goldfarb was not to exhibit physical features that usually stereotype Jews, he is almost immediately identified as a Jew through the cultural artifacts that the camera captures around him, that is, based on cultural and ethnic difference. Similarly, journalist and author Henryk Broder argues for the stereotyping of Goldfarb's character in his film review "Der ewige Gute." According to Broder, however, it is through the numerous instances of kitsch and tacky clichés about Jews in postwar Germany, such as the story of the German Jew returning from British exile after the war, because the English language has no word for *Gemütlichkeit*, that Goldfarb appears as stereotyped character. By means of incorporating these overused images of Jewishness into Goldfarb's biography, Broder argues that the character contributes to the current "German tendency to affect concern,"[5] which actually is meant to be attacked. He overlooks, however, that Goldfarb's character uses these clichés and stereotypes in order to show how they, mostly unnoticed, still shape contemporary German–Jewish relations.

At the same time as Goldfarb criticizes being positioned as the "Other" in German postwar society, he cannot escape being positioned as the "Other" a second time, that is, cinematographically. While the notion of discourse as constructing the subject is dominant in Hirschbiegel's film, the notion of agency plays an important role as well. In line with the understanding of discourse theory that subjects are able to "engage in their own constitution, acquiesce with or contest the roles to which they are assigned" (Mills 41), *Ein ganz gewöhnlicher Jude* presents the possibility of social change by assigning the subject the role of an "agent of socio-cultural constructs and institutions" (Pribram 159). After forcefully refusing to play an active role in the shaping of German–Jewish relations, the final scene shows Goldfarb in Gebhardt's classroom. This scene only indicates the fact that he reconsidered his attitude, but does not clarify or even hint at the reason for his change. The analysis and interpretation of the film's narrative and cinematographic devices with which it depicts the construction of the discourse of German–Jewish relations is an attempt to shed light on the significance of this surprising turning point.

Goldfarb finds himself struggling to join his sense of Germanness with his sense of Jewishness. When he receives Gebhardt's invitation letter, addressed to a member of the Jewish community, he is automatically cast in the role of a Jew that stands in opposition to that of a German.

> Dear Sir or Madam, next semester I will be discussing the topic of Judaism with my 8th grade social studies class. Since in my experience [...] nothing has an effect as descriptive and memorable as a personal encounter, I would like to invite a Jewish fellow citizen to visit the class and answer the students' questions. Unfortunately, I do not personally know any members of the Jewish community [...] and, therefore, would like to ask you to accept this invitation and to visit us. [...] Thus I hope you are able to accept my request and remain with a sincere Shalom [...], R Gebhardt. (Lewinsky 10–15)[6]

Quite clearly, Gebhardt's letter is not meant to offend or show disrespect to the person receiving his invitation, but rather to initiate an educational dialogue between Germans and Jews living in Hamburg. Goldfarb's reaction might therefore at first sight seem inappropriate. Goldfarb, however, stumbles across Gebhardt's cautious and politically correct wording, which points toward an unstated but underlying layer of meaning. Goldfarb begins to unravel what he perceives to be part of the conditions and circumstances for this complicated relationship between Germans and Jews in postwar Germany. His realization of the political correctness with which he is confronted incites a closer scrutiny of these relations and their cultural and social manifestations as well as the mechanisms and ideologies that structure them. Foucault's concept of discourse proves to be helpful to understand and analyze the workings of such mechanisms and ideologies. One of Foucault's most famous definitions of discourse as "practices that systematically form the objects of which they speak" (Foucault 54) emphasizes that it is precisely because of the systematicity of these practices, such as ideas, attitudes, beliefs, courses of action, and institutions, as well as their socio-cultural effects that the identification of often unapparent or obscured discursive structures is possible. The discourse of German–Jewish relations and its structures and rules become visible because Germans and Jews "behave within a certain range of parameters" (Mills 16) when defining themselves as subjects whose experiences relate in some way to the shared history of Germans and Jews. It is within the boundaries of this discursive framework, which excludes, for example, anti-Semitic behaviour while encouraging politically correct behaviour, or that promotes the longing of Jews for ordinariness and the expectation that Germans express their contrition, that Germans and Jews negotiate their discursive positions. The fact that these positions are marked as legitimate and desirable indicates which knowledge about the discourse is considered part of the dominant discourse and, by implication, which knowledge is excluded from it. Accordingly, since political correctness is marked as a true, or legitimate, way of speaking about German–Jewish relations, the lack of political correctness is automatically marked as illegitimate, so that people and institutions associated with this illegitimate behaviour will be penalized by the stigma of anti-Semitism. The third constituent of a discourse besides truth and knowledge is therefore, according to Foucault, power, an element that is "dispersed throughout social relations [and] produces possible forms of behaviour as well as restricting behaviour" (17). This categorization of practices within the dynamics of truth, knowledge, and power affects the entire discourse, of which a few instances are discussed in Hirschbiegel's film.

When viewed as a product of this discourse, Gebhardt's letter has been shaped by many of its discursive practices that Foucault describes as "a group of *rules* that are immanent in a practice, and define it in its specificity" (51). The invitation letter exposes some of the behaviours shaped by these practices, such as political correctness, a sense of social distance—and the belief that this distance needs to be formally overcome—and courses of action such as the act itself of writing an official invitation letter to a representative of the Jewish community in anticipation of a positive response. Moreover, Goldfarb reflects on and dissects various instances of the discourse of postwar German–Jewish relations in front of the spectator, who witnesses how his German-Jewish identity is formed in this discourse. He speaks about key words such as *Holocaust compensation, tolerance,* and *reconciliation* as social imperatives that govern the interaction between Germans and Jews and thus points toward the fact that such behaviour should rather be seen as naturalized and less as natural. Dismantling the negative connotations of this kind of interaction by characterizing it as "fawning sympathy"[7] and "repulsive empathy"[8] (Lewinsky 17), Goldfarb highlights how the constraints of expression within this discourse, based on a dominant culture of contrition, indeed have negative effects on the relation between Germans and Jews.

Goldfarb's sarcastic understanding of how many non-Jewish Germans attempt to react appropriately to the mention of the Holocaust and in accordance with the public-political discourse about it is also aimed at all of those instances when the Holocaust is publicly commemorated in Germany. By paraphrasing this attitude, which he pointedly terms "a German face of affected concern,"[9] "the parliamentary-remembrance-speech-face,"[10] and "the Lea-Rosh face"[11] (27), Goldfarb criticizes Germany's dealing with its Nazi past as an undertaking based on obligation rather than conviction. Lea Rosh, famous for her role as initiator and main proponent of the Memorial to the Murdered Jews of Europe, as well as the many parliamentary speeches given to commemorate the Holocaust, are two of this attitude's physical manifestations that earn Goldfarb's ire. Rosh's lack of tact became a topic of public discussion and controversy when she proposed to affix the tooth of a murdered Jew, which she had found in a concentration camp, into one of the concrete pillars of the memorial. Outraged about Rosh's suggestion, many Jewish communities, which were to be honoured with the memorial, threatened to boycott it if she carried out her plan. Her motivation in leading a seventeen-year campaign to build the memorial has often been derided as distasteful, and her attraction to Jews has been seen as a kind of philo-Semitism. Her efforts have been criticized as the obsession of a non-Jewish German with the Holocaust. Goldfarb uses the public figure Lea Rosh to exemplify how affected concern has become a response to the Holocaust that is indeed controversially discussed yet nevertheless publicly affirmed.

Upset about the German "Lea-Rosh face," Goldfarb sides with Martin Walser who, in his acceptance speech for the Frankfurt Book Fair's Peace Prize in 1998, criticized the instrumentalization of the Holocaust and its abuse as a "moral club"[12] and "compulsory exercise"[13] (Walser 20). In his speech, Walser examines, from an arguably subjective position, the relationship of contemporary Germany to its Nazi past and, more specifically, the conditions under which this past is discussed and remembered. In doing so, he formulates his statements in the subjunctive mood in order to highlight their self-reflexive quality. Immediately after warning against a ritualization of the Holocaust, for example, which comes about by allowing it to become an "ever ready means of intimidation"[14] (20), Walser follows up with a question that makes his previous remarks only relevant if this question were actually asked: "But what kind of suspicion is raised if one were to say that the Germans are a normal people, a normal society?"[15] (20). Similarly, he criticizes the instrumentalization of the Holocaust only as a result of his own experiences, emphasizing that this phenomenon should merely be understood as a possible personal discovery and not a definite or general judgment.

> [...] I try to listen to motives within the expostulation of our shame and I am almost happy when I believe I am able to discover that often, the motif is not commemoration or the forbiddance to forget but the instrumentalization of our shame to contemporary ends.[16] (18)

The subjectivity that is expressed in Walser's controversial statements and his resulting ambiguous stance toward them has been seen both by scholars such as Stephen Brockmann (2002) and Walser's fellow authors such as Friedrich Christian Delius (2000) as one of the major reasons for the ensuing controversy following his speech that turned into a public debate between liberal and conservative intellectuals and non-intellectuals about the way the Holocaust should be commemorated in contemporary Germany. Goldfarb, after putting a sugar cube in his coffee and mentioning that his mother always used to take three or four sugar cubes after her experiences in a concentration camp, believes he is able to foresee Gebhardt's reaction to his mention of the Holocaust: "I know exactly what kind of face you will put on when you read this, Mr. Gebhardt. The German face of affected concern. [...] You don't have to do this, Mr. Gebhardt. This is a coffee cup, not a moral club"[17] (Lewinsky 27). While Goldfarb initially seems to concur with this controversial labelling by Walser, he admits at the same time to feel the necessity to speak about the Holocaust, because it is still relevant to his life as Jew in Germany: "I did not mention the concentration camp where my mom vegetated as a young girl so that you have a bad conscience. I can stand this 'oh-how-bad-everything-was reflex' as little as Martin Walser. But I also can't always forgo this topic, because it bends the back in the long run"[18] (28). He diverges again from Walser's general position as he insists on the impossibility of looking the other way when it comes to broaching the issue of the Holocaust, because it represents a vital part of his self-understanding. Conversely, Walser seems to suggest that "repression can be a good thing" (Brockmann 136), stating that "I block out those bad things in whose rectification I am not able to play a part. I learnt to look the other way"[19] (Walser 10). The tensions between Goldfarb's irreconcilable attitudes toward the Holocaust as well as his simultaneous approval and disapproval of Walser's criticism of a "routine of accusation"[20] (17) and the consequent feeling of shame bring forward the problematic and perhaps contradictory nature of Goldfarb's wish to be just an ordinary Jew, which parallels the seemingly incompatible attitudes of Germans and Jews when dealing with the Holocaust.

While the film attempts to offer a reflection on German–Jewish relations, it soon becomes clear that issues of identity or rather identities are at the forefront. In this context, it seems that the title of the film, *Ein ganz gewöhnlicher Jude*, is rather more of a question than a statement upon which the viewer is likely to stumble. Is there something like an ordinary Jew after World War II, especially in Germany? Interestingly, throughout the course of the film, Goldfarb speaks of himself only as a Jew in Germany, never as German-Jewish. Yet he understands Germany's most recent history as the common history both of Jews and Germans.

While his family's stories are marked by the Holocaust in a fundamentally different way from those stories of non-Jewish Germans, he concludes that they are inextricably linked with each other. "We have the same history but not the same stories, you and me. Although they all are German stories"[21] (Lewinsky 28). Goldfarb sees himself constructed by a discourse in which Jewishness and Germanness can ultimately not be separated because of their obviously problematic but nonetheless shared historical and cultural space. Feeling trapped in the contemporary discourse of postwar German–Jewish relations that emphasizes difference rather than common ground, Goldfarb feels pressured to negotiate continuously his position within this conflicting relation of difference and commonality. He fears that "we will always be Jews in Germany and never Jewish-Germans. An everlasting special case"[22] (81).

Hirschbiegel's film reveals some of the practices and institutions of this discourse that construct difference as one of the truths about German–Jewish relations whose naming already suggests the hyphenation and separation of Jewishness and Germanness, implying that one identity cannot be part of the other, but must stand beside it. The construction of German-Jewish identity is shaped, among other things, by powerful public institutions and organizations such as the *Zentralrat der Juden in Deutschland* (Central Council of Jews in Germany) and the *Gesellschaft für christlich-jüdische Zusammenarbeit* (Society for Christian–Jewish Cooperation), whose very names comply with a hyphenated identity construction. As Goldfarb states: "Shall I tell this to your students, Mr. Gebhardt? That there is no such thing as matter-of-course for us, not on the one side and not on the other, precisely because there are two sides and they remain two sides. Because there is no Central Council of Jewish Germans or one of German Jews but only a Central Council of Jews in Germany"[23] (53–54). These associations suggest an incompatibility between Germans and Jews, either reducing their relationship to a matter of locality or to the need to remedy this situation implicitly stigmatized as problematic and critical. As Goldfarb says, "We became a case for animal-rights activists. For Greenpeace and the Society for Christian–Jewish Cooperation. Rhinoceroses are on display in the zoo; Jews are invited to high-school classes"[24] (19).

At the same time as the public sphere has an impact on Goldfarb's private life, his private life is made part of public scrutiny through a curious, gazing spectator. This observer already appears at the very beginning during the film's credits, when a friend of Goldfarb's hands him the invitation from high-school teacher Gebhardt. After trying to reject this request instantly, he nonetheless takes the letter to his apartment in a Hamburg high-rise building. The camera follows him into the elevator, gazing at his face and chest at eye level in a medium close-up and then, in the following shot, at the back of his head. Following him into the corridor and toward the door of his apartment, the picture is shaking slightly, imitating the movements of a walking person. It is the spectator who is positioned as the person looking at Goldfarb at this very moment. The door closes, and we are left standing in front of it, staring for several seconds at a sign engraved with his name, Emanuel Goldfarb. Our look then slides to the doorframe and to a mezuzah, a decorative case holding a Jewish prayer, which fulfills the Biblical commandment to inscribe this prayer on the doorframes of every Jewish home. Within the first few scenes of the film, we know that we are in a Jewish apartment.

As the camera continues to follow Goldfarb through his apartment, he is sitting down at his desk, preparing to formulate a letter of refusal to Gebhardt. Interestingly, the camera does not enter his study, but stops next to a curtain that separates it from the hallway and covers almost half of the frame. This *mise en scène* creates the impression of someone standing in the distant hiding position of a curious observer who, attracted by objects that evoke foreignness and exoticism, cannot help but intrude into Goldfarb's privacy. The camera takes on such observing positions throughout the film, continuously confirming the spectator in this position. It also continues to turn a considerable amount of its attention to things Jewish such as a bowl with skullcaps, which are worn during kippot; a bag containing the prayer shawl tallit; the seven-branched menorah, one of the most important symbols of Judaism; and a tin can from the KKL, the Jewish National Fund, used to collect donations for the development of Israeli land and infrastructure. The camera captures many instances of exotic objects marked as Jewish and at the same time marked as "different," and it constructs the viewer as the observer and the protagonist as the observed. The fact that the camera's curiosity seems to be triggered by the foreignness and exoticism of these religious and cultural artifacts creates a sense of cultural distance between the observer and the observed, gazing at him persistently from a distance.

The spectator identifies with the camera's perspective and looks at these unfamiliar objects with curiosity and ignorance, encouraged to accept the implied judgment as his own. Thus, the communicative process that takes place in this instance between the film and the viewer will often be, according to Stuart Hall's concept of encoding and decoding, successful, because it aligns the producer's encoded side of the message with the receiver's decoded one. Hall understands the communication process not as a traditional circulation circuit consisting of sender, message, and receiver, but as a "structure produced and sustained through the articulation of linked but distinctive moments—production, circulation, distribution, consumption, reproduction" (Hall 508). Not only is every message circulated in a discursive form that is determined by a linguistic or audiovisual code, the processes of production, distribution, and consumption are also discursively framed both by their respective routines, rules, and modalities as well as by the wider socio-cultural and political structure of which they are a part. Accordingly, the knowledge about German–Jewish relations and about a legitimate way to speak about it plays an integral part in the film's production, circulation, and consumption. It shapes, as we could see in the case of Charles Lewinsky and Ben Becker, the reasons for choices of actors, as well as the way everyone involved in the production process contributes to making the film's plot and its cinematography contemplate German–Jewish relations. *Ein ganz gewöhnlicher Jude* is thus not only a contemporary document *about* German–Jewish-relations, it is also a contemporary document *of* these relations, allowing the integration of the socio-cultural and political conditions of the film and the way it broaches the issue of German–Jewish relations into one reading of this discourse.

Considering that particular expectations about the audience of the film also form part of this socio-cultural and political context in which the film originated, it is interesting to take a closer look at the film's audience figures. *Ein ganz gewöhnlicher Jude* attracted only around 13,000 cinema-goers, according to the film-ranking list of the German Federal Film Board (Filmhitlisten FFA Filmförderungsanstalt), and it was only released in German art-house cinemas. While the reasons for this scarce reception are difficult to reconstruct, it could be argued that one important factor was the marketing of the film through the art-house circuit, which generally registers lower audience figures than mainstream cinema. This leads to the question about the expectations of the audience's composition. Although there is no detailed information available to support the claim that the film's viewers have been envisioned as non-Jewish Germans with a limited understanding of Judaism in Germany, the cinematography of the film positions the viewer as a culturally distant onlooker, suggesting his or her association with the cautious teacher Gebhardt, who approaches Goldfarb from exactly this reserved and arguably German standpoint. Furthermore, Hall's notion of literal and associative meanings of signs sheds some light on the consequences of the camera's constructed unfamiliarity with objects identified as pertaining to the Jewish tradition. As signs their denoted meaning is, if not unknown, unclear. Their meaning is mostly constructed at the level of association and connotation, where the signs are "open to articulation with wider ideological discourses and meanings" (Hall 512). As a result, associating these "things Jewish" with foreignness and exoticism, or generally with otherness, becomes their principal meaning. The spectators thus seem to be positioned as unknowing of what they are shown, suggesting a cinematographic construction of an encounter preconfigured as unfamiliar.

Through his request, Gebhardt creates a sense of distance between himself and Goldfarb by using a language of political correctness and, by implication, cultural distance. This distance is expressed in several sub-discourses of German–Jewish relations, political correctness being one of them. Similarly emphasizing difference and distance between Jews and Germans, the notion of political correctness seems to solve the problem of disrespect when naming a Jew "Jewish fellow citizen" or "member of the Jewish community." They imply that the avoided term "Jew" is offensive while actually marking the group of Jewish Germans as different from the unmarked group of non-Jewish Germans. Even though there is no explicit mention of the origin of this naming problem, it is contextualized within the Holocaust when Goldfarb says:

> You wanted to ask to send one over, so that the children can take a look at that. You wanted to write that the extinct species are currently on the curriculum, but we have already been to the dinosaurs in the Natural History museum. [...] This is what it looks like, the Jew. The Jewish fellow citizen. A member of the Jewish community.[25] (Lewinsky 12–13)

Alluding to Hitler's Final Solution of the Jewish Question in Europe and the function of the Yellow Badge to identify Jews immediately as public enemy, the word *Jew* is erased from the public discourse. By using the politically correct terms after the supposedly offensive one, Goldfarb shows all the more their artificiality and constructedness as correctives that paradoxically evoke the presence of the Holocaust exactly by avoiding any association with it. Goldfarb demands to reclaim the word *Jew*, pointing at the constructive use of what Paul Meredith calls the "emancipative potential of negative terms" (1998, 13).

Considering the strong analogy between German Jews and an "extinct species," it is surprising that the Holocaust is never explicitly mentioned in the entire film. Instead, the many and continuous direct and indirect references to it parallel its noticeable though often subliminal presence in German society. They remind viewers of its great impact on the formation of postwar German–Jewish relations and construction of German-Jewish identity. During Goldfarb's furious speech, he constructs a generalized image of these relations that are marked by Germany's attempt to recoup the harm caused by the National Socialist rule not only with material compensation but also, especially in the case of political correctness, with moral (over)compensation, thus casting Jews in a special position that prevents an ordinary life in postwar Germany. "I want to live in a Germany where you can be a Jew without everyone around you thinking that it is important to be automatically tolerant"[26] (Lewinsky 17). Stumbling over the word *tolerant*, Goldfarb looks up the lexeme *tolerance* in an etymological dictionary, where he finds its literal meaning leading him back to his initial problem:

> Tolerance—from the Latin word tolerare, to endure, to undergo. But I do not want to be endured and not undergone. I find the permanent solidarity annoying. [...] I do not want to have this special position. Not in the bad sense of the word and not in the good one. I just want to be an ordinary person. Just an ordinary Jew[27] (18).

Goldfarb does not desire the "normalization" of the Holocaust and the Nazi past, as reviewer Ulrich Kriest suggests. Realizing that he can neither ignore this issue nor constantly subject himself to the German tendency to affect concern, he longs for a third space in which the possibility exists that "difference loses its menacing connotations" (Sommer 162). It is not clear how such a third space would be constructed, and whether there he could be an ordinary Jew without having to exclude the significance of the Holocaust for the construction of his identity. The necessity, however, of constructing a hybrid identity within the discourse of German–Jewish relations becomes apparent in Goldfarb's realization that the current cultural gap between Jews and Germans is widened by the persisting attempt to reduce it: "Don't you notice that your good intention provokes exactly what it attempts to avoid?"[28] (Lewinsky 55). Germany's attempt to harmonize the severely damaged postwar German–Jewish relations seems to have reached its limits, making it necessary to "call into question established categorizations of culture and identity" (Meredith, 14) that pertain not only to the Jew in Germany but also to the German. It must not be overlooked that the discourse of German–Jewish relations not only constructs Goldfarb as Jew in Germany but also Gebhardt and the spectator as Germans, whose relationship to Jews is based on cultural ignorance and alienation.

After a long night of transforming his furious speech into an autobiographical work called *Just an Ordinary Jew*, we see Goldfarb standing in a classroom next to high-school teacher Gebhardt. Goldfarb's book has, so to speak, been publicized at the moment of its formation, contributing to the same discourse of German–Jewish relations in which Goldfarb has refused to participate. In doing so, he expresses his frustration with postwar German–Jewish relations, while at the same time answering his own rhetorical question that he directs at Gebhardt: "Is this what you would like me to tell your students, Mr. Gebhardt? [...] that you can adapt or not adapt, [...] that nothing matters, [...] because you cannot escape your role, not here in Germany, [...] where a teacher writes a polite letter to the Jewish community to hire a real Jew for his social studies class"[29] (Lewinsky 52–53).

It is only in the last scene of the film that he ultimately accepts the challenge to participate in the German–Jewish dialogue, attempting to find what Homi Bhabha calls the "third space," an "in-between" space where "the meaning and symbols of culture have no primordial unity or fixity; [where] even the same signs can be appropriated, translated, rehistoricized, and read anew" (55). Goldfarb is in Gebhardt's classroom, moving slowly to the front desk and sitting down stiffly, with a nervous facial expression. In a series of shot-countershots between the silent group of students and Goldfarb, it becomes clear that both they and he are equally unsure of the kind of behaviour this artificial encounter requires. The ending of Hirschbiegel's film *Ein ganz gewöhnlicher Jude* does not imagine possible ways to create a third space in which the binary opposition of us and them, or of Goldfarb and Gebhardt, or ultimately Jews in Germany and Germans, can be overcome. It recalls, however, that the complex discourse of postwar German–Jewish relations perpetuates a German fascination for Jews, although it means to create an environment in which the seeming opposition of Jewishness and Germanness is overcome.

Notes

1 "[Ich] springe gern in meinen Themen und Genres. Ich folge nicht dem Geld, sondern dem Stoff."
2 "[*Ein ganz gewöhnlicher Jude*] wirkt fast wie ein Nachtrag, wurde ihm doch vorgehalten, er habe in seinem Bunker-Drama jede Anspielung auf den Holocaust geflissentlich ausgelassen."
3 The film is based, verbatim, on Charles Lewinsky's screenplay *Ein ganz gewöhnlicher Jude* that was also published under the same name and without any alterations after the film's release. Due to its accuracy, this published screenplay will be used here as reference for film citations.
4 "Und gerade dadurch, dass er eben nicht dem Klischee eines Juden entspricht, macht er sehr gut deutlich, dass das Klischee bei den anderen liegt. Dass es ihm nicht einmal etwas nützt, wie ein blonder SA-Mann auszusehen. Wenn das Klischee einmal da ist, sieht man in ihm nur den typischen Juden, auch wenn er es gar nicht ist."
5 "deutsche Betroffenheitskultur."
6 "Sehr geehrte Damen und Herren, mit meiner achten Klasse werde ich im Sozialkundeunterricht im nächsten Semester das Thema Judentum behandeln. Ich habe die Erfahrung gemacht, [...] dass nichts so anschaulich und einprägsam wirkt, wie eine persönliche Begegnung und möchte deshalb gerne einen jüdischen Mitbürger einladen, an einer Unterrichtsstunde teilzunehmen und Fragen der Schüler zu beantworten. Leider kenne ich persönlich kein Mitglied Ihrer Religionsgemeinschaft [...] und wollte Sie deshalb bitten, diese Einladung anzunehmen und uns zu besuchen. [...] so hoffe ich, dass Sie meiner Bitte entsprechen können und verbleibe mit einem herzlichen Schalom [...], R. Gebhardt."
7 "ranschmeißerisches Verständnis."
8 "ekelhafte Einfühlsamkeit."

9 "das deutsche Betroffenheitsgesicht."
10 "das Gedenkansprachen-im-Bundestag-Gesicht."
11 "das Lea-Rosh-Gesicht."
12 "Moralkeule."
13 "Pflichtübung."
14 "jederzeit einsetzbares Einschüchterungsmittel."
15 "Aber in welchen Verdacht gerät man, wenn man sagt, die Deutschen seien jetzt ein ganz normales Volk, eine ganz gewöhnliche Gesellschaft?"
16 "[...] ich [versuche], die Vorhaltung unserer Schande auf Motive hin abzuhören, und bin fast froh, wenn ich glaube, entdecken zu können, daß öfter nicht mehr das Gedenken, das Nichtvergessendürfen das Motiv ist, sondern die Instrumentalisierung unserer Schande zu gegenwärtigen Zwecken."
17 "Ich weiß genau, was für ein Gesicht Sie machen werden, wenn Sie das lesen, Herr Gebhardt. Das deutsche Betroffenheitsgesicht. [...] Das müssen Sie nicht, Herr Gebhardt. Das hier ist eine Kaffeetasse, keine Moralkeule."
18 "Ich habe das Lager, in dem meine Mutter als junges Mädchen vegetierte, nicht erwähnt, damit Sie ein schlechtes Gewissen haben. Ich kann diesen 'Ach-wie-war-das-alles-schrecklich'-Reflex genauso wenig leiden wie Martin Walser. Aber ich kann auch nicht immer einen Bogen um das Thema machen. Das verkrümmt auf die Dauer den Rücken."
19 "Ich verschließe mich Übeln, an deren Behebung ich nicht mitwirken kann. Ich habe lernen müssen, wegzuschauen."
20 "Routine des Beschuldigens."
21 "Wir haben die gleiche Geschichte, aber nicht die gleichen Geschichten, Sie und ich. Obwohl es alle deutsche Geschichten sind."
22 "Dass wir immer Juden in Deutschland sein werden, und nie jüdische Deutsche. Ein ewiger Sonderfall."
23 "Soll ich das Ihren Schülern erzählen, Herr Gebhardt? Dass es keine Selbstverständlichkeit für uns geben kann, nicht auf der einen Seite und nicht auf der anderen, weil es eben zwei Seiten sind und zwei Seiten bleiben, weil es keinen Zentralrat der jüdischen Deutschen gibt und keinen der deutschen Juden, sondern nur einen Zentralrat der Juden in Deutschland."
24 "Wir sind ein Fall für die Tierschützer geworden. Für Greenpeace und den Verein für christlich-jüdische Zusammenarbeit. Nashörner guckt man sich im Zoo an; Juden lädt man sich in den Unterricht ein."
25 "Schicken Sie doch mal einen vorbei, wollten Sie bitten, damit sich die Kinder das ansehen können. Es stehen gerade die ausgestorbenen Tierarten auf dem Lehrplan, wollten Sie schreiben, und bei den Dinosauriern im Naturhistorischen Museum waren wir schon. [...] So sieht das nun also aus, der Jude. Der jüdische Mitbürger. Ein Mitglied der jüdischen Religionsgemeinschaft."
26 "Ich möchte in einem Deutschland leben, in dem man Jude sein kann, ohne dass die Leute um einen herum es automatisch für notwendig erachten, tolerant zu sein."
27 "'Toleranz'—vom lateinischen tolerare, erleiden, erdulden. Ich möchte aber nicht erlitten werden, nicht gelitten und nicht geduldet. Die permanente Solidarität geht mir auf die Nerven. [...] Ich will die Sonderrolle nicht haben. Nicht im Schlechten und nicht im Guten. Ein ganz gewöhnlicher Mensch möchte ich sein. Ein ganz gewöhnlicher Jude."
28 "Merken Sie denn nicht, dass Ihre gute Absicht genau das bewirkt, was sie verhindern will?"

29 "Soll ich das Ihren Schülern erzählen, Herr Gebhardt? [...] Dass man sich anpassen kann oder nicht anpassen, [...] dass das alles egal ist, [...] weil man nicht rauskommt aus seiner Rolle, nicht hier in Deutschland, [...], wo ein Lehrer einen höflichen Brief an die Gemeinde schreibt, um sich einen echten Juden für den Sozialkundeunterricht zu engagieren."

References

Autor Charles Lewinsky im Interview. NDR Fernsehen. 30 Apr. 2008. 6 Nov. 2009 <http://www3.ndr.de/moderation/ndr_produktionen/prod148.html>.

Bhabha, Homi. *The Location of Culture.* London: Routledge, 1994.

Brockmann, Stephen. "Martin Walser and the Presence of the German Past." *German Quarterly* 75 (2002): 127–43.

Broder, Henryk M. "Der ewige Gute." Rev. of *Ein ganz gewöhnlicher Jude,* dir. Oliver Hirschbiegel. *Spiegel Online* 19 Jan. 2006. 30 Apr. 2008 <http://www.spiegel.de>.

Delius, Friedrich Christian. "Herrn Walsers Schlacht um den Seelenfrieden." *Glossen: Eine internationale zweisprachige Publikation zu Literatur, Film, und Kunst in den deutschsprachigen Ländern nach 1945* 11 (2000): n. pag.

Ein ganz gewöhnlicher Jude (Just an Ordinary Jew). Dir. Oliver Hirschbiegel. Multimedia Film- und Fernsehproduktions GmbH, 2005.

Filmhitlisten. FFA—Filmförderungsanstalt. 30 Apr. 2008 <http://www.ffa.de/>.

Foucault, Michel. *The Archaeology of Knowledge.* Trans. A. M. Sheridan Smith. London: Routledge, 2002.

Hall, Stuart. "Encoding, Decoding." *The Cultural Studies Reader.* Ed. Simon During. London: Routledge, 2000. 507–17.

Kriest, Ulrich. "Wie man Geschichte entsorgt." Rev. of *Ein ganz gewöhnlicher Jude,* dir. Oliver Hirschbiegel. *Stuttgarter Zeitung* 9 Feb. 2006. 30 Apr. 2008. <http://www.stuttgarter-zeitung.de/>.

Lewinsky, Charles. *Ein ganz gewöhnlicher Jude.* Berlin: Rotbuch, 2006.

Meredith, Paul. "Hybridity and the Third Space: Rethinking Bi-cultural Politics in Aotearoa/New Zealand." *He Pukenga Korero: A Journal for Maori Studies* 4.2 (1999): 12–16.

Mills, Sara. *Discourse.* London: Routledge, 2004.

Papastergiadis, Nikos. "Tracing Hybridity in Theory." *Debating Cultural Hybridity: Multi-Cultural Identities and the Politics of Anti-Racism.* Ed. Pnina Werbner and Tarig Modood. London: Zed Books, 1997. 257–81.

Pribram, Deidre E. "Spectatorship and Subjectivity." *A Companion to Film Theory.* Ed. Toby Miller and Robert Stam. Malden: Blackwell, 1999. 146–64.

Rodek, Hanns-Georg. "Ein ganz gewöhnlicher Jude. 'Untergang'-Regisseur Oliver Hirschbiegel über seinen neuen Film." *Die Welt* 18 Jan. 2006. 30 Apr. 2008 <http://www.welt.de>.

Sommer, Roy. "'Simple Survival' in 'Happy Multicultural Land'?" *Diaspora and Multiculturalism.* Ed. Monika Fludernik. Amsterdam: Rodopi, 2003. 149–81.

Walser, Martin. "Erfahrungen beim Verfassen einer Sonntagsrede." *Friedenspreis des Deutschen Buchhandels 1998*. Frankfurt: Suhrkamp, 1998.

Zander, Peter. "Mein letztes Nein." Rev. of *Ein ganz gewöhnlicher Jude*, dir. Oliver Hirschbiegel. *Berliner Morgenpost* 19 Jan. 2006. 20 May 2009 <http://www.morgenpost.de>.

12
Border, Bridge, or Barrier?
Images of the German–Polish Borderlands in German Cinema of the 2000s

Jakub Kazecki

Abstract Drawing upon border studies and using the notions of the frontier, boundary, and borderland as sites of hybridity, this chapter investigates how Poles and their country are perceived in contemporary German cinema. It explores images of German–Polish relationships in selected German films such as *Vergiss Amerika* (Vanessa Joop, 2000), *Herz im Kopf* (Michael Gutmann, 2001), *Klassenfahrt* (Henner Winckler, 2002), *Milchwald* (Christoph Hochhäusler, 2003), and *Schröders wunderbare Welt* (Michael Schorr, 2006).

On 21 December 2007, as a further step in the expansion of the European Union, which had started in 2004, passport checks were abolished on Germany's border with its neighbours to the east, Poland and the Czech Republic, allowing the two countries' citizens to freely move within the Union's Schengen zone. The new European Union states' implementation of the Schengen agreements marked a symbolic end to the postwar order of Europe: the border control at the limits of "old Europe" had disappeared. While Polish officials and public opinion interpreted the border opening as a natural and long-desired step in the expansion of the European Union, and often formulated the step as "returning home to Europe," difficulties emerging in the new situation, such as the inability to control illegal immigration from third countries, were suppressed. The Polish Ministry of Interior and Administration emphasized in an official news report the historic moment of the border opening: "The importance of this event could be compared to our accession to the EU" ("We Are in the Schengen Area!"). The voice of the administration was accompanied by enthusiastic headlines and affectionate editorials in the press: "A Happy Cutting of Borders" (Kraśnicki), "Poland of Open Borders" (Stróżyk and Cybiński), or "Poland has Returned Home" (Seweryn). Carried by a wave of Euro-enthusiasm, Polish officials and the Polish press rushed to play down the issue of illegal activity and international conflict around the German–Polish border, and they started to stress the necessity of securing the new eastern perimeter of the EU.

The overall enthusiastic response to the border opening suggested that the border-related complications around Görlitz/Zgorzelec and Frankfurt an der Oder/Słubice had disappeared on that single December night of 2007. In Germany, however, more often than not concerns were expressed about long-standing controversies associated with the Oder/Neisse line. The German commentators articulated various potential problems such as a further increase in criminal activity after the border opening, an influx of illegal immigrants and cheap labour, and a worsening of the economic situation of the local population, stressing all too often an assumed civilizational discrepancy between Germany and Poland, that is to say, between the "old" and the "new" Europe (Crolly).

The negative and positive values associated with Poland and Germany were and are projected onto the borderland region in which various influences and interests cross, and national and European identity formations are tested and developed. This opens a promising field for filmmakers, who look for narrative tensions originating in conflicts and in visible and invisible barriers between the characters. Differences emerging from complex socio-historical, political, and linguistic conditioning, as is the case with Germans and Poles, seem to create a unique opportunity for exploring images of international contacts in liminal situations.

The present essay investigates the cinematic representations of the boundaries between Germany and Poland and concentrates on selected German film productions that pose, directly or indirectly, questions about the attitude of Germans toward Poles in the context of the changing European borders, that is, whether the border area is represented in the films as the true link between western and eastern Europe, or whether it is shown as a territory infiltrated by foreigners who put the local social structures in danger. Seen through a camera lens, is there a border, a bridge, or a barrier between Germany and Poland? In order to answer the question, I will focus on films set against the increasingly infiltrated or disappearing geopolitical barrier between the two countries in the late 1990s and 2000s. Around that time, many German filmmakers rediscovered the narrative potential of the Otherness of Poland. As individual, business, and cultural relationships with Germany's neighbour to the east intensified, audiences were ready to be receptive about depictions of Poland from a German perspective. Many films such as *Schröders wunderbare Welt* (*Schröder's Wonderful World*) by Michael Schorr (2006), *Halbe Treppe* (*Grill Point*) by Andreas Dresen (2002), and *Lichter* (*Distant Lights*) by Hans-Christian Schmid (2003) place the main personal conflicts against the background of a hybrid borderland society. Elements associated with Poland play key functions in these narratives. In the first part of the chapter, I will concentrate on *Schröders wunderbare Welt* as a particularly successful representation of the idea of hybridity in German–Polish filmic border discourse. Other films such as *Klassenfahrt* (*School Trip*, Henner Winckler, 2002), *Herz im Kopf* (*Heart Over Head*, Michael Gutmann, 2001), and *Milchwald* (*This Very Moment*, Christoph Hochhäusler, 2003) build the main narrative tension around the confrontation of Germans with a negatively codified Other that manifests itself in the landscapes of Poland, in Polish language and social structures, and in the alluring yet threatening sexual appeal of Poles. I will discuss these films in more detail in the second part of the chapter. Yet other productions such as *Befreite Zone* (*Liberated Zone*, Norbert Baumgarten, 2003) or *Vergiss Amerika* (*Forget America*, Vanessa Joop, 2000) contain only an episodic yet strongly codified appearance or camouflaged allusion to Poland. They are playing upon the stereotypical, widely recognizable image of the country and its citizens: a characteristic typical for the popular reception of Poland in German commercial media until the border opening. While I am considering German films only, it has to be noted that the Polish cinema during the time frame in question also delivered to its audiences a number of Western border-related productions, in which the Otherness of foreigners (not only Germans) is strongly emphasized. But the question of how the border and migration issues are portrayed in Polish cinema of the last decade will not be discussed here, nor will the many documentaries from Germany and Poland that thematize the German–Polish border, as these deserve a separate analysis. To the recent Polish feature films that explore the topics of border opening, border crossing, and living in the borderlands belong, among others, *Oda do radości* (*Ode to Joy* by Anna Kazejak, Jan Komasa, and Maciej Migas, 2005) and the adaptation of Radek Knapp's novel, *Lekcje pana Kuki* (Mr. Kuka's Recommendations) by Dariusz Gajewski (2008).

As recent German films set near the German–Polish border suggest, the geopolitical division between Germany and Poland is but one divide from which the filmmakers draw narrative tension. Another is the notion of a "natural boundary" between the two countries: not a geographical divide in form of a river or a mountain range, but an assumption that there is a difference in character of nations, a set of innate national characteristics. The concept of natural boundary, which was popularized in France during the Enlightenment, proclaims that the differences between nations result from differences in climate (that is, in nature). Different climates would influence peoples' behaviour, habits, and language, creating natural divides between populations in different areas. Although rejected by the scientific community as an ideological superstructure for the expansion of nations, this theory survived in both German and Polish schools and vernacular social consciousness, signifying the linguistic, social, and cultural differences between Germans and Poles (Schultz 9–21, Rykiel 57). It is also worth noting that, despite the fact that Polish stereotypes are a persistent topic and that some of these films have found a wide popular and critical audience, there has been little discussion about the way national stereotypes about Polish people influence the construction of film characters and locales. I consider stereotypes as products of national-typological fiction, as mental images, ideas, and *Vorstellungsbilder*, that is, as value judgments resulting from a selective perception channelled through pre-existing categories in which the given social group sees itself and the Other—which fulfill an identity-building function in the political-intellectual projection of a nation (Beller 12). According to a sociological study on the perception of Poles in Germany conducted in 2000 by Xymena Dolińska, the associations bound with the image of Germany's neighbours are predominantly negative: the Germans see Poland as an underdeveloped country in which the political, economic, and social conditions differ substantially from western European standards. In the view of the respondents, "typically Polish" characteristics include religiosity, backwardness, dishonesty, laziness, dirtiness, and a lack of success in life. Positive characteristics were rarely named; in general, the Germans, despite a shared history with the Poles, see themselves as not being similar to their eastern neighbours (Dmitrów 432–34).

The number of films set in the eastern margins of the former GDR or even in the areas ceded to Poland after 1945, including the Baltic coast of Pomerania, provoked scholars to read the filmmakers' choice of location as a statement about German identities in a post-unification era of continued European integration. Gabriele Mueller, analyzing the films *Lichter* and *Halbe Treppe*, notes that some filmmakers contest the use of large urban areas such as Berlin in identity-formation discourses. If the capital city serves as the mainstream site of forging contemporary identities, the dislocation of the narratives to the east establishes a "countermodel to the Berlin discourse by constructing German identity as explicitly European rather than distinctly German" (Mueller 119). Similarly, Kristin Kopp argues for reading *Lichter* as a picture of transnational space, offering a model for local identity as opposed to a global identity (Kopp). Alexandra Ludewig, who concentrates, among others, on the films *Vergiss Amerika* and *Klassenfahrt*, sees the directors' interest in the Baltic Sea coast as a contemporary reinvention of escapist *Heimat* images and a regression from a world that has become alienating. She states that the travel to the periphery, far from the official centres of power, is a "flight" that "signifies a total rejection of the prevailing ethos of the political and economic developments in contemporary eastern/central European regions" (Ludewig 171).

In order to decentralize and challenge the debate about German identity, the directors choose Germany's borderlands rather than the country's centre as the sites of their films: the borderlands emerge here as sites of hybridity, exposed to foreign trans-border influences and cross-border movements, and subjected to cultural clashes. *Lichter* and *Halbe Treppe*, widely discussed in film scholarship, are not the only examples of such borderland treatment. Michael Schorr's *Schröders wunderbare Welt*, released in 2006, also seems to follow the paradigm of borderland and communities at the margins of Germany as an opportunity to create an alternative to the processes of European identity building—as an alternative to films in which Berlin is seen as a pulsating metropolis that epitomizes the new European Germany. In Schorr's film, however, the attempt to overcome the local specific and to follow the institutionally encouraged pattern of regional and transnational cooperation leads to failure. The starting point of *Schröders wunderbare Welt* is inspired by real-life events: in the Dreiländereck, the area in German Lower Silesia where Germany, Poland, and the Czech Republic meet, a development project that includes building a golf course, a hotel with marina, and an underwater park is currently under way at the Berzdorfer See, a lake located south from Görlitz/Zgorzelec. In the film, Schorr turns the modern tale of regional success into a disaster story: Frank Schröder, a young employee of Paradise Corporation, convinces his boss, the American John Gregory, to invest in a "Magic Lagoon" in Tauchritz, Schröder's birthplace. The investment should also create a chance for multinational co-operation between three mayors: Frank Schröder's father, Theo, the Czech Milan Janáçek, and the Pole Jerzy Krukowski. Everything goes well until the investor, who has a soft spot for hunting, takes an offer to go on a hunt. Theo's brother-in-law Wigbert Wolf, a nationalist nurturing dreams about German Silesia, uses this opportunity to turn the investor against the locals and torpedo the entire project. The film suggests that the attempt to overcome the local specific and to follow the institutionally encouraged pattern of regional and transnational cooperation leads to failure.

In the tri-point region, as portrayed by Schorr, the visible borders have been abolished de facto: in the area around Tauchritz, geographical divisions (like rivers or mountain ranges) are nowhere to be seen. The CineScope camera looks over the silent valleys in inclusive panoramas or bird's-eye-view shots that

Michael Schorr, *Schröders wunderbare Welt*: selecting a location for the Czech-German-Polish tropical resort. © filmkombinat

offer no clue as to where one country ends and another begins. The borders, however, are redrawn for the purpose of a projected tropical paradise simply because they are needed. In the scene in the power plant Bogatynia, the Polish and German officials discuss the project for the first time, together with Frank Schröder and Wigbert Wolf, who throws in questionable comments about the *polnische Wirtschaft*, the Polish economy. The borders are brought into existence only on an amateurishly designed map and miniature model of the region, which are used as presentation tools. The unskillfully prepared model, with national flags stuck in the clay for better orientation, is a mock replica of large-scale EU-supported projects. It creates a satirical comment on divisions set arbitrarily, according to the nation paradigm. The abstract character of the borderline is stressed in both instances: the division between countries has to be created first in order to be overcome by a regional effort. The horizontal model of the *Lagunenzauber*, the Magic Lagoon, reappears once more in the form of a cake made of exotic fruits. This third appearance of the model drives the analogy to European Union–funded projects home, as Theo literally puts his hand in the cake, the symbolic cookie jar of European funds. Similarly, the language of European unification is reduced to buzzwords, as in the presentation of the future tropical paradise by the driving force of the investment, Frank Schröder, to his uninspired father, the mayor of Tauchritz: "Everything will have a lasting effect, it will be agreeable, ecological, and so on … from now on, we have to think on a larger scale: global, international, border-crossing."[1] The ideological and linguistic project of removing the borders and starting an international initiative is reduced to a forced performance, re-enacted in the joint effort of the three mayors, and a necessary show played for the purposes of potential future investment in the region. The scene draws a vision of the united European region as an escapist fantasy in which there are "no terror, no freak tides and tornadoes,"[2] that is, a dream, a tropical holiday destination for Europeans, only better, because it would be both familiar and new and apparently untroubled by post-colonial social and political disturbances.

The act of reaching out to connect is desired by the paradigm of European co-operation, but in the film the gesture appears delayed and unnecessary. John Gregory's description of the new construction site, in which the "former enemies unite to create a great project that will bring prosperity and freedom to the people of this wonderful place," is a mockery of the political speeches of the Kohl era, especially of Kohl's famous "blooming landscapes" speech.[3] In contrast to Kohl's optimism, Gregory's imagery is outdated by over a decade and displaced in an area devastated by heavy industry. In this area, where old factories stand like abandoned ruins in the landscape, the connotation of the phrase "blooming landscapes" changes, as nature slowly gains the upper hand over the de-industrialized region. Gregory, a second-generation American of Russian descent, operates on the level of perceiving borders as frontiers separating malevolent people, an impression that is not corrected but amplified by the locals presenting him with a machine gun to face "the beast in all of us" and staging the hunt. Gregory's character is highly ambiguous: he represents the blissful intervention from above (investment) and, at the same time, the dangers of imposing an interpretative framework from a position of power. His attire and the elements of military vocabulary in his language, as well as the simplified employment of the "survival of the fittest" principle, stand in contrast with the non-invasive, rather passive characters of the locals. Gregory's character is a symbol of aggressive globalization, stressed linguistically by the use of the English language that both Frank Schröder and his father, the main people behind the project, are desperately trying to acquire. The investor is both a chance and a threat to the tri-point area, and he deals professionally with building artificial tropical paradises: a colonial trope of unmarked and unsurveyed space that offers unusual possibilities of commercial enterprise. By introducing the figure of Gregory, Schorr draws a clear parallel between the colonial discourse and the EU border-crossing project that promises the commercial development of the region. *Schröders wunderbare Welt* satirically depicts the re-colonization of European spaces by a gesture of unmarking the space once divided between the three states in order to announce it as an area available for colonial conquest, therefore allowing for its discovery and development. The assumption that the space is unmarked has a convenient (from the point of view of the explorers) consequence of ignoring the local specific with its divisions of space, borders, and areas of communal exchange. And that's exactly what is happening in *Schröders wunderbare Welt*: by redrawing and abolishing the borders, the "discovery" of the Silesian tri-point for the purposes of an ideological project of the united Europe is complete.

In addition, the film seems to juxtapose the imposed act of redrawing and then abolishing the borders with the notion of *Heimat*. The viewer can hear the overreaching statement "Once a Silesian, always a Silesian" on a few occasions in the film. Each time, the statement effectively disarms any frustration and differences between Germans, Poles, and Czechs brought about by their forced cooperation. Schorr relies here on an important element of Silesian identity—the Catholic faith—and the Catholic character of the region is stressed in a number of interior shots of the apartments of Germans, Poles, and Czechs that show religious symbols in the background. In the last two centuries, the Catholic Church upheld a distinctive perspective that recognized ethnic differences in the region but, at the same time, did not recognize ethnicity as instrumental in developing a national identity. Here, too, the characters are depicted first as Silesian (with German as lingua franca) and only then as representatives of national groups. The distinctive elements are treated as marginal: the director uses them to introduce subversive humour by playing with the expectations of the viewers. National stereotypes are reduced to innocent quirks and treated with stereotype-subverting humour: the Poles are associated with caring and controlling female figures, low technological culture, and a fascination with weapons and uniforms, while a predilection for the affluent life is attributed to Czechs in the figure of Janáçek. Occasionally, conflicts between the three national groups reappear during hiccups in cooperation. But the snipes at unorganized Slavs, fascists, and World War II aggressors have a strong ritual character expressing the frustration of the participants with the overwhelming task rather that reflecting any real events. They seem absurd and anachronistic, a residue of state propaganda practices before 1989. Most of the conflicts live in the musings of the old nationalist and revanchist Wigbert Wolf, but the danger lying in his stories is disarmed by his inept actions. In a way, Wolf's displacement in time, his living in the past, catches up with the present; his dream of Silesia without borders is already realized. His attachment to the former great Silesia, paradoxically, saves the day. He saves Tauchritz from the investment that would inevitably change the place. His attempts to sabotage the investment that would transform Tauchritz serve to bring the three mayors closer together, and his final trick to delay the agreement by sending John Gregory on an overnight wolf hunt gives the locals time to realize that they do not need an exotic project to co-operate. This realization is sealed by the joint trip to the hospital to witness the birth of a new citizen of the region, Janáçek's child.

Schröders wunderbare Welt depicts the borderlands as a site of true hybridity that should be left to (human, local) nature, and where no ideological projects should be conducted. The characters' playground—the valleys and mountains between Tauchritz, Bogatynia, and Grabstejn—is depicted as inclusive rather than exclusive: the area sucks in the newcomers landing at the bus stop like a Bermuda triangle, and, in exchange for the separation from the outside world and the willingness to accept the quirks of the locals, provides the visitors with personal fulfillment. Only the intruders who are not willing to accept the status quo are rejected. This is the fate anticipated for John Gregory: lost in the fog after the overnight hunt, he enters a golf course guarded with a scythe by Karel, Janáçek's employee and a modern Silesian grim reaper.

While *Schröders wunderbare Welt* postulates the tri-national borderlands as a site of hybridity, the German–Polish border appears much more frequently as a frontier in German films. The frontier, a term used in border studies for historical and present-day colonial encroachments, signifies the meeting point between the known and the alien land. The previously mentioned notion of a "natural boundary" between Germany and Poland reflects the paradigm of a frontier, a product of colonial discourse that implies the opportunity to push forward, explore the new land, and benefit economically or socially. The risk connected with this type of border crossing is quite significant: the escapades on "the other side" are intrusions into the unknown beyond the German comfort zone.

Christoph Hochhäusler's *Milchwald*, especially, offers a very good example of the treatment of the German–Polish border as a frontier and not as a place of hybridity and exchange. The film, a variation on the Hänsel and Gretel theme, tells the story of Sylvia, stepmother to two children, Lea and Konstantin. During a shopping trip to neighbouring Poland, she is annoyed by the kids' behaviour in the car and dumps them on the side of the road. She is afraid to tell Josef, her husband, about the incident, and the children roam the Polish side of the border until Kuba Lubiński, a travelling sales manager who supplies the motels in the area with sanitary products, finds them. Kuba first wants to take Lea and Konstantin to the police, but, after seeing on TV that Josef is offering a reward for any information about his lost children, the salesman decides to earn some money on the side and deliver the children to Josef himself.

In an interview about *Milchwald*, Hochhäusler explained his vision of Otherness in the film: he needed a frontier, "a space that is relatively strange and different, and the German–Polish border is something like that. Many Germans do not know Poland, surprisingly. It is a direct neighbour. The language is very different; it is really a different cultural area. It is certainly the strongest of all German borders"[4] (Schleich). These remarks reflect the difference between the two ways of perceiving the German–Polish border. In contrast to Schorr's treatment of the border as practically non-existent, Hochhäusler draws a very strong divide between the two countries and cultures, and does not allow for any exchange. Following the paradigm of frontier, the director of *Milchwald* takes advantage of both elements, the intertextual echoes of his narrative and the linguistic and cultural Otherness of Poland. The viewers' interpretation of the children's first encounter with a Pole is preconditioned by the reception of the well-known Hänsel and Gretel story—the hungry children find an unlocked truck in the middle of the forest, and they find food set up on a table in front of it (the equivalent of the gingerbread house from the Grimms' tale). The truck belongs to Kuba, who is just taking a dinner break on the road. Even when Kuba, after the first brief moment of speaking Polish and scaring the children, switches to familiar German and in a friendly manner invites the children to join him at the table, an element of uncertainty about his intentions remains. The audience's misgiving is confirmed when good-hearted Kuba, motivated by a stroke of greed, refuses to let the children go. The German spoken by the Pole is revealed as an instrument of deception. Moreover, the representation of languages in *Milchwald* becomes an indicator of the director's position on the divisions between the characters as unbridgeable. The Polish spoken in the film is not translated and contributes to the isolation of the characters, unlike in *Schröders wunderbare Welt*, where Polish and Czech dialogue is subtitled, and where the Czechs and the Poles speak German, helping each other with translation problems.

Before a word of Polish is even spoken in *Milchwald*, however, the Otherness of Poland is already manifested in the landscape. When Sylvia picks up Konstantin and Lea on their way back from school in the opening sequence of the film, bald hills and power lines characterize the German spaces, with one empty asphalt road cutting through the deserted landscape. The moment of crossing the border is marked by the passport control. The viewer does not yet know what country the visitors enter, for the border officer is German. The first time the viewer is informed about which border has been crossed is the moment when Sylvia marks the area where the children have vanished on the map for her husband. The viewer sees the abstract cartographic image of the space, with a clearly marked red border and the name of the foreign country. Before knowing the country's name, the viewer first experiences the Otherness of Poland as a change in vegetation. On the other side of the border, the power lines disappear and are replaced by a thick green forest. Wheat fields are ready for harvest, pollen dust is slowly carried by the wind, and birds are singing. The sleepy high summer landscape reminds the viewer of a dreamy vision of an unreal and wild land, vital but threatening.

The foreign area is tied to Germany by the road system, a device created to control nature and put it on track, a civilizing effort to provide a connection between people, but, as used by Hochhäusler, also a metaphor for personal development. When the children get lost, they are going away from the road, pushed by the approaching combine, and they disappear in the road ditch. The night spent in the forest is the only time when the children are deprived of any social contacts, truly lost in the middle of nowhere in a state of suspension. Kuba, who finds the children, is constantly on the move, and takes Lea and Konstantin with him on the trip. The children experience the new country from his truck, looking at the roads and streets of Poland. The strangeness of the foreign land is mediated through their point of view: the traditional annual August pilgrimage to the Catholic monastery in Częstochowa on the side of the road appears inexplicable and fascinating in its exoticism. The city streets blocked by the masses of pilgrims praying, singing, and marching with Polish and EU flags seem like a chaotic disturbance to the rules of traffic—an intervention of nature, invading the roads and lifting the civilizing order.

The contrast between Polish and German spaces as domains of vitality and infertility respectively is amplified through the depiction of Sylvia and Josef's house: a brand-new black-and-white building, characterized by clean lines and symmetrical design, with a concrete driveway and a carefully trimmed front yard. The interior of the house is cold and sterile, with the blinds half-closed, lights off, unfinished walls, and furniture still factory-wrapped. The rooms are submerged in a blue-tinted light and ghostly quiet. The house is also a space of intimacy bordering on entrapment, which mirrors Sylvia's state and explains her wish for a chance at a new life without the burden of her stepchildren. The spaces where Sylvia has abandoned the kids are characterized by the cycle of nature and a maternal principle: rich in vegetation and eroticized, they are clearly juxtaposing the emptiness of the father's house. Several visual elements on the Polish side of the border remind the audience of Sylvia's denial of her parental duties and her symbolic infertility: the stork appearing in Sylvia's path when she reflects on her moment of hostility toward Lea and Konstantin; the Church celebrations of harvest and pilgrimage to Mary, the Mother of God; the caring maternal figures who feed the hungry children; and Kuba's pregnant wife who struggles with the decision whether she should paint the child's room blue (for a boy) or pink (for a girl).

The father's search for his lost children is also visually associated with a landscape deprived of any vegetation, as he seems to turn the places he visits in Poland into a desert: he looks for Lea and Konstantin in an empty open-air theatre and an abandoned parking lot with street lamps like bizarre concrete flowers. The rejection of the vital elements, associated with the land abroad, is depicted by Hochhäusler as a dominant feature of the relationship between Josef and Sylvia. The trip to Poland exposes the faults of their marriage. Even when the moment of border crossing and facing the Other appears to be a chance for communication between the two adults, Sylvia still cannot overcome her fear of being honest, and Josef promptly leaves his wife, deserting her in a dark hotel room that replicates the setting of their empty household.

A similar depiction of Polish areas as a colourful background against which the conflicts between the protagonists are played out can be found in Henner Winkler's *Klassenfahrt*. The film, released one year before *Milchwald* in 2002, starts, like *Milchwald*, on the road: a group of high-school students from Berlin have just passed the German–Polish border on their way to the Baltic Sea, to the Polish border town Międzyzdroje, for a week-long school trip. The students spend their time drinking, walking on the beach, frequenting the bars, and flirting with each other. Ronny, the shy outsider in the group, is interested in Isa but finds himself in latent competition with a Polish teenager, the older and more self-confident Marek, who works in a local hotel during the summer. The rivalry between the two boys ends tragically: Ronny provokes the drunken Marek to jump off the pier, and the Pole dies in the attempt.

Christoph Hochhäusler, *Milchwald*. © Filmgalerie 451

The view of Poland presented by the film offers a comment on the young generation's perception of Germany's neighbour, and a polemic directed against the understanding of the borderlands as sites of hybridity. The hotel where the students stay is an island of German-ness in the foreign element. The visitors are not supposed to go outside without supervision, but they are also not curious at all about their surroundings, except for escapades to places that they know, and in which they feel comfortable, like the local disco or the snack bar. They watch the German series *Tatort* on TV, even when it is dubbed into Polish, clinging to the familiar. Their teacher's intention to bring them to the Polish coast is not revealed; the viewer knows as much as the students, who do not understand the purpose of the trip. The failure of the educational aspect of the stay is especially visible during the visit to the Archaeological Museum, which becomes a stage for teenage gags. A feeling of spatial disorientation prevails— the day trip to Szczecin/Stettin is welcomed with the indifferent question: "Where is it anyway?"

The attitude toward Poland is brought to the point in the figures of the two German protagonists, Isa and Ronny. Isa, asked by Marek what she wants to do after graduation, answers that she intends to do "something special," maybe go abroad.[5] Poland, the destination suggested by Marek, does not seem attractive to Isa, however, who would prefer to go to the United States. She is the only one, though, who demonstrates any signs of curiosity and interacts with Polish boys, using German and broken English to communicate. The only time Ronny is exposed to the world outside of the familiar hotel surroundings is when he tries to show his independence and runs away, hitchhiking through the countryside. The camera takes over his point of view and witnesses a series of seemingly inexplicable episodes that make him very uncomfortable: two suspicious men drive him through the unknown area, a car crashes in front of him without any apparent reason, and the driver swears at him, and he is subjected to the curious gaze of the locals while visiting a village. Eventually, he comes back to the hotel in a car, looking at the streets he passes by from a safe distance, separated from the surroundings by glass.

The pier shown in the final scene of *Klassenfahrt* brings the film to a visual point. Although it resembles a bridge, the pier, the site of Marek's tragic death, leads nowhere and connects nothing. The film's concluding metaphor makes a pessimistic statement about the young Germans who use stereotypes in their perception of Poland, but they do not make any effort to challenge them. They only feel comfortable after the foreign threat (personified by Marek) is removed from view.

Another production directed at younger audiences and thematizing the contacts between Germans and Poles, although not placed in the border area but in Frankfurt am Main, is *Herz im Kopf* by Michael Gutmann from 2001. The film tells the emerging love story between a Polish au pair from Kraków, Wanda, and a German teenage rebel, Jakob. Gutmann, who also worked on the script of *Lichter* by Hans-Christian Schmid, exposes the erotic appeal of the foreign woman without the subversive effect of irony, which makes the film almost voyeuristic. The character of Jakob, who gets involved with Wanda, is contrasted with the figure of Dirk, who is attracted to Polish au pairs but blames the Otherness of the women as the main reason for seeing them strictly as exotic sexual conquests. Each woman becomes replaceable when "she has to go back to her native land."[6] What draws Jakob to Wanda is not clear (the logic of the narrative suggests he sees his relationship with Wanda as revenge on his former schoolteacher, who is Wanda's employer). It is up to Wanda to overcome her social limitations and accept Jakob's rebellion without reservations: in the final scene, Wanda gives up her job as cleaning lady and babysitter (she takes over Jakob's view of her employment as au pair as demeaning) in order to stay with her boyfriend. The gesture of accepting the German has strong colonial connotations: Jakob wins over the attractive woman without engaging in cultural exchange besides the occasional conversations about the duties of an au pair and jokes about stealing Polish cars. An additional intertextual reference pointing to that interpretation is hidden in Wanda's name: according to a Polish national legend written down by Wincenty Kadubek in the twelfth century and popularized after 1945 to sustain Polish–German antagonisms, Wanda is the name of a Polish princess from Kraków who rejected the advances of a German king and who chose death by drowning over marrying the stranger and surrendering her beloved land to him (Mistrz Wincenty 16). The modern Wanda's acceptance of her German suitor reverses the story and affirms the German conquest.

Similarly, the conservative national stereotypes, popular in the western part of Germany, that depict Poles as car thieves, illegal workers, or prostitutes can be observed in productions depicting life in the new German *Bundesstaaten* in the east. In the films *Befreite Zone* by Norbert Baumgarten and *Vergiss Amerika* by Vanessa Joop, the proximity of the border plays only an episodic role. The portrayals of the competitive conditions of free-market economy and their impact on the local communities, with concentration on the young generation trying to get jobs, include interactions with strangers: in *Vergiss Amerika*, the wannabe American car dealer, Benno, engages in shady business with Polish criminals and, after an initial period of prosperity, gets in trouble with his new customers (dressed in dark suits and driving a black Mercedes). David, his best friend, drives to the other side of the border to bring Benno back to Germany;

on the visual level, Poland is depicted in dark colours and in deep shade, adding to the threatening atmosphere. Eventually, Benno dies in a car accident on his second trip to Poland caused by malfunctioning brakes—a narrative solution that also constitutes a memento to keep the job honest. Anna—Benno and David's love interest and an aspiring actress—refuses to do the voice-over in a porn film, which also happens to come from Poland. The stereotypes about Poland (as a country of raging criminality and moral disorder, the "Wild East" that threatens the young Germans learning how to function in adult life and in the new, post-wall economic reality) are not subverted but rather confirmed by Joop. Benno's death means the end of the lucrative business with the Polish "dark side" and, eventually, allows Anna and David to break free and leave the provincial town, thus affirming the honest German way of life over the crooked dealings of their eastern neighbour. In *Befreite Zone* from 2003, another strategy is used to dismantle the (apparently serious) Polish threat: the illegal Polish workers appear on and disappear from the construction site, leaving their tools when the police approach, as if in a slapstick comedy, disarmed and stripped of power by the self-rewarding and self-assuring act of the audience's laughter.

With few exceptions, the presentation of Poland as strange and threatening to the Germans of the borderlands is typical of German feature films of the late 1990s and 2000s. An explanation of the phenomenon can be found in the content selection strategies of German media. The Polish historian Edmund Dmitrów notes in an analysis of national stereotypes on both sides of the border, conducted between 1998 and 2004, that the image of Poles in the German media and the resulting influence on the German perception of Poles is split between national and local broadcasters. German commercial TV stations focus on medially attractive controversial and conflicted issues related to Poland, taking advantage of the negative associations connected with Poland. This is visible in popular TV productions such as *Polski Crash* (1993) by Kaspar Heidelbach, which focuses on Polish car thieves and is subtitled "Welcome to Warsaw," the popular German version of "welcome to hell." On the other hand, regional news providers, according to Dmitrów's research results, offer an image closer to reality, emphasizing examples of international co-operation and positive aspects of life abroad, such as the dynamically developing Polish economy (Dmitrów 421).

Recent German films seem to replicate elements associated with Poland in the mainstream media in a very conservative way and to employ them to enhance the conflicts of the narratives. With the notable exceptions of *Halbe Treppe, Lichter, Schröders wunderbare Welt,* and *Am Ende kommen Touristen* (*And Along Come Tourists,* Robert Thalheim, 2007),[7] the employment of Polish accents in the films' narratives does not contest the stereotypical view of Poland but rather confirms it. Even when Polish geographical, cultural, and social spaces appear open for exploration in German feature film productions, they largely remain a *terra incognita* for German visitors, and, in many cases, the Otherness of Poland is subtly suggested by visual means. Fittingly, the predominant metaphor of the separation from the strange surroundings becomes the cinematically overexploited metaphor of the glass wall. In *Halbe Treppe*, the character of Chris, overlooking the border from the windows of the radio tower, uses Poland as an exotic yet reachable playground for his sexual escapades with Ellen, sheltering himself from the surroundings by creating intimate spaces in hotel rooms and in a car, only looking outside. Similarly, most characters experience Poland's borderlands from the enclosure of a car, separated from the unknown habitat by glass (*Klassenfahrt, Milchwald, Polski Crash, Vergiss Amerika, Lichter*). The glass window creates a transparent yet solid boundary that is not meant be crossed even when the characters are physically present on the foreign soil; it is the transgression of the barrier that gets them in trouble and puts the narrative in motion.

Several directors have pointed out in interviews about their films that the German–Polish borderland constitutes a space that offers unique possibilities for a filmmaker. Hans-Christian Schmid observed about Frankfurt an der Oder/Słubice, where his film *Lichter* is located, that "one can tell good stories in that place because for many it becomes a place of fate."[8] Similarly, Christoph Hochhäusler, the director of *Milchwald*, commented about the area: "There is an openness [there], anything could happen there."[9] The directors express their intention to explore the possibilities resulting from the confrontation of Germans and Poles in the borderland area where their influences cross and interests intersect. The opportunity to create a captivating story is seized by introducing the elements of chance and social instability, feeding off the insecurity of the German viewer in the unfamiliar world. Therefore, the predictability of the story is lifted, and tension in the narratives is increased by using elements of the frontier paradigm, with Poland as the Wild East, and where stories can take the audience off the beaten track.

Notes

1 "Alles nachhaltig, verträglich, ökologisch, und so weiter ... ab sofort müssen wir in größeren Dimensionen denken: global, international, grenzüberschreitend."
2 "[K]ein Terror, keine Flutwellen, das perfekte Paradies."
3 "Durch eine gemeinsame Anstrengung wird es uns gelingen, Mecklenburg/Vorpommern und Sachsen-Anhalt, Brandenburg, Sachsen und Thüringen schon bald wieder in blühende Landschaften zu verwandeln, in denen es sich zu leben und zu arbeiten lohnt" (Kohl).

4 "Ein Raum, der ... relativ fremd und anders ist, und die deutsch-polnische Grenze ist so etwas. Sehr viele Deutsche kennen Polen nicht, erstaunlicherweise, es ist ein direkter Nachbar. Die Sprache ist sehr anders ... es ist wirklich ein anderer Kulturraum ... Es ist von allen deutschen Grenzen jedenfalls die stärkste."

5 "—Was machst du nach der Schule?" "—Ich weiß nicht. Irgendwas Besonderes."

6 "... wenn sie ja irgendwann zurück muss in die Heimat."

7 *Am Ende kommen Touristen* can serve as a counterpoint to *Herz im Kopf*: in it, a young male German arrives as a social worker in Oświęcim (in the former death camp Auschwitz) and falls in love with a Polish woman on her terms.

8 "Man kann ja sehr gut Geschichten erzählen an diesem Ort, weil er für viele zu'nem Schicksalsort wird" (Schumacher).

9 "Man hat ja erstmal so eine Offenheit, da könnte alles passieren" (Schleich).

References

Am Ende kommen Touristen. Dir. Robert Thalheim. 23/5 Filmproduktion, 2007.
Befreite Zone. Dir. Norbert Baumgarten. Ö-Filmproduktion Löprich & Schlösser, 2003.
Beller, Manfred. "Perception, Image, Imagology." *Imagology: The Cultural Construction and Literary Representation of National Characters*. Ed. Manfred Beller and Joep Leerssen. Amsterdam and New York: Rodopi, 2007. 3–16.
Crolly, Hannelore. "Keine Angst vor dem Europa ohne Grenzen." *Die Welt* 6 Dec. 2007. 6 Nov. 2009 <http://www.welt.de>.
Dmitrów, Edmund. "Die Rolle von Mythen und Stereotypen in der gegenseitigen Wahrnehmung." *Nachbarn auf Distanz: Polen und Deutsche 1998–2004*. Ed. Anna Wolff-Powęska and Dieter Bingen. Wiesbaden: Harrassowitz, 2005. 419–50.
Halbe Treppe. Dir. Andreas Dresen. Peter Rommel Productions, 2002.
Herz im Kopf. Dir. Michael Gutmann. Claussen + Wöbke Filmproduktion, 2001.
Klassenfahrt. Dir. Henner Winckler. Schramm Film Koerner & Weber, 2002.
Kohl, Helmut. "Fernsehansprache von Bundeskanzler Kohl anlässlich des Inkrafttretens der Währungs-, Wirtschafts- und Sozialunion, 1. Juli 1990." *Konrad Adenauer Stiftung: Archiv für Christlich-Demokratische Politik*. 26 Oct. 2008 <http://www.helmut-kohl.de/index.php?msg=555>.
Kopp, Kristin. "Reconfiguring the Border of Fortress Europe in Hans-Christian Schmid's *Lichter*." *Germanic Review* 82.1 (2007): 31–53.
Kraśnicki, Andrzej. "Radosne cięcie granic." *Gazeta Wyborcza*. Wydanie Szczecin. Wydarzenia. 22 Dec. 2007: 6.
Lichter. Dir. Hans-Christian Schmid. Claussen + Wöbke Filmproduktion, 2003.
Ludewig, Alexandra. "A German 'Heimat' Further East and in the Baltic Region? Contemporary German Film as a Provocation." *Journal of European Studies* 36.2 (2006): 157–79.
Milchwald. Dir. Christoph Hochhäusler. fieber.film, ZDF, 2003.
Mistrz Wincenty (Kadłubek). *Kronika Polska*. Trans. Brygida Kürbis. Wrocław: Ossolineum, 2003.

Mueller, Gabriele. "'Welcome to Reality': Constructions of German Identity in *Lichter* (Schmid, 2003) and *Halbe Treppe* (Dresen, 2002)." *New Cinemas: Journal of Contemporary Film* 4.2 (2006): 117–27.

Polski Crash. Dir. Kasbar Heidelbach. Gemini Filmproduktion, 1993.

Quetteville, Harry de. "Police Warning as Politicians Hail Open Borders." *Telegraph.co.uk* 21 Dec. 2007. 25 Oct. 2008 <http://www.telegraph.co.uk/>.

Rykiel, Zbigniew. "The Geographical Conditionality of the Polish Western Boundary." *Grenzen und Grenzräume in der deutschen und polnischen Geschichte: Scheidelinie oder Begegnungsraum?* Ed. Georg Stöber and Robert Maier. Hannover: Verlag Hahnsche Buchhandlung, 2000. 57–70.

Schleich, Frieder. "*Milchwald*: Interview mit dem Regisseur." Milchwald *Bonus Materials*. Fieber.Film, 2004.

Schröders wunderbare Welt. Dir. Michael Schorr. Filmkombinat Nordost, 2006.

Schultz, Hans-Dietrich. "Die Theorie der 'natürlichen Grenzen' am Beispiel Polens: Ein Beitrag zur Geschichte des Nationalismus und der deutschen Geographie." *Grenzen und Grenzräume in der deutschen und polnischen Geschichte: Scheidelinie oder Begegnungsraum?* Ed. Georg Stöber and Robert Maier. Hannover: Verlag Hahnsche Buchhandlung, 2000. 9–56.

Schumacher, Brigitte. "An der Grenze: *Lichter* von Hans-Christian Schmid und Michael Gutmann." Lichter *Bonus Materials*. Claussen + Wöbke Filmproduktion, 2003.

Seweryn, Andrzej. "Polska wróciła do domu." *Dziennik* 21 Dec. 2007. 28 Feb. 2009 <http://www.dziennik.pl>.

Stróżyk, Jarosław, and Łukasz Cybiński. "Polska otwartych granic." *Rzeczpospolita* 21 Dec. 2007: 1.

Vergiss Amerika. Dir. Vanessa Joop. Avista Film, 2000.

"We Are in the Schengen Area!" *Ministry of Interior and Administration* 21 Dec. 2007. 25 Oct. 2008 <http://www.mswia.gov.pl/portal.php?serwis=en&dzial=1&id=476&search=12>.

13
The Transnational Deutschkei
in Yilmaz Arslan's *Brudermord*

Michael Zimmermann

Abstract The present chapter examines representations of the effects of globalization and transnational migration in Yilmaz Arslan's film *Brudermord*. The film portrays migrating children as victims within the German host nation who are forced into a marginalized existence on the periphery of society. This essay discusses the ways in which the film problematizes aspects of the Turco-Kurdish culture in Germany.

Globalization as a Point of Departure

There are men who have left their homeland.
They pursue a dream: prosperity and wealth.

These words, spoken by child narrator in voice-over near the beginning of Yilmaz Arslan's film *Brudermord* (*Fratricide*, 2005), refer to the phenomenon of migration from Turkey to Germany, and introduce the theme of transnational social space in the film. In defining transnational social space, Ulrich Beck states that a country is "not a fixed geographical magnitude, not a separate place on the globe, but a *transnational idea and the staging of the idea*" [emphasis in original] (*Globalization* 27).[1] Put simply, people bring versions of their culture—language, customs, and conflicts—with them when they migrate. Yet, in the transnational space, the transplanted national culture does not correspond entirely with the culture of origin, because the transplanted culture adapts to the peculiarities of its new environment, and does not experience as directly any changes that take place in the land of origin subsequent to migration (Beck *Globalization* 27). This idea is echoed by Betigül Argun when referring specifically to Germany and defining the term *Deutschkei*. He states that the "*Deutschkei* is a web of networks established by migrants from Turkey in Germany [...]. A syncretic union of Deutschland and Türkei [...] *Deutschkei* is a trans-state or transnational entity, which is neither a mirror image of Turkey proper, nor does it quite display the characteristics of Germany" (6).

In examining migrating populations and their constellations in the new national space they occupy, in this case Germany, much of what can be determined about these communities has directly to do with the particular nature of the combining cultures. Religious, ethnic, historical, and political peculiarities come together to constitute a definable cultural amalgam, and the willingness of both the host and migrating cultures to adapt to the new circumstances determines the extent and success of assimilation or adaptation. The nature of the *Deutschkei* will vary even from location to location within the host nation, that is to say, that the Turkish community in Kreuzberg will exhibit specific characteristics owing to its unique history, its size relative to Berlin and Germany, and to the additional cultural makeup of the community in which it finds itself.[2] Argun describes Kreuzberg as "the quintessential embodiment" of Turkish culture (9), but Kreuzberg has been a flashpoint for conflict between Kurdish and Turkish groups, and it is necessary to recognize the heterogeneous nature of the Turkish community, which is often viewed as homogeneous.

In an interview from 2003, Beck asks how far countries such as Germany are globalizing themselves internally. He says that we "must become accustomed to [...] a transnational or a cosmopolitan reality, in which cultures are recombining and in which the boundaries we still assume to exist, have already been at least partially swept away" ("Muslim"), thus producing a differentiated and constantly changing picture. This is a question that lies at the heart of Yilmaz Arslan's film *Brudermord*, a film that provides a representation of Germany's internal globalization, contributing to the discourse about the extent to which boundaries are changing. In an articulation of one of the film's central messages, the words of the child narrator, quoted at the beginning of this essay, continue as follows:

> They have worked hard.
> Often in degrading conditions.
> As moths draw to the light, many took the road to the Promised Land.
> And they endured all this only for one dream.
> When they reached their goal,
> They realized they had left much of themselves behind.

This chapter will examine Arslan's depiction of the *Deutschkei*, a transnational social space in Germany. It will discuss the ghettoization or marginalization of the transplanted cultures, inter- and intra-cultural linkages, and generational conflict, highlighting motifs within the narrative and suggesting avenues for interpretation. *Brudermord* is a film that presents a largely differentiated picture of Turkish/Kurdish trans-migrant life in Germany in which representatives of the migrant culture are seen not only as a silent and victimized monolithic presence on the margins of society, but also as members of a diverse transnational community.

Part of the conflict depicted in the film finds its origins in the root causes of migration. These relate to the economic realities of the countries of origin and destination that have for decades resulted in a push–pull dynamic. After 1945, the Federal Republic of Germany became a nation of immigrants; by 1989 one-third of its population was comprised of those who had immigrated to Germany since World War II; about a third of that number was made up of people from eastern Europe (Panayi 200; Hoffmann 28–29). As Panayi points out, the manufacturing sector and the need for reconstruction in West Germany produced, with a couple of exceptions, sustained economic growth until the 1990s, something that led to a strategy of foreign labour importation (212–13). Although eastern Europe supplied most labour to West Germany initially, this movement slowed as eastern European countries stemmed the flow of those leaving in order to address their nations' own industrialization needs. In view of the reduction of incoming eastern Europeans, the Federal Republic turned its sights toward more distant countries such as Yugoslavia, Italy, Greece, Spain, Portugal, and Turkey (216). As Panayi notes, "These states had social and economic characteristics diametrically opposite to those of the Federal Republic," for example, Turkey's soaring birth rate, which excluded dependants from participation in the workforce and created a situation that saw Turkey actively "export [its] population as a part of a planned economic strategy" (217). On 31 October 1961, the first labour importation contract with Turkey was signed in order to address a labour need following the construction of the Berlin Wall; the initial principle of rotation obliged workers to return home (Kürsat-Ahlers 113). Following a short-lived economic crisis in 1966, during which 300,000 foreign workers lost their jobs, Turkish migrants came to Germany in increasing numbers, especially after 1969 (Kolinsky 81). Another downturn in the German economy in 1973 following the oil shock prompted an *Anwerbestopp* (ban on recruitment of foreign workers) (82). Since the lifting of this ban, however, the number of Turkish immigrants to Germany has risen steadily, and today the Turkish population is Germany's largest minority population (Hofmann 194).

Globalization and Cinema

A discussion of Arslan's *Brudermord* as it relates to the question of German or Austrian cinema as stable categories is unavoidable. Referring to a framework articulated by Andrew Higson to assess what constitutes national cinema, Luisa Rivi states that national cinema is classified "according to the producing industry, a distinctive aesthetics and culturally specific imaginary of the nation, the places of circulation and consumption, and the critical discourse around the film" (45).[3] Suggesting the permeability of this kind of classification, Randall Halle envisages a "transnationalization of culture," a process whereby Europe is "reimagining itself as a community both economically and culturally" (7). Political and economic forces have led to a levelling of differences among European nations, and there is debate about the significance of national cinema at all.[4] Deniz Göktürk has argued that long-standing international collaboration in the film industry, including "travelling actors and directors" and "aspects of international co-production, distribution, and reception," can contribute to a blurring of the concept of national canons (213–14),[5] and so the very definition of national cinema can prove elusive. As Randall Halle points out, however, "the nation continues to act as a significant form of political and cultural affiliation" (10). For example, the consumption and critical discourse of films about German issues will be different inside or outside Germany. The particularities of film production will necessarily contribute to the depiction of subject matter, thereby affecting the ensuing public and academic discussions.

Germany and its national cinema must be seen as a shifting concept and in need of ongoing "resignification" (Halle 10). Germany and its filmic reflections of culture vary with time and changing social, political, and cultural conditions. The very nature of Arslan's film reflects a widening and globalized or transnationalized definition of what constitutes national German cinema. Although set largely in Berlin, Arslan's film does not observe an "allegiance to state boundaries" (Halle 8) in terms of the financial aspect of its production. Indeed, one could assert that the film experienced a kind of financial marginalization, as Arslan was unable to secure much funding for the project in Germany, having instead to find substantial financial support in France and Luxembourg. Thomas Elsaesser compares national cinema to other institutions of culture, such as opera and ballet, remarking that "national cinema usually means that it is or wants to be also an institution (officially, or at least semi-officially), enjoying state patronage and, when defined as culture, often receiving substantial state support" (36). Arslan's film did not enjoy state sponsorship as a constituent of the "producing industry" (Higson), and yet, as Halle has pointed out, changes in state subsidies during the latter part of the twentieth century have led to a situation in which state interests have a reduced role in the direction of national cinema (10).

Despite evidence of Americanization in film aesthetics and consumption in Europe, there is much that renders European and national cinema distinct from American cinema. The problematization of Turkish and Kurdish minority cultures within Germany reflects conditions of specific cultural significance in the German context. The issues raised in *Brudermord* are part of a national critical discourse in Germany whereas outside Europe the narrative may be less well understood. Thomas Elsaesser posits that to assert the existence of a national cinema is to strive for a certain cultural identity and coherence; this necessitates a repression of "differences of class, gender, race, religion, and history," producing a kind of "internal colonization" (36). Arslan's film serves to provide a counterbalance to this "colonization" through the differentiated representations of minority cultures. *Brudermord*'s very challenge to the traditional, culturally specific imaginary of the nation underlines the film's significance as an articulation of cultural and aesthetic change. The specific interlinkage of culture and language in the depiction of existing cultural realities necessitates a rethinking of traditional concepts of national identity. The fact that the dominant language of the film's narrative is not German does not preclude the film from a place in German national cinema; rather the bifurcation of language draws attention to situations of cultural separateness within Germany.

A Differentiated View of Migrant Culture

Brudermord is a film about human migration and interculturality, informed in part by its director's personal experience as a Turkish migrant to Germany as an eight-year-old with his family. Conceived of first as a documentary about young Kurdish asylum seekers, Arslan has stated that he realized it was too contentious a topic, and decided to explore the subject matter "using fiction," because he thought that documenting the lives of Kurdish children would have "gotten them into trouble." Instead of jeopardizing the lives of actual migrants, Arslan fictionalizes the presentation, but preserves a measure of authenticity and documentary realism by using amateur actors and authentic locations.

At its centre the film traces the migration of two young Kurdish boys, foregrounding their friendship and experiences within the Turkish/Kurdish community of Berlin.[6] For one of these boys, Azad, the impetus for migrating is family-initiated and financially motivated. Like his older brother Semo before him, he too must journey to Europe in order to support his family in the homeland. For the other boy, Ibo, the migration results from political turmoil in the homeland, an example of which is the execution of his parents.[7] Drawn together in Germany through similarity of language and culture, Azad establishes a protective, brotherly attitude toward the more recently arrived and considerably younger Ibo and introduces him to his existence working as a barber in the washroom of a local establishment. A confrontation with two young Turkish men in the subway touches off a series of events that ultimately leads to three murders. The assimilation of the boys into a segregated community and their entanglement with the criminal realm of society takes place as a result of intra-community enmity between Turks and Kurds, and is exacerbated by the presence of a Kurdish nationalist group.

Contrasted with the culture of the "Promised Land" (Germany, Europe) from the introductory quotation, the rural culture from which Azad comes is depicted as one of simplicity, kinship, poverty, and to a certain extent, innocence. The film opens with a scene of mourning, a flash-forward depicting a Turkish family engaged in a culturally specific ceremony that the film viewer might reasonably infer occurs within a Muslim country. The inference created by Arslan in this scene is an effective device for challenging the viewer's cultural expectations as expressed through spatial representation, that is, that an authentic Muslim ceremony is part of the German reality. The clue to a transnational location resides in the Western clothing worn by a grieving brother.

The ceremonial use of water in blessing the deceased in the opening scene is a link to a scene in which a goat is given water to drink before it is sacrificed. In the latter instance, Ibo's grandfather uses a traditional ceremonial sacrifice to prepare Ibo for his journey to Germany. The narrator's assertion that death is "the only faithful companion" is illustrated in this connecting of instances of death, both in the homeland and in Europe.

Azad's migration begins with the delivery of a letter from abroad. The film viewer is engaged passively as an invisible occupant and traveller in a point-of-view tracking shot within a car as it drives through the Turkish countryside. The passage of distance and time is achieved through numerous jump cuts, while the diegetic sound of the car's radio plays uninterrupted, and the moving shot from within the vehicle presages impending change. The barren countryside and impoverishment of its people offer a first glimpse into the cause–effect chain of circumstances that create migration. This simple and unobstructed landscape creates a stark contrast to the urban topography of Berlin with its high-rises, fast pace, and affluence. A letter received from Azad's brother Semo, who has preceded him to Germany, explains the purpose of Azad's impending journey to Europe: "As promised, here's money, so my brother Azad can join me. Together, we will grow rich and build the greatest house in the region" (*Brudermord*). Thus, the expressed intention of migration is not to establish a new permanent home in Europe, but rather to use European prosperity to improve conditions at home. Counting a wad of bills, the eldest son's currency of sacrifice in hand, the father states: "If God wishes, soon you shall be with your brother in Europe" (*Brudermord*). And so a version of the archetype of fratricide as contained both in the Bible (Genesis 4:116) and the Qur'an (5:26-32) is invoked. For Azad, who is about to embark on a journey to Europe to better support the family, the role of shepherd has proven an insufficient sacrifice. The lure of earning money in a foreign country is presented as a phenomenon of globalization, an unquestioned obligation that eventually leads to the disintegration of family. Hidden from those who remain in the Turkish homeland, the fate of those who migrate is foretold in the eroded innocence of the child's narrating voice.

As Azad embarks on his journey to Europe, the hope for the preservation of the transmigrating culture is symbolized by a handful of soil, placed by Azad's father into his son's suit pocket. As if to undermine promptly the desired effect of the talisman, however, the precocious voice of the film's child narrator announces the fate of those who leave: "At the end of this tunnel shines the light of money. When you reach it, you start to die slowly. People die, even if their bodies continue to live" (*Brudermord*). As the film progresses, one recognizes the child narrator's voice as that of Ibo.[8] Not simply recounting the story as it unfolds, the child narrates from a perspective of hindsight, reflection, and wisdom that is incongruous with the youthful voice. The effect produced is one of lost innocence and an omniscient inscription of social truth as told by one of its victims. This narration also accompanies several inserted scenes that enact the story of Newroz, celebrating the deliverance of the Kurds from a tyrant and the coming of spring. In the Kurdish diaspora, the celebration is often associated with cultural identity and solidarity.

The process of migration itself is never foregrounded, and appears to be seamless and unproblematic, thus creating the impression of routine. This notion is confirmed during the film when a young refugee scoffs at the prospect of deportation as a result of working illegally, bragging that if deported, he would "be back the next day." The only indication of the journey from the Turkish homeland to the European transnation is a point-of-view shot from within a vehicle travelling through the darkness of a tunnel toward emerging light, accompanied by the voice-over narrator, who warns of the coming "light of money," "death," and "exile." With the migration to Germany begins the process of becoming an *almanyali*, the word among Turks for German–Turkish, a binary signifier that stresses the German rather than the Turkish (Tan and Waldhoff 152).

Connected by the voice-over narrative, the film resumes from the point-of-view of Azad's older brother Semo, who earns money by pimping foreign women. Facing the frontal nakedness of a prospective prostitute, the viewer watches and listens as Semo, in heavily accented German, conducts a job interview. Continuing the affect of stolen innocence, the child narrator's voice describes the paths taken by those in exile, corruptive paths emulating the European love of money: "In exile, it didn't make any difference how you helped your relatives survive in the homeland. Whether you sold dead meat in a döner kebab or living flesh in a hotel room. That is something the Europeans have learned. Money doesn't stink" (*Brudermord*). And yet, just as other filmmakers use marginalized figures to dismantle those stereotyped images (Burns 142), so too does Arslan depict representatives of the migrant population that are anything but uniform in their attitudes. In Azad, Arslan provides an associational contrast to Semo, thereby creating a situation of intrafamilial discord. Instead of engaging in a life of crime in which money can be earned more quickly, Azad makes different moral choices, opting to carve out a meagre existence as a barber in a washroom, where earning money really does stink. Even when money is required to help his ailing father in Turkey, Azad refuses to accept what he calls "whores' money" from his brother. The result of this family squabble signifies a departure from the perpetuation of "populist stereotypes of the foreigner as antisocial malingerer or inveterate criminal" (Burns 142). In films dealing with migrant culture, the family is often the "site where battle is waged between the old and the new culture" (Burns 133). The Turkish family at the centre of the film provides an example of this. The peaceful lives of the immigrant parents, who run a grocery business, contrast sharply with the lives of their sons, who shirk their duties in the family business in order to arrange dogfights. The film presents both generations in this family as marginalized, that is, a parent generation that lives culturally and linguistically separate from mainstream society and a second generation that is confined to a peripheral criminal segment of society, despite having attained the cultural camouflage of success, a BMW. Articulations of minority cultural integration are, however, not uniform. In the film, Kurds and Turks also function as teachers, translators, and police officers, although significantly always in connection with the minority population.

Language as Signifier of Integration?

Azade Seyhan points out that a fundamental reality of migration is that people "live in a language that is not their own" (23). A logical question would be at what point, if ever, does the language of the country to which one migrates become one's own? Must one renounce one's native tongue in the new homeland? At the same time, the use of language becomes an indicator of the degree to which the host nation and its people are globalized, that is to say, have themselves responded to the "transnational or cosmopolitan reality" (Beck "Muslim"). Biculturalism and bilingualism can be considered attributes of cultural enrichment and of a social mosaic. In Arslan's film, far from creating the impression of an integrated multi-ethnic society, German, the official language of society at large, is rarely and selectively heard, and it is clearly Arslan's intention to produce a sense of marginalization through the specific use of language in the film, signifying the separation between host and migrant cultures.

German is the challenged language of authority in *Brudermord*. At the children's refugee residence, an institution created for the protection of migrating children, Ibo, a new arrival, is instructed in German to read through the *Hausordnung* (house rules). In a manner seemingly less concerned with Ibo's native language and more impressed with German thoroughness, the residence worker rattles off in German a list of languages into which the document has been translated. When Ibo then asks Azad to read the document, the older and more acclimatized Azad tears up the document in defiance of the German sense of order, giving Ibo an early lesson in the importance of German and the system in which it functions.

During a scene in which an allowance is dispensed to refugee children at the residence, the expectations and power relations between host and guest cultures are clearly displayed. In this culturally homogenizing scene, children of many nations descend to a central table as their names are called out. Absent are any other words or gestures of sympathy or friendliness, reflecting a degree of detachment on the part of the residence officials. When one child impatiently shoves forward with an outstretched hand demanding money, the composure of the benefactors dissolves and the mechanical, dispassionate dispensation of money is interrupted with angry emotion as the official barks out a menacing rebuke. Disorder among the children ensues, and the group is threatened: "Silence! If you don't calm down, we'll stop handing the money out!"[9] Germany, as an asylum-friendly state, tolerates the refugees in its midst, allowing them to sink invisibly beneath the surface of society. When, however, ripples in the societal order surface, access to the coveted currency of survival is threatened.

An instrument of authority and punishment, German is used by police during an interrogation of Azad and Ibo following the murder of the Turk Ahmet. Sitting in a sparsely furnished room, with guard and translators, the children are subjected to the bullying harangue of a police interrogator:

> In Turkey you can kill each other if you want. But in Germany the law rules. Understood? As long as you are guests in this country, you will behave as is expected of

you. We give you money, we give you food, we give you clothing, we give you god knows what else. And you, what do you do? You stab each other. Is that your way of thanking us?[10]

In this instance, the police interrogator uses German to exert authority and control. This, however, is illusory. Azad and Ibo are able to assume a measure of control by feigning incomprehension, discussing aspects of the case in Kurdish in front of the interrogator, and by necessitating the presence of a Kurdish interpreter, despite the fact that the boys are able to speak and understand Turkish in other instances. Translucent glass panes behind the German police interrogator symbolize the threat of incarceration for the two young detainees as well as the limited view of the German justice system for what exists in the streets beyond its walls. The intensity of the interrogator's emotion and the anger on his face reveal the resentment of a host nation that shows willingness to give to those it defines as temporary residents, but from whom it expects the observance of order.

German is also the language of discourse in other situations of criminal behaviour in the film. During a selection interview, Semo asks a prospective prostitute whether she can speak German, a requirement in making clear to German customers the basic agreements of solicitation; it is in German, too, that Semo gives instructions to and punishes prostitutes. As well, it is German that connects Turkish brothers Ahmet and Zeki to the illegal world of dogfighting. Zeki speaks German to and about his pit bull, creating a strong association between the brutality of this killing instrument and German society. The dog consumes the intestines of both Semo and Ahmet after they are murdered, mirroring the fact that these men are eventually consumed by the criminal realm and the society in which it exists.

Despite the predominant connection of German to aspects of crime and marginalization in the transnation, the film does present German in other contexts. For example, the host nation makes available language instruction to refugee children (and German language education is presented even by Kurdish national groups as a vehicle for opportunity). For Ibo, however, the experience seems perfunctory and impractical. During a scene of language instruction, the repetition of basic items of German vocabulary transports Ibo to a place of reverie and escape, one in which he is reunited with his parents, but not to a world in which Germany is the imagined ideal landscape. His desire to "bring back the dead" is far removed from any conception of the benefits of learning German.

German is also presented as the language of hope and compassionate assimilation. During an Easter celebration at the refugee residence, the well-intentioned Christian service underscores the disconnection between host and guest cultures, and appears as a further method of cultural assimilation. Far from attending to the meaning of the service, Azad uses its relative safety to explore young love with a refugee girl from Albania. Symbolic of hope and normalcy, German is the language in which the two young lovers interact in the host land. Contributing further to the meaning of hope, but foretelling Azad's coming sacrifice are the German words of the Easter Gospel spoken in the background.

Turkish and Kurdish dominate the film's dialogue and the Turkish/Kurdish community appears largely self-contained and self-sufficient. For the *Gastarbeiter* (guest worker) generation, presented in the characters of Ahmet and Zeki's parents, existence within the Turkish community is possible without significant use of German. During the investigation of their son's death, they are able to speak Turkish with a police official. Members of the second generation, like Ahmet and Zeki, lead linguistically compartmentalized lives, defined by their points of access to the German-speaking community. Turkish is spoken with their parents and German is spoken to a degree outside of the Turkish community. That a certain requisite knowledge of German can be presumed is demonstrated by Azad's basic fluency, but actual contact with German bureaucracy is never made visible and is only alluded to by Azad in response to Ibo's question about what Germany is like: "You go into the offices, fill out forms, get them stamped, go into one place, then another" (*Brudermord*). The only examples of Turkish/Kurdish citizens functioning within mainstream German society are a Turkish teacher and police officials or translators, but their work is defined by and specific to their linguistic difference. Showing that linguistic integration does not necessarily complete cultural integration, Fatih Akin's *Auf der anderen Seite* (*The Edge of Heaven*, 2007) provides an example of a Turkish-German professor of German literature who, despite advanced linguistic and cultural knowledge, feels a sense of cultural difference and incompleteness. In the transnation the preservation of original language signifies at once the continuity of cultural identity and a component of marginalization. For the young migrants, Azad and Ibo, the acquisition of German does not mean convergence with what is perceived as German identity. Learning German is purely instrumental in achieving limited goals. For Semo, Ahmet, and Zeki, too, German is limited to specific vocabulary and illicit activities within the "guest" culture.

Kurdish Nationalism

Unlike Yesim Ustaoglu's film *Journey to the Sun* (1999), in which the Turco–Kurdish conflict is explored directly in the homeland, Arslan's *Brudermord* could be described as projecting an image of the Kurdish "extra-territorial nation-state" (Argun 123). According to Argun, "Kurds live and thrive in the transnational space" and the "desire to establish one's own state and becoming a political refugee, exile, or asylum seeker as a result of it makes exit from the host society much more difficult and renders the transnational condition almost permanent" (123). In *Brudermord*, Kurdish Otherness within the migrant community is promoted through the activity of a Kurdish political group. Zilan leads a Kurdish activist organization that seeks to provide a sense of community for refugees, but has as its paramount goal a political agenda for which the recruitment of young Kurds is vital. Kurdish organizers visit a captive audience of Kurdish children in the residence in order to indoctrinate them in the politics of the diaspora; children must go to school for "only the uneducated can be oppressed," and they "must stand together to let the world know that [they] have a home" (*Brudermord*). The presentation of political strife between Kurds and Turks is made poignant through the depiction of Ibo as one of its child victims. In a flashback of political murder induced by post-traumatic stress disorder, Ibo relives the execution of his parents. He is then re-traumatized by Turkish gangsters in the transnation. Despite Ibo's family circumstances and horrific experiences, he is too young to understand the politics of his homeland.[11] For Azad, too, who has come to Germany to work, Kurdish politics seem far removed from his experience and interest.

The deterritorialized political agenda of the Kurds produces an imaginary landscape in the transnational sphere. The celebration of Newroz, considered by Kurds to be the most important holiday of the year, was illegal in Turkey until 1995. In the transnation, Newroz (Newroz or Nuroj means "New Day" in Kurdish) is more than the celebration of the spring equinox. It symbolizes the preservation of Kurdish cultural identity and renewal, and Germany thus becomes a stage for political solidarity. The political struggle for an imaginary Kurdistan carries fewer repercussions in transnational exile than it does in the Turkish homeland. Much of the political symbolism of the fight for a Kurdish homeland is contained in the flashouts to a narrated enactment of the story of Newroz, narrated by Ibo's voice. As a casualty of political violence, his voice appropriately narrates the subjugation and sacrifice of the Kurdish people as told in the story of Kawa, who lived under the tyranny of Dehak. According to the story two young men were sacrificed each day, the person charged with performing the sacrifice could save one person each day by replacing his brain with that of a sheep (Ibo's grandfather symbolizes this part of the legend, when he sacrifices a goat and smears its blood on Ibo's head.) The insertion of this legend provides a way of interpreting present circumstances through collective memory.

At a nighttime celebration of Newroz that is part of the storyline, Zilan reinforces in her speech the aims of Kurdish exilic existence: "Happy Newroz to those in the homeland! Happy Newroz to those living in exile! Long live Kurdistan! My friends, so long as a single fire burns on Earth, the Kurds shall endure!" (*Brudermord*). At this celebration, Zilan offers to help Semo escape prosecution in Germany, thereby reclaiming him for the Kurdish cause. Zilan's intention for Semo is undone, as Azad's naïve belief in justice and his presumption of Semo's safety in prison causes Azad to turn in his brother to the police. Semo's evisceration while under the protection of the German prison system reveals, at best, the host nation's inability to comprehend intracultural strife and to protect the incarcerated and, at worst, a willful neglect of this marginalized minority and the hypocrisy of the culture that professes order and justice. When the Kurdish group requests permission to politicize Semo's death in a public funeral procession, Azad's contempt for the group increases, and he refers to them as "parasites" who "even use corpses to [their] own ends" (*Brudermord*). A member of the Kurdish political group externalizes the blame for Semo's murder, saying that he was murdered in a German prison and that "those German pigs accept our extermination" (*Brudermord*). Disillusioned by both his Kurdish countrymen and the host nation, Azad ultimately displays loyalty to one brother lost and one gained by exacting revenge on Zeki, thereby sacrificing himself in order to deliver Ibo from the promised land to paradise. That migrating children such as Azad and Ibo become wards of the state in group-housing facilities is not the reason for the deaths in the film. The film seems to assert that such a risky migration strategy, whereby families send their children to Europe to make money or to escape violence contributes to the dissolution of the family unit and the problems that attend young children who try to cope in a foreign society. Although living within a foreign society, their ability and even desire to become an active part of the community-at-large seems minimal.

Brother-Murder

The title of the English version of the film, *Fratricide*, is decidedly too sanitized and removed from the lethality and cinematic realism clearly intended by the film's director. Ironically, the German word *Brudermord* is never actually used in the film, but its first component *Bruder* (brother) is used in German and Turkish/Kurdish more than forty times, and thus obtains special significance. Throughout the film the word is used as a polite form of address, even between strangers (as are similar words connoting family relationships such as *sister* and *uncle*). The word *brother*, whether referring to one's sibling and or as a polite form of address to a stranger, always conveys a sense of belonging, shared identity, and obligation. It is the bond that obliges Azad to work in Europe and to commit murder in retaliation for the murder of Semo, but it is also the protective urge that draws him to Ibo, thus fulfilling the prophetic words of a blind clairvoyant who appears twice in the film: "You'll lose a brother, but will find another" (*Brudermord*). With this loss and gain comes fundamental realization and understanding about what is important. Unable to prevent Semo's murder, Azad sacrifices himself for Ibo's future, a future outside of Germany.

The German word *Brudermord* provides greater immediacy and appropriate impact than does its English counterpart.[12] The "brother murders" committed in the film reflect the destruction of a variety of kinships between fellow countrymen (Turks and Kurds) and between biological siblings; in some cases, the murders are direct and in others indirect; some of these killings are committed in self-defence, while others are committed out of revenge. In all, three murders are central to the storyline. In the first instance, Kurdish Semo kills Turkish Ahmet on the street in defence of his brother Azad. The confrontation has been precipitated by a previous scene on a streetcar in which Azad refers to Ahmet as "brother" in Turkish, while trying to get Ahmet to keep his dog at bay. By using Turkish and the word *brother*, Azad is appealing to a perceived shared identity as a minority culture. Ahmet rebukes Azad, taking exception specifically to the word *brother*. Ahmet's objection to the word may have to do with his involvement in the conflict between Kurds and Turks, or it may have to do with his perception of his own migrant status vis-à-vis more recent migrants. The second murder occurs when Semo is disembowelled during his incarceration in a German prison. The specific perpetrator of Semo's murder is unknown, but it is clear that it has been committed by Turks in retaliation for Ahmet's murder. Semo has been imprisoned, because Azad has incriminated his own brother Semo out of feelings of justice and fraternal protection. Without intending or foreseeing his brother's murder, Azad nevertheless feels responsibility for Semo's death as a direct consequence of his betrayal. The last murder central to the film takes place, when Azad murders Zeki. A sign marked "Polizei" inscribes the scene with the presence of police surveillance while underscoring in a visual way Azad's disillusionment with the German justice system and his decision to exact his own justice by entering the Turkish corner store, where he slits Zeki's throat and cuts off one of his ears as a trophy of vengeance for Ibo. In a literal sense, this *Brudermord* can be understood here as the murder of Ahmet's brother. In the context of migrant minority culture, the murder can also be understood as having been committed against a minority "brother." The tragedy of murders by and of brothers in this film reflects the legacy of deterritorialized and transgenerational conflict between seemingly apolitical individuals.

Position of *Brudermord* within the Spectrum of Turkish-German Film

Referring to guest-worker literature of the 1970s and early 1980s, Rob Burns points to the "discrepancy between the immigrants' initial projections of a promised land of opportunity and affluence and their actual hellish reality of discrimination and exploitation" (130). The depiction of a discrepancy exists thirty years later in the film *Brudermord*, but in differentiated form, for no longer is the discrimination and exploitation depicted as hellish, as in Günter Wallraff's *Ganz unten (Lowest of the Low,* 1986). The cultural containment or marginalization that arises from externally or internally imposed restrictions is evident, though the causes for such are shifting. Germany offers migrant children shelter and an allowance. It also offers them access to language education, a requirement for greater access to German culture (and a right granted under new federal provisions of 1 January 2005).

Evidence of marginalization is more finely nuanced in Arslan's film. Language education, while available to migrant children, is presented as part of a segregated *Parallelgesellschaft* (parallel society) in which cultural differences are expected to collapse with the repetition of German vocabulary. Consonant with a newer trend in German-Turkish film that breaks with the image of the Turk as victim, an image common in the "cinema of the affected" (Burns 133), *Brudermord* focuses its lens on intracultural discord within migrant communities, highlighting the imported strife between Kurds and Turks. As a consequence, the role of the German host nation becomes one of incomprehension of the transplanted issues and incompetence or even apathy in the administration of justice. Concomitant with the tendency for transnational cinema to be male-oriented, as opposed to the foregrounding of women seen in the "cinema of the affected," the depiction of women in *Brudermord* is scant, though not unimportant. Migrant women's roles in the film are of several types: the first-generation *Gastarbeiter* mother, the vulnerable and exploited sex-trade worker, a Kurdish activist, and an Albanian child migrant. In each case, these female characters are on the periphery of the wider German society. As Burns has noted of other transnational films, women in *Brudermord* are largely marginalized or cast in "the role of escape route for oppressed or endangered male characters" (142). The Turkish *Gastarbeiterin* mother of Ahmet and Zeki allows Zeki an escape from disownment by his father for the rape of Ibo and dishonour of the family, thus giving him re-entry into the stability of his parents' world. The Kurdish leader Zilan plans Semo's escape to Paris to avoid prosecution for murder, and Mirka, Azad's Albanian girlfriend, offers him love and escape from an oppressive existence in Germany.

Conclusion

Yilmaz Arslan belongs to a generation of immigrants who could be described as "taking stock of their lives so far," something that "affects the nature of intergenerational relations and of relations within families" (Tan and Waldhoff 138). This assessment is an examination of the aspirations of *Gastarbeiter* families that are important and inform part of *Brudermord*'s overall palette. In his portrait of the plight of migrating children, Arslan turns his lens toward an effect of globalization, the world's hierarchical structure, and the "almost magical attraction" Europe holds "for those fleeing war, or desperately seeking a better life" (Arslan). This relates directly to Ulrich Beck's question regarding globalization and transnational social spaces. Germany, as a preferred destination for migrating children, must consider the effect of transnational cultures within its borders. At what place does Germany find itself when it comes to globalization? Literary and filmic statements such as the one under examination here provide points of reference for debate and discussion.

Arslan points out the problem of child migrants, that is, they are pawns in an effort to secure wealth or asylum in western European nations, but whose fate it is to remain on the periphery. Arslan does not apportion sole responsibility to the host nation for the choice or fate of migrant children. Clearly, the choice to migrate, as demonstrated in the film, rests with those in the country of origin who take the decision to send their children abroad. Part of Arslan's admitted goal is to "sensitize these rich countries to the effect they have on others," presumably in an effort to reveal the hardships attendant on migration.

What of the obligations of the host nation to migrants in the transnational space? Is it, as Helmut Kohl famously declared, "up to the[se] foreigners themselves who live here whether they can successfully integrate or not" (qtd. in Kolinsky 93)? Their ability to integrate and fit into the German "public and social life" (Kolinsky 93) requires a further dismantling of some of the conceptual and cultural boundaries that exist within a given society. Ulrich Beck says, "Transnational social spaces cancel the local associations of community that are contained in the national concept of society" (*Globalization* 28). This means that traditional versions of community must be challenged and transformed in accordance with new societal constellations. An "approach centred on transnational social spaces" affirms a condition in which both "places of departure and place of arrival" are transmuted (28). Money earned by children abroad can transform the lives of those in the land of origin/departure, and political asylum can save the life of one endangered by violence in the homeland. The transnational place of arrival, however, is presented by Arslan as one of privation. His film focuses on the child victims of the transnation, the migrant spaces in Germany. *Brudermord* portrays children as the ultimate victims of migration, casualties in the pursuit of economic survival and the administration of benevolent indifference. Throughout the film the brand "Fus Europ" is present on the pullover of young Ibo. At first it contains the hope for a life in the "Promised Land," but this meaning is worn away during the rape by Zeki, as Ibo beats another Kurdish boy, during the sorrowful phone call to the village chief in his homeland, and finally as he boards the bus to leave Germany. In the end, Germany and with it, Europe, have become empty promises.

Notes

1. In making this point, Beck refers to a study by Patricia Alleyne-Dettmers called "Tribal Arts: A Case Study of Global Compression in the Notting Hill Carnival," in Eade, John. ed., *Living the Global City: Globalization as a Local Process*. London: Routledge, 1997, 163–80.
2. Berlin-Kreuzberg has been the locus of many other films, including Sinan Çetin's *Berlin in Berlin* (1993), Thomas Arslan's *Dealer* (1999) and *Der schöne Tag* (2001), and Kutlug Ataman's *Lola + Bilidikid* (1999).
3. For further discussion of these categories, see Higson.
4. For more detailed discussion of this debate, see Halle.
5. For further discussion on a definition of German Cinema, see also Silberman (297–315).
6. Burns notes with reference to Deniz Göktürk that new transnational cinema, as opposed to "cinema of the affected," is male-oriented (142).
7. The Geneva Convention protects refugees from deportation, even if not entitled to asylum under Article 16a of the Basic Law, if they have a well-founded fear of various kinds of persecution, including persecution based on nationality. Kurdish nationality is central to the intra-national conflict presented in the film.
8. The narration has attributes of both diegetic (recognizably the voice of one of the characters within the story) and non-diegetic (from the perspective of omniscience or hindsight) sound.
9. "Wenn ihr nicht sofort leiser seid, dann ist Schluss mit der Taschengeldausgabe!"
10. "In der Türkei könnt ihr euch meinetwegen zerfleischen, wie ihr wollt, aber hier in Deutschland herrscht Ordnung, verstanden? Solange ihr in diesem Land Gäste seid, habt ihr euch zu benehmen, wie es von euch verlangt wird. Wir geben euch Geld, wir geben euch Essen, wir geben euch Kleider, wir geben euch weiß Gott was alles noch. Und ihr, was macht ihr? Ihr geht mit dem Messer aufeinander los. Ist das der Dank?"
11. In the film, Ibo's character makes specific mention of his home being a village near Mardin, a region in southeastern Turkey where the population comprises large groups of Assyrians, Turks, Arabs, and Kurds. The formation of an independent Kurdish state in the southeastern part of Turkey was promised in the Treaty of Sevres, but was withdrawn by the Turkish state. For more on the history of Kurdish nationalism and internationalization of the Kurdish issue, see Argun (119–37).
12. This is also true of the term *Selbstmord* and the more clinical-sounding Latinate *Suizid*.

References

Ali, Abdullah Yusuf. *The Meaning of The Holy Qur'an*. Beltsville: amana publications, 2004.
Appadurai, Arjun. *Modernity at Large: Cultural Dimensions of Globalization*. Minneapolis: U of Minnesota P, 1996.
Argun, Betigül Ercan. *Turkey in Germany: The Transnational Sphere of Deutschkei*. New York: Routledge, 2003.
Arslan, Yilmaz. Interview. "Fratricide/Kardes Katili/Brudermord." *Turkish Cinema Newsletter*. 29 July 2005. 2 Apr. 2008 <http://turkfilm.blogspot.com/2005/07/fratricide-kardes-katili-brudermord.html>.
Beck, Ulrich. "Muslim Societies and the Western World Can No Longer Be Considered to Be Separate Entity." *Interview with Brigitte Neumann*. 12 June 2003. 1 May 2007 <http://www.quantara.de/webcom/show_article.php/_c-327/_nr-16/_p-1/i.html?PHPSESSID=133099777>.
Beck, Ulrich. *What Is Globalization?* Trans. Patrick Camiller. Malden: Polity Press, 2000.
Brudermord (Fratricide). Dir. Yilmaz Arslan. Yilmaz Arslan Filmproduktions, 2005.
Brudermord. Screenplay by Yilmaz Arslan. Dir. Yilmaz Arslan. Tarantula and Ya Filmproduktion, 2005.
Burns, Rob. "Turkish-German Cinema: From Cultural Resistance to Transnational Cinema?" *German Cinema since Unification*. Ed. David Clarke. London: Continuum, 2006. 126–49.
Buß, Christian. "Jedem seiner eigene Heimat." *Spiegel Online*. 25 Sept. 2007. 28 Mar. 2008 <http://www.spiegel.de>.
———. "Beyond Paternalism: Turkish German Traffic in Cinema." *The German Cinema Book*. Ed. Tim Bergfelder, Erica Carter, and Deniz Göktürk. London: British Film Institute, 2002. 248–56.
Elsaesser, Thomas. "European Culture, National Cinema, the Auteur and Hollywood." *European Cinema: Face to Face with Hollywood*. Amsterdam: Amsterdam UP, 2005. 35–56.
Fischer, Sabine, and Moray McGowan, "From 'Pappkoffer' to Pluralism: On the Development of Migrant Writing in the Federal Republic of Germany." *Turkish Culture in German Society Today*. Ed. David Horrocks and Eva Kolinsky. Providence: Berghahn, 1996. 1–22.
Ganz unten (Lowest of the Low). Dir. Jörg Gförer. KAOS Film- und Videoteam, 1986.
Göktürk, Deniz. Introduction. "Transnational Connections." *The German Cinema Book*. Ed. Tim Bergfelder, Erica Carter, and Deniz Göktürk. London: British Film Institute, 2002. 213–16.
Halle, Randall. "German Film, *Aufgehoben*: Ensembles of Transnational Cinema." *New German Critique*. 87 (2002): 7–46.

Higson, Andrew. "The Concept of National Cinema." *Screen* 30.4 (Autumn 1989): 36–37. Reprinted in Williams, Alan, ed., *Film and Nationalism*. New Brunswick, NJ: Rutgers UP, 2002. 52–67.
Hoffmann, Lutz. *Die unvollendete Republik: Zwischen Einwanderungsland und deutschem Nationalstaat*. 2nd ed. Cologne: Papy Rossa, 1992.
Hofmann, Michael. *Interkulturelle Literaturwissenschaft. Eine Einführung*. Paderborn: Wilhelm Fink, 2006.
Horrocks, David, and Eva Kolinsky. "Migrants or Citizens? Turks in Germany between Exclusion and Acceptance." *Turkish Culture in German Society Today*. Ed. David Horrocks and Eva Kolinsky. Providence: Berghahn, 1996. x–xxviii.
Karakasoglu, Yasemin. "Turkish Cultural Orientations in Germany and the Role of Islam." *Turkish Culture in German Society Today*. Ed. David Horrocks and Eva Kolinsky. Providence: Berghahn, 1996. 157–79.
Kolinsky, Eva. "Non-German Minorities In Contemporary German Society." *Turkish Culture in German Society Today*. Ed. David Horrocks and Eva Kolinsky. Providence: Berghahn, 1996. 71–111.
Kürsat-Ahlers, Elçin. "The Turkish Minority in German Society." *Turkish Culture in German Society Today*. Ed. David Horrocks and Eva Kolinsky. Providence: Berghahn, 1996. 113–35.
Panayi, Panikos. *Ethnic Minorities in Nineteenth and Twentieth Century Germany: Jews, Gypsies, Poles, Turks and Others*. Harlow: Pearson, 2000.
Rivi, Luisa. *European Cinema after 1989: Cultural Identity and Transnational Production*. New York: Palgrave Macmillan, 2007.
Seyhan, Azade. *Writing Outside the Nation*. Princeton: Princeton UP, 2001.
Silberman, Marc. "What Is German in the German Cinema?" *Film History* 8.3 (1996): 297–315.
Tan, Dursan, and Hans-Peter Waldhoff. "Turkish Everyday Culture in Germany and Its Prospects." *Turkish Culture in German Society Today*. Ed. David Horrocks and Eva Kolinsky. Providence: Berghahn, 1996. 137–55.

14
Diasporic Queers:
Reading for the Intersections of Alterities in Recent German Cinema

Alice Kuzniar

Abstract Rather than see non-normative race, ethnicity, residency status, and sexuality as separate categories, each of which can individually cause its bearer to be subject to ostracism and abjection, this chapter seeks, by focusing on Yüksel Yavuz's *Kleine Freiheit* (2003) and Angelina Maccarone's *Fremde Haut* (2005), to investigate the intersection and interdependence of alterities across categories, a movement that calls into question the very viability of such divisions and our assumptions about them. I thus wish to complicate globalization studies and queer studies by thinking them together.

As in his earlier films *Im Juli* (*In July*, 2000) and *Gegen die Wand* (*Head-On*, 2004), director Fatih Akin creates characters in his more recent film *Auf der anderen Seite* (*Edge of Heaven*, 2007) who move between Germany and Turkey. This time, however, in contradistinction to his earlier films that focused on heterosexual romance, he frames his intricate, intersecting narratives around a love affair between two women. Ayten is a young radical activist who flees to Germany with a falsified passport in order to escape arrest in Istanbul. There she meets the German university student Charlotte, who falls in love with her at first sight. From the start, Lotte is unswervingly dedicated to the angry but oddly attractive Ayten. When Ayten is arrested and, after a year in detention while appealing in vain for political asylum, sent back to Turkey, Lotte follows her, eager to pay attorney fees yet again in an attempt to free her friend. Again, she is impervious to the grief she causes her mother. In turn,

Ayten, engrossed in her own countercultural world and without regard for Lotte's own safety, uses her girlfriend to assist her fellow revolutionaries, which leads inadvertently to Lotte's death. As even this brief overview of the Lotte-and-Ayten segment of the film indicates, the compatibility of the two women and thus their reciprocal attachment are questionable. Lotte appears unbelievably naïve and credulous in her devotion to the insensitive Ayten. The latter's political affiliations remain vague and unmotivated in a generic protest against globalization, the European Union, and the wearing of brand-named clothing. She in turn also appears naïve. What remains significant, however, is the choice of a German–Turkish lesbian affair, for apart from *Querelle* (Rainer Werner Fassbinder, 1982) and, more recently, *Alles wird gut* (*Everything Will Be Fine*, Angelina Maccarone, 1998) and *Lola + Bilidikid* (Kutluğ Ataman, 1998), there have been no same-sex relations on the German cinematic screen inflected by skin hue. In large part, this situation has arisen out of a Western inability to conceive of non-Europeans and non-Americans as gay or lesbian.[1] Akin, though, brings them into mainstream cinema, but, in doing so, he fails to develop the lesbian attachment convincingly, and, more importantly, he fails to tie the issue of political asylum to being gay or lesbian.

What this chapter attempts to do is to claim that being gay or lesbian, politically persecuted, and living illegally in Germany *are* interrelated issues. If Akin sets up these elements, only to neglect to make them interdependent, other lesser-known filmmakers have forged the link, in the process offering much more politically astute commentaries on Germany today in the context of international human rights. What these filmmakers call for is the challenge to reconfigure German society not only in terms of global, mass migration but also in terms of the movement of gays and lesbians across borders. This essay, in addition, wants to ask where a nation-based German queer cinema is today in light of such migration. Many of Germany's renowned gay and lesbian directors have situated their films abroad—from *Johanna d'Arc of Mongolia* (Ulrike Ottinger, 1989), *Die Jungfrauenmaschine* (*Virgin Machine*, Monika Treut, 1988), and *My Father Is Coming* (Monika Treut, 1991) to *Der Rosenkönig* (*The King of the Roses*, Werner Schroeter, 1986), *Schweigen=Tod* (*Silence=Death*, Rosa von Praunheim, 1990), and *Positiv* (*Positive*, Rosa von Praunheim, 1990). The experimental director Bjoern Melhus has impersonated American screen idols in various transvestitic roles; queer films have been made by Germans and Austrians living abroad, such as Joerg Fockele and Hans Scheirl; and the documentary filmmaker Jochen Hick in *Menmaniacs—The Legacy of Leather* (1995) and *Sex/Life in L.A.* (1998), like Monika Treut and Rosa von Praunheim, has documented queer lifestyles in America. Today, however, it seems that the diaspora has come home, with German filmmakers depicting the problems confronted by queers of colour and illegal immigrant status. In *Am Ende des Regenbogens* (*Rainbow's End,* Jochen Hick and Christian Jentzsch, 2005 and 2006), for instance, the directors have made a hard-hitting documentary on the lack of equality for homosexuals in Europe today—examining, among other things, experiences of gay Arab men in the Netherlands, Polish anti-gay organizations, and the deportation of gays and lesbians back to countries that persecute them for their sexuality. All too often one assumes that global migration does not impact the daily lives of gay-identified individuals living in Western Europe or that open, government-sanctioned gay-bashing occurs only in the developing world. These attitudes ignore how government policies in Europe regarding migration disregard gay and lesbian specificities. Thus, rather than see non-normative race, ethnicity, residency status, and sexuality as separate categories, each of which can individually cause its bearer to be subject to ostracism and abjection, I want to investigate the intersection and interdependence of alterities across categories, a movement that calls into question the very viability of such categories and our assumptions about them. I thus wish to complicate German studies by thinking both globalization studies and queer studies together.

Specifically, I want to focus on two films: *Kleine Freiheit* (*A Little Bit of Freedom,* Yüksel Yavuz, 2003) and *Fremde Haut* (*Unveiled,* Angelina Maccarone, 2005). In 2003, Yavuz's feature-length film won the Main Prize of the 15th Ankara International Film Festival and in 2004 the Audience Award of the 23rd International Istanbul Film Festival. Its uniqueness can be best highlighted by marking its differences from the aforementioned film by Kutluğ Ataman, *Lola + Bilidikid,* which also investigated an urban German-Turkish milieu by focusing on a young man coming to terms with his family history and burgeoning gay sexuality. I then want to turn briefly, also for comparison's sake, to the previously mentioned *Alles wird gut,* especially because *Fremde Haut* is by the same director and thus registers a shift in interest in current gay and lesbian consciousness and conscience. Both of Maccarone's films deal, generally speaking, with the problems faced by lesbians of colour. *Alles wird gut,* a comedy that was popular in the gay and lesbian film festival circuit, tells the story of two Afro-German women from different classes who fall in love. *Fremde Haut* narrates the tale of an Iranian woman who has to flee her native country due to persecution caused by her lesbianism, but whose rape while incarcerated cannot be documented. Thus, once she enters Germany, she is afraid to acknowledge the true reasons for her flight, lies about her identity, and thus cannot be recognized under Germany's immigration asylum law. She therefore faces deportation once discovered. What *Kleine Freiheit* and *Fremde Haut* add to previous German queer cinema are the problems faced by illegal immigrants.

There are many other significant ways in which these two films contribute to queer studies. The loss of family and national identity is exacerbated when the desire of these individuals for friendship and love becomes unattainable— in other words, when the only form of community left open to them also becomes closed. Thus, these more recent films confront the painful reality of the impossibility of identity formation and even of community building abroad. The main protagonists have no claim of belonging to a group that understands them; they have no place of dwelling, way of belonging, or orientation. At issue here, then, is precisely not hybrid, multiple, or fluid postmodern identities that earlier filmmakers such as Monika Treut or Ulrike Ottinger extolled. Crossing national borders and sexual boundaries is not liberating and emancipatory but life threatening; the transgression results in the individual not being able to be recognized by social convention. The liminality that these characters experience prohibits any cultural transition for them into new communities. Nor can they look back to reclaim an identity from their past. The resulting suffering makes us question not only the glorification of Gilles Deleuze's notion of deterritorialization or Rosi Braidotti's concept of the nomadic, non-unitary subject, just to give two examples,[2] but also our Western assumptions about what constitutes gay and lesbian identity. The films by Yavuz and Maccarone interrogate the supposed transparency of the categories "gay" and "lesbian," when the conditions of being recognized as such are not in place. They tell us that these conditions cannot be taken for granted. Moreover, because *Fremde Haut* is a new version of the *Hosenrolle* film, where the female lead character has to wear men's clothing and pass as male, in this case, in order to hide her illegal alien identity, the film casts drag in a hitherto unrecognized light. Hers is not playfully undertaken trickery, a self-conscious bravura performance, or a swaggering parody of gender norms. Nor is it about gender malaise as in many films about transgender. She fears being discovered not only as a woman but, more importantly, as an illegal alien. Finally, *Fremde Haut* and *Kleine Freiheit*, because they play on the registers of visibility and invisibility, encourage gay and lesbian studies to regard the issue of being out and being outed in terms of deportation.

Kleine Freiheit

Whereas *Lola + Bilidikid* and *Alles wird gut* offered the promise of new communities and bonds of gay and lesbian kinship and love in response to homophobic and xenophobic societies in Germany, *Kleine Freiheit* is much bleaker by introducing the atomization of life due to exile, economic deprivation and dependency, combined with the constant fear of arrest. Ataman's film focuses on three brothers: the eldest closeted, ultra-macho, and brutally homophobic;

the middle one, Lola, having to turn to a transvestite-like appearance in order to have his sexuality be legible in German-Turkish society; and the youngest, on whose narrative the film concentrates, discovering a gay identity that is more contemporary, open, and Westernized compared to that of his siblings. In his article, "Transculturation, *Transe* Sexuality, and Turkish Germany: Kutluğ Ataman's *Lola und Bilidikid*," Christopher Clark discusses how these various expressions of German-Turkish gay identities overlap and come into conflict in the film. Clark valorizes the state of "in-betweenness" or "transness" in the film— between transvestite and transsexual, between German and Turkish cultures, even between gay and straight. He sees multiple alterities as intertwining, thereby undermining "a number of cultural, sexual, and historical binarisms" (556). The film offers up "a queer array of possible sexual and cultural identities" and "points of intersection between various modes of sexual and cultural transition and liminality" (572).[3] Indeed, by the end of the film, the youngest brother, Murat, survives and moves forward with his life, liberating his mother from their claustrophobic family; the rich German and his Turkish lover form a couple; and the community of German-Turkish drag queens, who provide the comic relief in this otherwise dark film, strike it rich and optimistically plan for their future plastic surgeries. Bonding thus occurs on and across various levels.

Although *Kleine Freiheit* depicts the burgeoning ties of friendship between two youth, one Kurdish, the other African, Clark's phrase "queer array of possible sexual and cultural identities" would be inappropriate to apply, precisely because identity affiliation is denied the two boys. Unlike the characters in *Lola + Bilidikid*, these two boys, as illegal immigrants, are not in a position to belong to any permanent community based on ethnic, national, or even gay identity membership, however varied and hybrid these are conceived. Baran is a young Kurdish refugee, who escaped to Germany five years before, when his family was exterminated. Recently, upon turning sixteen, his application for asylum was turned down, and he now lives in the country illegally. His only family in this foreign home is a cousin, Haydar, with whom he lives. Baran makes ends meet by working inconspicuously at a kebab restaurant in Hamburg, delivering orders on the restaurant boss's bicycle. It is on the streets that he makes the acquaintance of Chernor, also in the country illegally. The friend is given even less back story: from Africa, Chernor has had no contact with his family for the last two years and does not know their whereabouts. He is forced to live and make do in the present on a day-to-day basis, reluctantly becoming involved in drug deals in order to make a living and remain on good terms with the men who are granting him a place to sleep.

Yüksel Yavuz, *Kleine Freiheit*: Baran and Chernor. © Peter Stockhaus Filmproduktion GmbH

The "little bit of freedom" to which the title alludes and that the youth possess is symbolized in the independence and thrill that Baran experiences in making his delivery rounds.[4] Indeed, the shots taken from the bicycle are among the most exciting and stunning in the film's beautiful cinematography. For example, near the beginning of the film, superimposed on the image of the spokes turning, are the views Baran espies from aloft, at night or by day, as he delivers kebabs. But even this small bit of freedom is taken from him when the owner of the restaurant dismisses him and reclaims the bicycle out of fear that his restaurant would be closed were the police to discover that he had hired an illegal alien. The city streets are thus the site not only for movement and liberty, but also of police surveillance and racial targeting. The streets, then, are the location where, at the close, the boys run from the cops and the final shootout takes place. They earlier become a maze when Chernor is searching for Baran, or when Baran tries to track down the Kurd who betrayed his family to the Turkish militia, leading to their death and Baran's appeal for asylum abroad.[5]

Barely into manhood, still children in a sense, and threatened with deportation, Baran and Chernor are extremely vulnerable. The only aspiration the boys seem able to articulate at their young age is merely to be friends. Even then, their friendship is shy, and their attraction to each other delicate and modest. What they have in common is their youth and common diasporic experiences. Baran, in particular, is of an age where he feigns not to be aware of his attractiveness and sexuality. With dyed blond hair, Chernor appears most self-consciously queer, and the focus on his hair evokes the role the red wig played in *Lola + Bilidikid* as a marker of homosexuality. One of his housemates indeed homophobically labels him as queer. The only indication that Baran could be what we would call gay is that he is thoroughly uninterested in the teenage daughter of his boss, who tries to get his attention. When his boss suggests his niece as an alternative to his daughter, reminding him that his residency status would thereby be resolved, Baran again responds with aloofness. It furthermore never occurs to his boss that the reason for this diffidence is that he might be gay. The one character definitely self-identified and recognized by the boys as gay is the "Captain," an old man who claims to have travelled the seas, but now slums on a street bench. He dies by the end of the film.[6] Like the boys, he is homeless and has lived an itinerant existence. The boss's daughter, frustrated by her inability to charm Baran, needles him by saying the reason he hangs out with the stinky captain is that both are gay. But this is not a label the boy ever claims for himself.

In an interview Yavuz was quick to point out that one cannot properly speak of homosexual love between the two boys:

> I tell of the situation of two youth who are very dependent on each other because of their illegality, where a certain freedom is denied them, and they must constantly keep on guard. Having already lost a lot in their young lives, they enter into a friendship, all the more drawn to each other, respecting, and loving each other. It is this intensity that leads to such a thing, especially because they are of an age where one is searching for sexual orientation. That doesn't mean, though, that they are homosexual, although one can already say that about the black boy, but not necessarily the Kurdish boy. The pals of the black one cuss him out as a "faggot," although he doesn't act that way or have any ambitions to do so, but apparently he's so inclined. The Kurdish boy not, although he'd be open to it, so perhaps he is homosexual after all.[7]

Because neither Chernor nor Baran are self-evidently gay or self-identify as gay, the film refuses to follow the conventional trajectory of the coming out narrative that typically patterns gay youth films—and that determines the plots of both *Lola + Bilidikid* and *Alles wird gut*. But what *Kleine Freiheit* does share with *Lola + Bilidikid* is the demonstration of the inaccurate assumption that to be gay in Germany means being hip, liberated, affluent, and, in the case of the Captain, young. The free expressions of gay identity and gay rights would first be dependent on extending human rights and a safe haven to migrants. And just as *Lola + Bilidikid* addressed various sexualities uneasily co-existing in German-Turkish society, so too does *Kleine Freiheit* intimate that we need to pay attention to a different form of sexuality, here the tenderness of young sexualities that are fluid, not yet fixed, and uncertain of themselves. To say as much means not that homosexuality is absent in the film but that, as Yavuz points out, the film leaves it open as a possibility.

One of the reasons why it is hard to read *Kleine Freiheit* as a gay film is that surveillance so pervades the boys' lives that there is no safe space in which they could develop close physical proximity. Both live in male-dominated communities where homosexuality and cross-racial friendship are not accepted. Thus, even in the relatively safe space of the apartment and in each other's sleeping quarters, the boys experience tension when Chernor's housemates and, reciprocally, Baran's cousin Haydar espy the friend of another racial colour. Haydar does come to accept Chernor, however, and lets him move in and share a bed with Baran, but only because he is oblivious to the potential sexuality of his cousin. There is one brief scene where sexual intimacy suggests itself: as the boys lie side by side, Chernor begins to caress Baran, who, it seems, is too inexperienced to know how to respond to these gentle advances. Although Yavuz quickly cuts to another scene, this episode of intimacy does appear to deepen Baran's passionate commitment to Chernor.

The camera, in its various guises, serves to emphasize this fear of surveillance. Baran is in possession of a video camera, and indeed the first images of the film are those taken of his Kurdish relatives back home. He shows Chernor this segment to explain who he is in the present. He also carries his camera with him everywhere, as if it signalled a means not only to memorialize his family past but to register, frame, and conquer his new world. When he catches Chernor dealing drugs on tape, however, the camera becomes a method of surveillance—and presumably it will serve as proof to the police of Chernor's illegal activities. The photo automat also shares in this dual function: the boys retreat there to take humorous shots of themselves and to enjoy physical proximity to each other, but it does function as a closet of sorts. The walls of the photo booth are confining, despite the show of candid, mutual affection the close(d) space enables.[8] Finally, as Baran is apprehended by the police, his video camera is still running, capturing images upside down in an apt metaphor for his life going awry. The film ends as the police turn the camera off.

Kleine Freiheit thus reminds us that the risk certain individuals take in today's "*Risikogesellschaft*," to use Ulrich Beck's term, is exponentially greater once the fortresses of insurance, security, and surveillance are erected precisely against them. In *Lola + Bilidikid*, Lola's red wig signified visibility and thus vulnerability; Chernor's dyed blond hair functions similarly—as the sign of the impossibility of passing and fitting into the society as both gay and non-white, i.e., non-black-haired. Although the boys are always trying to maintain a low profile and avoid the eye of law enforcement, in the denouement, in the one moment when they are unguarded, the police turn to them unprovoked on the streets asking for identification papers. The youths try to run away, and when Chernor is captured, Baran makes the unwise decision to try to liberate him from the police using a stolen pistol. Such a desperate move indicates not only his painfully immature, young judgment, but also the extent of his obsessive devotion to Chernor. If earlier in the film, Baran hid the pistol in order to take revenge on a fellow Kurd now living in Germany and who played a role in betraying his family, a vengeance he never accomplishes, here at the close of the film, he wants to come to the defence of his new "kin." The point, however, is that family ties are completely dissolved for such illegal immigrants as Baran and Chernor, who have no home to speak of in either their native country or country of adoption. Even Haydar cannot assist in obtaining asylum for his cousin, and Chernor is more rootless still, for we have no idea how he even got to Germany and with what difficulties.

The boys' bonds are solely to each other, but we cannot speak here of a burgeoning gay affiliation that would redefine family and kinship. The boys stand outside of a gay community; their sexuality is not organized around a movement called gay. I am reminded of Michael Warner's cautionary words that "community [...] falsely suggests an ideological and nostalgic contrast with the atomization of modern capitalist society" (xxv). To put it another way, being part of a collective identity or participative community would not be a possibility for Chernor or Baran. In fact, *Kleine Freiheit* illustrates how defence of the Kurdish enclave in Hamburg leads Baran to murderous intentions vis-à-vis the old man formerly in his community and to a near deadly fight in the new restaurant his boss opened up. Moreover, current discourses valorizing hybridity, social mobility, living between two cultures, and thus belonging in some fashion to them both, are all highly inadequate to describe the phenomenon that Yavuz is documenting. Take, for instance, Paul Gilroy's notion of "conviviality," which he uses "to refer to the processes of cohabitation and interaction that have made multi-culture an ordinary feature of social life [...] in post-colonial cities. [...] The radical openness that brings conviviality alive makes a nonsense of closed, fixed, and reified identity and turns attention toward the always-unpredictable mechanisms of identification" (xi). Although Yavuz's film, in the friendships it depicts across national boundaries, seems to celebrate Gilroy's "conviviality," precisely speaking, "radical openness" is the problem

Baran and Chernor experience, not its solution, for these youth require a modicum of care, security, and stability in their lives, not more exposure to political and social contingencies. To the same intent as Gilroy, Stuart Hall defines the diasporic experience "not by essence or purity, but by the recognition of a necessary heterogeneity and diversity; by a conception of 'identity' [that] lives with and through, not despite, difference; by *hybridity*" (402). Hall's valorized term of "hybridity" would do injustice to the atomization at work in *Kleine Freiheit*, which comes not only from being an illegal migrant, but also from belonging neither to a gay community nor, in Baran's case, to the heterosexually determined ethnic community that took him in. The film, in addition, contrasts established German-Turkish immigrants with the plight of new migrants. In light of Baran's and Chernor's dilemma, solutions based on notions of conviviality and hybridity fall short. More apt would be the cautious stance of Leslie Adelson regarding what she calls a "new critical grammar of migration": "No cultural frames of reference are pre-given in any authoritative sense for [...] migration [...]. Each text must be interpreted for relevant frames of reference or contexts to be rendered meaningful" (12).

Fremde Haut

The earlier films by Angelina Maccarone, *Kommt Mausi raus?* (*Is Mausi Coming Out?*, 1994) and *Alles wird gut*, celebrate being lesbian and the process of coming out. *Fremde Haut*, by contrast, reminds the European gay and lesbian community that queers are not only facing persecution in developing countries, but also in their own Western, liberal society. This film complicates the issue of coming out as lesbian by linking it inextricably with coming out as an illegal immigrant, in fact, in its complicated plot, even coming out as a woman! The English title *Unveiled* is thus well chosen. The film begins on a plane from Tehran, when a woman goes to the lavatory and takes off the headscarf she had been wearing until she arrived in the international air space. She uses the fabric to cover up the smoke detector while she lights a cigarette. As the film develops, we find out that Fariba Tabrizi is fleeing Iran, because her affair with another woman was discovered, and because she faced political persecution for not denouncing her lesbianism, unlike her lover, who in recanting is regarded as a sick woman in need of protection. Once Fariba arrives in Germany, she is unable to confess her real reasons for fleeing, and presents a falsified passport, knowing that she has no documentation of being held in prison after her detection, nor any proof of being raped there, which would support her claim for asylum. Nor is she given any legal aid. Fariba, a translator by profession in Iran, not only speaks fluent German, but she is well versed in German literature. A fellow plane traveller, Siamak, whom she befriends, also dreads that his asylum plea will be rejected, sending him back to Iran. While in detention, he commits suicide, though ironically in the very moments before finding out that his application was temporarily accepted. Realizing that she will be sent back to Iran, Fariba dons the clothing of her dead friend and appears before the officials in his place. She leaves, packing Siamak's corpse into his large suitcase and granting him burial once outside the detention centre. In her extended act of melancholic impersonation and grieving commitment, she continues to write his family that he is prospering in her new domicile. She does so, not only to respect Siamak's wishes that she do so in case of his death, but conceivably also because his parents must perforce become her ersatz family; her own family, it is presumed, will have disowned her. Ironically, Siamak's sacrificial death, which allows Fariba to live in Germany, parallels his own brother's death. When captured by the Iranian military, Siamak's brother courageously claimed he was the one they were searching for. On news of the brother's death, then, Siamak commits suicide in the shame and agony he feels for previously lacking the courage to claim his own identity. Fariba, by contrast, is persecuted and chooses exile, because she insists on maintaining her lesbian identity and not renouncing it.

In his book *An Accented Cinema*, Hamid Naficy selects the topoi of performed identity, the *doppelgänger*, and duplicity as characteristic of exilic and diasporic filmmaking: clearly *Fremde Haut* matches the criteria for Naficy's film genre. In Germany Fariba must adopt a foreign skin—one not only of a man but also of a legal immigrant awaiting final decision on his refugee status. She lives in limbo, existing in an in-between state of neither man nor woman, neither illegal alien nor legal immigrant. She must now adjust to life in Germany and start at the bottom in a refugee camp. Becoming "German" is thus yet the other foreign skin she needs to step into, although now, despite being perfectly fluent in German, she has to act as if she is just learning the language. Although she is familiar with Novalis, she has to pass as belonging to the uneducated. And although coming from Tehran, an urban centre, she works harvesting cabbages in a rural setting.[9] The veiling could also refer to the breast binding she has to perform and, arguably, in the extended metaphor of impeded vision, to the wearing of Siamak's glasses. It is ironic that she can sit as Siamak before the detention officials without them noticing the disguise, suggesting not only that for Germans dark-skinned foreigners all look alike and cannot be distinguished from one another, but also that they are always already feminized.

How, then, does Fariba become "unveiled"? The disclosure slowly unravels, as she falls in love with a German girl, Anne, who takes to this shy, polite foreigner, precisely because he, circumspect and gentle, is so unlike the actual men

Angelina Maccarone, *Fremde Haut*: Anne and Fariba. © MMM Film Zimmermann & Co.

around her. Much of the film is taken up with the interaction between these men. Their societal status is threatened by the fact that, as co-workers in a cabbage-processing facility, they work alongside "smelly" illegal aliens, and by the fact that Anne prefers an Iranian to the German Uwe. In order to separate themselves from him, they call Siamak Anne's "Mexican friend" and nickname him "Ayatollah." They mock his shyness and order him to sing and dance to express himself (since he cannot speak German adequately). These prejudicial markers, too, become the "fremde Haut" Fariba must don: she sings on command, but in a strikingly haunting voice.

Significantly, the film does not explore the possibilities of Anne's coming-out story. In contrast to her other films, Maccarone refrains from depicting any struggles Anne has with falling in love with someone of her own sex. To be sure, we do see that she does not lead a charmed life: she struggles to make ends meet as a single mother in a menial job, and is harassed by men who think she should feel obligated to pay them attention. Like Fariba, she too is trapped economically in a society where the men call the shots. Compared to *Aimée & Jaguar* (Max Färberböck, 1999), which also depicts the dire necessity of the closet and the threat of deportation, the lesbians are not fashionable, good-looking women. Plus, the narrative is not told, as it is in *Aimée & Jaguar*, from the perspective of the blond German female protagonist, a perspective that encourages the spectator's self-distantiation from the foreign-appearing lover.

Instead the focus in the *Fremde Haut* remains on Fariba: she is the one to come out as a lesbian, when she finally divulges her background to the sympathetic Anne. And she is the one who, in the end, is brutally outed. The final denouement occurs in a scene similar to *Boys Don't Cry* (Kimberly Peirce, 1999): the cross-dresser is discovered at her lover's home and roughed up for being a male imposter, which means duping the men around her and being a predatory lesbian in disguise. When Anne's son calls the police for help in this case of domestic violence, the authorities, predictably, do not care about the brutality, but arrest Fariba for being in the country illegally. It is symbolically relevant that Fariba's exposure comes when she has disrobed and is wearing just a camisole with her breasts no longer bound, in other words, freed for one brief, but tragic moment from the restrictive clothing she has had to wear. She is also gazing into the forged passport she had just bought, where she is pictured as a woman—the future identity she had purchased at a high price and that she, at this moment, is looking forward to adopting, because it means living again freely as a woman and hence as an outed lesbian.

If in *Kleine Freiheit* the city streets provided the ambiguous site of both freedom of movement and of surveillance, in *Fremde Haut* the night assumes a similar dual function. It is the time for stealth, which paradoxically means for Fariba the moment when she can wash and undo her bandaged breasts. The threat of detection, however, never goes away. Also late at night, the men go carousing, forcing Fariba to come along. The police stop their car and fine, not Uwe for drunk driving, but "Siamak" for leaving the district to which he as a refugee awaiting asylum is restricted. On this occasion, the men take their "Mexican friend" to a brothel, where again Fariba's identity as a woman and lesbian threatens to be exposed. These men expect "Siamak" to perform and verify his masculinity by having sex with a prostitute, a masculinity that for them would also be certified by infidelity to Anne. Finally, then, it is at night that Uwe and his pal come to Anne's home looking for beer, only to discover Fariba's true identity.

In the last scene of the movie, Fariba is back on a plane, where she again doffs her headscarf, but this time to put on Siamak's glasses and enter Iran with his passport, which she had hidden in her shoe. The airplane thus marks the site of transitioning—between East and West, between wearing and not wearing the headscarf as a form of female oppression, and between male and female. Paradoxically, planes do not signify as they usually do freedom of movement and international travel. The detention centre is stationed next to the airport, and the constant sight and sound of the planes serve as a reminder to the refugees that they are not legally in Germany, but in a no-man's land from where they can be sent back to Iran. Thus, when Fariba returns at the end of the movie, she faces a future even more threatening than her experiences in Germany, which were harrowing enough and an indictment not only of German immigration policy, but also of homophobia in a society that officially proclaims tolerance toward sexual diversity. The implicit parallels drawn between Iran and Germany are thus fascinating: she has to leave both countries and the woman in each with whom she had fallen in love. In each she has to disguise her gender identity. The film also suggests that, insofar as Germany fails to recognize as political the particular domestic persecution that women face or to recognize that state violence against women (such as rape in jail or merely the fact of incarceration) cannot always be documented and hence proven in an asylum court abroad, Germany aligns itself with the violence against women tolerated in Muslim countries.

Like Yavuz's film, Maccarone's explores the impossibility in contemporary Germany of assuming an identity other than that of illegal alien. To become "unveiled" does not mean that one can unfold one's true identity. Although very differently, Fariba, like Baran and Chernor, does not and cannot belong to the GLBTQ community as it is currently constructed in contemporary Europe. Part of this problem lies in the fact that the West harbours an undifferentiated notion of the Muslim Other as being not just homophobic but also therefore inconceivably gay, let alone lesbian. Some critics, such as Joseph Massad, have even argued that being "gay" is an unwelcome Western importation to Arab-speaking countries, and that the efforts of such NGOs as the International Lesbian and Gay Association (ILGA) and the International Gay and Lesbian Human Rights Commission (IGLHRC) are endangering the lives of men and women who love others of the same sex, because they draw them to the attention of the religious fundamentalist regimes. I would beg to differ with Massad and argue that *Fremde Haut* is important for drawing attention to the persecution and discrimination for reasons of sexual orientation that occur both in Iran and in Germany. Plus, it reminds us that self-identified lesbians do exist outside the Western world, in particular, among the educated classes, who are invariably influenced by contact with the West, as is clearly the case with the bilingual, culturally literate Ms. Tabrizi.

Fremde Haut, moreover, serves as an important corrective to assumptions commonly held in queer theory, namely, that transgender performance and the ability to pass successfully are matters of celebration and queer pride. Although Venus Xtravaganza and Brandon Teena are real cases of transgendered individuals who have lost their lives—and *Fremde Haut*, as previously mentioned, does do homage to Kimberly Peirce's film—Fariba's life reminds us that, unlike in these previous tragic stories, cross-dressing is not automatically a matter of personal decision, volition, and agency, much less style. The actress Jasmin

Tabatabai does pass magnificently in her role as a man, but Fariba's desire, we must remember, is to be a woman. Thus, penultimate to the violent scene that erupts upon her, the one where she sits pensively in the kitchen dressed only in a woman's camisole and gazing at a picture of herself as a woman, is extremely poignant. Here, for the briefest of moments she is truly unveiled and herself, although also alone and vulnerable. This scene thus begs to be read in tandem with the previous lovemaking one between Anne and Fariba, where Anne gently unbinds Tariba's chest and unveils her breasts. The two women open up to each other in their nakedness and shared vulnerability. In contrast to the Brandon Teena story, where Brandon never undresses, even during sex, Fariba is attacked when seen as a woman and not clothed as a man.

In light of *Kleine Freiheit*, much of the queer theorization of drag and performance appears too oversimplified. Majorie Garber's comments are indicative of such generalization, when she writes that cross-dressing opens "a space of possibility structuring and confounding culture," and that it is a "disruptive element that intervenes" (17). Katrin Sieg follows suit claiming that ethnic drag serves as a "crucial site of contests about identity, authority, and power" (28). Fariba's performance does not contest stereotypical identities or indicate how they are constructed as much as she complies with the identities associated with the minority subject—male, poor, provincial, and illiterate. If Jennie Livingston's *Paris Is Burning* (1990) serves as the model for which queer theory thinks of performance as invariably mimicking authority and power,[10] then *Kleine Freiheit* reminds us that the subaltern can also be a mimicked position. Fariba's tragedy is that she has to play the stereotype expected of her.

Her cross-dressing, then, is better characterized as passing in a bid for survival than as theatricality, apart from the one night scene where Uwe commands her to perform. Maccarone explored the playful and comic side to performance, when in *Alles wird gut* Nabou poses as Kim's crazed sister so as to avoid suspicion that the two are actually in love. Similarly in *Lola + Bilidikid*, the drag queens, calling themselves *die Gastarbeiterinnen* (the female guest workers), add comic relief. In *Fremde Haut*, however, camp and the carnivalesque are absent. Even in the scene where Fariba performs on command is poignant for how subserviently she complies. The dissonance resides in the searing tonalities of her song and in the peculiar register of her voice, not in any kind of challenge to gender normativity. Moreover, by expressing herself through song, whose words will not be understood, Fariba emphasizes how her silence throughout the film is also mimicked and enforced. It may also be observed that, in Fariba's case, the body does not so much perform the drag as show its discomfort with the role-playing. With downcast head and averted eyes, in other words, holding herself as if she wanted to sink into the ground, Fariba indicates a disunity within herself, the splitting of her identity actually writ on her body's gestures. Although she plays the role of the subaltern migrant expected of her, Fariba reveals her subjectivity and singularity—not as often presupposed in queer theory via the active drag performance—by the involuntary expressions on her face. The close-ups of the camera subvert the concealment of the passing, when they show her pain and longing; they function to preserve the uniqueness of the individual, the Levinasian face.

Finally, in terms of a reassessment of queer studies, both *Kleine Freiheit* and *Fremde Haut* cause one to re-evaluate what the terms "to be out" and "to be outed" mean. The characters in these films do not discover freedom or liberation from being "out." These characters are instead "out" in the sense of being outside society and ostracized by it. Their vulnerability comes from being visible, in large part because of their skin and hair colour, although, ironically, Fariba has to don *eine fremde Haut* and Chernor dyes his hair blond. To be outed in these films has less to do with sexuality than with deportation. Ironically, then, had Fariba truly been recognized as lesbian by the government of Germany, she might have been granted asylum, because she would face imprisonment, torture, and even death as an out lesbian in Iran. Once she lies and then later out of desperation steals a car and falsifies a passport, such hopes are dashed. *Kleine Freiheit* leaves open what Chernor's and Baran's future will be after deportation, as if it were too bleak to even consider; the viewer does not even know if Baran will survive the gunshot wound.

In sum, then, uprootedness and lack of identity, as opposed to plural, mobile, poly-national, or hybrid identities, are explored from all angles in *Fremde Haut*. Fariba is permitted neither to be a woman, a lesbian, a legal immigrant, despite her perfect command of German, nor a fully recognized human being with a longing for the closeness and comfort of another person. The emphasis on skin in the film also points to the visibility and surveillance that people of different shades of colour experience in the predominantly white German society. The film thus cautions against the simplicity and utopianism of certain theorists, such as Gilles Deleuze, Rosi Braidotti, and Julia Kristeva, who uncritically uphold the notion of nomadic, nation-less existence as an ideal. To be sure, the traveller is an unstable signifier who deconstructs claims to normalcy, but it is traumatic to have to live such instability. Kristeva asks in *Nations without Nationalism* that we "recognize ourselves as strange in order better to appreciate the foreigners outside us instead of striving to bend them to the norms of our own repression" (29). To say that "only strangeness is universal" (21) underplays major differences and belittles the suffering that illegal aliens experience compared with our own. Although many of us might like to identify ourselves as perennial foreigners to the hegemonic culture, we choose a cosmopolitan or expatriate membership and are not victim of chance origins. Kristeva speaks of the duty and responsibility of being boundary subjects, but duty and responsibility are not the same as when one is coerced into being a "boundary subject" (35). Despite her education and linguistic ability to cross cultures, Fariba is not in a position to do so, making such exhortations as Kobena Mercer's appear idealistic: "Deciding to act as a world citizen or cosmopolitan has the potential to de-naturalize the symbolic authority of *patria* or nationality" (8–9). Finally, it bears noting that it is not an issue for Fariba of choosing in her diaspora between the identity of German or Iranian; between lesbian or transvestite. Instead, the possibility of adhering to any one as an identity category is prohibited. Where is she to locate herself? Where is she going to find the community to which she belongs? It is not that these are separate, different aspects of her identity, because none of these categories are possible in society. It is not a matter of passing through different spaces or negotiating a plurality of affiliations, let alone entering into a dialogue between them. These variables or labels intersect solely as unfeasibilities. The shame and fear that envelop her make all of these categories negative ones. Here I cannot emphasize enough how this approach varies from the concept of pluralistic, though granted competing, identities from Stuart Hall and Paul Gilroy to Kobena Mercer and Rosi Braidotti.[11]

Postscript

In 2007, the European Parliament President Hans Gert Pöttering wrote a letter to British Prime Minister Gordon Brown on the fate of Pegah Emambakhsh, an Iranian lesbian who risked expulsion from Great Britain. She became a refugee in 2005 after her partner was arrested, tortured, and sentenced to death in Iran. It was Pöttering's task to communicate to Brown that her expulsion would constitute a serious violation of human rights and international conventions, and bring shame not only on Great Britain but on the European Union as a whole. After the campaign to free her, also involving international human rights organizations including Amnesty International, Emambakhsh was granted freedom on 11 September 2007. On 7 March 2008, however, it was reported that she might be deported to Iran after losing the latest round in her battle to be granted asylum. If this were to have happened, she would have faced a possible death penalty on the grounds of her sexual orientation. Fortunately, on 11 February 2009, Emambakhsh was finally granted asylum and allowed to stay in the UK. Although there are some European Union countries that do grant political asylum on the basis of sexual orientation, not all do. Thus in October 2005,

ILGA-Europe (the International Lesbian, Gay, Bisexual, Trans and Intersex Association for the European region) composed "Protecting LBGT People Seeking Asylum: Guidelines on the Refugee Status Directive." Although Germany and the United Kingdom are listed in ILGA's directive as one of the countries having established case law on awarding asylum on the basis of sexual orientation, both Emambakhsh's case and Maccarone's film indicate that the law does not invariably protect the individuals in most need of it.

Notes

1 This inability arises out of an assumption that religious or cultural taboos must prohibit non-procreative sex, which is often ignorant of how various cultures have actually encouraged same-sex attractions and gender inversion, the uniqueness of which would be foreign to the Western eye. The documentary *Dangerous Living: Coming Out in the Developing World* (John Scagliotti, 2003) by the director of *Before Stonewall* (1984) and *After Stonewall* (1999) is one of the few films made in the West that addresses this issue. But it can be criticized for its hodgepodge of examples, leading to a homogenized, touristic view of same-sex lifestyle and persecution in developing countries. By contrast, *Fire* (Deepa Mehta, 1996) and *Nina's Heavenly Delights* (Pratibha Parmar, 2006) made by women directors, who have immigrated to Canada and the United Kingdom, respectively, deconstruct all too simplistic parallel binaries such as East–West, persecution–tolerance, and hetero–homosexual.
2 In *Anti-Oedipus*, Deleuze and Guattari posit purely immanent, ongoing self-differentiations and becomings, subject-less individuations that ceaselessly move beyond boundaries. Braidotti's nomadic, mobile, non-unitary subject is a feminist version of the will to such continuous, limitless, dispersed becomings.
3 For further articles on *Lola + Bilidikid*, see Hamm-Ehsani, Hillmann, and Mennel.
4 The German title, *Kleine Freiheit*, also alludes to the section of Hamburg where the film is shot.
5 For an excellent discussion of this film focusing on its representation of minority identities, see Kraenzle.
6 The Hamburg captain's role is significant, for he represents a variation on a stock German character type. He serves as a reminder that economic deprivation, homelessness, and lack of family support can affect even Germans, and that these problems are not exclusive to a racialized, migrant Other.
7 "Ich erzähle die Situation zwei Jugendlicher, die sehr stark aufeinander angewiesen sind in der Illegalität, wo sie in einer gewissen Freiheit verwehrt sind und ständig aufpassen müssen und die in ihrem Leben schon viel verloren haben, dass sie dann in eine Freundschaft eingehen, um so stärker sie sich binden, gegenseitig respektieren, lieben. Es ist diese Intensität, die zu so was führt, zumal in der Alter ist man auch einfach auf der Suche nach sexueller Orientierung. Das heißt aber nicht, dass sie Homosexuelle sind, wobei man bei dem schwarzen Jungen das schon sagen kann, aber bei dem kurdischen Jungen nicht unbedingt. Die Kumpels von dem schwarzen Junge beschimpfen ihn als 'Schwuchtel', obwohl er sich nicht so bewegt, oder keine Ambitionen dazu hat, aber anscheinend ist er schon so orientiert. Der kurdische Junge nicht, aber lässt sich darauf ein, vielleicht ist er auch doch homosexuell" (Yavuz).

8   Prager writes about this scene in the photo booth: "Baran draws attention to Chernor's hair, and, at the moment the machine snaps their picture, a negative image of the print appears on screen. [...] As black is switched to white and the shades of their skin are inverted, it is evident that the close relationship between these two has enabled them to fleetingly transcend the bonds of the anomic identities" (376).
9   In an interview, Angelina Maccarone states that "Iran is one of four countries in the world where homosexuality stands under death penalty. It is at the same time a non-European country with a very 'modern' standard of living and allows the main character to be an educated middle-class person from a huge city like Tehran whose expectations and visions of the 'free world' are turned upside down in rural Germany" (Maccarone).
10 See, for instance, the chapter on *Paris Is Burning* in Butler.
11 It could be argued that *Kleine Freiheit* and *Fremde Haut* are a regression to what Rob Burns calls "a cinema of the affected," where there is a focus "unremittingly on alterity as a seemingly insoluble problem" and on the immigrant as "victim." What distinguishes these two films, however, from this earlier German cinema are the issues of sexuality, cross-cultural friendship, and the relative absence of intergenerational conflict.

References

Adelson, Leslie. *The Turkish Turn in Contemporary German Literature: Toward a New Critical Grammar of Migration*. New York: Palgrave, 2005.
Aimée & Jaguar. Dir. Max Färberböck. Senator Film Produktion, 1999.
Alles wird gut (*Everything Will Be Fine*). Dir. Angelina Maccarone. TV film, 1998.
Am Ende des Regenbogens (*Rainbow's End*). Dir. Jochen Hick and Christian Jentsch. Galeria Alaska Productions, 2005 (German version) 2006 (English version).
Auf der anderen Seite (*Edge of Heaven*). Dir. Fatih Akin. Anka Film, 2007.
Boys Don't Cry. Dir. Kimberly Peirce. Hart Sharp Entertainment, 1999.
Braidotti, Rosi. *Nomadic Subjects: Embodiment and Sexual Difference in Contemporary Feminist Theory*. New York: Columbia UP, 1994.
———. *Transpositions: On Nomadic Ethics*. Cambridge: Polity, 2006
Burns, Rob. "Turkish-German Cinema: From Cultural Resistance to Transnational Cinema?" *German Cinema since Unification*. Ed. David Clarke. London: Continuum, 2006. 127–49.
Butler, Judith. *Bodies That Matter: On the Discursive Limits of "Sex."* New York: Routledge, 1993.
Clark, Christopher. "Transculturation, *Transe* Sexuality, and Turkish Germany: Kutluğ Ataman's *Lola und Bilidikid*." *German Life and Letters* 59.4 (2006): 555–72.
Deleuze, Gilles, and Félix Guattari. *Anti-Oedipus: Capitalism and Schizophrenia*. New York: Viking Press, 1977.
Fremde Haut (*Unveiled*). Dir. Angelina Maccarone. MMM Film Zimmermann & Co., 2005.
Garber, Majorie. *Vested Interests: Cross-Dressing and Cultural Anxiety*. New York: Routledge, 1992.
Gilroy, Paul. *After Empire: Melancholia or Convivial Culture?* New York: Routledge, 2004.

Hall, Stuart. "Cultural Identity and Diaspora." *Colonial Discourse and Post-Colonial Theory: A Reader*. Ed. Patrick Williams and Laura Chrisman. New York: Columbia UP, 1994. 392–403.
Hamm-Ehsani, Karin. "Intersections: Issues of National, Ethnic, and Sexual Identity in Kutluğ Ataman's Berlin Film *Lola und Bilidikid*." *Seminar* 44.3 (2008): 366–81.
Hillmann, Roger. "*Lola and Billy the Kid* (1999): A Turkish Director's Western Showdown in Berlin." *Postscript* 25.2 (2006): 44–55.
Kleine Freiheit (A Little Bit of Freedom). Dir. Yüksel Yavuz. Cotta Media Entertainment, 2003.
Kraenzle, Christina. "At Home in the New Germany? Local Stories and Global Concerns in Yüksel Yavuz's *Aprilkinder* and *Kleine Freiheit*." *German Quarterly* 82.1 (2009): 90–108.
Kristeva, Julia. *Nations without Nationalism*. Trans. Leon Roudiez. New York: Columbia UP, 1993.
Lola + Bilidikid. Dir. E. Kutluğ Ataman. Boje Buck Production, 1999.
Maccarone, Angelina. "Interview with *Unveiled* Director, Angelina Maccarone." Interview with Shauna Swartz. *After Ellen*. 17 Nov. 2005. 17 Dec. 2010 http://www.afterellen.com.
Massad, Joseph. "Re-Orienting Desire: The Gay International and the Arab World." *Public Culture* 14.2 (2002): 361–85.
Mennel, Barbara. *The Representation of Masochism and Queer Desire in Film and Literature*. New York: Palgrave, 2007.
Mercer, Kobena, ed. *Exiles, Diasporas, and Strangers*. Cambridge: MIT, 2008.
Naficy, Hamid. *An Accented Cinema: Exilic and Diasporic Filmmaking*. Princeton, NJ: Princeton UP, 2001.
Prager, Brad. "Glimpses of Freedom: The Re-emergence of Utopian Longing in German Cinema." *The Collapse of the Conventional: German Film and Its Politics at the Turn of the Twenty-First Century*. Ed. Jaimey Fisher and Brad Prager. Detroit: Wayne State UP, 2010. 360–85.
Sieg, Katrin. *Ethnic Drag: Performing Race, Nation, Sexuality in West Germany*. Ann Arbor: U of Michigan P, 2002.
Warner, Michael. *Fear of a Queer Planet: Queer Politics and Social Theory*. Minneapolis: U of Minnesota P, 1993.
Yavuz, Yüksel. "'Ich bin vom Traum meiner Mutter ausgegangen': Interview with Stefania Maffeis." *Jura Gentium Cinema*. 2003. 17 Dec. 2010 <http://www.jgcinema.org>.

AN INSIDER'S VIEW

15
The Construction of Reality:
Aspects of Austrian Cinema between Fiction and Documentary

Barbara Pichler

Abstract Austrian cinema is known for its affinity to realist filmmaking. But is that attitude shared by Austria's youngest generation of filmmakers? Four case studies provide an opportunity to explore notions of authenticity and veracity in contemporary Austrian film. While some of these films owe a debt to more established filmmakers such as Michael Haneke and Ulrich Seidl, the diversity of aesthetic and narrative structures in these films indicates that Austrian filmmaking's most likely shared trait is a desire to challenge the expectations and mindsets of its viewers.

Realism, veracity, authenticity. What Austrian cinema, especially the feature film, is known for worldwide is a certain form of realist cinema, marked by an almost obsessive observation and at the same time forceful stylization of reality.

> It is often said that artists represent the conscience of a nation. In Austria that conscience tends to be expressed with a certain amount of contempt. [...] True to form, the salient quality of Austrian film's new wave is its willingness to confront the abject and emphasize the negative. In recent years this tiny country has become something like the world capital of feel-bad cinema. (Lim, "Austrian Filmmakers")

Even if slightly polemical, that statement summarizes the dominant stereotype about Austrian cinema. This perception was determined by the two big names in Austrian filmmaking, Michael Haneke and Ulrich Seidl—two auteurs enjoying great authority among cinephiles worldwide. Ulrich Seidl often describes his way of making films as an attempt "to find the authentic in the world" (qtd. in Rebhandl), a world that is at the same time specific and general. In regards to Haneke, it is stressed that he is on the lookout for the "real," for the "incorruptible gaze" (Rebhandl). These two directors, and the responses of a group of younger filmmakers to their predecessors' oeuvres, have generated what may be perceived as a dominant form of narration and style in Austrian cinema. Critic Stefan Grissemann describes this as a specific, maybe slightly academic, and sometimes arrogant form of auteurism. Critic Bert Rebhandl offers an even sharper diagnosis, when he says that all these filmmakers share "an uneasiness with modernity. [...] They tend to be determinist. They start with a preconceived assumption which they want to prove cinematically" (6).

These clichés, as always, contain a kernel of truth, while at the same time they overlook the far greater underlying complexities. In actual fact Austrian film production is much more diverse. Not only is there a dynamic and thriving experimental scene that is informed by the critical discussion and sometimes also continuation of the country's quite exceptional avant-garde tradition, but there is also an abundance of short and medium-length works, especially in the documentary sector. If one uses the word *cinema* to describe the audiovisual output not specifically produced for TV, the landscape of Austrian cinema is quite diverse, especially for a small country like Austria. One has to concede that this argument might not look as convincing from abroad, however, both because the films produced never make it to cinemas beyond Austria's borders or from the start only reach small, specifically interested audiences. What remains are the films that make it to international festivals, and it is these films that seem to be marked by a strange homogeneity or a typical style defined by a precise framing of the image, a deliberate pace, sparse use of dialogue, a specific stylization—a dominant form of realism, an authoritative mode of narration, or put simply: a pervading sense of pessimism.

This idea of realism is the focus of this essay. I would like to think about tendencies and perspectives of Austrian cinema and provide a more differentiated view. My argument is based on four examples—case studies, if you will. Produced between 2003 and 2007, the films under discussion are works of young filmmakers who enjoyed international critical success. I am interested in how they construct reality, but also in the reception of the films in Austria and Germany, their home market so to speak. There is no doubt that Michael Haneke and Ulrich Seidl have influenced a number of young filmmakers. The first two examples explore the impact of these two auteurs.

Case Study 1: *Struggle* (Ruth Mader, 2003) and the Haneke Approach

The inspiration for this film, which Ruth Mader wrote in collaboration with Barbara Albert, herself one of the main protagonists of the young and successful Austrian cinema, and Martin Leidenfrost, were the lives of illegal harvesters from Eastern Europe. The story revolves around two main protagonists: Ewa from Poland, a young mother staggering through capitalist Austria on the constant search for illegal work, and Harald, a recently divorced real estate agent, who tries to escape from the dreariness and emptiness of his life through sadomasochistic sexual encounters.

Struggle is set in contemporary Austria and thus on the borders between the West and the so-called former East. It is a film about affluent societies, the losers within this system, and the loss of human dignity. Mader shows two forms of exploitation: that of poor nations by Western industrialist societies and that of women by men. She tries to achieve this by keeping as close to reality as possible. The filmic style is something Mader described as "factual narration" (Schiefer): cool, detached, with an extremely sparse use of dialogue, offering no psychological insight into the characters but only an image of life in Western society. The settings are places of work: strawberry fields, an abattoir, a sex club (which is the place where the two worlds meet as, in Ewa's case, the club stands for work, whereas for Harald it is supposed to be a place of leisure). Mader claims that she was "interested in a detailed, precise and authentic description of work—the faces, the hands, work cycles, spaces and duration. Formally a clear, factual imagery took centre stage. Scenes were shot in real factories, mostly with the workers employed there. The scenes were meant to accurately reflect both the process as well as the rhythm of work. Also important was the respectful portrayal of the workers" (Mader).

Thus the imagery has a documentary quality. Through the accurate portrayal of work and through the almost physical qualities of the images, there is no escape offered the viewer through any form of contrived drama. Rather one is forced to acknowledge the drudgery of physical labour, the exertion of picking strawberries, or the monotony of gutting turkeys all day long. But, of course, at the same time the images are quite obviously immaculately choreographed and staged to make you feel precisely the obscenity of the working and living conditions of the people involved.

Internationally *Struggle* was received as an impressive feature debut, a film full of authenticity and a striking aesthetic sense. It is aesthetically clear, rigorous, and even uncompromising. Undoubtedly the film has its qualities and, in its aesthetic, a certain radicalism that consciously declines concessions to the

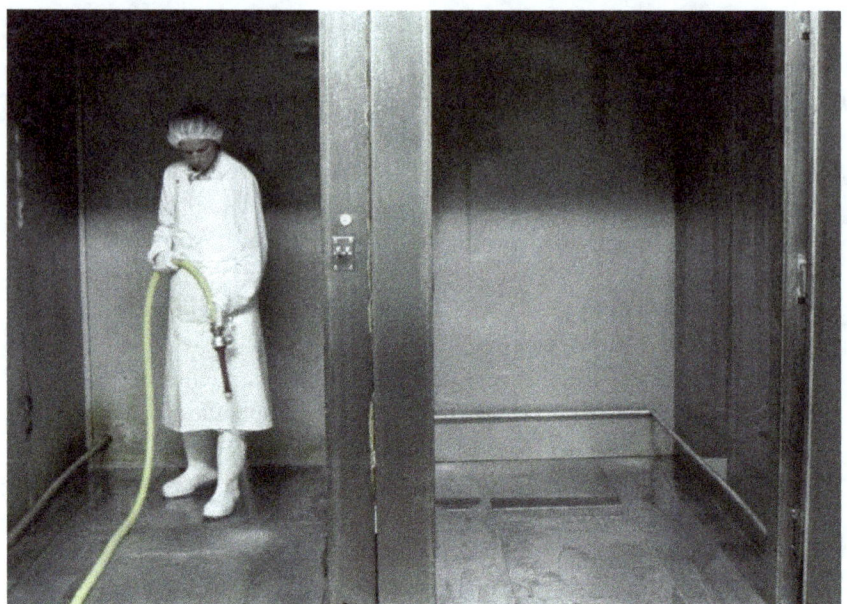

Ruth Mader, *Struggle*. © Struggle Films and Amour Fou

mainstream—by all means a characteristic of the internationally successful Austrian feature. In this light, it might also not seem that surprising that *Struggle* was not only declared to be a typically Austrian film, but also as a work of art belonging to a specific cultural or rather literary tradition. Critics saw references to authors ranging from Robert Musil, Thomas Bernhard, and Helmut Qualtinger to Elfriede Jelinek—all writers who denounced the baseness and deceitfulness of life, especially the Austrian way of life. Even if this tradition is one that fits Mader, her approach also belongs to a specific tradition of filmmaking: her research is painstaking, she always grounds her work in a close observation of the everyday, and she often works with non-professional actors. And with regard to cinematography: the image is clinical and not supposed to euphemize; rather, the opposite is the desired effect.

Searching for direct filmic influences, one does not have to look very far. Michael Haneke's principles of narration—especially the films he made in Austria up to *Die Klavierspielerin* (*The Piano Player*, 2001)—are in a way canonized in films like *Struggle*. They give the impression of the seamless, almost fateful consequence of events, carried by a strong notion of cultural pessimism. Mader follows these principles: in her story, there is no room for subjectivity. If looked at from the point of view of a more conventional logic of narration, the film constantly leaves gaps that are filled by the endless, monotonous repetition of work processes. This automatically leads to a critique of the capitalist ways of production and thus of the capitalist lifestyle itself. The effect of this mode of narration and its rigorous visual form is a highly conscious objectification of the characters. They cannot speak for themselves; the few words they are allowed to utter stand for society as a whole. The characters act as replaceable dummies, stressing the universally valid, not the individual.

This cultural pessimism and the objectification of her characters dominated the reviews at home. Bert Rebhandl took Mader's film as a prime example of this dominant style of narration with an implicitly authoritarian stance. The structures of authority are clearly visible, because "the characters in Austrian cinema don't find the freedom that would allow them to do anything unexpected" (Rebhandl 10). Stefan Grissemann spoke of a "recycling of typically Austrian motives and a kind of 'folklore of pessimism'" (61). This recycling in turn is a strength, at least, if one sees it from an economic point of view; it allows you to market films much more easily. It is all about an "Austrian style and film language." The recognizable is cultivated, because it is suitable for festivals, and because it creates a trademark and identity—which leads to the conclusion that Austrian filmmakers might use this auteurism very consciously and purposefully, not as a necessity or inner compulsion, but rather as a marketable trademark.

Thus, at least at home and in Germany, the praise for the radicalism and aesthetic rigor of certain Austrian productions is tainted by symptoms of fatigue and a distinct discontent with the lack of curiosity and the tendency to codify reality. The reality these authoritarian narrations discover or uncover is determined long before the camera is ever turned on.

Case Study 2: *Kurz davor ist es passiert (It Happened Just Before*, Anja Salomonowitz, 2007)

This criticism of insufficient curiosity and a pronounced determinism is often voiced in regards to the work of Ulrich Seidl. He also has left his mark on the work of young filmmakers. With *Kurz davor ist es passiert* by Anja Salomonowitz, we cross over into the realm of the documentary. While Ruth Mader creates a fiction inspired by a documentary style, Salomonowitz takes a different stance, and transfers the so-called real into a fictitious documentary.

Kurz davor ist es passiert is an examination of the global phenomenon of trafficking in women. Salomonowitz takes an unorthodox approach; her film is based on the real accounts of real women. She transformed those life stories into a script, but it is not the women themselves or professional actors who speak those texts. Rather, those stories are told by people who could have some connection to the places and events of the film: a customs officer, a villager, a

Anja Salomonowitz, *Kurz davor ist es passiert*. © http://www.lukasbeck.com

barkeeper in a brothel, a diplomat, and a cab driver. They tell of possible realities, of real problems like false promises, debt, violence, exploitation, and modern-day slavery, in short, the mechanisms of trafficking in women, but they do it in a fictionalized setting. So the film connects a filmic fiction—stories that might have happened, told by people that might have met the women in question—with a documentary approach that reminds the viewers that the scenes are based on real stories of real women. This paradox is repeated in the visual style: the images are too obviously arranged in perfect "tableaus," static shots or controlled pans, to allow you to mistake them for a documentary, but at the same time all the settings are connected to the real stories that are the basis for the film.

Kurz davor ist es passiert is a prime example for a certain permeability of genres that also might be called typical for Austrian cinema. Alexander Horwath, former film critic and now director of the Austrian Film Museum, even described this "formal hybridity as Austrian cinema's most unique and important asset" (qtd. in Lim "Greetings"). Salomonowitz's film was labelled both as an experimental documentary and as a documentary fiction—it is left to subjective judgment which of these descriptions applies, but the interlacing of documentary material and explicit *mise en scène* creates a distancing effect that allows for a questioning of conventions of filmic narration, and of documentary strategies and societal circumstances. Salomonowitz consciously stages this line between the fictitious and the documentary, quite obviously following her role model, Ulrich Seidl. She has worked with Seidl on some of his films and confirms that he taught her a lot: about patience, working with actors, and developing a character. The starting point for both Seidl and Salomonowitz is clearly reality and the research of actual living conditions. Even though generalizing an experience or a character is a central issue for her as well, and even in the midst of all stylization, reality always remains the main frame of reference: real people, real stories.

"Obsessed by reality"—quite significantly that is the title of a text that is to be found on the film's home page (Sternfeld). But Salomonowitz works with a reality that indicates a distance and is obviously shifted toward the filmic. She constantly tries to find new relationships between the fictional and the documentary logic of narration, and in doing this follows the Austrian tradition of consistent stylization. The mechanisms of filmic construction are virtually exhibited through artificial imagery, distancing long shots, and the occasional, quasi-investigative tracking shot. Again, Salomonowitz clearly gets her inspiration from Seidl. She incorporates the principles of the precisely staged, moving still life, of staging the banal and the everyday, of emptiness, of different forms of stagnation, and in a certain way the play with clichés. The reality that is negotiated here has to be constructed in a certain style and grandeur to be suitable for the big screen. "I want to tell about reality in wide, composed imagery so that it is able to expand. But before it can expand, it must be framed" (Salomonowitz). Thus the compositional element, the friction that is produced by the clash of fiction and documentary, is clearly not only at the centre of her work, but also in the centre of all reviews.

Struggle and *Kurz davor ist es passiert* both share a clear stance of auteurism. And they share a general attitude that might be described as didactic. Both would agree with Barbara Albert, who believes that making films is not about satisfying the audience. Cinema does not have to be cozy, it is supposed to make you think and to confront you with different ways of living, with different perspectives. Both films could therefore be described with the wonderful German word *Thesenfilm*. The line between the fictitious and the documentary is dealt with through a stylization of reality. While Mader tries to make reality look even more real, consequently showing a restricted image of reality and taking the possibility of interpretation away from the audience, Salomonowitz goes the other way. She works with an overstatement that opens new associative spaces and reveals societal structures. For both directors, this revelation is at the core of their work, but Salomonowitz takes it further. For her it is not only about the question whether cinema, be it documentary or fictional, is able to question openly life or society, but rather whether it might even be able to open a new space and create some room for political action. She says that she intended to question conventional documentary approaches with the aim of making the audience see two films at once: the one that is projected onto the screen and the one that originates in the audience's heads (Salomonowitz). This actually quite simple strategy still calls for a certain readiness to assume a risk—not only in the style of the film, but mainly because of the loss of control with regard to the audience's perception. And this might also be where the difference with "conventionally" realist cinema lies: one cannot accuse Salomonowitz of lacking curiosity, of shying away from experimenting with audience perception.

But what about a dominant style or mode of narration in the more unambiguously documentary formats? Austrian documentary production is especially dynamic, the production volume surprisingly large, and as a result also aesthetically diverse. It is much harder to pinpoint clear aesthetic or formal tendencies. Case Studies 3 and 4 stem from different filmic frames of reference, and use quite different and individual strategies of authentication. The question is to what extent one can diagnose dominant or typically Austrian modes of narration.

Case Study 3: *Unser täglich Brot (Our Daily Bread*, Nikolaus Geyrhalter, 2005)

This film is an example for an internationally successful documentary, made quite obviously for the big screen and with a clear aesthetic standard. *Our Daily Bread* is a glimpse into the world of industrialized food production and high-tech agriculture. It gives an insight into the places where food is produced, describing a system that is the basis for Western society's standard of living. The film visits a number of places of industrial food production and high-tech-agriculture, a surreal, parallel world of monumental spaces that are almost devoid of people and dominated by machines, conveyor belts, and strange soundscapes. While trying to depict modern food production, Geyrhalter is radical in his choice of means and in their reduction while aiming for a rigorous aesthetic configuration of the image. Geyrhalter is not only the director of the film, but—as always—the cinematographer. He works with sequence shots and central perspectives, refuses any zooms, pans, or close-ups; he dispenses not only with music but also with interviews, voice-overs, inserts, or any other source of information that might offer an explanation or contextualize what we see. He attempts to deliver factual and objective images of this working environment, to make this world visible and tangible through an exact gaze devoid of emotions. This aesthetic is supported by a kind of montage that to my mind is guided by the visual logic of the imagery, by a sense of rhythm, not by a rationally developing argument.

While this rigorous and even radical form is clearly the reason for the film's success, it is also the reason for two main points of contention. One line of criticism refers to the aesthetics of the imagery, the allegation being that its beauty banishes the horror of this mode of production. Geyrhalter counters by saying that his images perfectly reflect the efficiency of this production system.[1] I would even take it further and argue that the constant use of the long shot and the central perspective is a translation of a closed and in a way "totalitarian" system into a visual system. He develops an individual authoritative mode of narration absolutely suited to the topic.

The second line of criticism always refers to a lack of information. Again Geyrhalter takes a puristic view: There is enough information on any topic one can think of out there. To supply more information is of no interest to him, he wants to challenge his audience. To him filmmaking is all about stimulation; it is an invitation to examine a topic; it is about expanding one's ideas about the world (Geyrhalter). Again, a sentence on the home page for the film adequately describes Geyrhalter's ideas: *Our Daily Bread* is a "pure and detailed filmic experience that leaves the audience enough room to draw its own conclusions."[2]

That might sound close to Albert's argument that cinema does not need to think about the audience, but nevertheless one would be hard-pressed to construct an affiliation to a kind of school or cinematographic style, which is quite easy with my first two examples. Of course, critics still try to categorize Geyrhalter's films, but they do it along other lines. Stefan Grissemann, for example, states the emergence of what can almost be called a new subgenre in Austrian documentary cinema of the last years: "the long distance travel and globalization documentaries" (58). This genre would connect Geyrhalter to the likes of Michael Glawogger, Georg Misch, and Paul Rosdy to name a few. But he would also fit into the category of films about work, food production, capitalism, and the waste of resources. These are topics that have thrived within the last couple of years: *We Feed the World* (Erwin Wagenhofer, 2005), *Working Man's Death* (Michael Glawogger, 2005), *Über Wasser* (*About Water: People and Yellow Cans*, Udo Maurer, 2007), or even the feature films *Struggle* by Ruth Mader or *Caché* by Michael Haneke.

Anyone who knows these films will also know that, apart from the fact that they were all produced for the big screen, they do not share any common ground with regard to formal ideas or their intellectual approach, but rather the contrary. Take Glawogger as an example. His style is quite often compared to Geyrhalter's because of the impressive imagery, but actually he needs the spectacular and looks for the alien and unknown to present us the exotic, the Other. Wagenhofer or Mauerer, on the other hand, clearly want to inform and arouse curiosity;

they want to trigger emotions, and lead the audience to the realization that it is high time for action. In contrast, Geyrhalter is not interested in empathy, but he wants to facilitate the experience of places of food production, and in his films one can detect a certain disconnected lust of exploration or discovery in his fascination with these places in his imagery.

The aforementioned films are connected not by a style or an auteur idea but by their topics. And also perhaps by an attempt to flee the narrowness of a small country like Austria—a context that in reviews is often mentioned in an ironic, even derogatory tone. The discussion of domestic political questions, which had a sort of renaissance in the past few years, was conspicuously restricted to smaller productions with less interest in what can be called production values. What is reflected in all these big productions is the much more general question of dealing with distance. They are about the relationship between image and text, maybe even about the relationship between image, text, and message. They are about the question as to how much complexity an image can communicate, if there even is something like the autonomous image, and how or when language penetrates the image. And, not least, they are about the gaze, especially the gaze onto the Other, and about the political potential of this gaze.

Geyrhalter in a way is unique due to his absolute reliance on the filmic. Through the way he frames an image, through the way he and his editor Wolfgang Widerhofer, his most important creative ally, connect the images, he tries to enable a new way of seeing. And for this, he needs the cinema. He needs the dark movie theatre with a big screen and a good sound system, and he needs the physical aspect of seeing and hearing. Annett Busch describes Geyrhalter's approach as follows:

> The quality of Geyrhalter's work is that his film speaks to us not first and foremost as consumers but as spectators. So the cinema itself again becomes a place where something happens. The act of exposing oneself to the images, to listen to the sounds becomes a kind of action, a complex activity of perception and cognition. [...] Cinema is regained as a free space that allows us to concentrate on the essential of a film. The film does not articulate for us, but rather aims at observation. Those are images that activate. (47)

Geyrhalter's rigorous aesthetic, which in itself might be free of a valuation, still leads to an ethical moment: the recognition that this mode of production is a mirror of our society, and that we as consumers are automatically implicated in the internal logic of this system. Nevertheless, Geyrhalter consistently refuses to comment or to offer any solution or even an evaluation.

Case Study 4: *The End of the Neubacher Project* (Marcus J. Carney, 2007)

The fourth and last case study brings us into a totally different universe: *The End of the Neubacher Project*. This film tells the story of filmmaker Marcus J. Carney and his mother's family. He tries to come to terms with the family's past, but step by step he encounters greater entanglements and deeper levels of denial. It is a film about what he calls *Morbus Austriacus*, the Austrian illness of silence and denial, exemplified by means of the filmmaker's own family's involvement with National Socialism.

It would be hard to find an obvious connection to any kind of typical Austrian mode of realism or a dominant style. But this film sits at the intersection of a couple of tendencies that have left their traces in recent Austrian documentary cinema, most obviously the examination of history, both the general examination of the country's Nazi past and the personal examination of one's own family history. Carney confronts official history and questions his relatives, especially his mother, about their past. To quote Dietmar Kammerer: "This is not about the investigation of the dead [...] but about a therapeutic or cathartic investigation of the living." This attempt to process the past of the Third Reich in the present, maybe even in the present of one's own family, connects *The End of the Neubacher Project* to a couple of other films, most prominently with *Das wirst du nie verstehen* (*You Will Never Understand This*, 2003) by Anja Salomonowitz and *Hafners Paradies* (*Hafner's Paradise*, 2007) by Günther Schwaiger.

Just as important is the question of what there is to tell and how to tell it cinematically, that is, the formal questions and the development of a narrative arc.

Marcus J. Carney, *The End of the Neubacher Project*. © Marcus J. Carney/Extrafilm

Quite contrary to the previously mentioned films, Carney's imagery is not stylized or choreographed at all. His images are very personal, coming from the midst of his family; his visual style seems rather unaffected, sometimes even accidental and thus intuitive and immediate. He mixes his own footage—shot from 1998 to 2006, showing interviews with family members and personal scenes of family life, including a number of phone conversations he had with his mother during the long work on the project—with historical material and Super 8 films from the family archives. This opens a connection not only to more classical documentary formats or the diary film, always directly implicating the filmmaker who often is on-camera or asking questions from off-camera, but also to the found-footage film, which is of great importance to Austrian experimental cinema and to Austrian avant-garde tradition in general. As with many other young filmmakers, Carney does not see himself as part of that tradition, even though he is absolutely aware of it and its historical background.

Carney describes his film as an "epic home-movie," and the mixture of filmic material allows him to show not only the blurring of boundaries between the private and the public, but also between the fictitious and the documentary. In interviews Carney always explicitly refers to the question of the *mise en scène* in the documentary, and quite clearly he is aware of the problems surrounding this issue. But still: everything is always about authenticity. In Carney's case, the biographical or autobiographical serves as a mighty strategy of authentication. He introduces his perspective through the off-camera commentary; he films a lot of his material himself and through his hand-held camera makes the cinematography personal and corporeal; he uses what might be called performative elements to integrate his own person into the film—for example, by taping every single phone conversation with his mother during the eight years he worked on this film. And in the questioning of his family, he consciously oversteps certain boundaries, and discloses personal and intimate details.

In contrast to all other films discussed in this chapter, the reception of Carney's film is rarely about any aesthetic issues, which is a shame since the interweaving of materials, the rhythm, and the way Carney leaves traces that lead from the past to the present in order to develop narration are worth discussing. Instead, the reviews concentrated on those moments when he seems to cross a line; they were about the taboo, about the possible exposure or maybe rather over-exposure of his protagonists; and about the fact that some audiences find the film too personal, too embarrassing, too hard to watch. Carney has a clear answer to that: "The audience can take everything as long as the filmmaker doesn't avoid responsibility and marauds in the lives of his characters as an end in itself. This is true for documentary as well as fictional work. Shifting the boundaries of what is known hurts, but this is what every story should do" (Schiefer "Carney").

In this respect, one might find a closeness to Haneke or Seidl, but what distinguishes Carney is the fact that he risks uncertainty and implicates himself. The shifting of the boundaries does not aim toward the past but toward coming to terms with the present. He tries to accomplish this with his film, and at the same time analyzes what a process like that does to the filmmaker. So the audience is allowed to follow a process in the course of which the camera becomes a weapon. At the end of this process, we share not only an emotional insight but also an insight into the mechanisms of filmic construction and a leave-taking from the alleged security of the filmmaker's or even one's own viewpoint.

Conclusion

The question remains to be answered: Is there really something like a dominant mode of narration in Austrian cinema? Without doubt there are traces of that, especially in feature film. But even here this idea often seems too restrictive and if one includes documentary, the thesis does not hold. Can there be any general conclusions about Austrian cinema's treatment of reality or any strategies of authentication? Bert Rebhandl once wrote that this search for the real, for the genuine and authentic, as it is postulated for the cinema of Haneke and Seidl, is nothing but a big misunderstanding. Both filmmakers, who are known as "realists," are in fact quite the opposite, namely, they are marked "constructivists" of cinema (6). This is perhaps the one attribute that would fit all of these filmmakers. If there are similarities, then one will not find them in any kind of formal or narrative dogmatism, but rather in much more general things: first of all in the awareness of common aesthetic enemies—the cinema of Franz Antel, the so-called *Kabarettfilm*, and a certain kind of informational television. The filmmakers under discussion in this essay all share a distinct attitude of auteurism; they all anchor their films in the complexities of everyday life and long to experience real life through film. One could diagnose a certain chill as a kind of leitmotif and a lack of security and positive role models. Maybe one even could argue that much of Austrian cinema is a didactic cinema, even a cinema with an ethical or moral core and thus also political. In the end, there might only be one thing these filmmakers all agree on: the idea that cinema by all means has to be dangerous![3]

Notes

1. Nikolaus Geyrhalter during a Q&A at the Duisburger Filmwoche in November 2006.
2. See the section "Der Film" at <http://www.unsertaeglichbrot.at>.
3. This is also the title of a compilation of interviews originally published in the German film magazine *Revolver*. This compilation contains, among others, interviews with Barbara Albert, Jessica Hausner, Michael Haneke, and Ulrich Seidl. Seibert, Marcus., ed. *Revolver: Kino muss gefährlich sein*. Berlin: Verlag der Autoren, 2006.

References

Busch, Annett. "Hello Place, Hello Complexity: Arbeit, Nahrungsmittel, Kapitalismus im neueren Dokumentarfilm aus Österreich." *kolik film* 7 (2007): 47.
Caché. Dir. Michael Haneke. Les Films du Losange, 2005.
Das wirst du nie verstehen. Dir. Anja Salomonowitz. Sixpack Film, 2003.
The End of the Neubacher Project. Dir. Marcus J. Carney. Extrafilm, 2007.
The End of the Neubacher Project. 6 Nov. 2009 <http://www.neubacherproject.com>.
Geyrhalter, Nikolaus. Interview with Silvia Burner. "Unser täglich Brot." 6 Nov. 2009 <http://www.unsertaeglichbrot.at/jart/projects/utb/website.jart?rel=de&content-id=1130864824950>.
Grissemann, Stefan. Interview with Dominik Kamalzadeh. "Rückzugsgefechte." *kolik film* 5 (2006): 58.
Hafners Paradies. Dir. Günther Schwaiger. Never Land Films S.L., 2007.
Kammerer, Dietmar. "Gegenwartsbewältigung." *kolik film* 7 (2007): 65.
Die Klavierspielerin. Dir. Michael Haneke. Arte, 2001.
Kurz davor ist es passiert. Dir. Anja Salomonowitz. Amour Fou Filmproduktion, 2007.
Lim, Dennis. "Austrian Filmmakers with a Heart for Darkness." *New York Times* 27 Nov. 2006. 6 Nov. 2009 <http://www.nytimes.com>.
———. "Greetings from the Land of Feel Bad Cinema." *New York Times* 26 Nov. 2006. 6 Nov. 2009 <http://www.nytimes.com>.
Mader, Ruth. "Ruth Mader über *Struggle*." *Struggle*. 2003. 6 Nov. 2009 <http://www.struggle.at/html/html/english/index.htm>.
Rebhandl, Bert. "Nicht anders möglich. Der neuere österreichische Spielfilm und sein Mangel an Realitätssinn." *kolik film* 1 (2004): 6–10.
Salomonowitz, Anja. Interview with Karin Schiefer. *Austrian Film Commission*. 2007. 6 Nov. 2009 <http://www.afc.at/jart/prj3/afc/main.jart?rel=de&reserve-mode=active&contentid=1164272180506&tid=1169655749221&artikel_id=1169655749200>.
Schiefer, Karin. Interview with Ruth Mader. *Struggle*. 2003. 6 Nov. 2009 <http://www.struggle.at>.
———. Interview with Marcus J. Carney. *The End of the Neubacher Project*. Oct. 2006. 6 Nov. 2009 <http://www.neubacherproject.com>.
Seibert, Marcus, ed. *Revolver. Kino muss gefährlich sein*. Berlin: Verlag der Autoren, 2006.

Sternfeld, Nora. "Besessen von der Wirklichkeit." 6 Nov. 2009 <http://www.anjasalomonowitz.com/kurzdavor/frames_texte.htm>.
Struggle. Dir. Ruth Mader. Amour Fou Filmproduktion, 2003.
Über Wasser. Dir. Udo Maurer. Lotus Film, 2007.
Unser täglich Brot. Dir. Nikolaus Geyrhalter. Nikolaus Geyrhalter Filmproduktion, 2005.
Unser täglich Brot. 6 Nov. 2009 <http://www.unsertaeglichbrot.at>.
We Feed the World. Dir. Erwin Wagenhofer. Allegro Film, 2005.
Workingman's Death. Dir. Michael Glawogger. Arte, 2005.

Filmography

71 Fragmente einer Chronologie des Zufalls (*71 Fragments of a Chronology of Chance*). Dir. Michael Haneke. WEGA-Filmproduktion, 1994.

100 Jahre Adolf Hitler—die letzte Stunde im Führerbunker (*100 Years of Adolph Hitler*). Dir. Christoph Schlingensief. DEM, 1989.

Aimée & Jaguar. Dir. Max Färberböck. Senator Film, 1999.

Alles auf Zucker! (*Go for Zucker!*) Dir. Dani Levy. X-Filme, 2004.

Alles wird gut (*Everything Will Be Fine*). Dir. Angelina Maccarone. 1998.

Am Ende des Regenbogens (*Rainbow's End*). Dir. Jochen Hick and Christian Jentsch. Galeria Alaska Productions, 2005.

Am Ende kommen Touristen (*And Along Come Tourists*). Dir. Robert Thalheim. 23/5 Filmproduktion, 2007.

Auf der anderen Seite (*The Edge of Heaven*). Dir. Fatih Akin. Corazón International, 2007.

Aus der Ferne (*From Far Away*). Dir. Thomas Arslan. Pickpocket Filmproduktion, 2006.

Befreite Zone (*Liberated Zone*). Dir. Norbert Baumgarten. ö-Filmproduktion Löprich & Schlösser, 2003.

Benny's Video. Dir. Michael Haneke. WEGA-Filmproduktion, 1992.

Die bleierne Zeit (*Marianne and Juliane*). Dir. Margarethe von Trotta. Bioskop Film, 1981.

Boys Don't Cry. Dir. Kimberly Peirce. Fox Searchlight Pictures, 1999.

Brudermord (*Fratricide*). Dir. Yilmaz Arslan. Yilmaz Arslan Filmproduktions, 2005.

Bungalow. Dir. Ulrich Köhler. Peter Stockhaus Filmproduktion, 2002.

Caché (*Hidden*). Dir. Michael Haneke. Les films du Losange, 2005.

Code inconnu: récit incomplet de divers voyages (*Code Unknown*). Dir. Michael Haneke. MK2 Productions, 2000.

The Collector. Dir. William Wyler. Columbia Pictures, 1965.
Das wirst du nie verstehen (*You Will Never Understand This*). Dir. Anja Salomonowitz. Sixpack Film, 2003.
Deutschland '09. 13 kurze Filme zur Lage der Nation (*Germany '09. 13 Short Films on the State of the Nation*). Dir. Angela Schanelec et al. Piffl Medien, 2009.
Deutschland im Herbst (*Germany in Autumn*). Filmverlag der Autoren, 1978.
Egoshooter. Dir. Christian Becker and Oliver Schwabe. Reverse Angle Factory, 2004.
Die Ehe der Maria Braun (*The Marriage of Maria Braun*). Dir. Rainer Werner Fassbinder. Film Verlag der Autoren et al., 1979.
The End of the Neubacher Project. Dir. Marcus J. Carney. Extrafilm, 2007.
Falscher Bekenner (*Low Profile a.k.a. I'm Guilty*). Dir. Christoph Hochhäusler. Heimatfilm, 2007.
Die fetten Jahre sind vorbei (*The Edukators*). Dir. Hans Weingartner. Y3 Film, 2004.
Die fetten Jahre sind vorbei (*The Edukators*). Dir. Hans Weingartner. Universum Film, 2004.
Freaks. Dir. Tod Browning. Metro-Goldwyn-Mayer, 1932.
Freakstars 3000. Dir. Christoph Schlingensief. volksbühne films, 2003.
Free Rainer—Dein Fernseher lügt (*Reclaim Your Brain*). Dir. Hans Weingartner. Coop 99 Filmproduktion, 2007.
Fremde Haut (*Unveiled*). Dir. Angelina Maccarone. MMM Film Zimmermann & Co., 2005.
Der Fuehrer's Face. Dir. Jack Kinney. Walt Disney Productions, 1942.
Funny Games. Dir. Michael Haneke. WEGA-Filmproduktion, 1997.
Funny Games. Dir. Michael Haneke. Celluloid Dreams, 2007.
Ein ganz gewöhnlicher Jude (*Just an Ordinary Jew*). Dir. Oliver Hirschbiegel. Multimedia Film- und Fernsehproduktions GmbH, 2005.
Ganz unten (*Lowest of the Low*). Dir. Jörg Gförer. KAOS Film- und Videoteam, 1986.
Goebbels und Geduldig (*Goebbels and Geduldig*). Dir. Kai Wessel. SWR, 2001.
Good Bye, Lenin! Dir. Wolfgang Becker. X-Filme Creative Pool et al., 2003.
The Great Dictator. Dir. Charles Chaplin. Charles Chaplin Productions, 1940.
Die grosse Liebe (*Great Love*). Dir. Rolf Hansen. Universum Film, 1942.
Hände weg von Mississippi (*Hands Off Mississippi*). Dir. Detlev Buck. Boje Buck Produktion, 2007.
Hafners Paradies (*Hafner's Paradise*). Dir. Günther Schwaiger. Never Land Films S.L., 2007.
Halbe Treppe (*Grill Point*). Dir. Andreas Dresen. Peter Rommel Productions, 2002.
Heil Hitler, das Schwein ist tot! (*Heil Hitler, the Pig Is Dead!*). Dir. Rudolph Herzog. Ilona Grundmann Filmproduction, 2006.
Heimat. Eine Chronik in elf Teilen (*Heimat: A German Chronicle*). Dir. Edgar Reitz. Edgar Reitz Film Productions, 1984.
Heimat 3. Chronik einer Zeitenwende (*Heimat 3: A Chronicle of Endings and Beginnings*). Dir. Edgar Reitz. Edgar Reitz Film Productions, 2004.

Herr Meets Hare. Dir. Friz Freleng. Warner Brothers, 1945.
Herz im Kopf (*Heart over Head*). Dir. Michael Gutmann. Claussen + Wöbke Filmproduktion, 2001.
Hitler—ein Film aus Deutschland (*Hitler: A Film from Germany*). Dir. Hans Jürgen Syberberg. British Broadcasting Corporation, 1977.
In einem Jahr mit 13 Monden (*In a Year of 13 Moons*). Dir. Rainer Werner Fassbinder. Film Verlag der Atuoren, 1978.
Die innere Sicherheit (*The State I Am In*). Dir. Christian Petzold. Schramm Film, 2000.
The International. Dir. Tom Tykwer. Columbia Pictures, 2009.
Jacob the Liar. Dir. Peter Kassovitz. TriStar Pictures, 1999.
John Rabe. Dir. Florian Gallenberger. Hoffmann & Voges Filmproduktion, 2009.
KeinOhrHasen (*Rabbit without Ears*). Dir. Til Schweiger. Barefoot Films, 2007.
Klassenfahrt (*School Trip*). Dir. Henner Winckler. Schramm Film Koerner & Weber, 2002.
Die Klavierspielerin (*The Piano Player*). Dir. Michael Haneke. Arte, 2001.
Kleine Freiheit (*A Little Bit of Freedom*). Dir. Yüksel Yavuz. Cotta Media Entertainment, 2003.
Kurz davor ist es passiert (*It Happened Just Before*). Dir. Anja Salomonowitz. Amour Fou Filmproduktion, 2007.
Das Leben der Anderen (*The Lives of Others*). Dir. Florian Henckel von Donnersmarck. Arte et al., 2006.
Der letzte Akt (*The Last Act*). Dir. G.W. Pabst. Cosmopol Film, 1955.
Lichter (*Distant Lights*). Dir. Hans-Christian Schmid. Claussen + Wöbke Filmproduktion, 2003.
Lola + Bilidikid. Dir. E. Kutluğ Ataman. Boje Buck Production, 1999.
Lola rennt (*Run Lola Run*). Dir. Tom Tykwer. X Filme Creative Pool, 1998.
Lucy. Dir. Henner Winckler. Schramm Film Koerner & Weber, 2007.
Mammoth. Dir. Lukas Moodysson. Memfis Film, 2009.
Marseille. Dir. Angela Schanelec. Schramm Film Koerner & Weber, 2005.
The Matrix. Dir. Andy and Larry Wachowski. Groucho II Film Partnership, 1999.
Mein Führer—Die wirklich wahrste Wahrheit über Adolf Hitler (*Mein Führer: The Truly Truest Truth about Adolf Hitler*). Dir. Daniel Levy. X-Filme Creative Pool, 2007.
Milchwald (*This Very Moment*). Dir. Christoph Hochhäusler. fieber.film, 2003.
Muxmäuschenstill (*Quiet as a Mouse*). Dir. Marcus Mittermeier. Warner Home Video, 2004.
Netto. Dir. Robert Thalheim. Hochschule für Film und Fernsehen "Konrad Wolf," 2005.
Nordrand (*Northern Skirts*). Barbara Albert. Lotus-Film, 1999.
Nuit et brouillard (*Night and Fog*). Dir. Alain Resnais. Argos Films, 1955.
Polski Crash. Dir. Kaspar Heidelbach Gemini Filmproduktion, 1993.
The Producers. Dir. Mel Brooks. Crossbow Productions, 1968.
The Producers. Dir. Susan Stroman. Universal Pictures, 2005.
Schindler's List. Dir. Steven Spielberg. Universal Pictures, 1993.

Schröders wunderbare Welt (*Schroeder's Wonderful World*). Dir. Michael Schorr. Filmkombinat Nordost, 2006.
Schtonk! Dir. Helmut Dietl. Bavaria Film, 1992.
Shoah. Dir. Claude Lanzmann. Historia, 1985.
Sehnsucht (*Longing*). Dir. Valeska Grisebach. Peter Rommel Productions, 2006.
Die Sehnsucht der Veronika Voss (*Veronika Voss*). Dir. Rainer Werner Fassbinder. Laura-Film, 1982.
Der siebente Kontinent (*The Seventh Continent*). Dir. Michael Haneke. WEGA-Filmproduktion, 1989.
Sonnenallee (*Sun Alley*). Dir. Leander Haußmann. Boje Buck Produktion, 1999.
Speer und er (*Speer and Hitler: The Devil's Architect*). Dir. Heinrich Breloer. Bavaria Film, 2005.
Sturm (*Storm*). Dir. Hans-Christian Schmid. 23/5 Filmproduktion, 2009.
Struggle. Dir. Ruth Mader. Amour Fou Filmproduktion, 2003.
Le temps du loup (*Time of the Wolf*). Dir. Michael Haneke. Bavaria Film, 2003.
To Be or Not to Be. Dir. Ernst Lubitsch. Romaine Film Corporation, 1942.
To Be or Not to Be. Dir. Alan Johnson. Brooksfilms, 1983.
Train de vie (*Train of Life*). Dir. Radu Mihaileanu. Belfilms, 1998.
Triumph des Willens (*Triumph of the Will*). Dir. Leni Riefenstahl. Leni Riefenstahl Produktion, 1935.
Über Wasser: Menschen und gelbe Kanister (*About Water: People and Yellow Cans*). Dir. Udo Maurer. Lotus Film, 2007.
Die Unberührbare (*No Place to Go*). Dir. Oskar Roehler. Distant Dreams Film Produktion, 2000.
Unser täglich Brot (*Our Daily Bread*). Dir. Nikolaus Geyrhalter. Nikolaus Geyrhalter Filmproduktion, 2005.
Der Untergang (*Downfall*). Dir. Oliver Hirschbiegel. Constantin Film, 2004.
Valkyrie. Dir. Bryan Singer. United Artists International, 2008.
Vergiss Amerika (*Forget America*). Dir. Vanessa Joop. Avista Film, 2000.
La vita è bella (*Life Is Beautiful*). Dir. Roberto Benigni. Cecchi Gori Group, 1997.
Warum Männer nicht zuhören und Frauen schlecht einparken (*Why Men Don't Listen and Women Can't Read Maps*). Dir. Leander Haußmann. Constantin Film Produktion, 2007.
We Feed the World. Dir. Erwin Wagenhofer. Allegro Film, 2005.
Workingman's Death. Dir. Michael Glawogger. Arte, 2005.
Yella. Dir. Christian Petzold. Piffl Medien. 2007.
You Natzy Spy. Dir. Jules White. Columbia Pictures, 1940.
Die zweite Heimat. Chronik einer Jugend in 13 Filmen (*Heimat 2: Chronicle of a Generation*). Dir. Edgar Reitz. Edgar Reitz Film Productions, 1992.

Notes on Contributors

Marco Abel is associate professor of English and Film Studies at the University of Nebraska–Lincoln. He is the author of *Violent Affect: Literature, Cinema, and Critique after Representation* (University of Nebraska Press, 2008) and is currently working on *The Berlin School: Toward a Minor Cinema*, which is under contract at Camden House. He teaches film history and theory at the University of Nebraska–Lincoln.

Sophie Boyer is associate professor of German Studies at Bishop's University in Sherbrooke, Quebec. Her research focuses on nineteenth-century poetry and the representation of crime and sexuality in Weimar literature. She is the author of *La femme chez Heinrich Heine et Charles Baudelaire: le langage moderne de l'amour* (L'Harmattan, 2004).

Roger Cook is professor of German and director of Film Studies at the Missouri State University in Springfield. He is the author of *By the Rivers of Babylon: Heinrich Heine's Late Songs and Reflections* (Wayne State University Press, 1998) and *The Demise of the Author: Autonomy and the German Writer 1770–1848* (Peter Lang, 1993), and he is editor with Gerd Gemünden of *The Cinema of Wim Wenders: Image, Narrative, and the Postmodern Condition* (Wayne State University Press, 1996).

Peter Gölz is associate professor of German and chair of the Department of Germanic and Slavic Studies at the University of Victoria. He has published on film, contemporary literature, computer-assisted language learning, and vampires.

NOTES ON CONTRIBUTORS

Jakub Kazecki holds an M.A. from Dalhousie University, Halifax, and a Ph.D. from The University of British Columbia, Vancouver. He is currently working as an assistant professor of German at Central Connecticut State University in New Britain, Connecticut.

Alasdair King is senior lecturer in German and Film Studies at Queen Mary, University of London. His recent publications include a monograph on Hans Magnus Enzensberger, and numerous articles on German cinema. He is currently working on a monograph on Edgar Reitz's *Heimat* trilogy as part of a wider research interest in contemporary cinematic engagements with space and time.

Morgan Koerner is an assistant professor of German at the College of Charleston in South Carolina. His research focuses on intermediality and laughter in contemporary German theatre performances after unification.

Alice Kuzniar is professor of German at the University of Waterloo, Ontario. She has edited *Outing Goethe and His Age* (Stanford University Press, 1996) and authored *Delayed Endings: Nonclosure in Novalis and Hölderlin* (University of Georgia Press, 1987), *The Queer German Cinema* (Stanford University Press, 2000), and *Melancholia's Dog: Reflections on Our Animal Kinship* (University of Chicago Press, 2006).

Joanne Leal is director of the M.A. in European Cultures program at Birkbeck, University of London. She has published on feminist literature and contemporary fiction and film, and she has recently completed a project on the collaborative works of Wim Wenders and Peter Handke (with Martin Brady, King's College London), funded by the Arts and Humanities Research Council (United Kingdom).

Myriam Léger is a Ph.D. candidate at the University of Waterloo, Ontario. Her research interests are in twentieth-century German literature and film, representations of Jewish identity, intersections of politics and literature, and cultural studies.

Gabriele Mueller is associate professor of German and affiliated with The Canadian Centre for German and European Studies at York University in Toronto. Her research focuses mainly on contemporary German cinema. She has published on various aspects of post-unification cinema in Germany, in particular, on cinematic contributions to memory discourses.

NOTES ON CONTRIBUTORS

Mary-Elizabeth O'Brien is professor of German and the Courtney and Steven Ross Chair in Interdisciplinary Studies at Skidmore College in Saratoga Springs, New York. Her book *Nazi Cinema as Enchantment: The Politics of Entertainment in the Third Reich* (Camden House, 2004) explores how cinema participated in the larger framework of everyday fascism. Currently she is writing a book on national identity in post-wall German cinema.

Barbara Pichler is the director of Diagonale, the festival of Austrian film at Graz, which is the main platform for the presentation and discussion of Austrian film. She studied theatre and film at the University of Vienna and at the British Film Institute. An experienced member of film-festival juries, she is also an adjunct lecturer on film at the University of Vienna and the co-editor of *moving landscapes: Landschaft und Film* (Synema, 2006) and *James Benning* (FilmmuseumSynemaPublikationen, 2007).

James M. Skidmore is associate professor and chair of the Department of Germanic and Slavic Studies at the University of Waterloo, Ontario.

Florentine Strzelczyk is associate professor of German and director of the Language Research Centre at the University of Calgary, Alberta. Her research interests include the concept of *Heimat* in literature and film, and the afterlife of Nazism in North American cinema. She is the author of *Unheimliche Heimat: Reibungsflächen zwischen Kultur und Nation* (Iudicium, 1999) and co-editor of *Glaube und Geschlecht: Fromme Frauen—Spirituelle ErfahrungenReligiöse Traditionen* (Böhlau, 2008).

Michael Zimmermann teaches in the Department of International Languages at the University of Regina, Saskatchewan. His areas of research interest are the twentieth-century novel, film, German as a heritage language, and language pedagogy.

Index

100 Jahre Adolf Hitler—die letzte Stunde im Führerbunker (*100 Years of Adolph Hitler*, Christoph Schlingensief, 1989), 156–57
1968 student revolts. *See* West German student movement
71 Fragmente einer Chronologie des Zufalls (*71 Fragments of a Chronology of Chance*, Michael Haneke, 1994), 51, 55n4

A

acousmêtre, 84, 86, 94
aesthetic experience, 12
Akin, Fatih, 26, 245, 246. *See also Auf der anderen Seite*; *Gegen die Wand*
alienation, 36, 44, 108, 128; between Germans and Jews, 191, 202
Alles wird gut (*Everything Will Be Fine*, Angelina Maccarone, 1998), 246
Am Ende des Regenbogens (*Rainbow's End*, Jochen Hick and Christian Jentzsch, 2005 and 2006), 247
Arslan, Yilmaz, 17, 27, 28, 29, 31, 32, 225–43; challenging viewer expectation, 230, 232; child migrants, 240; depiction of *Deutschkei*, 227, 232; film funding, 228; globalization, 240; personal experiences as Turkish immigrant, 229; sense of marginalization through language, 233; taking stock of life, 240. *See also Aus der Ferne*; *Brudermord*; child migrants in Germany; globalization; migrant culture in Germany
asylum in Germany, 246, 258
Auf der anderen Seite (*Edge of Heaven*, Fatih Akin, 2007), 245–46
Aus der Ferne (*From Far Away*, Yilmaz Arslan, 2006), 31; Austrian cinema and, 7, 267–81; affinity to realist filmmaking, 267; auteur style, 268; conclusions, 279; construction of reality in, 268; diversity of, 268; documentaries, 12, 17; reception of films in Austria and Germany, 268; reputation of, 12; traductive realism, 13. *See also* reality in Austrian cinema; *The End of the Neubacher Project*; *Kurz davor ist es passiert*; *Struggle*; *Unser täglich Brot*

B

Baudrillard, Jean, 45, 49, 165; fatal strategy, 43, 53; the "hyperreal," 47, 165; *The Perfect Crime*, 49;

representations of reality, 47; simulacra, 47, 48, 165–67; *Simulacra and Simulation* (1994), 47; *The Spirit of Terrorism*, 53; *Symbolic Exchange and Death* (1976), 47, 54; three historically successive social orders, 47
Bauman, Zygmunt, 6
Baumgarten, Norbert, 209. See also *Befreite Zone*
Becker, Wolfgang, 26. See also *Good Bye, Lenin!*
Befreite Zone (*Liberated Zone*, Norbert Baumgarten, 2003), 209, 221
Benny's Video (Michael Haneke, 1992), 52
Berlin School, 12, 13, 25–42; aesthetic, 34, 38; aesthetics of reduction, 30, 31; a-representational realism, 25; attitude toward reality, 33–34; autonomy of art, 34–35; backlash and criticism, 29, 30; *Bungalow* as quintessential Berlin School film, 32–33; cartographic quality, 38; characteristics, 28; commercial success, 28, 29; counter-cinema and, 25, 27; elements of style, 31; ethnological gaze, 33; first generation, 27; mobility, 25, 35, 36; inexpensive production, 28; making strange of the familiar, 37; sociocultural paralysis, 34; rejection of consensus cinema, 12; relationship to the present, 38; tendency to flaneurism, 32; true realism, 32; untimeliness, 38; US distribution, 29; use of static endings, 36–37, 40n17
Berlin Wall in film, 106. See also *Heimat 3*; *Die innere Sicherheit*; *Die Unberührbare*
Berlinale (Berlin Film Festival), 1, 2, 4, 28
Bildungsliteratur, 79, 83
Bildungsroman, 92, 93
borders as liminal, 208

Brecht, Bertolt, 79, 84, 88, 90; challenge to in *Das Leben der Anderen*, 83; poetry of, 82, 88; themes, 83. See also *Der gute Mensch von Sezuan*; *Die Sonate vom guten Menschen*; literature in *Das Leben der Anderen*
Brudermord (*Fratricide*, Yilmaz Arslan, 2005), 17, 225–43; child migrants, 237, 240; counterbalance to internal colonialism, 229; genesis, 229; Kurdish politicization, 237; language as signifier in *Brudermord*, 232–35; meaning of *Bruder*, 237–38; position in Turkish-German film, 239; roots of conflict in, 227; transnational social space in, 225. See also Kurdish nationalism and transnationalism; migrant cultures in Germany; minority cultures in Germany; Turco-Kurdish culture in Germany
Bungalow (Ulrich Köhler, 2002), 26, 32, 33, 36. See also Berlin School

C

Caché (*Hidden*, Michael Haneke, 2005), 45, 50–53
camera as time machine, 103–5
Carney, Marcus J, 277, 278. See also *The End of the Neubacher Project*
chamber drama, intimacy of, 192
Chaplin, Charlie, 155, 156, 174. See also *The Great Dictator*
child migrants in Germany, 237, 240, 241. See also *Brudermord*; immigration; illegal immigration; *Kleine Freiheit*
Chion, Michel, 84
cinema of consensus, 3, 123, 136
cinema of dissent, 3, 4
cinema of identification, 13, 36
cinema of the affected, 16
cinematic metalanguage, 51

Code inconnu: récit incomplet de divers voyages (*Code Unknown: Incomplete Tales of Several Journeys*, Michael Haneke, 2000), 45–48, 50, 56n9; audition scene, 46–47, 48, 56n8
collective memory, precariousness of "appropriate," 184
colonial connotations, 220
comedy and tragedy, 174, 184
comedy as subversive, 61, 174
comedy genre, marginalization post-Holocaust, 175
commodification of cinema, 10
copy and original, relationship between, 163
counter-cinema. *See* Berlin School
creative chaos, 134, 148
criticism of totalitarianism, 86; free thinking and free speech in, 81; influence of *Der gute Mensch von Sezuan* (Brecht), 79; literary nature of, 79, 83; narrative in, 87–88, 90; perception images, 89–90; use of voice-over, 80, 84. *See also* literature in *Das Leben der Anderen*

D

demonization of the media, 133
desubstantiated image, 52
Deutsche Filmakademie (German Film Academy), 10
Deutsche Film und Fernsehakademie Berlin (DFFB), 27
Deutschkei, 226, 227. *See also* Yilmaz Arslan; *Brudermord*; Turco-Kurdish culture in Germany
Deutschland im Herbst (*Germany in Autumn*, 1978), 2
Deutschland '09.13 kurze Filme zur Lage der Nation (*Germany '09: 13 Short Films on the State of the Nation*), 2, 3, 7
Dietl, Helmut, 15, 155, 157, 159. *See also* Schtonk!

disability and medical gaze, 59, 60, 71; resistance to, 72; ridicule of, 72. *See also Freakstars 3000*; Christoph Schlingensief
disability, 59; categorization of disabled individuals, 60; cultural location of, 60; discourse on, 59; ethical questions about, 60; film and, 62; media representation of, 61, 62; medical definitions of, 59, 60, 71; parody of able-bodied media formats, 62; rehabilitation and, 60; scientific discourse and, 60; sketch comedy and, 68; television and, 68. *See also* disability rights, German; disability and popular German media, 64, 67; *Freakstars 3000*; Christoph Schlingensief; subversion in *Freakstars 3000*
disability rights, German, 61–62. *See also Freakstars 3000*; Christoph Schlingensief
disabled performers in *Freakstars 3000*, 63, 64, 67, 70–72: audience assumptions, 69; ethical questions regarding, 62; improvisation, 67; tryouts, 65. *See also* Freakmann
Dresen, Andreas, 40n17, 209. *See also Halbe Treppe*

E

Ehe der Maria Braun, Die (*The Marriage of Maria Braun*, Rainer Werner Fassbinder, 1979), 86, 93, 94
Eichinger, Bernd, 8, 9
Emambakhsh, Pegah, 261–62
emotional impairment in postmodern society, 52, 53
End of the Neubacher Project, The (Marcus J. Carney, 2007), 277–79; authenticity, 278; personal and national history, 277; responsibility, 278

INDEX

"Die Erinnerung an Marie A.," 88. *See also* Bertolt Brecht

exilic and diasporic filmmaking, 255

F

Fassbinder, Rainer Werner, 11, 27, 30, 123, 246. *See also Die Ehe der Maria Braun*; New German cinema

fatal strategy at play, 43, 46; in *Cache*, 53. *See also* Jean Baudrillard

fetten Jahre sind vorbei, Die (*The Edukators*, Hans Weingartner, 2004), 26, 115, 116, 124–28, 134–41; appropriateness of interventionist political action, 124; ATTAC (Association for the Taxation of Financial Transactions for the Aid of Citizens), 137; black comedy of, 133, 135; criticism of post-unification Germany, 116, 128, 129; global capitalism as disease, 136; as lament, 149; ideologies of educators, 137, 139–40; intellectual legacy of 1968, 135, 139; intergenerational confrontation, 117, 125–28; kidnapping, 138–39; originality in protest, 138; as plea for change, 148; radical youth, 125, 136; search for meaning in, 135; social justice and political action, 124; leftist background of capitalist, 126; ticket sales, 134; two endings, 127; violence or poetic resistance, 140. *See also* 1968 student revolts, intellectual legacy of filmic text as a cultural agent, 80

fragmentation to create illusion in *71 Fragmente einer Chronologie des Zufalls* and *Code inconnu*, 56n9

"Freakmann," 67, 68. *See also* disability; *Freakstars 3000*; media representation; parody

Freaks (Tod Browning, 1932), 70

freak shows, 68, 69

Freakstars 3000 (Christoph Schlingensief, 2003), 13, 59–75; audience objection to, 72; camera work in, 65–66; critique of societal treatment of disabled, 72; disability as central theme, 62; long-term influence of, 73; ethical questions about, 60; format, 64–65; improvisation in, 67; ironic and irreverent tone, 60; mockery of television political discourse, 66; parody of mainstream television, 63; as satire/comedy, 72–73; refusal of medical or wondrous narrative, 69; ridicule of non-disabled gaze, 71; satirization of able-bodied media, 62; tryouts for, 65. *See also* disabled performers in *Freakstars* 3000; *Freakmann*; freakshows, media parody; Christoph Schlingensief

Freakstars 3000, parody in, 59, 60; parody of the able-bodied, 63; parody of casting shows, 64. *See also* disability; *Freakstars 3000*; subversion in *Freakstars 3000*

Freakstars 3000, subversion in, 63; assumptions and 71; disability labels, 60–61; expectations and, 69, 71; medical definitions of disability and, 59; medical gaze and, 68–72; subversive comedy, 61. *See also* Christoph Schlingensief

Free Rainer: Dein Fernseher lügt (*Free Rainer: Your Television Is Lying*, Hans Weingartner, 2007), 134

Fremde Haut (*Unveiled*, Angelina Maccarone, 2005), 247, 248, 254–60; airplane as site of transitioning, 257; cross-dressing in, 255, 248, 259; freedom and surveillance in, 257; focus on Fariba, 256–57; homo-

294

phobia, 258; as *Hosenrolle* film 248; non-German perspective, 256; plot setup, 254–55; unveiling, 255
frontier paradigm, 215, 222
Funny Games (Michael Haneke, 1997), 49, 54

G

ganz gewöhnlicher Jude, Ein (*An Ordinary Jew*, Oliver Hirschbiegel, 2006), 16, 191–206; audience figures and reception, 200; camera style and use, 192, 199; chamber drama style, 191, 192; constructed unfamiliarity, 200; as contemporary document of German–Jewish relations postwar, 200; contemporary setting, 191; overused images of Jewishness, 193; plot, 192; possibility of social change in, 193
Gastarbeiter, 239, 240
Gegen die Wand (*Head-On*, Fatih Akin, 2004), 26
German Democratic Republic (GDR), 81, 85, 92, 93; failed system of, 83. See also *Das Leben der Anderen*
German film culture, 8, 26
German Filmkunstpreis, 10
German Film Prize, 10
German–Jewish identity, construction of, 198, 202
German–Jewish relations postwar, 197, 198, 200, 203; categorization of practices, 195; construction of hybrid identity, 202; cultural difference, 191, 201; dominant culture of contrition, 195; political correctness, 194, 195, 201; position of Jews as Other, 193; prevention of ordinary life, 201; shared cultural space, 192
German–Polish border, 208, 209–10, 215, 220; cinematic representations of, 207, 208

German–Polish relationships, 16, 207, 208
Germany, economic and social problems of, 149, 150
Gespenster (*Ghosts*, Christian Petzold, 2005), 28, 29, 32, 150n2
Geyrhalter, Nikolaus, 17, 274–76. See also *Unser täglich Brot*
GG19: 19 gute Gründe für die Demokratie (*GG 19: Nineteen Good Reasons for Democracy*, Harald Siebler, 2007), 134
glass window as symbol, 222
globalization, 5, 7, 17, 18, 231; aggressive globalization, 213; consequences of, 3, 18, 228; in *Heimat 3*, 98, 100; and Berlin School, 39; cinema and, 7, 228; generic protest against, 246; global culture and, 9; internal German globalization, 226; migrating children and, 240; negative aspects of, 6; popular discourse and, 6; and queer studies, 247; social change and, 5. See also neo-liberalism. See also *Brudermord*; *Die fetten Jahre sind vorbei*; *Schröders wunderbare Welt*
Goldfarb, Emanuel, 192–206; constraints on discourse, 195; identity issues, 194, 197; Holocaust as vital part of self-understanding, 197; Lea Rosh, 196; ordinary life prevented, 192, 201; private life made public, 198–99; trapped within postwar German–Jewish relations, 198. See *Ein ganz gewöhnlicher Jude*; German–Jewish relations postwar
Good Bye, Lenin! (Wolfgang Becker, 2003), 26
Great Dictator, The (Charlie Chaplin, 1940), 155–56, 158, 174. See also Hitler humour

INDEX

Grisebach, Valeska, 27, 28, 29. *See also Sehnsucht*
Guggenberger, Bernd, 101
gute Mensch von Sezuan, Der (*The Good Woman of Setzuan*, Bertolt Brecht, 1943), 79, 83
Gutmann, Michael, 209. *See also Herz im Kopf*

H

Halbe Treppe (*Grill Point*, Andreas Dresen, 2002), 209–11
Haneke, Michael, 13, 43–58, 267; Baudrillard and, 45; cinematic techniques, 49, 50; film as mediated reality, 48–50; glaciation, 55n4; HD technology, 51; image texture, 50; long take, 56; nature of Haneke's films, 45; simulacra and, 48, 54; trilogies, 45; topics in work, 44; use of the *mise en abyme*, 47; violence in oeuvre, 53; as witness to malaise of postmodern reality, 44, 52. *See also* Jean Baudrillard; *Benny's Video; Caché; Code inconnu; Funny Games; Der siebent Kontinent; Le temps du loup; The Perfect Crime*
Hauck, Elke, 31. *See also Karger*
Heil Hitler, das Schwein ist tot! (*Heil Hitler, The Pig Is Dead!*, Rudolph Herzog, 2006), 174
Heimat, 7, 214; escapist images of, 211
Heimat 3: Chronik einer Zeitenwende (*Heimat 3: A Chronicle of Endings and Beginnings*, Edgar Reitz, 2004), 14, 97–114; end of the provincial, 97; fall of the Berlin Wall, 106–9; foregrounding the temporal, 99; filmic "time machine," 97, 105, 111; generational differences in, 99–100; globalization and, 98, 100; impact of historical change in, 111; plot summary, 106–11; setting as period of time, 101; shared identity and shared experience, 99. *See also* time in *Heimat 3*; unification in *Heimat* cycle
Heimatfilm as a genre, 98
Heimat film cycle, 97. *See also* unification in *Heimat* cycle
Heisenberg, Benjamin, 31
Herz im Kopf (*Heart Over Head*, Michael Gutmann, 2001), 209, 220
Hick, Jochen, and Christian Jentzch, 247. *See also Am Ende des Regenbogens*
Hirschbiegel, Oliver, 16, 26, 168, 191–206; strategy in choosing films, 192. *See also Der Untergang; Ein ganz gewöhnlicher Jude*
historical films, 9; Holocaust in, 15
history, postmodern notions of, 167
Hitler diaries scandal, 155, 158. *See also Schtonk!*
Hitler humour, 155, 159; 168, 169, 174; history of, 174–77; American Hitler humour, 174; appropriateness within Germany, 174; first German feature film of, 178; Hitler comedies, 173; Internet, 177; modern German television, 177; outside and inside Germany, 173; popular and populist Hitler humour, 176; rules for laughing at, 155–56; standup comedians and, 177; tradition of, 178. *See also The Great Dictator; Heil Hitler, das Schwein ist tot!*; Hitler–Holocaust cinematic etiquette, authority of; *Life Is Beautiful; Schtonk!*
Hitler, representations of, 161, 166, 167. *See also See also Mein Führer—Die wirklich wahrste Wahrheit über Adolf Hitler; Schtonk!*
Hitler–Holocaust cinematic etiquette, authority of, 175, 176, 178, 179, 182; changes in, 175–76; issues of high and low culture, 176. *See also Mein*

296

Führer—Die wirklich wahrste Wahrheit über Adolf Hitler Hochhäusler, Christoph, 16, 26, 209, 216. *See also Milchwald*
Holocaust, 201; instrumentalization of, 196; irreconcilable attitudes toward, 197; "normalization" not desired, 202; obligation for, 196; public commemoration in Germany, 196, 197
homogeneity, fear of, 11
humour, use of, 159, 174
hybridity, 207, 209, 211, 215; impossibility of, 254; valorization of, 253
hyperreality, 13, 43, 48, 56n8, 165; eventual reversal, 53; simulation and, 45; triumph of, 47, 54. *See also* Jean Baudrillard; Michael Haneke

I

illegal immigration, 122, 231, 254–58, 260, 269; atomization of life, 254; dissolution of family ties for, 253; interrelationship with political persecution, queerness, 246, 247; Polish, 207, 208, 220, 221. *See also Fremde Haude*; *Kleine Freiheit*; Turkish immigration
illegal immigration and queerness, 247, 260, 261; atomization of queer lives, 248, 254; intersection with political persecution, 246; lack of community, 249, 253, 258; political asylum, 246. *See also Fremde Haut*; *Kleine Freiheit*
innere Sicherheit, Die (*The State I Am In*, Christian Petzold, 2000), 115, 116, 120–24; ambiguity to ideology of 1968, 121; moral bankruptcy of anachronistic political extremism, 120, 121, 123; criticism of post-unification Germany, 116; East German vs. West German values, 119; materialism in the new Germany, 119, 122, 124; New German cinema and, 123; parent–child confrontation, 117; themes of consumerism, memory, terrorism, 124
intergenerational conflict, 117, 121, 125–28, 129
International, The (Tom Tykwer, 2009), 1

J

Jerichow (Christian Petzold, 2009), 29
Joop, Vanessa, 16, 209. *See also Vergiss Amerika*

K

Karger (Elke Hauck, 2007), 31
Klassenfahrt (*School Trip*, Henner Winckler, 2002), 26, 33, 209, 210, 218; failure of young to engage with foreign, 219
Kleine Freiheit (*A Little Bit of Freedom*, Yüksel Yavuz, 2003), 247, 248–54; expressions of German-Turkish gay identity, 249; fear of surveillance, 252; lack of belonging, 253; lack of gay self-identity, 251; loss and isolation, 248; need for stability, care, security, 254; no safe space, 252; outside "cinema of the affected," 263n1; uncertainty of sexual identity, 251. *See also* child migrants in Germany; illegal immigration; queerness, non-European
Köhler, Ulrich, 26, 34. *See also Bungalow*
Kosslick, Dieter, 1, 4
Kurdish nationalism and transnationalism, 235–37, 241n7. *See also Brudermord*
Kurz davor ist es passiert (*It Happened Just Before*, Anja Salomonowitz, 2007), 271–74; auteurism, 273; influence of Ulrich Seidl, 271, 272, 273; documentary–fiction cross, 272; reviews at home, 271

L

laughter as corrective, 60
Das Leben der Anderen (*The Lives of Others,* Florian Henckel von Donnersmarck, 2006), 14, 25, 26, 79–97; affect images, 89–90; as *Bildungswerk*, 83; Brecht and, 79–80; colour schemes, 91–92; music in, 88, 89, 93; plot summary, 80–81, 84; social control and, 84; *Die Sonate vom guten Menschen* (*Sonata for a Good Man*), 80, 83, 90, 92; voice-over/sound-over in, 80, 84–87 (see also acousmêtre)
Levy, Dani, 15, 173–90; negative effect of *Mein Führer* on Levy's career, 179; reaction to *Der Untergang*, 178; stated good intentions, 179. *See also Mein Führer—Die wirklich wahrste Warheit über Adolf Hitler*
Lichter (*Distant Lights,* Hans-Christian Schmid, 2003), 209–11, 220
Life Is Beautiful (Roberto Benigni, 1997), 175, 176
liminality and queerness, 248
Link, Caroline, 26. *See also Nirgendwo in Afrika*
literature in *Das Leben der Anderen*, 81, 82; dominant role played by narrative, 87–88; state-dictated literary production, 92; state-propagated literature of the GDR, 81; voice-overs of written texts, 84, 85; Western literary freedom, 92. *See also* Bertolt Brecht; *Das Leben der Anderen*; Florian Henckel von Donnersmarck
Lucy (Henner Winckler, 2005), 31, 32
Ludwigshafener Position, 10, 11

M

Maccarone, Angelina, 246, 248, 254, 256, 258; problems of lesbians of colour, 247. *See also Alles wird gut*; *Fremde Haut*
Mader, Ruth, 270. *See also Struggle*
Mammoth (Lukas Moodysson, 2009), 1
Marseille (Angela Schanelec, 2004), 26, 28, 32, 36
media-manipulated reality, 43. *See also* Jean Baudrillard, Michael Haneke
Mein Führer—Die wirklich wahrste Wahrheit über Adolf Hitler (*Mein Führer—The Truly Truest Truth about Adolf Hitler,* Dani Levy, 2007), 25, 168, 173–90; challenge to Hitler–Holocaust etiquette, 178; critical reaction, 179–80; failure of first cut, 182–83; failure of Hitler frame, 183; failure to transcend rules of Holocaust etiquette in film, 182; first German Hitler comedy feature film, 178; limitation of comedic potential by tragedy, 181, 182; plot, 180–81; suspension of disbelief too great for many, 180; tragic-comic results, 183. *See also* Hitler humour; Hitler–Holocaust cinematic etiquette, authority of
Mein langsames Leben (*Passing Summer,* Angela Schanelec, 2001), 27, 32
memory culture, 15
Metelmann, Jörg, 53
migrant culture in Germany, 229–32, 239; becoming *almanyali*, 231; cultural preservation, 231; cultural separateness, 229; interculturality, 229; marginalization, 239; migration as routine, 231; non-uniformity of, 232; reasons for migration, 227, 230–31. *See also Brudermord*; language as signifier of integration
Milchwald (*This Very Moment,* Christoph Hochhäusler, 2003), 26, 31, 33, 209, 215; Otherness of Poland, 216. *See also* Polish stereotypes

minority cultures within Germany, 229, 240. *See also* Turco-Kurdish culture in Germany
Mittermeier, Marcus, 134, 141, 147; aesthetic, 148; criticism of turbo-capitalism and mass media, 148; use of satire, 148. *See also Muxmäuschenstill*
Möller, Olaf, 27
Monty Python's Flying Circus, 66, 71, 72
Moodysson, Lukas, 1. *See also Mammoth*
murder of reality, 49
Mux (in *Muxmäuschenstill*), 141–47; German origins of Mux's demagoguery, 142; diatribe against media images, 145; emotional stuntedness of, 143; Kira, 143–44; philosophical evolution of, 142–43; psychopathy of, 145, 147; solutions for German social and economic problems, 147; violence of, 144. *See also Muxmäuschenstill*
Muxmäuschenstill (*Quiet as a Mouse*, Marcus Mittermeier, 2004), 134, 135, 141–47; black comedy of, 133, 135, 141; editing style, 145; lament over current state of affairs, 149; protagonist as vigilante, 142; public fear for security, 146; reflection of modern crisis atmosphere, 147; satire of Internet, 146; ticket sales, 134; underground quality of, 141; unusual genesis of film, 141

N

national as category, 2; usefulness of, 2–3
national cinema, German 1, 7, 18, 228, 229
national identity, Austrian. *See also* national identity, uncertainty about
national identity, post-1990 German, 16, 100, 211, 248; construction of foundational myths, 107; in globally responsible framework, 133, 135; and *Vergangenheitsbewältigung*, 157; in *Vergiss Amerika*, 214
nationalism and globalization, 9
Nazi past, 122, 160
Nazi period, 8, 9, 15, 122, 160; popularity of Nazi films, 8. *See also Vergangenheitsbewältigung*
neo-liberalism, 5, 39; contemporary Germany and, 25
New German cinema, 27, 123
Nicodemus, Katja, 26, 127, 139
Nirgendwo in Afrika (*Nowhere in Africa*, Caroline Link, 2001), 26

O

Otherness, 200, 209, 222, 236, 258; otherness of foreign women, 220. *See also* German–Jewish relations, postwar; Kurdish
Otherness of Poland, 208, 209, 215–17, 222
"outing" and being "outed," reassessment of, 257, 260

P

para-comedy, 73
Parallel*gesellschaft* (parallel society), 239
paralysis of left post-unification, 119
Parfum, Die Geschichte eines Mörders, Das (*Perfume—The Story of a Murderer*, Tom Tykwer, 2006), 28, 30
parody, 159, 160, 163
Petzold, Christian, 11, 12, 27, 37, 115, 116, 121, 123. *See also Die innere Sicherheit; Jerichow; Yella*
"poetic resistance," 149
Polish stereotypes, 209, 210, 214, 220–21; as threatening, 217, 221, 222. *See also* Otherness of Poland
political correctness. *See* German–Jewish relations postwar; political incorrectness
political extremism, 123, 126. *See also* terrorist groups, German

political extremism as anachronistic, 123
political incorrectness, 141, 178, 195. *See also Freakstars 3000*
postmodern society, lack of emotional connection to the world, 52
post-unification, 83, 100, 125; criticism of political and social development, 116; debates, 115, 116; economic woes, 26; European integration, 210; fascination with fascism, 159, 167; generational issues, 100; paralysis, 34. *See also Heimat 3*; Hitler humour; Edgar Reitz; *Schtonk!*
purpose of cinematic time-machine, post-wall, 105

Q

queerness and human rights, 246, 247
queerness in German film, 17, 245–46; interracial relationships, 245–46. *See also Fremde Haut*; illegal immigration and queerness; *Kleine Freiheit*
queerness, non-European, 247, 258, 262n1; diaspora, 245. *See also Fremde Haut*; illegal immigration and queerness; *Kleine Freiheit*; liminality and queerness

R

Reitz, Edgar, 14, 97–114; comments on film and time, 102–5; commitment of analogue filmmaking in *Heimat 3*, 111; Deleuzian influence upon, 105, 106; foregrounding of temporal, 99; *Generationsvertrag* (contract between generations) as theme, 100; influence of Krackauer's *Theory of Film*, 104, 105; spatial constructions, 98–99; film and time, 102, 105; *Zeit-Raum* (time-space), 102; *Zeit-Heimat*, 101, 102, 106, 110. *See also Heimat 3: Chronik einer Zeitenwende*
Rentschler, Eric, 123, 125, 160, 161

Roehler, Oskar, 115, 116. *See also Die Unberührbare*
Rothemund, Marc, 26. *See also Sophie Scholl—Die letzten Tage*

S

Salomonowitz, Anja, 17, 271–74; unorthodox approach, 271
Schanelec, Angela, 26, 27, 28, 29, 32. *See also Marseille, Mein langsames Leben*
Schlingensief, Christoph, 13, 59–75, 156; aesthetics, 61; avoidance of pity or sensationalism, 70–71; background, 62–63; camera work, 65; *Chance 2000*, 63, 67; chaotic, neo-avant-garde aesthetic, 62, 63; disruptive, non-linear editing, 66; experience with live performance, 66; genre blurring, 64; theme of disability in work, 61–63; work with disabled actors, 63, 64, 67. *See also 100 Jahre Adolf Hitler—die letzte Stunde im Führerbunker*; *Freakstars 3000*
Schmid, Hans-Christian, 1, 209. *See also Lichter*; *Sturm*
Schorr, Michael, 16
Schröders wunderbare Welt (*Schröder's Wonderful World*, Michael Schorr, 2006), 209, 211–15; European Union as escapist fantasy, 213; re-colonization of European spaces, 213
Schtonk! (*Stench*, Helmut Dietl, 1992), 155, 157–69, 176; approach to Nazi past as topic, 157; criticism of *Schtonk!*, 160–61; debate over Germans as victims or perpetrators, 164; as fake documentary, 160–65; ironic dimensions of, 159, 163; mimics the documentary, 160–62; origin of title, 158; parody in, 159, 163; plot line, 158–59; product of immediate unification period, 157;

Vergangenheitsbewältigung and, 176; satire in, 15; West German fascination with fascism post-unification, 15

Schtonk! and fetish, 165–67; fetishization of Nazi history, 165; Freudian definition of fetish, 165–66; Hitler's omnipresence through fetish objects, 166; Nazi simulacra as fetish functions, 165–67

Sehnsucht (*Longing*, Valenka Grisebach, 2006), 28, 29, 30

Seidl, Ulrich, 267, 272, 273

self-destruction as communication, 54

siebente Kontinent, Der (*The Seventh Continent*, Michael Haneke, 1989), 45, 52

Siebler, Harald, 134. *See also GG19: 19 gute Gründe für die Demokratie*

simulacra, 47, 48, 165–67; definition, 165. *See also* Jean Baudrillard; Michael Haneke

simulation, 43

social change, 4, 6, 7. *See also* post-unification; unification

Sophie Scholl—Die letzten Tage (*Sophie Scholl—The Final Days*, Marc Rothemund, 2005), 26

spectator, role of, 12

Struggle (Ruth Mader, 2003), 269–71, 273; auteurism, 273; documentary quality of, 269; reception, 269–70

Sturm (*Storm*, Hans-Christian Schmid, 2009), 1

surveillance issues, 51, 147, 149, 252, 257, 260; Gestapo and Stasi legacies, 141, 146; of people of colour, 250, 260; police surveillance, 238, 250

T

temps du loup, Le (*The Time of the Wolf*, Michael Haneke, 2003), 43

terrorism, 53

terrorist groups, German, 117, 119, 124, 126, 130, 140; Red Army Faction (RAF), 116, 138; *see also* 1968 student revolts; *Die fetten Jahre sind vorbei*; *Die innere Sicherheit*; political extremism

Third Reich history, German fascination with, 155

Tiele-Winckler-Haus, 63, 64, 71

time in *Heimat 3*, 98, 101; three images of time, 106–11; glass panes as symbols of, 107, 108, 111; mirrors as symbols of, 109

transitory spaces, emotional and social, 33. *See also* Berlin School

transnational cinema as male-oriented, 239

transnational cinema, 8, 9

transnational migration, effects of, 225

transnational spaces, 17

Turco-Kurdish culture in Germany, 225–27, 229; enmity between Turks and Kurds, 230

Turkish immigration. *See also* Turco–German relations

Tykwer, Tom, 1, 28, 30. *See also Parfum, Das*; *International, The*

U

Unberührbare, Die (*No Place to Go*, Oskar Roehler, 2000), 115, 116, 117–20; anti-capitalist critique in, 117, 119, 120; parent–child confrontation, 117; criticism of 68ers, 118–19; criticism of post-unification Germany, 116; Hanna Flanders as personification of generation, 118; New German cinema and, 123; own mother as allegory, 117; reactions to fall of Berlin Wall, 118–20

unification, 39, 100, 101; and social change, 98; in *Heimat* cycle, 98

Unser täglich Brot (*Our Daily Bread*, Nikolaus Geyrhalter, 2005), 274–76; attempts to classify, 275; no affiliation to school or style, 275; points of contention, 275; rigorous aesthetic, 274, 276

Untergang, Der (*Downfall*, Oliver Hirschbiegel, 2004), 16, 26, 38, 168

V

Valkyrie (Bryan Singer, 2008), 9

Vergangenheitsbewältigung (coming to terms with the past), 15, 168, 173, 174, 184; in *Freakstars 3000*, 67; and Hitler humour, 156, 168, 173; in *Schtonk!*, 160, 162, 176

Vergiss Amerika (*Forget America*, Vanessa Joop, 2000), 209, 210, 220

vigilantes, 142, 148. *See also Die fetten Jahre sind vorbei*; *Muxmäuschenstill*

violence, 144; questions about, 140

von Donnersmarck, Florian Henckel, 14, 26, 79–97; influence of Brecht, 79, 80; literary bias of, 87; literary aesthetic, 89; reservations about drama, 82; tight control over affect, 91–92; visual technique, 91. *See also Das Leben der Anderen*

Vorstellungsbilder, 210

W

Walser, Martin, 196

Weingartner, Hans, 117, 124, 136, 149; aesthetic, 148; character of educators, 137, 142; criticism of turbo-capitalism and mass media, 148; change to end of *Die fetten Jahre sind vorbei*, 127; documenting his time, 147; style, 140, 148. *See also Die fetten Jahre sind vorbei*; *Free Rainer: Dein Fernseher lügt*

West German student movement (68ers), 115–17, 127, 129, 135, 150n9; critical reassessments of, 116, 121, intellectual legacy of, 133, 135, 139, 149. *See also* demonization of the media; *Die fetten Jahre sind vorbei*

Winckler, Henner, 26, 31, 32, 209. *See also Klassenfahrt*; *Lucy*

Worthmann, Merthen, 27

Y

Yavuz, Yüksel, 247, 248, 251, 252, 253. *See Kleine Freiheit*

Yella (Christian Petzold, 2007), 12, 28, 29, 32

younger generation and global injustice, 128, 129

Z

zeitgeist, 156

Books in the Film+Media Studies Series
Published by Wilfrid Laurier University Press

Image and Territory: Essays on Atom Egoyan / Monique Tschofen and Jennifer Burwell, editors /
2006 / viii + 418 pp / photos / ISBN 978-0-88920-487-4

The Young, the Restless, and the Dead: Interviews with Canadian Filmmakers /
George Melnyk, editor /
2008 / xiv + 134 pp. / photos / ISBN 978-1-55458-036-1

Programming Reality: Perspectives on English-Canadian Television / Zoë Druick and Aspa Kotsopoulos, editors /
2008 / x + 344 pp. / photos / ISBN 978-1-55458-010-1

Harmony and Dissent: Film and Avant-garde Art Movements in the Early Twentieth Century / R. Bruce Elder /
2008 / xxxiv + 482 pp. / ISBN 978-1-55458-028-6

He Was Some Kind of a Man: Masculinities in the B Western / Roderick McGillis /
2009 / xii + 210 pp. / photos / ISBN 978-1-55458-059-0

The Radio Eye: Cinema in the North Atlantic, 1958–1988 / Jerry White /
2009 / xvi + 284 pp. / photos / ISBN 978-1-55458-178-8

The Gendered Screen: Canadian Women Filmmakers / Brenda Austin-Smith and George Melnyk, editors /
2010 / x + 272 pp. / ISBN 978-1-55458-179-5

Feeling Canadian: Nationalism, Affect, and Television / Marusya Bociurkiw /
2011 / viii + 184 pp. / ISBN 978-1-55458-268-6

Beyond Bylines: Media Workers and Women's Rights in Canada / Barbara M. Freeman /
2011 / xii + 328 pp. / photos / ISBN 978-1-55458-269-3

Canadian Television: Text and Context / Marian Bredin, Scott Henderson, and Sarah A. Matheson, editors /
2011 / xvi + 238 pp. / ISBN 978-1-55458-361-4

Cinema and Social Change in Germany and Austria / Gabriele Mueller and James M. Skidmore, editors /
2012 / x + 304 pp. / photos / ISBN 978-1-55458-225-9

www.ingramcontent.com/pod-product-compliance
Lightning Source LLC
Chambersburg PA
CBHW070048080526
44586CB00013B/961